AF412162

Across the Lines of Conflict

Across the Lines of Conflict

Facilitating Cooperation to Build Peace

Edited by

Michael Lund and Steve McDonald

Woodrow Wilson Center Press
Washington, D.C.

Columbia University Press
New York

Woodrow Wilson Center Press
Washington, D.C.
www.wilsoncenter.org

Columbia University Press
Publishers Since 1893
New York   Chichester, West Sussex
cup.columbia.edu

Library of Congress Cataloging-in-Publication Data

Across the lines of conflict : facilitating cooperation to build peace /
edited by Michael Lund and Steve McDonald.
pages cm
Includes index.
ISBN 978-0-231-70450-2 (hardcover : alk. paper) — ISBN 978-0-231-80137-9 (ebook)
1. Peace-building—Case studies. 2. Conflict management—Case studies.
3. Reconciliation—Case studies. I. Lund, Michael S., 1941– editor.
II. McDonald, Steve, 1945– editor.
JZ5538.A27 2015
303.6'6—dc23
2015031983

Woodrow Wilson Center Press and Columbia University Press books
are printed on permanent and durable acid-free paper.

This book is printed on paper with recycled content.

Printed in the United States of America.

c 10 9 8 7 6 5 4 3 2 1

Cover design: Naylor Design, Inc.

References to websites (URLs) were accurate at the time of writing. Neither the authors nor
Woodrow Wilson Center Press and Columbia University Press are responsible for URLs that
may have expired or changed since the manuscript was printed.

The Wilson Center, chartered by Congress as the official memorial to President Woodrow Wilson, is the nation's key nonpartisan policy forum for tackling global issues through independent research and open dialogue to inform actionable ideas for Congress, the Administration, and the broader policy community.

Conclusions or opinions expressed in Center publications and programs are those of the authors and speakers and do not necessarily reflect the views of the Center staff, fellows, trustees, advisory groups, or any individuals or organizations that provide financial support to the Center.

Please visit us online at www.wilsoncenter.org.

Jane Harman, Director, President, and CEO

Contents

Part I. Approaching the Subject

Part II. Assessing Country Cases
Averting Conflict Escalation

Ending Active Conflicts

Transcending Past Conflicts

Part III. Findings and Implications

Figures and Tables

Figures

Tables

Foreword
Lee H. Hamilton

This book is a publication of the Working Group on Preventing and Rebuilding Failed States, a project created by former congressman Howard Wolpe at the Woodrow Wilson International Center for Scholars, and is dedicated to Howard's memory. Edited by Michael Lund and Steve McDonald, it brings together the presentations given to the various sessions of the working group and weaves them into a broader narrative on the kinds of international interventions that can occur and how they can best play out. Taking a holistic approach to the various stages of conflict and postconflict interventions, it studies episodes in Estonia, Guyana, Tajikistan, Sri Lanka, Cyprus, and Burundi in chapters by expert authors. Introductory and concluding chapters by Michael Lund set out the context and conceptual framework around "unofficial" peace processes, the lessons learned, and ways in which the international community can better approach conflict resolution.

I knew Howard for the entire time he was on the national stage as a member of Congress, later as a Special Envoy for President Bill Clinton, and then as the director of the Africa Program and the Project on Leadership and Building State Capacity at the Wilson Center. When he first came to the House of Representatives as a liberal Democrat representing District 3 in southwestern Michigan in January 1979, I had been in Congress for four-teen years. Howard's tenure on the House Foreign Affairs Committee, and unprecedented ten years as the chair of the Africa Subcommittee from 1982 to 1992, also coincided with my time on the Foreign Affairs Committee from 1973 until I left Congress in 1999. Needless to say, we worked closely together on issues relating to policy and his abiding interest in, knowledge about, and love for the African continent. Congress had never before had a chair of the Africa Subcommittee so steeped in the history and culture of the continent. His doctoral dissertation at the Massachusetts Institute of Technology was on Ibo politics in Nigeria, where he had lived for two years in the city of Port Harcourt. He had actively sought the chairmanship of the subcommittee because of his background, and he held that position longer than any other chair had done before or has since.

Our partnership and close relationship in the House and on the Foreign Affairs Committee led to us reuniting in 2001. Howard had then just fin-ished serving four years as Special Envoy to the volatile Great Lakes Region of Africa, following his appointment to that position in 1996 by President Clinton. The Wilson Center, where I served as president and CEO from 1999 to 2010, had offered Howard a Public Policy Scholar position in 2001, which he accepted. The next year, he came to see me and discuss a rather unique project he had been working on, and see if the Center would be interested in housing it. In his years as special envoy, Howard had been the primary American negotiator on the peace processes in Burundi and the Democratic Republic of Congo (DRC), ending long years of civil war in both countries that had taken hundreds of thousands of lives. Howard was very concerned that the peace accord in Burundi was fraying, with rebel groups returning to the battlefield to challenge the sitting government. He felt strongly that Burundians, both in the leadership of all parties and factions and among the public at large, were at a point of exhaustion and desperation and dearly wanted to avoid returning to a war footing. At the same time, Burundians feared each other, saw each other as untrustworthy enemies, and believed that the only way to protect their own interests was to exclude others from any role in governance. Howard's experience in building rec-onciliation and trust in divided communities and institutions during the US civil rights struggle suggested to him that in Burundi, before elections could be held and democratic government put in place, a similar reconciliation and trust-building exercise should be held among the leaders of all parties, including all ethnic, regional, economic, and social/cultural groups. He felt that the only way to ensure a stable, enduring peace and a return to responsible and democratic government was to create trust and communication among the key players and build their negotiation, communication, and joint problem-solving skills.

Howard told me that he had raised this issue and his thoughts on how it might be addressed at the World Bank's Post-Conflict Unit, where he was serving as a part-time consultant on the Great Lakes region of Africa. They expressed a great interest in his ideas and indicated that they might be willing to fund such a project. Howard asked an old friend of his, Steve McDonald, to help him develop a proposal along these lines to present to the World Bank. They did just that, working at it for about seven months, and in August 2002 they were awarded a $980,000 grant for an eighteen-month project to work on trust building with the Burundian leadership. Howard needed a tax-free educational institution, a 501(c)3 in US Internal Revenue Service terms, to receive the funds before the grant could be finalized. I agreed to have the Wilson Center assume that role, and Howard and Steve came to work for me at the Center as consultants to administer and implement this project in Burundi. In subsequent years, with further funding from other sources, the project would expand to the DRC and Liberia.

From 2002 to 2009, I worked very closely with Howard. When the directorship of our nascent Africa Program became open in 2003, I asked Howard if he would take over the position, and he agreed to do so. He served as the Africa Program's director for the next six years.

In 2005, Howard came to me with an idea of creating a Project on Leadership and Building State Capacity (PLBSC) under the Africa Program. Its purpose was to broaden the application of the peacebuilding and postconflict work that he had been conducting in the Africa Program to a global stage, and to promote more sustainable approaches to international conflict prevention and postconflict reconstruction through comparative, empirical research and "lessons learned" studies. The concept of the PLBSC flowed directly from the work the Africa Program had been doing in Africa, but was meant to provide a conceptual framework and release it from its geographic restrictions. To launch the project, we were able to use a small amount of funds left over from the Conflict Prevention Project, which was being closed following the departure of its director, Anita Sharma. The grantor was the Ford Foundation, which agreed to the restructuring. Howard sought further

Howard Wolpe at a training program with soldiers from Burundi.
Source: Woodrow Wilson International Center for Scholars.

donor funding for the PLBSC, which allowed him to design a similar trust-building and reconciliation project in Timor-Leste and to investigate several other potential country projects.

Under PLBSC auspices, Howard took several other initiatives. One made a critical assessment of the Africa Program's work in the DRC, where it was training leaders to work collaboratively in avoiding war, supporting postwar reconstruction, and building democratically accountable links between the governors and the governed. The PLBSC also provided training for trainers in conflict resolution, and held a series of workshops with donor nation representatives to introduce them to this trust-building and reconciliation approach so they could include it in their diplomatic "toolbox" for peacebuilding. The major "conceptual" initiative was the commissioning of comparative studies of several societies in conflict or postconflict transitions to deepen the international community's capacity to implement and manage complex peacebuilding interventions. With further funding from the Ford Foundation, Howard formed a standing Working Group on Preventing and Rebuilding Failed States. The working group was composed of distinguished diplomats, policymakers, trainers, and academic specialists, and met periodically over two years to distill lessons from case studies in internationally facilitated peace processes. Michael Lund, a senior associate for conflict and peacebuilding for Management Systems International, Inc., was hired as the consulting project director to manage this working group and work on other projects with the PLBSC. Howard remained at the Center until 2009, when he returned to government to serve at the State Department as a special representative to the Great Lakes Region. He passed away unexpectedly in 2011.

Howard would be proud of this book. He would be pleased that it reinforces his deeply held belief that "trust building" must precede institution building in conflicted societies. Unless the key stakeholders have enough trust in their fellow protagonists to fully commit to work together to implement and manage the institutions of governance, development, economic recovery, and rule of law to sustain peace and pull their societies out of poverty, corruption, and mismanagement, then conflict will raise its ugly head again. As Howard constantly intoned, the "winner-take-all" mentality has to give way to an understanding that we all "walk in the shoes of the other," and are interdependent in a shared and common future. The sooner we collectively understand this, the sooner we can effectively address conflict in the world.

As this extraordinary record indicates, Howard was an energetic, imaginative, compassionate professional, who always worked to improve the quality of life of the people who were the focus of his attention. What a remarkable privilege it was for me to learn from, work with, and count as a friend this remarkable man. All of us who know him say: Bravo, for jobs well done.

Lee H. Hamilton is a former member of Congress and former president and director of the Woodrow Wilson International Center for Scholars.

Preface

Steve McDonald

This book is entitled *Across the Lines of Conflict: Facilitating Cooperation to Build Peace.* It is the output of a Working Group on Preventing and Rebuilding Failed States, convened by the Wilson Center's Project on Leadership and Building State Capacity (PLBSC), which looked at a number of case studies of conflict and postconflict societies and ways in which the international community could help address those conflicts and move the affected societies toward sustainable peace.

This project was the brainchild of the late Howard Wolpe, then the director of the PLBSC, who felt strongly that techniques that he had used in addressing racial conflict in communities in the United States during the civil rights struggle could be applied successfully to state-level conflicts. This was after his five-year tenure, from 1996 to 2001, as the US Special Envoy to the Great Lakes Region of Africa, when he had been instrumental in negotiating the Arusha Peace and Reconciliation Agreement for Burundi. This agreement, signed in August 2000, brought to a close the hostilities in the Burundian civil war, which had claimed as many as 450,000 lives since

1993. When hostilities began to erupt again and the peace accord deteriorated, Howard sought support for trying his unique vision of trust-building, reconciliation, and negotiation and communication skills training with the key leaders of Burundi to again stop the fighting and create among those leaders a common vision and commitment to a shared future. This support was forthcoming from the World Bank as a funder and the Wilson Center as a host.

The workshops that were conducted in Burundi under this program (and subsequently extended to the Democratic Republic of Congo and Liberia) met with unprecedented success, and the working group was put together to assess whether this approach to peacebuilding—facilitating cooperation of the antagonists to address their own problems—had met with success in other country settings and what lessons could be learned from these experiences.

One of the chapters of this book is devoted to the Burundi experiment. However, as a way of introduction, I thought that an anecdote or two from some of the many workshops that we conducted in Burundi might be telling in assessing the power of this peacebuilding approach.

It was September 2003, and the last day of an intensive six-day workshop in Ngozi, a small provincial town in northern Burundi where the violence had not been too severe during the civil war. We had chosen Ngozi for that reason; it was relatively secure and peaceful. Still, we had to have a protection force, made up of South African soldiers deployed with the African Union peacekeeping force, on standby, and we traveled either by armed convoy over land or by air to get to the workshop venue.

The workshop consisted of thirty-five Burundians, drawn from a cross-section of all political parties, the government, the army, armed rebel groupings (as the war was still underway), and significant civil society actors. It was representative of the ethnic, regional, gender, and economic diversity of the country. The curriculum content was a series of role-playing, interactive simulation exercises involving negotiations, mediation, the need for listening well and communicating clearly, and joint problem analysis and solving skills. Each exercise was preceded by instructions about and examples of the skills needed to conduct the exercises, and was facilitated by our professional, international, experienced conflict resolution specialists. The exercises, which focused on theoretical situations or sets of circumstances, were followed by debriefings, where the Burundian participants were asked to draw on what lessons they had learned and how these lessons might be applicable to the real-life circumstances they faced in their own country. Howard, the organizer and initiator of the workshop series, would do the debriefing himself. His five years as Special Envoy to the Great Lakes Region, when he was the lead American negotiator on the peace agreement that had brought a momentary end to the conflict in Burundi, had given him a level of insight into and understanding of the conflict. Moreover, it had given him a unique status of trust and access in the eyes of the Burundian protagonists.

This was the second workshop in our series, trying to engage the hundred most important leaders in Burundi in an exercise to strengthen their capacities to work together, break down the barriers that years of war had thrown up between them, and create a sense of interdependence and the need for a shared future. We had a strong grouping of party officials, provincial governors, army officers, rebel group leaders, union leaders, and youth and church representatives. Five grueling days had passed, during which each participant had been thrown into situations where they had to "walk in the shoes" of the others—often their most feared antagonists—by taking on their roles and perspectives and negotiating a settlement in their own interests. As they assumed these roles, by necessity they had to think as their opponents thought and draw from their opponents' experiences and perceptions. As we debriefed and discussed the lessons learned, the participants gave voice to fears and facts that were normally unstated, admitting that past practices had excluded whole ethnicities from governance, economic, and developmental opportunities solely because of who they were. In the evenings, as we socialized together, we learned further of family, school, and professional linkages that often were unknown or had been forgotten. The participants learned that listening was as important to communications as speaking, and you could see the demeanor and discourse change in character as the week progressed.

The facilitators never lectured on the ways in which Burundians could work together to help the country recover and ensure a sustainable peace. But the participants began to offer suggestions moving forward on how they could do just that, drawing lessons from the exercises they had experienced together.

The workshop ended with a session in which the participants were asked to reflect on the week, describe what they had learned, and commit to ways in which they could build on the relationships they had developed and the skills they had acquired to secure a peaceful, democratic Burundi. Many moving comments and accounts were told, but one exchange in particular stands out in my mind. One participant, a Hutu who represented one of the armed rebel groups, the CNDD-FDD, stood up and pointed across the room to a tall, Tutsi army colonel. He said that when he arrived at the workshop site six days ago and saw "that man," he had telephoned his wife in Tanzania (where he was based) and tearfully said, "Do not expect me home; I am going to be killed." The colonel, in fact, had participated in the group that overthrew the elected Hutu President Melchior Ndadaye in October 1993 and was implicated in his assassination, although that accusation was never proven. The rebel group representative then informed the workshop participants that he now stood before this group to declare that the colonel was "now my best friend." He said that he had learned what kind of man the colonel was, how the colonel had been adopted by a Hutu family when he was orphaned and had grown up with Hutu brothers and sisters. He knew now that his perceptions of the colonel were misplaced, that the rumors of the roles he had played were exaggerated, and that the two of them shared a vision and commitment to a peaceful and united Burundi, inclusive of all ethnicities.

This admission by a Hutu who had been a staunch supporter of armed resistance to the Tutsi-led government was typical of the kind of personal transformation that we witnessed over the five years that we conducted this project in Burundi and elsewhere. We witnessed repeatedly the power of this approach to heal wounds, induce understanding of interdependence and shared values, and create the ability to work collectively to begin to address mutual problems and causes of past conflict. In a similar workshop in 2005, the participants, who were made up of the key leaders of all the political parties about to contest the forthcoming elections, evolved over the six days from fearing each other to working collegially in order to design a code of conduct for the elections and agreeing to appear together on radio and while campaigning to reassure the people that they were committed to an election without intimidation or violence. This led to a procedurally correct, free, fair, and violence-free election, a first in Burundi's history.

As we see Burundi slipping back into conflict in 2015, we are reminded of the need for long-term commitment to the approach to peacebuilding that is described in the chapters of this book. Although one can only speculate on such effects, had this work with the Burundian national leadership continued after 2007 and through the next two election cycles, Burundi might well have avoided the reemergence of divisions and conflict that bedeviled it in 2010 and again in 2015.

Finally, we cannot say that the approach used by the Wilson Center in Burundi would work everywhere. It represented a very unique situation, with a relatively small population, war-weary and thirsty for a way out of conflict, and an innovative initiative by an individual who was able to bring the protagonists together and encourage them to commit to this process. These chapters will show how and why that approach may or may not work in other conflict arenas. One thing is certain, however, and that is the need to engage all parties to a conflict in any peacebuilding approach, and to get their "buy-in" to a process of cooperation and address the core causes of the conflict in a direct, open, and inclusive manner.

Acknowledgments

The editors are fundamentally grateful for the generous financial support that the Ford Foundation and the Carnegie Corporation provided to launch and sustain this project, without which it would not have been possible. We thank the authors of the case studies for their careful research in doing the chapters and for their patience in responding to the followup tasks in producing a multiauthored volume. The editors are also grateful for the crucial help that was provided by program associates Georgina Petrovsky and Sarah Cussen, program assistant Alyson Lyons, and intern Lee Orr in the Project on Leadership and Building State Capacity of the Woodrow Wilson International Center for Scholars. The thorough, excellent copyediting by Shannon Granville of Woodrow Wilson Center Press pressed the authors to clarify opaque sentences and made the wordy text more readable.

Michael Lund wishes to thank project directors Howard Wolpe and Steve McDonald for the complete academic independence they afforded him for doing research for this book. He deeply appreciates the support and patience of his wife, Judy Bailey, over the many frustrating months that the book consumed. Also to be noted are the staff in the Modern Times Café at the Politics and Prose Bookstore in Washington, D.C., for their unfailing service and good cheer. Michael's grandchildren Ellie Grace Lund, Tristan Lund Miller, and Eden Katherine Miller were a source of great joy as well as motivation during this work.

Steve McDonald would like Howard Wolpe's widow, Julie Fletcher, to know of his gratitude for Howard's creativity and direction, which were always inspiring. He would also like to thank Michael Lund, who authored his own chapters, recruited and supervised the work of the case study authors, organized the case study consultations where each country study was presented and analyzed, and conducted the first edits of the entire book. Without his patience and persistence, this book would not have seen the light of day. Steve's wife, René Smit, was, as always, his reservoir of strength and a pillar of tolerance for the attention he took away from family life to play his role in the book's completion.

Across the Lines of Conflict

Part I

Approaching the Subject

Chapter 1

Intrastate Conflicts and the Problem of Political Will

Michael Lund

International Context

Since 1945, most conflicts around the world have involved not wars between states, but rather civil wars and other deadly internal conflicts—especially in poor, developing countries or weak democracies—over who controls a state and its policies. Since the end of the Cold War, there has been growing international recognition that these intrastate conflicts pose serious threats to regional security and global stability, exact huge human and other costs, and impede social and economic development. Since September 11, 2001, it also has been recognized that as states fail, they can not only experience major conflicts and humanitarian disasters but also provide inviting havens for terrorists, with impacts far outside their borders.

In response to intrastate conflicts and failed states, the US government, other major governments, the United Nations (UN), regional bodies, development agencies, and a host of nongovernmental organizations (NGOs) have become extremely active in trying to terminate intrastate wars, rebuild war-ravaged societies, and to a lesser extent prevent violent conflicts from erupting in the first place. An unprecedented number of UN and other peacekeeping missions are deployed around the world. International organizations now do much more than mediate peace agreements, aid victims of war, keep the peace, and finance physical reconstruction; they also try to repair the torn fabrics of societies and help construct state institutions. The result has been a proliferation of diplomatic, military, humanitarian, political, and economic programs and projects as diverse as demobilization and reintegration of former combatants, election support and monitoring, constitution writing, economic reform, health and education services, human rights promotion, justice reform, local government strengthening, political party training, community development, security sector reform, and trauma counseling. This vast complex of activities has come to be summarized as "peacebuilding."

The expansion of international peacebuilding has yielded definite results, although one would not necessarily know it from reading daily headlines. Intrastate as well as interstate conflicts have declined considerably in both their number and their fatalities since the mid-1990s. Informed observers attribute this decline in significant part to the "extraordinary upsurge of international activism" in peacebuilding, which in many cases has been considered indispensable in controlling the violence and has helped especially in shortening the duration of conflicts.[1] However, although international peacebuilding as a whole has had clear benefits, it often fails in particular countries to achieve a sustainable peace. In countries where conflicts started during the Cold War, such as in El Salvador, Guatemala, Mozambique, Namibia, and Nicaragua, international mediation ended the hostilities and led to economic growth, but underlying sources of conflict such as poverty and unemployment persist, and violent crime has increased. In several subsequent conflicts where the hostilities have stopped, the basic issues remain unresolved or "frozen," as in Nagorno-Karabakh, or broad-based governance and political stability have not taken root, as in Burundi, Cambodia, the Democratic Republic of Congo, and Mali. In yet other countries where peace accords were reached, wars broke out again, as in Angola, Ivory Coast, Sri Lanka, and Sudan. In some countries, armed conflicts still threaten despite major efforts to end them, such as in Afghanistan, Central African Republic, Colombia, Gaza, Iraq, Pakistan, Philippines, Somalia, South Sudan, and Thailand. Since 2010, a wave of rebellions in the Middle East against autocratic governments has led in Egypt, Libya, Syria, and Yemen variously to civil wars, mass atrocities, new repression, and state failure.

Meanwhile, many semi-democratic countries such as Guinea-Bissau, Kyrgyzstan, and Zimbabwe exist in an unstable state of neither war nor peace.

Mixed results have also been achieved by several post–Cold War peacebuilding efforts to head off violent conflict before it erupts.[2] In the Baltic states, Kenya, Macedonia, Slovakia, and South Africa, preventive diplomacy and associated actions helped to avert potential or rising violence. Yet in Bosnia, Kosovo, the Republic of the Congo, Rwanda, and Ukraine, preventive actions proved inadequate and they escalated into deadly conflicts.

The mixed performance of the international community in conflict-prone societies and fragile states has motivated a quest for more effective ways to resolve or prevent conflicts and achieve a sustained peace. Despite considerable progress in research on the causes of conflicts and factors essential for sustaining peace, as well as in doing peacebuilding on the ground, two fundamental criticisms continue to be made regarding how international actors tend to go about their tasks. One widely made criticism points to the lack of sufficient attention to instilling ownership of peacebuilding goals within the countries of concern.[3] A related criticism points to the failure to strengthen in particular the collective ability of the leaders within the conflict countries to ensure a sustainable peace.

The Challenge of Local Ownership

Critics of current practice argue that international actors typically fail to create specific opportunities for the people themselves in these societies to take charge of the peacebuilding enterprise. With the possible exception of occasional participatory community development and conflict resolution projects at the most local levels, international approaches do not build in concrete mechanisms and processes for eliciting cooperative interaction among fighting or estranged groups and their political leaders. Yet these are the actors who are expected to take the reins of responsibility for achieving peace. Efforts to translate policy goals into concrete results suffer from a missing link, as international activities in conflict-prone countries often fail to enlist as the agents of change the people who are often in the best positions to undertake these efforts and who, after all, are presumed to hold the prerogatives of national sovereignty and wield the levers of decision-making.

Few themes have been sounded as loudly in the policy discourse of international peacebuilding and development as the need for "local ownership," to the point that this concept has become a mantra. For some years, the development aid community (which funds most peacebuilding activities) has repeatedly affirmed the need for local ownership and related ideals that stress the importance of supporting endogenous processes, using expressions such as "partnership" with local actors, "alignment" with host country priorities, "country-led development," "stakeholder participation," and country "resiliency."[4] However, the international approach to peacebuilding and development is criticized for still being driven largely by mandates, preconceptions, and programs defined outside the countries being served, and often taken from a standard menu and designed along certain sectoral lines.[5] Despite the rhetorical emphasis on the need to engage local stakeholders as partners, development agencies and their implementing NGOs dominate the relationship.[6] Little provision is made for cultivating more active involvement of the officials and citizens in these societies.[7] In many instances, the new delivery systems bypass the incumbent public authorities, and instead establish parallel structures through NGOs, a practice that can absolve authorities of their governing responsibilities.

In particular, most international development programs seek their goals by supplying financial support, in-kind goods, technical expertise, or personnel training. These programs typically have a mechanical quality that shows little appreciation for the ways in which formal institutions depend on the actions and practices of their component individuals and groups. International development programs assume that success is largely a matter of putting certain programs in place, even as these programs ignore how local personalities and groups view what the programs seek to do and how they do it. Little or no attention is given to fostering buy-in by the very societies that the international community endeavors to help. A related theme is found in critiques of the dominant "liberal peace" theory that often propels international actors: namely, that external peace and development efforts can only be effective if they understand and "work with the grain" of the prevailing and often informal institutions, processes, and mores that operate in "hybrid" societies, where liberal principles intermingle with indigenous behaviors.[8]

Without a more deliberate focus on internal processes for gaining commitment to peacebuilding in unstable states, and lacking built-in procedures to ensure such ownership, the usual ways in which the international community implements its programs often fail to achieve a sustainable peace. One study of six postconflict recovery cases concludes that aid infusions will not work in the absence of local commitments to peace.[9] What has been said generally of development programs applies to peacebuilding as well:

> No amount of external donor pressures or resources, by themselves, can produce sustained reform. It takes ownership, both of the policy change to be implemented and of any capacity building efforts intended to enhance implementation. Unless someone or some group in the country where policy reforms is being pursued feels that the changes are something that it wants to see happen, externally initiated change efforts . . . are likely to fail.[10]

This shortcoming reflects a deeper disconnect between the mindset of Western donors and the realities in divided societies and weak states. Most international policy goals and sectoral programs are based on the values and institutions of wealthy liberal democracies, such as a free market–based economy, multiparty elections, checks and balances between executive and legislatures, an independent judiciary, a professional military, a free and vigorous media, and a vibrant civil society.[11] Organizing programs that serve these norms, often in a deductive way for any and all country situations, is deemed an adequate response to prevent divided societies from descending into violence or to enable them to recover from war and establish a stable state.

Although international manuals now duly stress the need to analyze and understand each country context using a "conflict-sensitive" lens, the prescriptive policy frameworks in these guidelines tend to look toward achieving the same sets of objectives and ideal components. Perhaps the most criticized practice is to press for multiparty elections in the interest of democracy, while giving little consideration to whether the societies involved have reached a consensus on the rules of the political game so that electoral competition can be genuine and peaceful. In conflict-affected and divided societies, a sense of a shared national identity and interdependence is often lacking; the definition of "the nation" may be contested. Years after independence, many unstable states—though legally sovereign—have not established regularized, accepted arrangements for choosing rulers, handling relationships between majority and minority communities, and providing basic state functions. Formally accountable governing institutions may barely function in many areas and spheres, resulting in what Ashraf Ghani and Clare Lockhart call a "sovereignty gap."[12] These contested political environments mean that modern organizations do not operate in the way wealthy democracies know them.[13]

Instead, inter- and intrafactional divisiveness over the spoils of political power and the assets of the state are the order of the day. Deep factionalism has been found to be among the most direct antecedents of several forms of intrastate conflict such as civil wars and genocide.[14] When high-stakes events such as elections or crises like economic shocks and natural disasters occur, they easily become destabilizing because insecurity and political uncertainty can lead rival leaders and ordinary people to take the situation into their own hands through violence.[15] In societies that lack enforceable norms or procedures for managing such episodes and channeling their public expression, these events and crises may evoke outbreaks of hostility, counterreactions, and recurrent conflicts.

These realities in weak or failed states make external efforts to deal with political disputes sometimes harmful. Indeed, programs in such settings that seek to implant the competitive features of democracy may further divide competing groups and destabilize the state, thereby undermining the very political cohesion that the programs ultimately wish to achieve.[16] In Burundi, for example, international assistance promoted a hoped-for democratic transition through encouraging elections in 1993, but the resulting sudden reversal of political power spurred backlash from an officers' coup, followed by ethnic massacres which escalated to a civil war that lasted until 2005. The Burundian civil war killed more people than all the outbreaks of interethnic violence during the preceding decades under authoritarian regimes.

In this light, international admonitions for more "holistic," "integrated," and "scaled up" peacebuilding strategies also miss the key point. The myriad particular international projects and programs that deliver peacebuilding activities usually operate in isolation from each other, and international actors increasingly have recognized the need for multidimensional strategies that combine diplomatic, development, and security instruments (the so-called "3 Ds" of development, diplomacy, and defense). The theme of integration has led to menus of tasks or a "palette" of problem areas to be addressed, including ambitious goals such as establishing a democratic government, reforming the security sector, and creating a civil society.[17] A few governments and international organizations have created overarching cross-agency decision-making procedures that endeavor to tie multiple programs into "whole-of-government," multiactor strategies. The United Nations Peacebuilding Commission and the US State Department's Bureau of Conflict and Stabilization Operations, for example, have sought to get beyond the stovepiping of individual agencies and sectoral programs by fostering more coherence among the international actors working in the same country. NGO circles, which years ago recognized the need for "multitrack diplomacy," have elaborated on this theme of coherence more recently by outlining "systemic," synergistic procedures for doing peacebuilding.[18]

Although more concerted multifaceted, multifactor efforts are clearly needed, what has yet to be incorporated into this discussion is whether such greater external cooperation is politically palatable or administratively feasible in view of local realities. Similar to the program-specific literature, this multilevel agenda does not indicate specifically how to engage with a country's internal political and social dynamics—the indigenous vicissitudes of individual and collective relationships and the tactical maneuverings of politics through which desired goals might be reached. The processes of gaining active consent are neglected, not only among the international outsiders but also within the host countries.

Clearly, the main task of building peace and democracy in such contexts is not to apply sector-specific institutional, technological, or analytical "fixes," nor even combinations of these fixes. Instead, the challenge is to involve local people in actively overcoming the tensions and mistrust that conflicts both stem from and inspire, and to help them work together across ethnic and political divisions. In short, the central challenge is not simply positing *what* needs to be achieved, but learning *how* to achieve it—in the specific sense of motivating local actions that marry ideal goals with particular people.[19]

Political Leaders as Pivotal

A corollary of the lack of attention to local ownership is the lack of effective efforts to promote responsible and cohesive endogenous political leadership that avoids or manages violent conflicts and undertakes peacebuilding. Conflict and institutional transformation require influencing how political and social leaders pursue their interests, understand what is at stake in conflicts, relate to one another, and engage in collective decision-making. A useful classification here involves four main entry points in a society that outside strategies can target. Interventions can seek to achieve one or more of the following basic kinds of change:

- *Structural* transformation.
- A change in the *players* or personnel who have influence.
- *Issue* or *policy* transformation.
- *Personal/elite* transformation of leading figures.[20]

Most sectoral development programs—economic, social, or political—target only the first two dimensions. It is common to assert that structural conditions (the so-called root causes) must be addressed in order to achieve lasting peace, and therefore programs encourage structural development efforts such as stimulating small and medium enterprises to create employment opportunities. Electoral assistance also organizes procedures for choosing and changing rulers—the players or personnel noted above. Although these first two dimensions are important elements of an overall long-term strategy, effective strategies also must address the other two entry points: substantive issues and the behavior of leading actors. Social scientists make a related distinction between *structure*, the societal conditions and institutions within which individual human beings operate, and *agency*, the realm of action that individual human beings can affect. This critique of current development and peacebuilding practice is that such practices largely neglect agency in favor of structure. In I. William Zartman's words, the dominant approaches that target broad societal conditions tend to

> . . . explain the supersaturation of the situation but none identify the crystallizing agent . . . the personally motivated political actor who sees and describes the situation as vulnerable to his blandishments and ready for conflict . . . remedies for identity conflicts are themselves insufficient if they address only the underlying conditions, since the agent is best placed to keep stoking the fires of identity conflict . . . targeting the agent with appropriate countermeasures is as important as dealing with the conditions themselves.[21]

Although Zartman is referring to political actors who instigate conflict, his point applies equally to leaders who might step up to build peace. The outlooks and practices of potential local agents of change are not simply direct results of underlying structural conditions or of institutional weaknesses, but operate with some independence from those factors. The behavior, actions, and attitudes of individual leaders, factions, and parties are themselves a significant part of both the problem and the solution.

Fortunately, some research on developing and transitioning states has begun to look more closely at political leaders and their relationships. The phenomenon of "conflict entrepreneurs" who use their positions to mobilize support for partisan ends and stir up conflicts is widely acknowledged. By dint of their influence, leaders also can promote peaceful outcomes. In some societies, considerable influence is exerted on ordinary people by traditional elders or other leaders who possess authority and thus play crucial roles in avoiding intergroup conflicts.[22] Traditional leaders tend to be most influential at the local level, but the argument applies to the national level as well. Insiders who are connected to the main constituencies in a society are often critical in legitimating a peace process, thus helping to sustain it.[23] In weak states, where strong and legitimate state authorities are not in place, political leaders who wield assets such as patronage to maintain followings can be either major obstacles or enablers of peace and development.[24]

Some of this recent research has underscored the central importance for basic stability of achieving "political settlements." These are not necessarily the formal peace accords in postconflict countries, but may involve the ongoing allocations of power that are implicitly agreed upon, primarily among elites, in conflict-affected countries or weak states.[25] Because civil society is often politically divided and weak in such settings, these dominant arrangements among political elites can support or subvert efforts to resolve conflicts and maintain stability. Similarly, the World Bank argues that it is crucial to obtain buy-in from an "inclusive enough" coalition of the political elite to achieve reliable agreement on certain rules of the political game.[26]

This is not to say that political leaders are usually able to bring about positive changes on their own. International approaches should not put much stock in the frequent resort to simply exhort leaders to bring about peace. A study of Afghanistan, Kosovo, and Sierra Leone finds that strong rewards and sanctions exerted by international actors were indispensable in bringing contending leaders to the peace table and converting them from warlords to "peacelords." In the absence of inducements, the leaders would not have altered their own behavior, for they had little to gain or the motivation and power to initiate peace. Their respective constituencies were incapable of bringing about positive changes, and the leaders did not have sufficient political and administrative skills to run their countries. The study suggests that international investments in training leaders in how to use their authority for conflict management, instead of conflict instigation, would pay significant dividends.[27] Stellar transforming domestic figures such as South Africa's Nelson Mandela are rare, and it is unwise to rely heavily on charismatic, seemingly powerful individuals to be "reform champions."[28]

In sum, a number of studies suggest that international organizations that promote conflict resolution, peacebuilding, and development give more systematic attention to incentivizing leaders and political elites as a promising entry point.

To be sure, international interventions to move leaders from open, intergroup conflicts to peaceful political systems already use certain tools such as negotiation and mediation to reach agreements. However, such third-party engagement often stops once power-sharing arrangements are agreed that parcel out offices among contending factions, thereby creating a "government of men" but not necessarily a "government of laws." To effect a more complete transition, a kind of ongoing, hands-on intercession needs to go beyond mediating the initial protocols to establish enforceable rules for governing that can regulate leaders' inveterate power struggles. Such diplomacy continues to engage the leaders of countries in transition, rather than leaving them on their own once agreements are signed. A study of the implementation of five peace settlements concludes that the most effective cases were those in which third parties continuously cultivated, cajoled, and supported a country's political actors in order to ensure a continued peace.[29] Another study advises:

> flexible and pro-active political management of peacekeeping . . . to win and keep popular support and create (not just enjoy) the support of local forces of order . . . ways to generate *voluntary* cooperation from divided local political actors and mobilize existing local resources for *locally legitimate*, collective purposes.[30]

In sum, the two lines of criticism above argue that to achieve sustainable peace in divided societies, international interventions must deliberately incorporate a *process* perspective that focuses specifically on improving the human interactions surrounding the policy issues and political disputes in a conflict-affected country, and an *agent* perspective that addresses the attitudes, beliefs, views, behaviors, and relationships among particular influential leaders and political elites who can make a difference:

> [S]uccess in pursuing reforms requires recognizing that reform is about process and people (who wins and who loses from reforms), as well as about content. . . . The policy implementation process is at least as political as technical, and is complex and highly interactive. Besides technical and institutional analysis, it calls for consensus-building, participation of key stakeholders, conflict resolution, compromise, contingency planning, and adaptation.[31]

The Option of Nonofficial Peacemaking

This book examines a particular method for acting toward conflicts that explicitly claims to be able to close the gap in achieving local ownership and political motivation by facilitating collaboration among leaders in conflict-affected states. This method purports to remedy shortcomings in current peacemaking approaches by instilling in a country's own leaders the motivation and sense of responsibility for resolving their conflicts, and thereby achieving certain prerequisites for sustained peace. As a result, it provides an especially important focus for grounded, systematic inquiry. To do so, this book looks closely at major examples of this type of nonofficial engagement in six countries: Burundi, Cyprus, Estonia, Guyana, Sri Lanka, and Tajikistan. The case study chapters describe and assess particular initiatives that applied this distinctive interactive technique in divided societies to help their leaders work together in fashioning a sustainable peace.

In essence, this approach involves engaging influential political and other societal leaders from across the lines of a conflict in intensive workshops that seek to foster group cohesion and thus encourage cooperative actions to resolve the conflict. Typically, these initiatives bring together small groups of key political leaders or influential citizens in informal, nonthreatening, but structured meeting formats devoted to training and relationship building. Most of these meetings involve national leaders who occupy top or mid-level positions, but some include local leaders. These interventions are nonbinding, confidential, and unofficial, but may operate under or alongside more formal official diplomatic and political processes.[32]

Such facilitated, unofficial processes have been given various names, including "interactive conflict resolution," "conflict transformation," "track-two diplomacy," "problem-solving workshops," "collaborative analytical problem solving," "pre-negotiations," "third-party consultations," "informal mediation," "controlled communication," or "conflict transformation training."[33] Sometimes, they are known as "quiet diplomacy."[34] Described in "track" terms, these initiatives lie below the level of official "track one" diplomacy and involve actors at the "one and a half," "two," and "three" track levels. Using Mary Anderson and Lara Olson's fourfold classification of NGO projects, these initiatives mainly involve "key people" rather than "many people," and at least initially, they stress "individual/personal" (or small group) work rather than "sociopolitical" or policy problems.[35]

These unofficial interactive methods have been applied in many countries around the world, usually by NGOs and often with regard to intrastate conflicts. The effective nonofficial role played by the Catholic lay order of Sant'Egidio in the Mozambican peace process following the 1977–92 civil war has received considerable publicity, as have initiatives in Israeli-Palestinian relations that have been conducted for decades.[36] However, numerous other conflict resolution initiatives using nonofficial techniques have been carried out at national or subnational levels in areas such as Cambodia, Lebanon, central Africa, and the Horn of Africa.[37] From the urban neighborhoods in Belfast and interethnic villages in the Balkans to the forests of the Casamance in southern Senegal, desolate areas of northern Nigeria, grasslands of southern Sudan, and the steppes of Central Asia, projects using these interactive methods have been organized to reduce local tensions and manage internal conflicts. Nonofficial diplomacy of this sort also has been applied in state-to-state relations, such as in east Asia and regarding the Kashmir dispute between India and Pakistan.[38] Yet although NGO projects funded by development agencies have used these unofficial methods extensively, they are not regularly employed by the diplomatic or security communities, nor have they been accepted as a standard tool in the foreign policies of the United States or other countries.

Aims and Organization of the Volume

Despite their many applications, the record and potential of these structured interactive initiatives have received surprisingly little systematic, evidence-based academic or policy research. Interactive methods for building collaborative capacity rarely have been evaluated in rigorous ways to determine their actual performance and potential.[39] As the development agencies that often finance these efforts began to ask what their outlays were achieving, they commissioned evaluations of development programs that use such dialogue techniques.[40] Researchers have begun to conduct more rigorous studies of such projects (see chapter 2). Nevertheless, most of the literature on these activities is descriptive and prone to claiming results such as "conflict transformation," "empowerment," and "capacity building" based on intentions or anecdotal evidence rather than systematic analysis.[41]

The paucity of analysis to date need not leave us with the extremes of uncritical naïveté or unexamined cynicism. If the failure to incorporate techniques for building collaborative capacity into conventional peacebuilding interventions accounts for a significant portion of the fragility of many peace agreements, these structured interactive initiatives deserve to be included as a tool that diplomats use more often in peacemaking and peacebuilding efforts. To help fill the evaluation gap, this volume probes systematically into the ability of six examples of the use of nonintrusive methods to engage key leaders in conflict-affected countries and thereby to stimulate local ownership of and political commitment to resolving conflicts and building a sustained peace. The case studies in chapters 3 through 8 look at the following projects:

- Burundi: Burundi Leadership Training Program (BLTP)
- Cyprus: Harvard Study Group Process for Cyprus (HSG)
- Estonia: A joint project of the University of Virginia's Center for the Study of Mind and Human Interaction and The Carter Center (CSMHI-TCC)
- Guyana: United Nations Development Program's Social Cohesion Program (SCP)
- Sri Lanka: One-Text Initiative (OTI)
- Tajikistan: Inter-Tajik Dialogue (ITD).

All six cases (hereafter referred to as the "initiatives") involved nonofficial facilitation processes to assist the sides in intrastate, national-level ethnopolitical conflicts to achieve a peaceful, lasting settlement of their differences. To expect such initiatives to have discernible results, the cases chosen all entailed a series of workshops held over several years and thus went beyond "one-shot" projects with one or two meetings. But being time-limited, all have finished their basic activities, allowing for some retrospective consideration of possible lasting impacts. No a priori judgment was made as to whether the selected cases were successes or failures; this consideration is one of the main questions being pursued. The research was also interested in learning about the impacts of process interventions at different stages of conflict. Thus, the case studies examine two potentially violent conflicts (Estonia and Guyana), two active conflicts (Tajikistan, Sri Lanka), and two past or waning examples (Cyprus, Burundi). Five of the initiatives have not received previous intensive evaluations, the exception being the Tajikistan project.

All the countries in which these initiatives were undertaken are relatively small in terms of both geography and population, and are ethnically divided. Linguistic, religious, racial, and/or regional groups constituted the constituencies of the main antagonists in conflict. In all six countries, outside third parties undertook initiatives that deliberately employed interactive methods in hopes of implementing peace agreements to resolve violent conflicts or managing contentious intercommunal political or policy disputes so they would not escalate into violence.

To research these cases, the volume editors commissioned experienced analysts who were familiar with this type of intervention and its theory, and had knowledge of each case study's particular initiative and its country's conflict. By presenting and analyzing these cases, the volume seeks to add to knowledge about both the potential and limits of this distinctive approach.

To identify the effects that these methods are thought to be capable of achieving, chapter 2 elaborates on the theory of change that is embodied in interactive conflict resolution. This discussion delineates the distinctive characteristics of this method, the case that has been advanced in support of its unique value as a way to get beyond conflicts, and a consideration of what the intended ultimate goal of "sustainable peace" means in a concrete, measureable sense. The chapter then lays out the common framework of questions that the case study authors were asked to use to investigate their respective cases. Such a framework was needed so that the volume could uncover possible general patterns from these different cases. The framework draws upon findings from existing research.

Part two contains the six case study chapters. The authors were asked to "interview" their cases using the same set of questions from the framework. First, each chapter characterizes the sources and drivers of the conflict in the country and the nature of the particular process intervention being studied. The authors then assess the direct or indirect effects that the process intervention seems to have had in moving the conflict toward a sustainable resolution, and discuss the main factors that explain these effects. Each author concludes with the action implications that the case suggests.

In part three, chapter 9 reviews the case studies to pull out generalizable findings about the kinds and extent of the contributions that this type of intervention has made to conflict resolution and peacebuilding. This accounting enables the chapter to return to the volume's core question: To what extent have these methods remedied the lack of local ownership and political buy-in in international peacebuilding and thereby improved the prospects for a lasting peace? It then ranks the initiatives in terms of their comparative effectiveness. The second part of chapter 9 seeks to identify what kinds of country settings and conflict situations are most amenable to this interactive approach and what key features of these efforts explain their greater or lesser success. Do certain types of conflicts appear to be most amenable to the application of these collaborative capacity building interventions? What timing is optimal? Which workshop techniques accomplish the most effective results? How do the processes relate to conventional forms of diplomacy and the country's ongoing political processes? Based on these findings, what guidance is suggested as to where, when, and how these types of interventions can be most effective? What advice emerges for practitioners about how to design and implement these interventions for the most productive results?

To conclude the volume, chapter 10 briefly characterizes the recent changing milieu of conflict and state fragility. In view of the book's findings about the strengths and limits of these interactive methods, the chapter proposes a way that the methods can be conducted to be especially relevant to this contemporary context. In brief, the chapter argues that peacebuilders in given countries can more fully realize the potential of the approach and overcome its evident limits if its particular methods are used to inaugurate modest, carefully targeted, and years-long efforts to incrementally build rule-governed institutions, and are backed up by fine-tuned, compelling international incentives.

The volume is intended for several readerships. For diplomats, lay citizens, students, and others who may be relatively unfamiliar with interactive methods, the book provides several illustrative and leading examples of this particular craft. For the growing numbers of conflict resolution specialists, trainers, students, policy analysts, development agencies, and international policymakers who generally are familiar with this methodology, the book seeks to expand and deepen their understanding of its distinctive contributions and its limits, enabling them to make informed choices among the repertoire of options they use to address conflicts.

However mixed the record of international peacebuilding is thus far, the immense toll in human misery and destruction from intrastate wars and failing states continues to mount, and international actors are spending billions of dollars on techniques and strategies that may achieve less than is possible to achieve a sustainable peace and to prevent violent destructive conflicts from thwarting that goal. New conflicts break out every year. By documenting this approach's advantages and its limitations in fostering in-country conflict management and self-regulating governance, this volume seeks to provide a sounder basis for giving this unofficial approach an appropriate place in the international conflict management, state-building, and development toolbox.

Notes

1. See for example, Human Security Report Project, *Human Security Report 2013: The Decline in Global Violence: Evidence, Explanation, and Contestation* (Vancouver: Human Security Press, 2013); Simon Fraser University, *Human Security Report 2009/2010: The Causes of Peace and the Shrinking Costs of War* (New York: Oxford University Press, 2011), 7. International peacekeeping forces in particular are generally concluded as having had a significant effect in curtailing internal wars. See Ian Johnstone, *Peace Operations Literature Review* (New York: Center for International Cooperation, 2005), 7; Virginia Page Fortna, "Does Peacekeeping Keep Peace? International Intervention and the Duration of Peace after Civil War," *International Studies Quarterly* 48, no. 2 (2004): 288; and Séverine Autesserre, *Peaceland: Conflict Resolution and the Everyday Politics of International Intervention* (Cambridge: Cambridge University Press, 2014), 7ff., 16.

2. The concept and elements of conflict prevention were laid out in Michael S. Lund, *Preventing Violent Conflicts: A Strategy for Preventive Diplomacy* (Washington, DC: United States Institute of Peace Press, 1996). The case for prevention was argued by Bruce W. Jentleson in *Preventive Diplomacy and Ethnic Conflict: Possible, Difficult, Necessary*, Policy Paper 27, Institute on Global Conflict and Cooperation, June 1996.

3. See, e.g., Laurie Nathan, *No Ownership, No Commitment: A Guide to Local Ownership of Security Sector Reform* (Birmingham, UK: University of Birmingham: 2007), http://issat.dcaf.ch/content/download/2210/19148/file/Nathan%20No_Ownership _No_Commitment.pdf; Frank Bliss and Stefan Neumann, *Participation in International Development Discourse and Practice: "State of the Art" and Challenges*, INEF Report 94/2008 (Duisberg, Germany: Institute for Development and Peace, Universitat Duisberg-Essen, 2007); Timothy Donais, "Empowerment or Imposition? Dilemmas of Local Ownership in Post-Conflict Peacebuilding Processes," *Peace and Change* 34, no. 1 (2009): 3–26: Autesserre, *Peaceland*, 3ff., 8, 13.

4. See, e.g., Organisation for Economic Co-operation and Development (OECD), "Monitoring the Principles for Good International Engagement in Fragile States and Situations," (Paris: OECD, 2015), http://www.oecd.org/dacfragilestates/47278529.pdf. Donors have endorsed these aspirations in a series of global development conferences such as in Busan, Korea in 2011.

5. Donais, "Empowerment or Imposition?," 3ff.

6. Hannah Reich, *"Local Ownership" in Conflict Transformation Projects: Partnership, Participation, or Patronage?*, Berghof Occasional Paper 27 (Berlin: Berghof Research Center for Constructive Conflict Management, 2006), http://edoc.vifapol.de /opus/volltexte/2011/2544/pdf/boc27e.pdf.

7. See, e.g., Nathan, *No Ownership, No Commitment*; and Autesserre, *Peaceland*, 4n3, 4, for other sources making this critique.

8. Volker Boege, Anne Brown, Kevin Clements, and Anna Nolan, *On Hybrid Political Orders and Emerging States: State Formation in the Context of "Fragility"* (Berlin: Berghof Research Center for Constructive Conflict Management, October 2008). Somaliland, an autonomous region of Somalia, is cited as an outstanding example of internally driven peacebuilding.

9. See Anne-Marie Smith, *Advances in Understanding International Peacemaking, Volume II* (Washington, DC: United States Institute of Peace, 2001), 51.

10. Derick W. Brinkerhoff and Benjamin L. Crosby, *Managing Policy Reform: Concepts and Tools for Decision-Makers in Developing and Transitioning Countries* (Bloomfield, CT: Kumarian Press, 2002), 6.

11. Donais, "Empowerment or Imposition?," 5; cf. "[I]nternational policy tends to be guided by models that are framed by certain norms of what a state *ought* to look like and how it *ought* to be run," in Alex De Waal, "Fixing the Political Marketplace: How Can We Make Peace without Functioning State Institutions?" (Christian Michelsen lecture, Bergen, October 15, 2009), 1.

12. Ashraf Ghani and Clare Lockhart, *Fixing Failed States: A Framework for Rebuilding a Fractured World* (New York: Oxford University Press, 2009), 21.

13. Michael W. Doyle and Nicholas Sambanis, *Making War and Building Peace: United Nations Peace Operations* (Princeton, NJ: Princeton University Press, 2006), 19.

14. See Jack A. Goldstone et al., "A Global Model for Forecasting Political Instability," *American Journal of Political Science* 54, no. 1 (2010): 190–208.

15. Timothy D. Sisk, *Power-Sharing and International Mediation in Ethnic Conflicts* (Washington, DC: United States Institute of Peace Press, 1996), 80.

16. Howard Wolpe and Steve McDonald, "Democracy and Peacebuilding: Rethinking the Conventional Wisdom," *The Round Table* 97, no. 394 (2008): 137–45.

17. Dan Smith, *Towards a Strategic Framework for Peacebuilding: Getting Their Act Together* (Oslo: Royal Norwegian Ministry of Foreign Affairs, 2004), 28.

18. See, e.g., Robert Ricigliano, *Making Peace Last: A Toolbox for Sustainable Peacebuilding* (Boulder, CO: Paradigm Publishers, 2012).

19. "[T]he process of international efforts (the 'how') is just as important to examine as their substance (the 'what')." Autesserre, *Peaceland*, 9.

20. Hugh Miall, "Conflict Transformation: A Multi-Dimensional Task," in *Transforming Ethnopolitical Conflict: The Berghof Handbook*, ed. Alex Austin et al. (Wiesbaden: VS Verlag, 2004), 77–78.

21. I. William Zartman, "Managing Ethnic Conflict," First Perlmutter Lecture, *Foreign Policy Research Institute Wire* 6, no. 5 (1998): 1–2.

22. James Fearon and David Laitin, "Explaining Interethnic Cooperation," *American Political Science Review* 90 (December 1996) 715–35; Ashutosh Varshney, *Ethnic Conflict and Civic Life: Hindus and Muslims in India* (New Haven, CT: Yale University Press, 2002); Joseph G. Bock, "The Exercise of Authority to Prevent Communal Conflict," *Peace and Change* 26, no. 2 (2001): 187–203.

23. Simon Mason, *Insider Mediators: Exploring Their Key Role in Informal Peace Processes* (Berlin: Berghof Foundation for Peace Support, 2009), 18.

24. See de Waal, "Fixing the Political Marketplace," 7, 9, 19.

25. "Understanding the elite bargain that lies at the heart of any political settlement provides a window for assessing state fragility and resilience as well as possibilities for reform and change." Jonathan Di John and James Putzel, "Political Settlements: Issues

Paper," Governance and Social Development Resource Centre (Birmingham, UK: Governance and Social Development Resource Centre, June 2009), 17; See the final report of this five-year research project at James Putzel and Jonathan Di John, *Meeting the Challenges of Crisis States* (London: Crisis States Research Centre, 2012). See also Ghani and Lockhart, *Fixing Failed States*, x.

26. World Bank, *World Development Report 2011: Conflict, Security and Development* (Washington, DC: World Bank, 2011), 120–24.

27. Gordon Peake, Cathy Gormley-Heenan, and Mari Fitzduff, *From Warlords to Peacelords: Local Leadership Capacity in Peace Processes* (Londonderry, UK: INCORE, December 2004): 13–15, http://www.incore.ulst.ac.uk/research/projects/wlpl/WlplFull.pdf.

28. Diane de Gramont, *Beyond Magic Bullets in Governance Reform* (Washington, DC: Carnegie Endowment for International Peace, November 2014), 5–7.

29. Fen Osler Hampson, *Nurturing Peace: Why Peace Settlements Succeed or Fail* (Washington, DC: United States Institute of Peace Press, 1996), 207; see also Elizabeth Cousens, "It Ain't Over 'til It's Over: What Role for Mediation in Post-Agreement Contexts?" (Geneva: Centre for Humanitarian Dialogue, 2008).

30. Doyle and Sambanis, *Making War and Building Peace*, 310 (emphasis in original).

31. Brinkerhoff and Crosby, *Managing Policy Reform*, xi, 5.

32. Use of these techniques in broad people-to-people diplomacy, as illustrated by projects between Israelis and Palestinians and Georgians and Abkhazians, are not considered here; see, e.g., Adel Atieh et al., *Peace in the Middle East: P2P and the Israeli-Palestinian Conflict* (New York: United Nations Institute for Disarmament Research, 2005).

33. Tamra Pearson D'Estree, "Problem Solving Approaches," in *The SAGE Handbook of Conflict Resolution*, ed. Jacob Bercovitch, Viktor Kremenyk, and I. William Zartman (Thousand Oaks, CA: SAGE, 2009), 51.

34. Craig Collins and John Packer, *Options and Techniques for Quiet Diplomacy* (Sandvagen, Sweden: Folke Bernadotte Academy, 2006).

35. Mary B. Anderson and Lara Olson, *Confronting War: Critical Lessons for Peace Practitioners* (Cambridge, MA: The Collaborative for Development Action, 2003), 55–57.

36. See, e.g., Andrea Bartoli, "Mediating Peace in Mozambique: The Role of the Community of Sant'Egidio," in *Herding Cats: Multiparty Mediation in a Complex World*, ed. Chester A. Crocker, Fen Osler Hampson, and Pamela R. Aall (Washington, DC: United States Institute of Peace Press, 1999), 245–74; Herbert C. Kelman, "Interactive Problem-Solving in the Israeli-Palestinian Case: Past Contributions and Present Challenges," in *Paving the Way: Contributions of Interactive Conflict Resolution to Peacemaking*, ed. Ronald J. Fisher (Lanham, MD: Lexington Books, 2005), 41–64.

37. Ronald Fisher, "Interactive Conflict Resolution," in *Peacemaking in International Conflict: Methods and Techniques*, ed. William Zartman and Lewis Rasmussen (Washington, DC: United States Institute of Peace Press, 1997), 242.

38. See, e.g., Navnita Chadha Behera, Paul M. Evans, and Gowher Rizvi, *Beyond Boundaries: A Report on the State of Non-official Dialogues on Peace, Security and Cooperation in South Asia*; and Paul M. Evans, "Canada and Asia Pacific's Track-Two Diplomacy," *International Journal* 64, no. 4 (Autumn 2009): 1027–38.

39. Ronald J. Fisher, "The Problem Solving Workshop as a Method of Research," *International Negotiation* 9, no. 3 (2004): 394; and Tobias Böhmelt, "The Effectiveness of Tracks of Diplomacy Strategies in Third-Party Interventions," *Journal of Peace Research* 47, no. 2 (2010): 167–78.

40. See, e.g., Michael Lund, "Getting Beyond Good Intentions or Cynicism: Methods and Findings from a Peace and Conflict Impact Evaluation of Three NGO 'Track-Two' Dialogues in Africa" (paper presented at the Annual Meeting of the International Studies Association, New Orleans, March 27, 2002); Larry S. Beyna, Michael Lund, Stacey Stacks, Janet Tuthill, and Patricia Vondal, *The Effectiveness of Civil Society Initiatives in Controlling Violent Conflicts and Building Peace: A Study of Three Approaches in the Greater Horn of Africa*, Greater Horn of Africa Peace Building Project (Washington, DC: Management Systems International for US Agency for International Development, June 2001).

41. "How to" manuals, with useful steps and best practices in designing and conducting these types of projects, are available. But as some manuals acknowledge, a distinction needs to be made between the question of *how* best to do these projects once a commitment has been made to carry one out, and the prior question about *whether* the method is feasible or will add sufficient value to warrant its being utilized at all (i.e., whether there is a comparative advantage in relation to other ways to approach a conflict). See, e.g., Heidi Burgess and Guy Burgess, *Conducting Track II Peacemaking*, University of Colorado Conflict Information Consortium (Washington, DC: United States Institute of Peace, 2010), 6, 10.

Chapter 2

Unofficial Conflict Resolution
and Sustainable Peace
Michael Lund

Introduction

To place the case study chapters in the context of existing work on conflict resolution, this chapter lays out the essential features of interactive conflict transformation methods, expectations about how these methods can resolve conflicts and build peace, and criticisms regarding their limits. It then discusses the ultimate goal sought by peacebuilding: a sustained, durable, or lasting peace. It concludes with the framework of questions that the case study authors were asked to investigate and illustrative findings from existing research.

Unofficial Conflict Resolution: Theory of Practice

Essential Features

Third parties can endeavor to ameliorate conflicts across ethnic or political divisions in a country through several methods that directly engage contending leaders with the aim of shaping their motivations, views, and actions. The nature of these interventions varies, but all have the conflicting parties enter into back-and-forth communications in order to work toward agreements on difficult political or policy disputes. Perhaps the most common forms of these direct measures are third-party mediation and negotiations conducted through official diplomatic channels. The basic rationale is that third-party intervention can lead the conflicting parties to discover common interests, identify potentially acceptable compromises, persuade them to bargain and ideally to reach some mutual accommodation. These instruments may be accompanied by various kinds of pressure, ranging from positive incentives such as offers of aid to negative inducements such as economic sanctions or the threat of military action.[1] If such channels do not exist when parties are weighing their options, they have little motivation to meet and explore the possibility of bridging their differences. As a result, they often pursue their interests unilaterally through hostile, coercive, or violent actions.

Unlike these "power" approaches that involve external pressure, some approaches to direct engagement do not wield either carrots or sticks, but simply offer the antagonists channels for interparty communication. Under official auspices, these techniques may be called consultations, conciliation, or good offices. Under nonofficial auspices, these methods include facilitated interactive communications and problem-solving conflict resolution workshops often referred to as interactive conflict transformation—the subject of this volume. This latter approach seeks common ground between the parties by organizing nonthreatening opportunities for face-to-face information sharing, dialogue, and other unforced interactions. By convening selected groups of high-level political and/or civil society leaders in joint training and other exercises, these nonbinding intercessions seek most immediately to impart skills, concepts, and attitudes and to build relationships, trust, and confidence among the opposed actors or estranged parties. The processes are more engineered than a simple open forum or opportunity for dialogue, which could merely lead to the protagonists asserting their respective positions without gaining an appreciation of each other's interests and possible interdependency. It is hoped that this experience will transform the way the differing groups see each other and understand their differences, thereby enabling them to work effectively together and change their contrary actions and policies. Even though these methods work at levels of politics and society below the highest level of elected or appointed officials, they seek ultimately to influence official decisions.[2]

Expectations for Conflict Resolution and Peacebuilding

Underlying the nuts and bolts of any intervention or program lies some *theory of change*—stated or presumed—that reflect beliefs about what kinds of actions will likely lead to what results and through what causal mechanisms. These strategies arise out of assumptions, which also may or may not be explicit, about the problem being addressed.[3] What is the basic case being made about the added value of the distinctive interactive conflict transformation approach in postconflict or other vulnerable societies?

Unlike the more adversarial and formal nature of the directive forms of third-party intervention, the gentler methods of interactive conflict transformation are intended to help the parties communicate with each other and recognize common needs. In contrast to the interventions undertaken through official diplomacy, which typically turn immediately to the substantive issues in contention and initiate bargaining, interactive conflict transformation is more open-ended and relationship-oriented. By cautiously exploring latent or openly expressed conflicting attitudes and perceptions, these methods create an opportunity for off-the-record conversations that can enable the parties to work together to resolve the deeper issues underlying their conflict. As a matter of principle, the methods eschew the use of coercive or even positive material incentives to motivate the parties, and rely instead on the prospect of nonpressuring, noncommittal methods to gain their attention and motivate them.

This nonobligatory character is viewed as one of the method's main assets because voluntary participation is expected to elicit more committed participation.[4] The noncommittal and confidential character of these engagements also can free the participants from being strictly tied to the established positions of the official parties, and this can make it easier for official governmental actors to participate in these activities.[5] Moreover, because participants are involved in face-to-face prolonged and facilitated engagement in nonpublic settings usually not afforded by the tougher forms of third-party involvement, these methods encourage the parties to take more responsibility for resolving their own conflicts. Key political, military, and civil society actors may develop a sense of ownership of the outstanding issues and interests at stake, which then can help build a constituency to cooperatively resolve them. The outcomes may include the following beneficial results:

- Moving from confrontational to cooperative modes of communication;
- Altering stereotypical images of "the other," thereby humanizing one's opponent;

- Strengthening interpersonal and group relationships between adversaries;
- Redefining the parties' perceived problems, needs, and interests;
- Enabling the sides to consider questions of identity and other deeper human needs, such as entrenched inequities;
- Encouraging the adoption of overriding collective norms and rules;
- Enlarging the range of options considered by the parties; and
- Developing and carrying out specific ways to cooperate.

In addition, these methods are thought to increase the chances that any conflict settlements or other agreements achieved will be more sustainable than those developed solely with the other, more pressuring methods. Without ample opportunities to discover mutual needs, opposed groups are likely to bargain over less important issues, and they will tend to acquiesce to temporary settlements and agreements that are desired by official mediators and pressed on the parties. In contrast, the nonofficial interactive approach can penetrate to the emotional, attitudinal, cognitive, and ideational levels that lie behind actors' behavior. By identifying the parties' respective needs, the interactive approach can possibly change relationships of antagonism to ones of joint problem-solving to ameliorate the wider conflict.[6] Official diplomatic efforts at conflict management tend to address the short-term symptoms of conflicts; by contrast, interactive techniques can begin to address underlying causes that give rise to such symptoms, such as socioeconomic disparities and mistreatment by institutions, and thus lead to a more lasting peace. Indeed, in this view, it is necessary to obtain the buy-in, personal transformations, and closer relationships of the parties involved before they will make serious commitments to long-term solutions. Empathy about mutual needs and a shared awareness of the costs of continued hostility can unlock the parties' willingness to resolve those deeper sources.[7]

Early proponents of this method contrasted it with the "realist" school of international relations. Contrary to the realists' beliefs, the most fundamental actors in the world's protracted conflicts were not states, but identity groups. Only face-to-face communication among these groups about their shared basic human needs—such as security, collective recognition, and participation—can motivate them to freely resolve conflicts in self-sustaining ways. By mutually exploring issues, learning concepts, and gaining skills, the groups can clarify their real interests and move beyond their conflicts to agree on solutions that establish more cooperative arrangements for mutual decision-making and remedy fundamental power and economic imbalances.[8]

Critiques

Serious skepticism has been expressed about the extent to which these methods actually can achieve the results that are attributed to them and thereby contribute to sustained peace. Most fundamentally, the small-scale nature of these conflict transformation initiatives, and their emphasis on individuals and social-psychological phenomena, may be ill-suited and ineffectual for addressing the difficult multilevel issues of national and international political conflicts and policies. It is observed that this method is prone to confusing the interpersonal dynamics of small group relationships with the deeper and stronger political and societal currents that govern group relationships in larger arenas, such as among the political leaders of major communities and interest groups in a state, who also interact with an international system of states.[9]

Efforts to demonstrate such effects must come to terms with the problem of the level of analysis, particularly the challenge of "scaling up" from interpersonal relations to collective action. Research on interethnic relations suggests that positive changes in individual attitudes, and even interethnic commercial and physical contact such as in a marketplace, do not necessarily translate into more positive behavior by larger organized groups such as ethnic-based political parties. Studies of the "ethnic contact thesis" show that individuals may indeed adopt more positive attitudes toward other individuals from an opposed group with whom they meet and perhaps even transact business. However, those changes do not necessarily carry over to what those individuals do when participating in larger political activities that involve competing interests among differing groups, such as voting in elections.[10] Speaking of the human relations school of psychology that spawned much of the theory behind these initiatives, the international relations theorist Kenneth Waltz (a prominent exponent of the realist school) concluded that "the more fully (such) behavioral scientists take account of politics, the more sensible and the more modest their efforts to contribute to peace become."[11]

Conflict transformation researchers themselves point to the related problem of "reentry" or "transfer": whether the gains produced in the special environment of the workshop can make a difference in the normal bureaucratic and political settings to which the participants return.[12] These researchers urge advocates of interactive techniques not to underestimate the influence of pervasive vested political and economic interests that shape the behavior of the participants in their usual positions and daily milieus. In

the words of Norbert Ropers, a leading practitioner-theorist of these techniques: "What good is individual insights into similar basic needs, when
the real problem is the superstructure of competing elites, institutions and
ideologies?"[13] For example, nondirective interaction techniques are easily
exploited in asymmetric conflicts, in which one side holds preponderant
power. Meetings may lower tensions, but they also may simply mask fundamental imbalances in power and social advantage and vitiate the impetus
to make meaningful progress.[14]

Other critics have observed that the values and norms imparted by the
methods reflect their Western cultural origins and may not be readily trans-
ferable to non-Western societies.[15] Similar criticism questions whether the
participants chosen for these unofficial exchanges are often from the more
professional circles in their societies, and so may already be largely "converted" to the norms of the exercise, but do not reflect the perspectives of the
antagonists on each side who are most centrally involved in the conflict.[16]

Regrettably, there is as yet little solid basis for adjudicating between these
differing views of the import of this method. With a few exceptions, these
initiatives have not been rigorously evaluated.[17] In the years following the
end of the Cold War, little systematic analysis was conducted on the multiple
approaches to achieving peace that were being tried. Development agencies
funded various "conflict resolution" projects in conflict-affected societies,
largely assuming that energetic efforts driven by good intentions could make
a difference. Little hard evidence was gathered on the impacts and efficacy
of differing approaches. Judgments of the value of individual conflict resolution projects often have been based simply on the enthusiasm that often is
expressed by their participants; less attention has been paid to documenting possible "transfer effects"—what participants did or did not affect as
a result of their workshop experience. Even leading proponents of these
methods have expressed concern that the inability to demonstrate external
effects through rigorous evaluation threatens to undermine the credibility
of the enterprise; this problem needs to be corrected in order to establish
professional standards and qualifications for this approach.[18] Despite some
efforts in the past decade to evaluate this method and other peacebuilding
activities, "evaluations are not yet contributing to learning and accountability in peacebuilding to their full potential."[19]

Some reasons for this lag are understandable. Initial problems were the
low number of actual initiatives in conflict resolution from which to draw
data, and their often one-shot nature. Although this limitation has been
alleviated as more and longer projects have been carried out, the increasing

number of and variety in their features makes generalization difficult.[20] A serious problem is the immense difficulty of collecting data on the complex primary, secondary, and tertiary effects that may flow from and affect an intervention activity.[21] Unlike mediation, which may be deemed successful if a specific agreement is signed, these nonofficial methods are believed to influence their environment indirectly through diverse and perhaps subtle longer-term effects that are harder to detect.[22] Also, there are scant opportunities to collect preactivity data and compare them with postactivity outcomes, or to organize comparisons with groups that have not gone through the experience.[23]

A philosophical reason for the dearth of evaluations that some practitioners have argued is that the vicissitudes and serendipity entailed in such deliberately open-ended encounters inherently preclude researchers from obtaining clear answers to the kinds of questions that donors ask about the outcomes and impacts of the projects that they fund in other domains. It is one thing to demonstrate that a development initiative has produced x number of roads or schools or y decreases in infant mortality; it is quite another to document whether a conflict transformation initiative has been responsible for, say, preventing an outbreak of violence by shaping the outlooks and motivations of given parties to a conflict. As this defense goes, the effects of these methods will always elude the desire to develop rigorous plans and measure attainment of preconceived goals. From this perspective, these workshops are most appropriately evaluated in terms of their ability to generate a long-term process of new connections, insights, and learning, not necessarily to achieve prespecified impacts.[24]

In any case, relatively little systematically gathered empirical evidence exists about the strengths and limits of these distinct process-centric techniques in affecting conflicts, sufficient to get beyond the untested faith of proponents and the dismissive opinions of skeptics. However, unless more attempts are made to evaluate this method in systematic ways, "all training and practice is relevant and success is always just a few more dollars away."[25]

What Is "Sustainable Peace"?

The core hypothesis of this volume is that the improved relationships, increased trust, and broadened outlooks fostered by nonofficial, noncoercive but intensively applied conflict transformation techniques can substantially advance a country's efforts to achieve a sustainable peace. To test this proposition by looking at actual evidence, we need to characterize the features of a "sustainable peace." Once we have a more concrete understanding of this concept, we can look at particular cases to try to determine what progress toward that goal has been achieved.

To be clear, the presumption is not that these nonofficial efforts can achieve sustainable peace *by themselves.* Nor can they substitute for other major ways to bring about peace and development, such as official diplomacy and economic policies. Proponents of this approach regard it as a complement of, rather than an alternative to, more robust kinds of interventions.[26] Therefore, the premise under scrutiny is that by virtue of its distinctive focus on transforming the outlooks of the leaders within conflict-affected societies, this approach makes international peacebuilding demonstrably more effective than if they were not used. Possibly, its contribution to the sustainability of peace processes is greater than has been recognized. The appropriate question for this investigation is not whether these methods achieve a sustainable peace on their own, but rather how much closer the use of them can come to reaching that ultimate destination.

To thus assess how much progress has been achieved toward the desired endpoint of sustainable peace, specific milestones or benchmarks are needed to lay out what effects would constitute *steps toward* that ultimate goal—that is, conceptual metrics that measure the progress that may have been made toward that destination. Close investigation can then examine whether such progress was actually achieved by particular initiatives, to judge their relative contribution to sustaining peace.

Surprisingly, much literature on peacebuilding is of little help here. The goals of peacebuilding and the notion of sustainable peace are frequently described in terms of prescriptive ideals that are defined vaguely, if at all, and are difficult to imagine being achieved in the foreseeable future. Such lofty ideals include not only an end to physical violence at all levels in society but also numerous attributes of "positive peace," including economic prosperity, social harmony, equality, justice, human rights, inclusive participatory democracy, demilitarization, disarmament, cooperation, reconciliation, and mutual respect and care.[27] However, like similarly expansive notions such as "human security," the lack of specificity of these values means that their fulfillment entails a quest for social perfection that would embrace almost any good thing and would never end. Also, such honorific, question-begging concepts often conflate the goal of sustainable peace with various ways that are used to achieve it, which makes it impossible to determine whether progress toward the goal has or has not been made.

The amorphous meaning of sustainable peace makes it difficult to define thresholds of success in keeping, building, and restoring peace.[28] Furthermore, if such ideals are presumed to require a participatory democracy and market economy, as in the formal institutions of liberal Western-style countries, efforts to introduce these structures in volatile countries can become ideological crusades that actually are detrimental. Rapid transitions from some forms of authoritarianism to democracy, for example, frequently lead to major violence or greater repression. Perfection could truly become the enemy of the good.

For long-term, aspirational purposes, it is laudable to set high ideals and ambitious goals for a society. But doing so does not help decision makers in vulnerable societies who face crucial short- and medium-term choices about how to invest chronically scarce international resources so as to make progress most cost-effective and avoid doing harm. Indeed, the failure to specify peacebuilding goals in tangible and realistic terms prevents peacebuilding missions from setting meaningful standards by which their activities can be held accountable. For their part, interactive conflict resolution practitioners in particular often have failed to spell out in specific terms how their methods could lead to significant changes in their wider conflict environments.[29]

Where can we find more grounded and usable criteria?[30] Over the past decade or so, a sizable body of qualitative and quantitative social science and policy research has helped to illuminate not only the principal sources of intrastate conflicts but also the kinds of international involvement that are most likely to achieve a "durable," "lasting," or "viable" peace. Most of the policy-oriented literature deals with postconflict programs in sectors such as security, elections, and economic development, but some cross-national empirical research has systematically examined the effectiveness of the United Nations or other international peacebuilding activities as a whole in a number of conflict-prone countries. Using "large-N" quantitative analysis or comparative case studies, these studies look at the extent to which the countries have achieved conditions such as the end of armed conflict and establishment of democratic procedures, and no longer need a continuing presence of international peacekeepers or other external interventions. They then identify the kinds of peacebuilding activities associated with the variation in outcomes. This research helps to pin down the components that are most critical for achieving a sustained peace.

A 2004 study of fourteen postconflict peacebuilding missions, for example, concludes that sustained peace requires effective, professional security forces and justice institutions; electoral systems that encourage moderate leaders and ensure peaceful elections; an effective, neutral bureaucracy; laws prohibiting hate speech; economic policies that avoid widening societal disparities; and a stable civil society.[31] Similarly, a more wide-ranging comparison finds that peace depends on considerations such as whether the parties in conflict receive security guarantees in exchange for laying down their arms, accepted third-party mediators negotiate power-sharing arrangements, efforts are made to resolve subsequent electoral and other disputes, and the most serious socioeconomic grievances underlying the conflicts are addressed. Countries that were most successful in overcoming violence and moving to stable self-governance did so by gaining wide acceptance for governing institutions that operate more or less autonomously and that displace the armed force or coercion that the most powerful leaders often use to pursue political dominance.[32]

Although these studies examine varied samples, intensities of conflict, and timeframes, a review of such studies distills the most important elements for avoiding war recurrence. Structures of governance must allow salient social groups to participate so that they feel sufficiently invested in the polity not to take up arms. These structures may include varied arrangements that link the central state's judicial and policing agencies to locally legitimate authorities, such as traditional or informal systems of justice.[33]

Other relevant studies have looked at countries where no recent wars had occurred but where early warning signs indicated a risk of conflict—and yet wars did not erupt. These studies seek to identify why these countries averted the onset of war, while others that similarly were at risk escalated into conflicts.[34] In the successful cases, key ingredients included timely, firm, and even-handed third-party preventive diplomacy in keeping political disputes from escalating into violence; the establishment of acceptable agreements to resolve the policy and political issues that were generating tensions; reinforcement of moderate leaders; support for compacts for governing and economic betterment; and efforts to keep neighboring countries from interfering.[35] Although the measure of success in these postconflict and prevention studies starts with the avoidance of new or renewed violence ("negative peace"), they suggest that, absent this condition, fuller meanings of sustainable peace—including democracy, equality, social justice, and a developing economy—are not likely to develop. According to one study, "any notion of peace means little if persistent combat exists."[36] Armed conflict largely needs to cease before other improvements are likely. At the same time, these studies understand that sustainable peace is more than merely the cessation of violence; avoidance of war is necessary, but insufficient.[37] The basic consideration is whether a country's processes and institutions are able to *self-regulate*: that is, to resolve social and political conflicts peacefully and independently, free from the threat of organized violence. A usable definition of sustainable peace thus involves the absence of organized violence and systematic violation of basic rights; even without external guarantees, a country's institutions must avoid the escalatory dynamics of coercive and violent interactions. In short, peace prevails due to a self-sustaining process.[38] A workable synthesis of this cross-national research would list the following intermediate elements as most essential for achieving a sustainable peace:

- Neutral armed forces that ensure general security
- Power-sharing agreement among leaders of the most important identity groups
- Generally impartial administrative and judicial agencies that provide basic services
- A modicum of broad access for political representation
- Improvements in standards of living and economic growth policies that do not worsen gross disparities.

Precise indicators for these conditions still need to be honed, but such a list provides more concreteness by narrowing down the most important priorities for sustaining a peace from among myriad ideal societal conditions and normative values that may be desirable but are unattainable or counterproductive in the near term. Many of these goals are not necessarily requirements; they are best treated as desired elements of a good society, not as requisites for a sustained peace.

The criteria resulting from these studies, although not utopian, are still very challenging. To be sure, any such conclusions from multiple countries should not be applied automatically as "unyielding guideposts" in formulating strategy in a specific country.[39] Nevertheless, subject to such a context-specific assessment, it is wise to consider prioritizing these elements, rather than pursuing a broad menu of ideal goals that seem worthy but may be extraneous, infeasible, or even harmful.

As necessary and helpful as this comparative empirical research is, its findings still leave unanswered the key question posed in chapter 1: what actual processes and incentives are most effective for *motivating* a host country's own leaders and other local actors to dedicate themselves to achieving a sustainable peace? Although research has narrowed down the most important goals and the priorities where international efforts are likely to be most fruitful, a gap remains in understanding (in a more immediate, tangible sense) how to engender a country's own will to take on peacebuilding tasks, including what tradeoffs may be necessary.[40] One of the cross-national studies characterizes the most successful international missions as achieving "enhanced consent" through packages of international diplomatic, economic, and political activities. Yet these studies still do not reveal what kinds of in-country processes and incentives are most effective in fostering such domestic "consent." This book's focus on nonofficial methods of interaction speaks to that question.

The Case Studies' Framework of Inquiry

The case studies in this volume add to the existing limited evidence on the effectiveness of nonofficial ways for improving the ability of leaders to achieve conflict resolution and build sustainable peace. They provide evidence on the consequences of six such initiatives in six countries and the reasons for those consequences. Each author describes the main features of an initiative, the improvements that its efforts have made in its conflict environment, the most effective key features, and the favorable or unfavorable contextual factors that influenced its impacts.

Even though these methods generally have not been evaluated, this volume was not conceived on a completely blank slate; the comparative advantages of these nonofficial processes in mitigating conflicts and building peace are beginning to be scrutinized. The framework of inquiry, which asked the case study authors to address leading questions, was derived in part from a handful of existing analyses of this method. Following the clues these analyses offer, this framework focuses on factors likely to be the most relevant and fruitful, in order to avoid fishing expeditions into unlikely factors or a plethora of case-specific insights. Evaluations of individual peacebuilding or conflict prevention programs often fail to yield generalizable findings, yet non-case-specific hypotheses are essential for comparative research and for seeing how particular initiatives might fare in other settings.[41] Building the questions on existing research allows this volume to test and possibly extend and deepen the findings to date, accumulating knowledge about this method of intervention.[42] The questions were not presented as exclusive or exhaustive; the authors were encouraged to look for any other factors that were crucial in their particular case but not anticipated in the framework.

Conflicts and Interventions

To identify the effects of this type of intervention on a country's conflict or peace process, the analyst first needs to characterize the nature and drivers of the conflict: the problem at which the intervention is aimed. In this part of each chapter, the authors provide a brief and focused chronological overview of the general course of the conflict during the period in focus. These narratives lay out major high and low points in social and political tensions or levels of violence that have occurred and identify the conflicts' main sources and issues.

A second essential topic in each chapter is the specific characteristics of the interactive process activity itself that was carried out in the country, such as their sponsors and the facilitation techniques applied. These efforts can vary considerably, such as in the identities of the convening initiators, the kinds of participants brought together, the number of sessions, and the type of training and other exercises used. This section is crucial not simply to describe what intervention was involved in each case, but also to lay the basis for judging which features of the intervention were most important for producing its evident effects. As with the other elements in the framework, this description of the intervention has to be cast in generic terms to enable lessons to be drawn across cases. Some of these elements may be crucial when this approach is tried in other settings.

Impacts

Once the chapters characterize the conflicts and the features of the intervention, they then probe whether and how the process of engagement contributed to progress toward sustainable peace. To escape the descriptive literature's tendency to conflate the intent of the project and their assumed effects, the case studies must define explicitly what impacts are conceivable and then examine the cases for the actual evidence of such impacts. For example, "cohesion" or "capacity-building" may be described as both the goal and the actual result. By stipulating explicit impact criteria that are distinguishable from intentions, the case studies can help to adjudicate the debate between those who make unverifiable claims about the value of a program based solely on its intended objectives, and those who are skeptical of the value of such "soft" interventions, perhaps simply because no indicators for ascertaining tangible impacts have been specified and measured.

Assessments of these impacts must go beyond "outputs," such as whether the workshop experience was well organized, whether the participants were pleased with it, or whether it received continued funding. Analysts have sought to define categories that encompass a range of more significant possible impacts.[43] To illustrate, the most immediate kind of impact would affect the workshop participants themselves. There is already considerable evidence of such impacts; several studies suggest that these interventions often have made significant impressions on the participants, sparking great enthusiasm even among previous adversaries and modifying their attitudes.[44] A 2007 study of nonofficial interstate dialogues on security issues in the Middle East, for instance, found that these dialogues began to shape the views, attitudes, and knowledge of a growing number of civilian and military elites by socializing them in new concepts and a new kind of discourse about the value of regional cooperation.[45] Still, even proponents of this craft have questioned whether a connection can be made between the diverse, often vague goals and particular techniques in these activities, and the changes observed in a group.[46] Therefore, this volume asked the authors to probe whether direct impacts such as the following were evident and attributable to the initiatives:

- Changed perceptions and attitudes
- Greater empathy between the parties and an improved emotional climate
- New cross-lines relationships exhibiting increased trust
- More constructive communication, as seen in reduced expressions of hostility
- New conceptualizations of compatible interests
- New integrative framing, vocabularies, or other learning
- Improved abilities to engage in problem-solving and to make decisions to resolve disputes.

Beyond such changes within the group, further results within the workshop process itself would show that the greater trust and closer relationships achieved had led the participants to take joint steps within the process to promote peace, such as by formulating common positions on the issues or even drafting statements affirming their agreements.

Other possible impacts have to do with actual transfer effects from the experience and activities in the workshops to the wider conflict environment. Such impacts would be seen in what the participants may have done individually or together as they reentered their normal professional milieus and dealt with a general public. The success of interventions need not hinge entirely on whether conflict settlements are reached at the level of official peace processes and politics. An emerging theme in the evaluation literature is the need to give more attention to intermediary effects, or the "pieces of peace" at the "meso-social" level.[47] Incrementally, for example, these initiatives could act as generators of change by providing a kind of critical "yeast" in a society, which progressively creates a national capacity to mediate disputes.[48] Such effects might be the expansion of the circle of participants or signs within the wider parties and support groups that the habit of empathetic dialogue is taking hold, even though the overall conflict has not been resolved.[49]

Indeed, several studies suggest that over time these activities can create networks of leaders who maintain good relationships and communication, and have stimulated participants to undertake further activities together.[50] A 1997 study of such initiatives in South Asia found that the atmosphere surrounding official negotiations was improved, informal channels for forwarding policy options were created, and public awareness and attitudes were influenced in ways that made interstate agreements more likely and feasible.[51] Accordingly, in post-activity interviews the authors of the case study chapters asked participants for their considered judgments of such impacts and looked for other evidence of effects such as the following:

- New leaders and influential people engaged
- Increased capacity to draw on public resources such as media
- New partnerships, processes, and organizations that improve the societal relationships within which the conflict occurs.

Finally, further impacts would have to do with whether any activities of the workshop group or subsequent participant activities moved the conflict closer to a formalized resolution, such as by encouraging official-level talks, communicating specific ideas to the official level, getting particular proposals accepted, or helping to bring about policy changes. Evidence has been found of such influences on reaching intrastate and interstate agreements.[52] For example, the Community of Sant'Egidio helped to guide and initiate informal meetings that resulted in a 1996 education agreement between Serbian president Slobodan Milošević and ethnic Albanian leaders in Kosovo.[53] A 1999 survey of ten conflict resolution projects in former communist countries concludes that they prepared people to participate in track-one (official diplomatic) negotiations and contributed specific ideas that broke deadlocks in official negotiations.[54] A 2010 study of civil society projects in eleven countries concluded that cross-lines meetings paved the way for official negotiations by developing useful ideas.[55] Nonofficial workshops sponsored by Canada and Indonesia were crucial in stimulating ideas for cooperation and ways to prevent confrontation that went into an official China-ASEAN Declaration regarding the South China Sea disputes.[56] Nonofficial dialogues were also influential in successfully concluding a treaty between Bangladesh and India concerning sharing the waters of the Ganga River.[57] To pursue possible impacts of this kind, the chapter authors looked for impacts such as the following:

- Catalytic effects in leading official peace negotiations to start or restart;
- Specific ideas about settlement options or policies that are accepted by authoritative decision-makers; and
- Effects on implementing political reforms or policies that alleviate governance and socioeconomic problems.

In sum, by probing into the evidence for these categories of possible impact, the authors seek to take the measure of this kind of intervention.

Missteps

Another key question concerns missed opportunities: what chances for influence were forgone by such initiatives? What issues might they have helped to address, but did not seize the opportunity to do so? The authors were asked to engage in "what if?" counterfactual speculation about what more the intervention might have been able to accomplish, but did not try to do. A related question is: "Did the initiative impede or worsen the prospects for peaceful progress?" An adequate assessment of these interventions must consider harms that may have been done. It may be necessary to bring central issues out in the open, for example, but this approach can also lead to confrontation and thus the breakdown of relationships.[58]

Explanations

To be useful for practitioners and policymakers, the case studies need to explicate why the process interventions contributed or not to the outcomes identified above. There are two main aspects that explain an intervention's effects on peace or conflict: (1) the *characteristics* of the initiative itself and (2) the *context* in which it was applied.

INITIATIVE CHARACTERISTICS

Part of the explanation for the outcomes may have to do with the features of the activity itself, namely its design and implementation. Features that have been found to make a difference in effectiveness include an appropriate choice of participants, the duration of the initiatives, and the skill of the facilitators.[59] As mentioned, some regard the choice of well-connected participants as crucial.[60] Others note that the most promising initiatives have involved a long-term series of workshops.[61] It is pretty clear that a continued process of intensive work is required for these initiatives to achieve results at the political macro-level of conflicts. Many sources also stress the importance of compatibility and communication between the workshop process and the official international negotiations that may be going on.[62] Although such interventions ostensibly are nonofficial, they may have differing degrees of linkage to official third-party mediations and negotiations, such as when major government or regional bodies implicitly endorse the exercise or an initiative's sponsor has international stature that gives the initiative a quasiofficial character and greater potential influence. The greater protection enjoyed by third-party outsiders and the expertise and knowledge of the international environment that they can bring to the discussions may help significantly to compensate for the limited perspectives of locally led initiatives.[63] However, international sponsorship should not displace local buy-in. In the previously mentioned example of nonofficial interstate security dialogues in the Middle East, it was important that the participants began to see that the concepts and skills introduced could serve their own interests.[64] The chapters look for these important connections and other possible design-based explanations, such as the following:

- Duration of the workshops
- Kinds of participants involved
- Timing of the initiative in relation to wider conflict circumstances

- Skills and personalities of the implementers and trainers
- Types of workshop exercises used
- Venue
- Aspects of organization and management such as sponsorship and sources of funding.

CONTEXTUAL FACTORS

The second kind of possible explanation of the discovered results has to do with factors in the domestic, regional, or global environments in which the intervention is conducted. No one type of intervention, however well designed and implemented, will work equally well in every stage of conflict and country setting. To learn what interventions lead to effective results, one must identify the most important contextual factors that enabled or constrained the achievement of these outcomes. Assessing how these contextual factors affected an initiative's achievements helps to differentiate between the influences of the contexts involved and the contributions of the process interventions themselves.

Internal factors. Evaluations of peacebuilding programs often do not take into account how the country and conflict environment greatly shapes their impacts, positively or negatively. Yet existing research strongly suggests that the more that the contextual conditions are favorable, the more effective the informal processes themselves are likely to be. Crucial factors may include not only certain socioeconomic "givens" in a country, such as whether it has a growing economy that can create a surplus of resources that encourages cooperative activities. Efforts to create closer relationships can only work if the wider forces of social integration are strong enough to bring and hold the parties of the conflict together.[65] However, such social factors are relatively unchangeable in the short run. Key factors also arise from more immediate aspects of the conflict itself. Research indicates that initiatives may have varying success in differing conflict situations depending on characteristics such as whether the parties in conflict are at a stalemate, the balance of power is more or less equal, and the main issues in dispute are amenable to compromise. For example, conflicts have been found to be more conducive to resolution if they deal with the problem of incorporating a group more fully into the country's political system, rather than a group's desire to become more autonomous or to secede.[66] Conflicts between ethnic groups that have compatriots outside the arena of conflict are also harder to influence.[67]

Differing degrees of open hostility may also affect a conflict's amenability to resolution. The extent to which a conflict is escalated and violent is generally thought to make it more difficult for third-party actors to influence its course.[68] Another possibly significant characteristic is whether the involved parties are in a mutual hurting stalemate, "when alternative, usually unilateral means of achieving a satisfactory result are blocked and the parties feel they are in an uncomfortable and costly predicament."[69] However, a 2005 study of peacebuilding initiatives found that their effectiveness and ease of implementation were not always affected by the stage of a conflict or existence of a stalemate.[70] In eight initiatives that were judged relatively successful, "the combination of a powerful [interactive] intervention and a receptive conflict result in both significant transfer effects and an eventual resolution of the conflict."[71]

Domestic politics, such as actions by host country governments, may also be crucial. The Middle East security dialogues examined in one study did not lead to major shifts in policies or resolution of conflicts because the prevailing security culture in the governments of the region was committed to unilateral action, so long-standing conflicts and high levels of violence often prevailed. In these circumstances, and because the regimes lacked broad legitimacy, opposition parties and speakers could readily attack dialogue projects by presenting them as succumbing to an adversary's position.[72] Only if the overall long-term security atmosphere changes, the study argued, are such projects likely to produce significant results in shaping particular policies. A wider constituency in favor of regional cooperation needs to emerge beyond the small circles of converted who remain disconnected from top leaders and broad social movements.

Several analysts agree that for process initiatives and other peace negotiations to achieve lasting results with regard to intrastate conflicts, the initiative participants need to mobilize wider publics in support of peace, such as social movements and civil society interests within their countries.[73] Researchers have found that NGO initiatives that deal with "key people" and "personal change" are more effective when linked to actions that seek "social and political change" and involve "more people"[74] For example, informal dialogues sponsored by respected religious figures from several faiths were able to insert ideas into Kenya's constitutional reform process in the 1990s and push it along, in part because the clerics could advocate change when addressing their followers.[75] However, it can be difficult to mobilize broad-based social groups within conflict-affected societies because their differing

views are often shaped by language differences, physical separation, education policies, and group-based associations.[76]

To test such hypotheses, the case study chapters look for both important
aspects of the conflict and key domestic political and societal factors, including the following factors:

- The state of domestic security
- The extent to which agreed-on and enforced democratic processes
  (e.g., regular elections) are functioning
- The country's level of social and economic development
- The nature of the issues at stake
- The country's organized capacities for peace (e.g., civil society
  pressure).

External factors. The degree of influence that external international
actors wield over the parties, such as the extent of deliberate international
involvement, may also be important. The parties' openness to accommodation also may be influenced by the amount of leverage that the initiative
organizers promoting conflict resolution have, as revealed by the support
they enjoy from other international actors.[77] Therefore, the case studies also
look at regional and extraregional influences such as the following:

- The positive or negative influence of regional political, military, financial support and other engagement
- The existence of external security guarantees (e.g., a military peacekeeping or police presence)
- The influence of other external third-party actors that are involved
  (e.g., United States, United Nations, other major powers, regional
  organizations)
- The extent of external support for other nongovernmental activities
  that promote resolution
- The role of the diaspora in fostering division or cooperation.

Conclusion

The case studies in the following chapters pursue leads such as those
described above to uncover and explain the most important impacts of
their initiatives. Understandably, the authors faced serious methodological

challenges in tracking down reliable answers to many of these questions. These constraints included gathering representative data from a range of participants, tracing the causal dynamics through which the initiatives had their effects, weighing the relative significance of various contextual factors, and judging whether such effects might have occurred without the process intervention. The authors also faced differing practical circumstances affecting their ability to collect data. Nevertheless, by carefully investigating the most plausible possible effects and making reasonable inferences from the available data, these theory-informed studies of interactive conflict transformation methods may yield grounded judgments about what works, what does not work, and why—not only building upon but also extending existing knowledge.[78] Following the six case study chapters, the two concluding chapters identify the overall patterns observed in the case studies and draw out the practical implications of this research for the contemporary international milieu.

Notes

1. See, e.g., Alexander L. George, *Forceful Persuasion: Coercive Diplomacy as an Alternative to War* (Washington, DC: United States Institute of Peace Press, 1991).

2. An overview of this method of intervention and its main functions is found in Diana Chigas, "Track II (Citizen) Diplomacy," in *Beyond Intractability* (The Beyond Intractability Project, The Conflict Information Consortium, University of Colorado, Denver, August 2003), http://www.beyondintractability.org/essay/track2-diplomacy.

3. Marc H. Ross and Jay Rothman, eds., *Theory and Practice in Conflict Management: Theorizing Success and Failure* (Houndsmill, UK: Macmillan, 1999).

4. See, e.g., I. William Zartman and J. Lewis Rasmussen, eds., *Peacemaking in International Conflict: Methods and Techniques* (Washington, DC: United States Institute of Peace Press, 1997); Herbert C. Kelman, "Social Psychological Dimensions of International Conflict," in Zartman and Rasmussen, eds., *Peacemaking in International Conflict*, 191–238; Dennis Sandole and Hugo van der Merwe, eds., *Conflict Resolution Theory and Practice* (Manchester: Manchester University Press, 1993); and Ross and Rothman, eds., *Theory and Practice in Conflict Management*.

5. Barbara Kemper, *Mediation in Intrastate Conflicts; The Contribution of Track-Two Mediation Activities to Prevent Violence in the Aceh Conflict*, INEF Report 88/2007 (Duisberg, Germany: Institute for Development and Peace, Universität Duisberg-Essen, 2007), 47; and Tobias Böhmelt, "The Effectiveness of Tracks of Diplomacy Strategies in Third-Party Interventions," *Journal of Peace Research* (2010) 47: 170.

6. See, e.g., Eileen Babbitt, "Contributions of Training to International Conflict Resolution," in Zartman and Rasmussen, eds., *Peacemaking in International Conflict*, 365–87; Ronald J. Fisher, ed., *Paving the Way: Contributions of Interactive Conflict Resolution to Peacemaking* (Lanham, MD: Lexington Books, 2005); and Ross and Rothman, eds., *Theory and Practice in Conflict Management*.

7. Norbert Ropers, *Peaceful Intervention: Structures, Processes, and Strategies for the Constructive Regulation of Ethnopolitical Conflicts*, Berghof Report 1 (Berlin: Berghof Research Center for Constructive Conflict Management, October 1995), 72ff.

8. Edward E. Azar and John W. Burton, *International Conflict Resolution: Theory and Practice* (Boulder, CO: Lynne Rienner, 1986), 29–39, 52, 63, 80–100, 113.

9. Nadim N. Rouhana, "Interactive Conflict Resolution: Issues in Theory, Methodology, and Evaluation," in *International Conflict Resolution after the Cold War*, ed. Paul C. Stern and Daniel Druckman (Washington, DC: National Academies Press, 2000), 325.

10. H. D. Forbes, *Ethnic Conflict: Commerce, Culture, and the Contact Thesis* (New Haven, CT: Yale University Press, 1997), 200–1, 206; and Anna Ohanyan and John E. Lewis, "Politics of Peace-Building: Critical Evaluation of Interethnic Contact and Peace Education in Georgian-Abkhaz Peace Camp, 1998–2002," *Peace and Change* 30, no. 1 (January 2005): 77–78.

11. Kenneth Waltz, *Man, the State, and War: A Theoretical Analysis* (New York: Columbia University Press, 1954), 79.

12. See, e.g., Ronald Fisher, "Interactive Conflict Resolution," in *Peacemaking in International Conflict: Methods and Techniques*, ed. William Zartman and Lewis Rasmussen (Washington, DC: United States Institute of Peace Press, 1997), 260; and Nadim N. Rouhana, "Interactive Conflict Resolution," 304.

13. Ropers, *Peaceful Intervention*, 78.

14. Ropers, *Peaceful Intervention*, 78ff.; Rouhana, "Interactive Conflict Resolution," 326; Mohammed Abu-Nimer, "Conflict Resolution Training in the Middle East: Lessons to be Learned," *International Negotiation* 3, no. 1 (1998): 111–16; and Thania Paffenholz, ed., *Civil Society and Peacebuilding: A Critical Assessment* (Boulder, CO: Lynne Rienner, 2010), 397ff.

15. Ronald J. Fisher, "Training as Interactive Conflict Resolution: Characteristics and Challenges," *International Negotiation* 2, no. 3 (1997): 338ff.; and Abu-Nimer, "Conflict Resolution Training in the Middle East," 109ff.

16. Paffenholz, *Civil Society and Peacebuilding*, 397; and Rouhana, "Interactive Conflict Resolution," 326.

17. Ronald J. Fisher, "The Problem Solving Workshop as a Method of Research," *International Negotiation* 9, no. 3 (2004), 394; and Fisher, *Paving the Way*.

18. Fisher, "Training as Interactive Conflict Resolution," 346.

19. Cheyanne Scharbatke-Church, "Evaluating Peacebuilding: Not Yet All It Could Be," *Advancing Conflict Transformation: The Berghof Handbook II*, ed. Beatrix Austin et al. (Farmington Hills, MI: Barbara Budrich Publishers, 2011), 480.

20. Ronald J. Fisher, "Developing the Field of Interactive Conflict Resolution: Issues in Training, Funding, and Institutionalization," *Political Psychology* 14, no. 1 (1993): 130.

21. Fisher, "Training as Interactive Conflict Resolution," 346; and Rouhana, "Interactive Conflict Resolution," 312–24.

22. Ropers, *Peaceful Intervention*, 76.

23. Rouhana, "Interactive Conflict Resolution," 319–22.

24. John Paul Lederach, *Building Peace: Sustainable Reconciliation in Divided Societies* (Washington, DC: United States Institute of Peace Press, 1997), 137–48. Debate persists between those, on the one hand, who look for results using some kind of logical framework that links inputs to outcomes in a linear fashion, and those, on the other hand, who argue that peacebuilding initiatives are about promoting relationships

and processes and thus have to remain open to unpredictable opportunities and turns of events. Reina C. Neufeldt, "'Frameworkers' and 'Circlers'—Exploring Assumptions in Peace and Conflict Impact Assessment," in *Berghof Handbook for Conflict Transformation* (Berlin: Berghof Research Center for Constructive Conflict Management, August 2007): 483–504.

25. Robert M. Schoenhaus, *Conflict Management Training: Advancing Best Practices*, Peaceworks No. 36 (Washington, DC: United States Institute of Peace, January 2001), 37.

26. Fisher, "Interactive Conflict Resolution," 241.

27. The concept of positive peace was formulated by Johan Galtung, as in *Theories of Peace: A Synthetic Approach to Peace Thinking* (Oslo: International Peace Research Institute, 1967), 14. For a recent expression of the peacebuilding field's expansive aspirations, see, e.g., Diana Francis, "New Thoughts on Power: Closing the Gaps between Theory and Action," in *Advancing Conflict Transformation*, ed. Austin et al., 508. For a useful overview of the evolution of the "peacebuilding" field and the increasing usage of this term by nongovernmental organizations, see Paffenholz, *Civil Society and Peacebuilding*, 43–58.

28. Francesco Strazzari, "Between 'Messy Aftermath' and 'Frozen Conflicts': Chimeras and Realities of Sustainable Peace," *Humsec Journal* 2 (November 1, 2007): 49, 51, 55–59, http://ssrn.com/abstract=1997560.

29. Rouhana, "Interactive Conflict Resolution," 301.

30. A step in this direction is Thania Paffenholz's proposed definition of peacebuilding; although confined to post-armed-conflict situations, it focuses on the zone between short- and long-term goals and refers to *"conducive conditions for* economic reconstruction, development, and democratization" (emphasis added). Paffenholz, *Civil Society and Peacebuilding*, 49ff.

31. Roland Paris, *At War's End: Building Peace after Civil Conflict* (Cambridge: Cambridge University Press, 2004).

32. Michael Doyle and Nicholas Sambanis, *Making War and Building Peace: United Nations Peace Operations.* (Princeton, NJ: Princeton University Press, 2006). See also James Dobbins et al., *The UN's Role in Nation-Building: From the Congo to Iraq* (Santa Monica, CA: RAND Corporation, 2005); Jock Covey, Michael Dziedzic, and Leonard Hawley, eds. *Quest for Viable Peace: International Intervention and Strategies for Conflict Transformation* (Washington, DC: United States Institute of Peace Press, 2005); Merilee S. Grindle, "Good Enough Governance Revisited," *Development Policy Review* 25, no. 5 (2007): 533–74; and Christoph Zuercher, "Is More Better? Evaluating External-Led State-building after 1989" (paper presented at the Graduate Institute of International Studies, Geneva, March 14, 2006). One multicountry study finds that the single most important international task for successful peace agreements in postconflict environments is the demobilization of soldiers: Stephen John Stedman, Donald Rothchild, and Elizabeth M. Cousens, eds. *Ending Civil Wars: The Implementation of Peace Agreements* (Boulder, CO: Lynne Rienner, 2002), 665. Another study lists fully ten functions needed to rebuild failed states, although this finding is based on general sources, not cross-national empirical analysis: Ashraf Ghani and Clare Lockhart, *Fixing Failed States: A Framework for Rebuilding a Fractured World* (New York: Oxford University Press, 2009).

33. Charles T. Call, "Knowing Peace When You See It: Setting Standards for Peacebuilding Success," *Civil Wars* 10, no. 2 (June 2008): 190–91. The elimination of "root"

causes of conflicts, such as poverty, is not directly associated with sustained peace, although it is desirable on other normative grounds as long as policies are appropriately designed.

34. See, e.g., Michael Lund, "Greed and Grievance Diverted: How Macedonia Avoided Civil War, 1990–2001," in *Understanding Civil War: Evidence and Analysis*, ed. Paul Collier and Nicholas Sambanis, vol. 2, *Europe, Central Asia, and Other Regions* (Washington, DC: World Bank, 2005), 231–259; and Michael Lund, "Why Do Some Ethnic Disputes Become Violent, While Others Remain Peaceful? Comparing Slovakia, Macedonia, and Kosovo," in *Journeys through Conflict: Narratives and Lessons*, eds. Hayward R. Alker, Ted Robert Gurr, and Kumar Rupesinghe (Lanham, MD: Rowman and Littlefield, 2001).

35. See, e.g., Bruce W. Jentleson, "Preventive Diplomacy: Analytical Conclusions and Policy Lessons," in *Opportunities Missed, Opportunities Seized: Preventive Diplomacy in the Post–Cold War World*, ed. Bruce W. Jentleson (Lanham, MA: Rowman and Littlefield, 2000), 319–48. A summary of prevention lessons is also found in Michael Lund, "Conflict Prevention: Theory in Pursuit of Policy and Practice," in *The SAGE Handbook of Conflict Resolution*, ed. Jacob Bercovitch, Viktor Kremenyk, and I. William Zartman (Thousand Oaks, CA: SAGE, 2009) 287–321. For example, the extraordinary success of South Africa in effecting a relatively peaceful transition from apartheid to a democratic governmental system from 1994 was attributable to internally initiated negotiations and international mediation, external political and economic pressures, a relatively neutral military, and remarkably able individual leaders on both sides of the conflict. Even though the importance of such preventive action has been recognized since the early 1990s, and a number of actual preventive efforts have been attempted, systematic analyses of such efforts are vastly exceeded by studies of postconflict or midconflict situations.

36. Call, "Knowing Peace When You See It," 189.

37. Ibid., 173.

38. Strazzari, "Between 'Messy Aftermath' and 'Frozen Conflicts,'" 63ff.

39. Call, "Knowing Peace When You See It," 191.

40. Zuercher, "Is More Better?," 23.

41. This problem is "the tendency of a number of evaluations to present project- or programme-specific 'lessons learned' which frequently could not be transformed into unproblematic 'lessons' or 'synthesis' for 'good practice' and/or relevance to other similar initiatives in other conflicts. The depth of a number of evaluations made it problematic to generalize from context-specific recommendations, and 'lessons' that were not presented as context-specific appeared generally to be too vague and abstract to be of much practical use." Raymond Apthorpe et al., *Evaluating Conflict Prevention and Peacebuilding Activities* (Oslo: Fafo Institute, 2006), 3.

42. The framework thus follows the comparative method of "structured focused comparison" for case studies. See Alexander L. George and Andrew Bennett, "The Method of Structured, Focused Comparison," chap. 3 in *Case Studies and Theory Development in the Social Sciences* (Cambridge, MA: MIT Press, 2005).

43. See, e.g., Christopher Mitchell, "Problem Solving Exercises and Theories of Conflict Resolution," in *Conflict Resolution Theory and Practice: Integration and Application*, ed. Dennis J. D. Sandole and Hugo van der Merwe (Manchester, UK: Manchester University Press, 1993), 82; Tamra Pearson D'Estree, Larissa A. Fast, Joshua N.

Weiss, and Monica S. Jakobsen, "Changing the Debate About 'Success' in Conflict Resolution Efforts," *Negotiation Journal* 17, no. 2 (April 2001): 101–13; Norman Frohlich et al., "Understanding, Modeling and Evaluating Conflict Resolution Techniques," Department of Government & Politics, University of Maryland (January 2001); and Rouhana, "Interactive Conflict Resolution."

44. See, e.g., Fisher, *Paving the Way*, 219.

45. Dalia Dassa Kaye, *Talking to the Enemy: Track Two Diplomacy in the Middle East and South Asia* (Santa Monica, CA: Rand Corporation, 2007), xi–xiii.

46. Fisher, "Training as Interactive Conflict Resolution," 346.

47. Schoenhaus, *Conflict Management Training*, 38; Rouhana, "Interactive Conflict Resolution"; and Pearson D'Estree et al., "Changing the Debate About 'Success.'"

48. John Paul Lederach, *The Moral Imagination: The Art and Soul of Building Peace* (New York: Oxford University Press, 2005).

49. Norbert Ropers, "Dialogue Projects in the Context of Theories of Conflict Management," in *From Resolution to Transformation: The Role of Dialogue Projects* (Berlin: Berghof Research Center for Constructive Conflict Management, 2004), 30.

50. Fisher, "Interactive Conflict Resolution," 248–50.

51. Navnita Chadha Behera, Paul M. Evans, and Gowher Rizvi, *Beyond Boundaries: A Report on the State of Non-official Dialogues on Peace, Security and Cooperation in South Asia* (Toronto: University of Toronto–York University Joint Centre for Asia Pacific Studies, 1997), 5.

52. Fisher, *Paving the Way*, 225.

53. Anne-Marie Smith, "Unofficial Diplomacy," in *Advances in Understanding International Peacemaking* (Washington, DC: United States Institute of Peace, 1998), 16.

54. CDR Associates, *Reaching for Peace: Lessons Learned from Mott Foundation's Conflict Resolution Programming, 1989–1998* (Flint, MI: Charles Stewart Mott Foundation, November 1999), 23.

55. Paffenholz, *Civil Society and Peacebuilding*, 398–401.

56. Chester A. Crocker, "Peacemaking and Mediation: Dynamics of a Changing Field," Coping with Crisis Working Paper Series (New York: International Peace Academy 2007), 13.

57. Behera et al., *Beyond Boundaries*, 5.

58. Ropers, *Peaceful Intervention*, 78.

59. Fisher, *Paving the Way*, 219, 227. The case studies draw on the authors' in-depth knowledge of the respective conflicts and the initiatives to identify the most important features. This close analysis does not eliminate the "problem of attribution," but can reduce it by "process tracing" between the intervention and the conflicts.

60. Ropers, "Peaceful Interventions," 75.

61. Fisher, "Developing the Field," 131; and Fisher, *Paving the Way*, 219.

62. See, e.g., Kemper, *Mediation in Intrastate Conflicts*, 48; and Simon Mason, *Insider Mediators: Exploring Their Key Role in Informal Peace Processes* (Berlin: Berghof Foundation for Peace Support, 2009), 17.

63. CDR Associates, *Reaching for Peace*, 23–24; Ropers, *Dialogue Projects*, 29; and Mason, *Insider Mediators*, 17.

64. Kaye, *Talking to the Enemy*, xiii.

65. Ropers, *Peaceful Intervention*, 78.

66. Fisher, *Paving the Way*, 228–29.

67. Ibid., 220.

68. See, e.g., Paffenholz, *Civil Society and Peacebuilding*, 400.

69. I. William Zartman, "The Timing of Peace Initiatives: Hurting Stalemates and Ripe Moments," *The Global Review of Ethnopolitics* 1, no. 1 (September 2001): 8. See also Kemper, *Mediation in Intrastate Conflicts*, 46.

70. Fisher, *Paving the Way*, 221–22.

71. Ibid., 226–30.

72. Kaye, *Talking to the Enemy*, xi–xiv.

73. See, e.g., Amy S. Hubbard, "Personal Change and Political Action: The Intersection of Conflict Resolution and Social Movement Mobilization in a Middle East Dialogue Group," Working Paper No. 7, Institute for Conflict Analysis and Resolution (Fairfax, VA: George Mason University, December 1992); Anthony Wanis-St. John and Darren Kew, "Civil Society and Peace Negotiations: Confronting Exclusion," *International Negotiation* 13, no. 1 (2008): 23–33.

74. Mary B. Anderson and Lara Olson, *Confronting War: Critical Lessons for Peace Practitioners* (Cambridge, MA: The Collaborative for Development Action, 2003), 56.

75. Michael Lund, "Getting Beyond Good Intentions or Cynicism: Methods and Findings from a Peace and Conflict Impact Evaluation of Three NGO 'Track-Two' Dialogues in Africa" (paper presented at the Annual Meeting of the International Studies Association, New Orleans, March 27, 2002).

76. Paffenholz, *Civil Society and Peacebuilding*, 396.

77. Kemper, *Mediation in Intrastate Conflicts*, 47.

78. The book seeks to reach conditional generalizations by identifying the effects under differing conditions of the variants of a generically defined type of international intervention. On this methodology, see Alexander George, *Bridging the Gap: Theory and Practice in Foreign Policy* (Washington, DC: United States Institute of Peace Press, 1993), xvii–xxv, 117–37.

Part II

Assessing Country Cases

Averting Conflict Escalation

Chapter 3

Estonia: Psychopolitical Dialogue Contributing to Conflict Prevention

Susan H. Allen

Introduction

From February 2, 1920, to June 17, 1940, the Baltic country of Estonia was recognized as an independent sovereign state. Following the Soviet occupation of the Baltic states in June 1940, the Soviet Union formally incorporated the Estonian Soviet Socialist Republic (Estonian SSR) as a constituent republic in August 1940. In the following years, an influx of Russians moved to the Estonian SSR to join the then 88.1 percent of the population who were ethnically Estonian, a migration that changed the proportions so drastically that fifty years later, ethnic Estonians made up only about 60 percent of the Estonian population.[1] Many of the Russians who came in the 1940s now consider Estonia the only home they have, and their children and grandchildren have lived their entire lives there.[2] Yet when Estonia formally reasserted independence from the Soviet Union on August 21, 1991, the new Estonian government viewed the ethnic Russians who had come to Estonia during the Soviet occupation as foreigners who had arrived through a Soviet policy of colonization.[3]

Soon after Estonia regained its independence, the international community recognized rising intercommunal tensions between ethnic Russians and Estonians. In the early 1990s, Estonia faced other challenges that might have fueled violent conflict, such as the presence of Russian troops, the task of establishing a new national identity, and a strong sense of insecurity among the Russian-speaking population, who feared being forced to move from Estonia. Observers pointed to the difficult economic transitions of all former Soviet republics as destabilizing forces that could set the stage for violent conflict. In his 1993 assessment of future sources of post–Cold War conflict, Samuel Huntington placed Estonia on the fault line between clashing civilizations.[4]

Taken together, these signs were read as an early warning of potential violent ethnic conflict. In the geopolitics of this transition period, it was important to Western countries that Estonia and the other Baltic states enjoy peaceful transitions. Estonia and its nationalities policies received significant international attention because of the early recognition of the potential for violent conflict in the region and the geopolitical importance of peaceful transition. Max van der Stoel, the High Commissioner for National Minorities of the Conference on Security and Co-operation in Europe (CSCE), played a leading role in the early recognition of the need for international attention, and was a leading figure engaging the Estonian government as it developed nationalities policies. Two decades later, as a result of broad international engagement with Estonia, ethnic tensions in the country had greatly diminished.

This chapter focuses on one of these international responses to Estonian-Russian tensions in Estonia. The Carter Center (TCC), the University of Virginia's Center for the Study of Mind and Human Interaction (CSMHI), and Ambassador Harold Saunders, then of the Kettering Foundation, partnered to facilitate six dialogues in Estonia between 1994 and 1996. The dialogues brought together prominent Estonians, Russian speakers in Estonia, and other Russians for a psychopolitical discussion of issues relevant to ethnic conflict in Estonia.

This chapter assesses the ways in which these dialogues contributed to the prevention of violent conflict in Estonia.[5] The discussion begins with a brief analysis of the conflict and its development prior to and after the dialogue series. Next, it describes the key elements of the dialogue series and analyzes the apparent direct and indirect effects of the initiative. It then considers other factors affecting the conflict dynamics, including interventions by other international actors, and concludes with a brief summary and recommendations.

Nature and Development of Estonian-Russian Tensions

The nature and development of ethnic tensions in Estonia are best understood by considering the sources and parties, the issues and key developments, and the actions of the involved parties. This background allows a more nuanced understanding of the parties' attitudes regarding the best approach to establishing a durable peace and toward third-party involvement, and the many challenges faced by those who sought to contribute to a peaceful resolution of tensions in Estonia. Later in the chapter, more detail is offered on the significant track-one (official governmental) preventive diplomacy efforts that sought to shape the course of the conflict.

Sources and Parties

From the Estonian perspective, for more than fifty years the main sources of their intercommunal conflict have revolved around the Soviet occupation of Estonia. During Soviet times, Russian became the dominant language in Estonia, and "it was not uncommon for Estonians to be insulted with the phrase 'speak a human language' if they attempted to speak Estonian."[6] Russian and Soviet culture dominated Estonian culture; higher-paying jobs in military-related industries often went to Russians; and Estonians came to see themselves as second-class citizens, subordinate to the occupiers. In light of this history, in the early 1990s ethnic Estonians generally feared that their language and culture would fade away unless action was taken to stop the tide of Russification in Estonia. In addition, difficulties in the post-Soviet transition to a market economy fanned intercommunal tensions.[7] As individuals faced higher costs of living and more uncertainty of income, each ethnic group found a scapegoat in the other.

From the ethnic Russian perspective, the sources of conflict stemmed not simply from the Soviet policies that transplanted Russians to Estonia, but also from the Estonians' desire to turn the clock back and remove the Russian people who had come to consider this area their home. Many of the ethnic Russians had lived their entire lives in Estonia, and for the most part were segregated from ethnic Estonians and from opportunities to learn the Estonian language. As Estonia changed to a market economy, economic hard times were also a reality for the ethnic Russians, especially in the predominantly Russian areas surrounding the military-related factories that shut down after Estonia regained independence.

The sources of the conflict arguably reach much further back in history. Russian and Estonian cultures are distinct. Through recent centuries, Russians and Germans repeatedly dominated the Estonian people, who placed considerable importance on autonomy and their unique identity as Estonians. The Estonians and Russians in Estonia have long lived side by side in separate communities with little communication between the groups. In the early 1990s, this separation continued and, with the language barrier, hampered communication from the Estonian community to the Russian community in northeast Estonia—for example, the latter received television broadcasts only from Russia. Schools and summer camps were separated by ethnicity, with each clearly organized for only Russian or only Estonian children.

The Estonian-Russian conflict in Estonia centered on a two-party conflict between Estonians and Russian speakers living in Estonia. However, the conflict also included more or less partisan third parties that substantially shaped the course of the conflict. The Russian government in Moscow took a keen interest in the Russians in Estonia, linking their fate to developments in Estonian-Russian relations. Several governmental and intergovernmental parties in Europe and the United States attempted intermediary initiatives. Thus, while the basic parties were the ethnic Estonians and ethnic Russians, Russia and Western governments and intergovernmental organizations played influential third-party roles.

Issues and Key Developments

The issues in the conflict all arose out of a basic disjunction between the Estonian search for recognition and security and the Russian search for security and acceptance in Estonia. These issues included citizenship, voting rights and local government, the Estonian-Russian border, Russian troop withdrawals, language laws, residency permits, and travel documents. All these issues arose in a context of an economy in transition and the economic difficulties that the whole population faced in everyday life.

Citizenship involved not only the recognition of the continuous Estonian state that had existed under Soviet occupation, but also the lack of security for those "Russians" inside Estonia who suddenly found themselves without acknowledged citizenship—a situation that involved one-third of the population living in Estonia. These resident Russians wanted some voice in Estonian government, and after the summer of 1993 they were given the right to vote in local elections. Estonians, however, did not want to recognize any rights that could be seen as legitimating claims to a legal right to live in a land the Russians had occupied. Similarly, the border dispute was over whether to honor a Soviet-era transfer of territory from the Estonian SSR to the Russian Soviet Socialist Republic. Because Estonia had been occupied and had not joined the Soviet Union voluntarily, Estonians insisted that the land transfer was illegal and should now be annulled. This claim was reflected in a map that appears without any comment in a 1994 English-language book on Estonia, showing the larger, pre-Soviet borders of Estonia.[8] However, the areas in question are inhabited predominantly by Russians. Soviet (and subsequently, Russian) troops remained on bases in Estonia until 1994, a policy the Russian government tied to concerns over the treatment of ethnic Russians in Estonia. Estonia's language laws were designed to ensure the continuity of the Estonian language, which Soviet power had almost eradicated, but they fueled anxiety and insecurity in the Russian community because the laws required use of Estonian in all official government business and reserved citizenship to those who could pass a language test demonstrating a very high level of Estonian language competency. Residency permits and travel documents also emerged as issues when Estonians attempted to meet Western human rights standards, which required governments to provide travel documents for all legal residents. Estonia provided temporary documents that avoided conferring citizenship on those they regarded as occupiers and the descendants of occupiers. On their part, Russians found that these temporary documents only increased their uncertainty about their futures in Estonia.

In July 1993, Estonia enacted the Law on Aliens, enumerating specifically which individuals would be considered as aliens, what their rights were, and how such individuals would apply for Estonian citizenship. Some Russians who had been born in Estonia and lived their whole lives there were labeled aliens by the law, and would be required to pass the difficult Estonian language test in order to apply for full Estonian citizenship. This law became a flashpoint issue in Russian-Estonian tensions within Estonia. Ethnic Russians in Estonia were outraged, while Estonians were not satisfied that their cultural identity would be adequately protected. In personal interviews at summer camps in Estonia in July 1993, ethnic Estonians reported wanting all the Russians to "go home," and ethnic Russians prophesied a war to protect the only home they knew.[9] The controversy over the Law on Aliens reflected underlying differences of Estonian- and Russian-speakers regarding the definition of the Estonian state.

Overall, ethnic Estonians wanted Estonia to be recognized as a continually autonomous country that had been occupied for more than fifty years. Based on that understanding, the newcomers were seen as the remnants of the occupiers' colonization and not as citizens of the original Estonia. The large numbers and past behavior of the Russians moved Estonians into a defensive position to protect the Estonian language and culture. The ethnic Russians in Estonia, for the most part, looked on Estonia as their home. They seemed to want the sense of belonging that comes with citizenship as well as the security that citizenship and acceptance of the Russian language could offer. The alternative of moving to Russia would mean leaving behind lifelong friends, secure employment, and a relatively healthy economy and government to go to uncertain employment, a drastically worse economy, and an unstable government.

Actions of Involved Parties

As reflected in the chronology (see the appendix to this chapter), the basic parties in this conflict all acted in contentious ways that affected the course of the conflict and the shape of potential resolutions. Yet each of the parties also at times showed restraint and appealed for a peaceful settlement of the issues that divided them.

ESTONIAN ACTIONS

In the early 1990s, members of the Estonian government repeatedly made appeals for continued avoidance of violence and even thanked the population, both Russian and Estonian, for their continued patience.[10] Following the Russian government's decision to cut off natural gas supplies to Estonia in June 1993, Estonian prime minister Mart Laar reminded the country on national television that the interruption of the gas supply was not the fault of those Russians living in Estonia.[11] No less remarkable, when the media reported that trenches were being dug on bases occupied by Russian military personnel, the government response was a calm explanation that the trench strategy is a common Russian tactic during times of tension. When Narva, a city in northeast Estonia with a population of approximately 90 percent Russian speakers, announced plans for a referendum on autonomy in July 1993, the Estonian Parliament declared that the referendum would be illegal; Estonian president Lennart Meri, however, pledged not to use force to stop it.[12]

In the early years of newly independent Estonia, the Estonian government's tactics could be seen as an exercise involving a negotiating "good cop" and "bad cop." The Estonian Parliament took the hard-line role of bad cop, passing the language and citizenship laws that the Russians so disliked and making inflammatory statements. "How to Become a Citizen of Estonia," a Russian-language pamphlet published by the Estonian legislature, contained twenty-one pages of detailed listings of requirements for citizenship, including a section on deciding which citizenship was desired (Estonian or Russian). The pamphlet ended with a page referring to organizations that helped people who were interested in immigrating to the United States. The Estonian Parliament clearly was not encouraging Russians to seek Estonian citizenship.

Estonia's president and ministers seemed more understanding, seeking dialogue and broader dissemination of the draft law, but they were constrained by a Parliament that watched for any pro-Russian sentiment.[13] In a conciliatory gesture, President Meri submitted the Law on Aliens to the CSCE and the Council of Europe for comment before signing it into law. He also participated in roundtable discussions considering both the Russian and Estonian viewpoints, and appointed a special liaison to the Russian-dominated Narva City Council. The executive branch of the government also discussed the need to appropriate more money for Estonian language classes to aid those who were attempting to learn the language to gain citizenship.

In spite of these accommodating measures, the Estonian government and legislature both held firmly to a position that the people who came to Estonia during the years of Soviet occupation would not become Estonian citizens unless they made a special application to do so. That special application excluded former career military personnel and intelligence officers of the Soviet Union, as well as those people who did not speak Estonian with appropriate proficiency. The language proficiency requirement required effective fluency at first, and then was relaxed to require the ability to converse on everyday topics such as family members and shopping, as well as the ability to understand news, official forms, and announcements.

RUSSIAN SPEAKERS' ACTIONS

The ethnic Russians held to the position that as individuals, they had not engineered the original Russian colonization of Estonia and therefore wanted to continue as equals in the country where they had come to live. The July 1993 referendum on autonomy in Narva and in nearby Sillamäe (another city with a high proportion of Russian speakers) sent signals to the Estonian government of the wide base of support that the Russians claimed to enjoy. Russian workers, who were the primary staff of power plants that were integral to the functioning of Estonian industry, threatened to strike if Russian rights were not upheld. Individual ethnic Russian leaders spoke of their inability to guarantee that the Russian people would not defend their rights by force if necessary. The Russian third of Estonia's population showed itself a force not to be ignored.

THIRD-PARTY ACTIONS

The Russian government wanted the Russians in Estonia to be able to take Estonian citizenship freely. In the early 1990s, Russia had no housing or jobs to offer Russians who returned from the former Soviet republics. Estonian supporters speculated that the Russian government believed that its "long-term strategic interests are best solved by leaving ethnic Russians resident in as many neighboring states as possible."[14] Several Russian government attempts to support the concerns of the Russians remaining in Estonia contributed to international concerns about the possibility of a violent confrontation. On the day that Estonian president Lennart Meri signed the final Law on Aliens, the Presidium of the Russian Parliament called for a renunciation of the 1920 peace treaty with Estonia that had first recognized Estonia's independence. Moscow had long tied the withdrawal of the remaining Russian military troops in Estonia to the secure assurance of the rights of Estonia's Russian population. As mentioned earlier, these troops had dug trenches on their bases in the period directly before the enactment of the Law on Aliens, while troops just across the border from Narva performed unusual military training exercises. Likewise, the Russian natural gas company Gazprom halted its deliveries to Estonia just before the Law on Aliens was enacted. Russian president Boris Yeltsin charged that the law was so discriminatory that it would constitute an "Estonian version of apartheid."[15] The Russian government showed that it could make Estonia very uncomfortable, and demanded that the Estonian government grant citizenship to all those who had been living in Estonia when it declared independence.

The Western governmental and intergovernmental organizations that intervened in the conflict largely framed their engagement in terms of advancing human rights, ensuring political stability, and searching for a durable peaceful settlement. Western interveners attempted to promote communication, adherence to international standards of human rights, and a decrease in tensions.[16] The CSCE and the Council of Europe both reviewed the Law on Aliens, making suggestions for clarifications that would bring the law closer to international standards on human rights. The CSCE had a long-term mission in Estonia aimed at decreasing tensions and, in coordination with the US Embassy, mediating with the Russian and Estonian leaders.[17] Through their embassies, the United States and the United Kingdom were both involved in encouraging and supporting the presidential roundtable meetings and in pushing for better communication between the Russian and Estonian communities.[18] Pope John Paul II traveled to Estonia in September 1993 and urged continued dialogue and consideration of the Russian minority. Nonviolence International met with Russian and Estonian leaders in Narva and Tallinn during the time of the Narva referendum on autonomy.[19] Although the Western press did not report the developments in Estonia as front-page news, Western governments and nongovernmental organizations (NGOs) followed developments with keen interest.

The CSCE established an official presence in Estonia because its fact-finding missions had concluded that the country was a place of potentially violent conflict. When the CSCE missions noted signs of potential conflict escalation, they passed this information to the CSCE as a whole. Such early warning included specific notice of plans for a general strike in the predominantly Russian-populated northeastern Estonia,[20] as well as less-tangible reports of Estonian feelings on the street that "they (the Russians) should go home."[21] In addition, as the Estonian government was generally made up of people who had had little to do with politics during Soviet rule and had little experience in governing, some experienced Western diplomats tended to fear that the young Estonian government would be unable to learn how to govern before it made a series of irreversible mistakes.[22] Nonetheless, other diplomats were more patient and understanding of the Estonian government, citing its inexperience as a reason for granting more latitude to Estonia as it took time to forge effective policy towards its Russian residents.[23]

In large part, violent conflict in Estonia may have been avoided through the preventive track-one diplomacy that addressed the salient issues in the conflict. Although tensions between the Estonian and Russian-speaking communities in Estonia escalated, the conflict did not become violent. The only physical violence occurred when a small bomb was detonated in Tallinn in September 1993, an incident that neither resulted in deaths nor was conclusively linked to political issues. Despite the potential for a chaotic transition, the characterization of disputes as human rights issues—coupled with Estonia's wish to join European institutions and live up to European standards—framed much of the conflict in terms that were appropriate to legal channels of settlement. All parties to the conflict accepted the legal characterization of many of the issues of the conflict, including issues of citizenship, voting rights and local government, the Estonian-Russian border, Russian troop withdrawals, language laws, residency permits, and travel documents. During the 1990s, much concrete progress was made on each of these issues, often by working out pragmatic details during the implementation process. However, given the depth of strong feelings, the magnitude of the issues involved, and the parallels between this conflict and others in the aftermath of the breakup of the Soviet Union, the Estonian-Russian conflict attracted significant international attention. Furthermore, the less concretely defined but certainly salient issue of the deep divide between the Estonian and Russian communities in Estonia remained a point of contention. (The chronology in the appendix at the end of this chapter summarizes key events in the conflict and its resolution.)[24]

Remaining Tensions

David Laitin's analysis indicated that as of 2003, ethnic Russians were integrating into Estonian society while both Russians and Estonians were integrating into the areas of Europe where the English language is commonly used for international communication, and that the Estonian government's policies were reinforcing those trends.[25] Yet even with all the progress that has been made, some tensions remain in Estonia today. In particular, the 2014 Russian annexation of Crimea from Ukraine serves as a stark example of Russia's expressed interest in the fate of Russian communities beyond Russian borders, particularly where Russian speakers live in high concentrations. However, all analysis indicates that there is little chance of widespread interethnic violence in Estonia in the near future. Tensions remain, but potentially inflammatory issues continue to be addressed through processes that generally are recognized as legitimate political avenues for change. Estonia's economic situation has improved greatly in the past two decades, interethnic contact is more common, and democratic structures are more developed and institutionalized. In short, while issues remain to be resolved and some tensions continue, some substantive issues have been settled.

The Dialogues: Theory, Structure, Example, and Goals

How did domestic and international actors address the tensions in Estonia? There were multiple initiatives encompassing the full range of multitrack diplomacy. The focus of this chapter is on one of these initiatives: the Center for the Study of Mind and Human Interaction–The Carter Center (CSMHI-TCC) psychopolitical dialogue. This initiative addressed the deep divide between Estonians and Russians in Estonia. This section summarizes the theory that informed the CSMHI-TCC dialogues and describes the structure of the dialogues. It also uses the example of the October 1994 dialogue to illustrate how the dialogues were built on their theoretical foundations. It then describes the structural innovations for the final two dialogues and discusses the goals that the organizing team had for the dialogue series.

Theory

The theory informing these dialogues was largely psychoanalytical. At the time of the 1994–96 Estonian-Russian dialogues, the CSMHI offices filled a pleasant brick house tucked away on a wooded hill in the Blue Ridge Hospital complex near Charlottesville, Virginia. Part of the University of Virginia Medical School, CSMHI's work and research focused on the psychological aspects of international conflict. The center was directed by Dr. Vamik Volkan, a psychoanalyst whose studies of the psychology of groups in conflict formed the cornerstone of the theoretical foundation for CSMHI's work.[26]

Volkan's work holds that people have a "need for Enemies and Allies,"[27] a perspective that draws on a psychoanalytic theory of human development. As the child develops, certain outside entities serve to externalize that which is good or bad. These psychological processes are crystallized in adolescence, creating part of a group identity and a shared pool of cultural targets upon which a group might focus during times of mass regression, perhaps in response to a threat to the group identity. Volkan does not claim that the shared cultural symbols are all negative projections; he notes that positive projections also occur. When some projections, positive and negative, are reinforced by society during adolescence, those projections become a cultural resource which can be called on in times of group stress. They are part of the group identity, which Volkan aptly describes metaphorically as the "ethnic tent." The ethnic tent is a home to shared symbols, rituals, and psychological coping mechanisms to which people turn if the tent must be defended.

Clearly, irrational processes are at work in conflict situations between groups. Volkan holds that both the irrational and rational aspects of a conflict must be addressed. If the irrational aspects are not addressed, there can be no effective solution for the substantive issues, because rituals, symbols, traumas, and the like will make any substantive suggestions unacceptable psychologically. Thus, the transcripts of a discussion of a conflict hide "second transcripts" beneath them, and these hidden agendas or subconscious desires motivate interests, as initially represented by participants in workshops. Psychoanalysts are uniquely trained to read these "second transcripts" by unveiling the otherwise hidden meanings in events, including events linked to conflict. Volkan describes psychoanalytic techniques as uniquely useful in bringing out the otherwise hidden meanings and agendas.[28]

Applying this perspective to the case at hand, when the ferry MS *Estonia* sank in September 1994, the nation of Estonia was shocked by the tragedy. Psychoanalytic insight unveiled the deep and "hidden" fear that Estonians had of disappearing, or sinking to the bottom as the ship had sunk. This fear was discussed at a CSMHI dialogue in Estonia just a week after the ferry sank. The Baltic participants indicated that the disaster had provoked feelings of shame, because the loss of the ferry seemed to reflect the inability of its namesake—the country of Estonia—to survive as an independent industrialized country. In effect, to the Baltic participants, the foundering boat had become a metaphor for their own country.

Structure

CSMHI sponsored eight meetings in the Baltics, and was joined by TCC in sponsoring the last six sessions. The first meeting was held in Lithuania in April 1992, followed by a dialogue in Latvia in 1993. These two discussions focused on the Baltics as a whole, and paved the way for an invitation from Estonians and Russians for the team to convene similar workshops focused on the Estonian-Russian relationship. CSMHI and TCC convened two workshops in Estonia in 1994, three in Estonia in 1995, and a final one in Estonia in 1996. The focus of this paper is on the CSMHI-TCC Estonian-Russian dialogues of 1994 to 1996, though these dialogues should be seen in the context of their emergence from the 1992 and 1993 Lithuanian and Latvian dialogues.

The CSMHI-TCC meetings had a common basic structure, described by one observer as "a hybrid of group therapy, diplomatic conference, and academic seminar."[29] Each meeting brought together approximately thirty key political players and scholars in the Baltics and Russia with a team of approximately ten CSMHI-TCC associates for four days of discussions. There were more participants from the hosting Baltic state than from the others, but each Baltic state was represented at each of the early meetings. The last five meetings included only Estonians and Russians and focused exclusively on Estonian-Russian relations.

The agenda was flexible according to the progress of the discussions. The schedule included both plenary and small group sessions facilitated by experienced CSMHI-TCC faculty. About 80 percent of the formal dialogue time of seven hours per day was spent in small groups.[30] In the small group sessions, Estonians, Russian speakers in Estonia, and Russians shared their analysis of recent events of significance to Estonian-Russian relations. Between the scheduled sessions, the whole group ate communally for lunch and dinner and spent other time together informally. Interpreters were available at all times, and discussions proceeded in English, Estonian, and Russian.[31]

Example: The October 1994 Dialogue

The second CSMHI-TCC meeting in Tallinn, Estonia in October 1994 captures the nature of the dialogues. Some of the participants in that meeting had attended the previous CSMHI-TCC meeting five months before. The October meeting involved mid- and high-level leaders from the Estonian government, the Russian community in Estonia, the Russian government, and several other Baltic participants.

For CSMHI-TCC, the focus of the meeting was the small group sessions in which more personal issues were discussed. It was in the small sessions, Volkan explained, that the bulk of the work on psychological resistances to resolution could occur.[32] According to Volkan, less important work occurred in the plenary sessions. Given the CSMHI focus on the psychological aspects of conflict, each group was facilitated by a psychoanalyst. However, CSMHI tailored the meeting to the high-level participants and their expectations for large plenary discussions in the image of a more traditional analytical workshop. This adjustment reflects the CSMHI tendency to view conflict as a fundamentally psychological phenomenon and to place less emphasis on the behavior and substantive issues, which might be discussed in plenary sessions.

The perspectives that emerged during the small group sessions added an important psychological dimension to understanding of the conflict. The October 1994 dialogue was held a week after the ferry *Estonia* sank. As described above, Estonians discussed their fears of disappearing and failure. These fears were linked to the stringent language requirements that the Estonian government had enacted to ensure that the Estonian language would not disappear. Further desires for a monoethnic Estonian nation-state surfaced. Russians reacted to these Estonian sentiments and expressed their own feelings of outrage that the people who had helped to bring Estonia into the industrialized world would now be marginalized. Furthermore, Russians described themselves as individuals separate from the Soviet regime, under which they also had suffered and been victims, and expressed their humiliation at facing the difficult, nonstandardized Estonian language exams. The historian, the diplomat, and the area specialist who were included in this dialogue assisted the psychoanalysts in understanding the context of the behavior that the team observed. Their assistance was crucial, given the absence of an opportunity for long-term participant psychoanalysis.

The final two dialogues were structured somewhat differently. To increase the reach of the dialogues to younger generations, the last two dialogue groups included eight university students (four Estonians and four Russian-speakers).[33] To augment the students' dialogue experiences, the CSMHI-TCC team brought these students to the United States to further develop their relationships and to jointly consider issues of minority integration.

Goals

The CSMHI teams hoped that the dialogues would serve as "catalysts to identify impediments to peaceful relationships in the region and to bring to light possible solutions to national and ethnic problems."[34] The meeting goals were not full resolution of the conflict, but the removal of the participants' psychological resistances to rational analysis of the conflict and subsequent rational analysis of the conflict and possible settlements. The facilitators aimed to meet these goals by creating for the participants "a safe space in which to talk."[35]

Volkan cautions that "resolution" is sometimes used to refer to a grandiose vision held by practitioners who overvalue their own roles in a conflict.[36]

He cautions that those who intervene in a conflict cannot produce a resolution for the conflict, and that any resolution must come from the parties involved. The psychoanalysts who intervene offer tools that the parties may use to move toward resolution. These tools include the skills that psychoanalysts develop in uncovering deep and hidden meanings (second transcripts) behind surface conversation and behaviors. This perspective on conflict resolution work reinforces an emerging sense that the task of the conflict resolution intervener is not to intervene in the substance of a conflict, but rather to create the space and process that are necessary conditions for participant-owned conflict resolution.[37]

Dialogue Effects

In the most comprehensive published documentation of these workshops to date, Joyce Neu and Vamik Volkan cite four primary workshop-related effects on Estonian-Russian relations in Estonia:[38]

- Professional and private contacts between participants;
- Participant reflection on and revision of individual attitudes held by participants;
- Direct input to and feedback from the Presidential Roundtable on Minority Issues; and
- Concrete substantive action ideas suggested and implemented to improve ethnic relations in Estonia.

Fourteen interviews with workshop facilitators, participants, and observers corroborated these effects and identified others. All in all, the dialogue series contributed to conflict resolution by increasing intercommunal understanding, generating useful approaches to the conflict issues, building relationships, and developing new dialogue skills among participants. The various direct and indirect effects that the dialogue series had on the conflict situation can be elaborated under the following three categories:

- *Attitude* impacts on dialogue participants;
- *Process* impacts on the intermediate processes of conflict resolution in Estonia; and
- *Substantive* impacts on issues central to the conflict.

Attitudes of Participants

The dialogues appear to have had an eye-opening effect on most participants.
Although some participants may not have changed their understandings of
Russian and Estonian perspectives on the conflict issues and the future of
Estonia, many did. They came to understand the other side better. One participant reported never having talked in any meaningful way to a person of
the other ethnicity prior to the dialogue session. Others had new insights
about the hopes and fears of the others and also of their own group. Several
participants spoke of understanding their own and the others' traumas, after
participating in the dialogues. One Estonian participant described learning
in particular that the Russians in Narva were afraid of their close neighbor
Russia and did not want the border shifted to make Narva a border town. This
insight showed a way in which Russians and Estonians in Estonia have more
in common with each other than Russians in Estonia have with Russians in
Russia.[39] Other participants reported similar insights on the commonalities
and the differences of Russian and Estonian experiences in Estonia.

With these new insights and the experience of discussing such important
issues respectfully, the participants also developed more personal and professional contacts with each other. Neu and Volkan documented many examples of increased personal and professional exchanges, discussion, and even
friendships across the interethnic divide.[40] This increased contact allowed
continued exchange of views and more open communication among influential individuals in the Estonian and Russian communities.

Intermediate Impacts on Conflict Resolution

Although the number of participants was limited (roughly thirty per dialogue, with the core group remaining the same from dialogue to dialogue),
the abovementioned impacts on the participants' attitudes should be seen
in light of the influence that some of these individuals had in their communities. Quite a few were very influential at the time of the dialogues, with
positions that included serving on the Presidential Roundtable on Minority Issues, leading political parties, and writing influential opinion pieces
in local newspapers. Arnold Rüütel, the former chairman of the Supreme
Council of the Republic of Estonia (the successor to the Supreme Soviet of
the Estonian SSR), was a participant in parts of four of the dialogues.[41] At
the time of his participation he was deputy speaker of the Estonian Parliament (Riigikogu), and later he became Estonia's third president. Each of the

dialogue participants highlighted the importance of the dialogues in making important impacts on the wider processes of conflict resolution. One participant, for example, explained that this new way of approaching difficult issues was adopted in some measure during the Presidential Roundtable on Minority Issues.

Interviews with the participants indicate that the dialogue organizers' emphasis on increasing participants' understanding of Estonian-Russian relations quickly led participants to realize concrete results built on their increased understanding: establishing connections between the dialogues and the Presidential Roundtable on Minority Issues, creating new relationships for continued professional or personal discussions even beyond the dialogue context, and stimulating local mixed ethnicity community projects to further intercommunal understanding. Other intermediary impacts of the dialogues were more indirect. Participants whose views changed as a result of the dialogues wrote newspaper articles, spoke with other influential individuals in society, brought insights to the Presidential Roundtable on Minority Issues, and shared new understandings with the Estonian Parliament.

In addition, dialogue participants highlighted the importance of their learning the process of dialogue as practiced in these sessions and using those skills in other contexts. This point is best illustrated with direct quotations from participants reflecting on their experience a decade after the dialogues:[42]

- "For people from a totalitarian society such as the Soviet times, dialogue meant that you have to enforce your truth and defend your position against opponents. For me personally, it was a great lesson from Vamik that dialogue might mean another thing. It could be to understand another position and create an atmosphere of exchanging opinions and values without expecting immediate outcomes, but to start a process. Democracy is a process. This was the most important lesson for me. These dialogues taught me we could talk in such a way, and that this way is important for democracy. . . . He [Vamik Volkan] taught facilitation of dialogue. . . . [Years later] I worked on a TACIS [Technical Assistance to the Commonwealth of Independent States] program as a member of a European Commission team for almost three years in Russia, creating dialogue teams in the North Caucasus and Volga region. So I distributed my [dialogue skills] experience to Russian local governments."

- "It was quite useful to learn to speak to each other honestly about how we feel, why we don't like something, how we perceive the other. . . ."

- "We understood [through the dialogues] what it means to speak openly with each other about these [conflict] problems. This was a new way of speaking with each other. There was little interethnic dialogue prior to the dialogues. These dialogues inspired other dialogues locally, and influenced the discussions in the President's Roundtable."
- "Previously, we had not learned this style of discussion. We had not studied in Western universities. We learned this new style of discussion, which first had been a battlefield of arguments and in later seminars . . . we could listen to each other. . . . This style of discussion had a long-term impact."

Another participant described using this dialogue approach to facilitate additional interethnic discussion in Estonia and elsewhere. Still another stated that the tensions in Estonian-Russian relations in the early years of Estonia's independence from the Soviet Union were due in part to the lack of experience with democracy. The dialogue skills were essential to further developing a real democratic culture where discussions could be based on understanding others' concerns and perspectives. This participant credited the dialogues with helping build meaningful democratic exchange, which in turn shaped policies that helped deescalate the conflict.

Impacts on Substantive Issues

The impact that the dialogues seem to have had on the main substantive issues in the conflict was indirect. As mentioned, through their small group discussions, participants gained new insights on the significance and under-lying fears and aspirations associated with each of the conflict issues. However, these discussions also generated concrete ideas on how to address these issues. Although no interviewee was comfortable attributing a direct causal link between discussions at the dialogues and subsequent eventual implementation of a helpful policy change, all agreed that the new insights gained through the dialogues helped make useful policy changes possible.

During the final dialogue sessions, participants brainstormed various practical ways to work on the substantive issues of the conflict. Three concrete projects that grew directly out of these discussions were supported for two years of work with $50,000 each in funding. These projects contributed locally to substantive efforts to address issues central to the conflict. Workshop participant and Estonian psychologist Endel Talvik coordinated the implementation of these projects from 1996 to 1998.[43] Even though none of the projects led directly to any policy change, each project provided an example of constructive Estonian-Russian relations. As the influential dialogue participants were aware that the projects they had conceived were being implemented, these localized projects indirectly raised awareness broadly of potential means for constructive interethnic relations.

The projects were implemented in three communities with different foci specific to the needs of each. In Klooga, community members built a cultural house so that people of both Estonian and Russian backgrounds could gather for films, cultural celebrations, weddings, knitting classes, and other community activities. Today, the cultural house is widely known in the community and it continues to be actively used by community members from both ethnic backgrounds.[44] This outcome is significant, because one of the difficulties in Estonian-Russian relations in the early 1990s was the lack of shared spaces for Estonian-Russian interaction. This spin-off project generated by the dialogues has helped remove one of the institutional impediments to building Estonian-Russian relations at the grassroots.

In Mustamäe, a district in Tallinn, the community created a model Estonian-language program for Russian children. In the program, Russian and Estonian children learned in kindergarten together.[45] This model educational approach pioneered by this project later received Estonian government funding to continue.[46] The success of the joint Russian-Estonian kindergarten was significant in terms of the substantive issues in conflict. Teaching the Estonian language to Russian children was difficult in the absence of appropriate language programs. In this context, the joint kindergarten provided one model. The influence of participants in the dialogues ensured that the kindergarten program's success was widely known. However, even today, a difficult practical challenge remains in transitioning the language of instruction from Russian to Estonian, as mandated by law for Estonian high schools. Shortages of qualified Estonian language teachers have required much slower implementation of the legislation calling for all high schools to be Estonian-language. Partial implementation was planned to be phased in gradually, with one subject at a time transitioning to the use of the Estonian language.

In Mustvee, a city near Lake Peipus on the Estonian-Russian border, community members founded an NGO to organize cultural excursions, language courses, and local activities; offer Internet access; and develop a tourist information center. The cultural excursions and activities bring people from the community together across the Estonian-Russian divide, including the Russian Old Believers who have lived in that area for centuries but still maintained a segregated culture. The tourist information center and renovation of local churches of all faiths served to draw foreign tourists to Mustvee. This project thus impacted the conflict issues by addressing the lack of interethnic activities, celebrating Mustvee's diverse cultural heritage, and bringing tourist revenue to the city. As with the kindergarten program in Mustamäe, the high profile of the dialogue participants ensured that the founding of the cultural NGO was widely known. Unfortunately, the NGO later had difficulties in raising enough funds to maintain as active a program as it would have liked.[47]

There do not appear to have been any missed opportunities or negative effects of the dialogues. Several participants noted that dialogue discussions could be difficult, heated, or emotional, but this was seen as a necessary part of the positive impacts that the dialogues had on the attitudes, processes, and substantive issues of the conflict.

Factors Explaining the Dialogues' Impacts

Based on this understanding of the conflict and the effects that the dialogues had on it, it is important to identify key factors that help to explain those impacts. These factors include features of the dialogues themselves and contextual factors.

Key Features of the Dialogues

Certain aspects of the dialogue methodology were crucial to their successful impacts. Some of these ingredients had to do with the planning of the entire series of meetings.

> *Timing.* The dialogues were held when the potential for violent conflict had been widely recognized. By 1994, politically active Estonians and Russians knew that international attention was focused on their tensions, and that at least some outside experts found the tensions in Estonia disturbing. Because of the influence of these outsiders, such as the CSCE, the parties to the conflict were inclined to take the concerns seriously. Thus, although from the Estonian perspective there was no "conflict" per se, there was motivation to participate in dialogue and gain understanding of the Russian perspectives. There were also concrete details, such as language laws, that remained to be fully addressed, so the dialogues had a chance to impact these issues. The dialogues were neither too early

(prior to emergence and recognition of the conflict) nor too late (after settlement of the contentious issues) to have an effect.

Composition. The participants who were selected had direct input to official-level decisions and public discourse in Estonia. Participants were, for the most part, highly influential. Some were senior in the Estonian government or Russian community leadership. Others were opinion leaders. This created direct input from the dialogues into the official negotiations on concrete issues and into public opinion.

Continuity. The participants were generally consistent from dialogue to dialogue. Participants were able to build trust and understanding with each other through repeated participation in dialogues. The depth of discussions in one dialogue laid the basis for further in-depth discussions among the same general participant group during future dialogues. Thus, subsequent dialogue sessions did not have to go over ground already covered. Also, the frequency of the dialogues, which occurred approximately every six months, meant that the dialogues always had substantial new material with which to work, the participants had time to reflect on previous discussions, and the momentum of the process could be maintained.

Other key ingredients had to do with how the individual dialogue sessions were conducted:

The facilitation team. The skills and personalities of the facilitation team, particularly those of Volkan, were crucial. As noted previously, the team was multidisciplinary and included area experts, historians, diplomats, and skilled psychoanalysts.

The method. The small group sessions concentrated on intergroup psychological processes. Participants had the chance to engage in in-depth dialogue. Many found new psychological insights through these discussions. In the process, participants learned in dialogue sessions, and practiced through subsequent meetings, a new way of approaching discussion of difficult issues. This method gave participants a new skill to apply in many areas of their lives, including in continued work on the conflict issues.

Nonofficial status. Given the international attention to potential violent conflict in Estonia, the formal engagement of Western governments with the Estonian government, and the fact that the ongoing discussions constantly referenced the legal framework of international human rights standards, Estonians were reluctant to provide any official acknowledgment of Russian concerns. The nonofficial nature of the dialogue process, however, provided a means of avoiding a legalistic discourse. This unofficial aspect of the dialogues contributed to their success in catalyzing new, more authentic approaches to discussion and thus produced unique insights.

Contextual Factors

Important contextual factors include the other international interventions that were directed at the conflict, certain elements within Estonia, and factors in the broader global context.

TRACK-ONE PREVENTIVE DIPLOMACY

The CSMHI-TCC facilitated dialogues did not occur in a vacuum, but operated in an environment in which many high-level diplomatic initiatives were also engaging Estonians and Russians at the track-one level. These instances of preventive diplomacy sought to make a positive difference by moving certain substantive issues in the conflict toward settlement. Several interventions also helped to introduce, develop, and legitimate channels of communication among Estonian and Russian elites. The preventive diplomacy interventions that targeted Estonia varied widely in their actors, their methods, the issues addressed, and their effects.

The CSCE. Because the CSCE was unique in its acceptance by the main parties to the conflict, the most visible and long-term interveners worked through the CSCE structure. As Estonia turned toward the West, seeking to gain acceptance as a part of Europe, Estonia gave the CSCE a significant (though certainly incomplete) degree of legitimacy and authority in the country regarding standards of human rights. Estonian president Lennart Meri's submission of the Law on Aliens to the CSCE for review, for example, demonstrated a concern for Western validation of Estonia's standards. The Estonian government's response to the Report of the CSCE Office for Democratic Institutions and Human Rights on the Study of Estonian Legislation included "assurances of their highest considerations."[48]

The CSCE sought to affect several aspects of Estonian-Russian tensions at both national and local levels. Following the passage of the Aliens Act in 1993, the CSCE's High Commissioner on National Minorities played a crucial role in averting escalation of the standoff between the Estonian government and the political leaders of the Russian-speaking community regarding the autonomy referendum. Another excellent example of an intervention that might not have been accepted if it had been attempted by a less bilaterally acceptable intervener is the role that the CSCE played in the local elections of the fall of 1993. The CSCE not only involved itself publicly as it urged the Estonian government to extend the vote in local elections to all residents, citizen or not, but also worked to ensure the presence of candidates that would make the elections legitimate.[49] Very few leaders of the Russian community held Estonian citizenship and were eligible for office. The CSCE, however, was able to identify those Russians who were moderate enough to be acceptable to the Estonian government and who might stand for election if they were citizens. These politicians were then pointed out to the Estonian government and were offered citizenship by special merit, a loophole category remaining in the citizenship law of Estonia. Although supporters of the Russian community might have raised a cry about what amounted to Estonian selection of the candidates, and Estonian nationalists might have disputed the wisdom of awarding "special merit" citizenship to Russian politicians, neither side to the conflict protested vocally.

United States. The key US government involvement in Estonia was led by US Ambassador to Estonia Robert Frasure. Ambassador Frasure enjoyed a good relationship with both the Estonian government and the Russian community. He often worked in coordination with the other parties, especially the CSCE, both soliciting CSCE support for US initiatives and giving official US government feedback on and support to CSCE projects. He was able to secure US and Swedish funding of the administrative costs of the Presidential Roundtable (described further below), an idea urged by the CSCE but not accepted by the Estonian government until the crisis of summer 1993.[50] Similarly, the partial US government funding of Estonian language classes in Sillamäe came about through collaborative effort between CSCE and the US government. Furthermore, Frasure suggested the compromise of "temporary travel documents" in lieu of passports for Estonia's noncitizen population.[51] The CSCE then supported the idea of such a compromise measure, but the initial version of the documents did little to meet the needs, for example, of many noncitizens wishing to visit the United States. President Bill Clinton also intervened to encourage Russian troop withdrawal from Estonia by the August 31, 1994, deadline.

Baltic states. Although in other circumstances the diplomatic links and ties that the Baltic states established with each other might be considered normal diplomacy, in the context of the conflicts within Estonia and also within neighboring Latvia, those ties took on a wider significance. The Baltic states banded together, supporting and legitimating each other's claims and reinforcing their positions. They developed a common Baltic defense force and close coordination of their foreign affairs. These stronger ties created a situation in which events in one country would invariably affect events in the other Baltic states, giving the Baltics a bit more strength against any possible Russian aggression as well as greater international attention.

European states. The Baltics, including Estonia, succeeded in capturing the attention of Western Europe. Consequently, the Western European nations have responded to the Baltic situation, taking public positions designed to prevent any escalation of the conflict as well as to encourage the settlement of unresolved issues. The Council of Europe was actively involved in efforts to prevent escalation of the conflict in Estonia. In February 1993, the Council recognized the Baltics as having been "occupied" by the Soviet Union, and one month later admitted Estonia to the Council of Europe. That summer, Estonia submitted its Law on Aliens to the Council for examination, and then incorporated some of the Council's suggestions in the final version of the law.[52]

United Nations. The United Nations (UN) also engaged with Estonia. In February 1993, a UN Commission on Human Rights (UNCHR) delegation reported that it found no human rights abuses in Estonia. The following month, a UNCHR meeting achieved a somewhat vague agreement between the Estonian parties to work together to solve the problems of Russian-speakers in the Baltics. Subsequently, President Meri stated that Estonia might invite UN troops into Estonia in the event of a conflict within Russia.

As with other interveners, the UN offered to mediate troop withdrawal talks in November 1993, but the offer was rejected by Russia. Several weeks later, a UN General Assembly resolution called for "early, orderly, and complete withdrawal" of the Russian troops from the Baltics.

These several interveners at times coordinated their efforts, but the larger picture that emerges is one of varied actors taking varied and independent initiatives. These official-level activities were significant but were not the cure-all for the broader conflict. They did not address either all of the substantive issues or the basic relationships between the two communities. In these respects, it did not appear that track-one preventive diplomacy could be effective. Settling upon a procedure for travel documents, for example, did little to assuage the Estonian sense of their earlier victimization. Nor were Russians made to feel more secure in their claim that Estonia had become their home as well. Recognition and security are key issues for both Estonians and Russian-speakers in Estonia, but preventive diplomacy did not address these needs directly. Although it was important that the issues framed as legal or human rights disputes be settled without violence, for the long term it was also important that the Estonian and Russian communities find some way to reconcile the underlying divisions that gave rise to those issues. Official channels could address the issues insofar as they were framed as legal disputes, but could not address the recognition and security concerns that lay at the heart of the Estonian-Russian conflict. A deep divide remained between the Estonian and Russian communities even as officials worked out compromises on particular pieces of legislation. Conflict resolution also had to reach the individual Estonians and Russians who needed to understand their neighbors in order to solidify a basis for long-term peaceful coexistence of Estonians and Russians in Estonia. Thus, official processes required supplementary initiatives to address the underlying concerns.

NATIONAL AND INTERNATIONAL FACTORS

In addition to the official-level interventions, certain features of the broader context that were conducive to the dialogues also seem to have contributed to their success. Some of these features are internal to Estonia:

A peaceful, pragmatic approach. Political leaders in both the Estonian and Russian-speaking communities framed the issues in terms of legal arguments, human rights claims, and the importance of building a positive future for Estonia within Western Europe. They also appealed for nonviolent settlement of the issues. Concretely, the Estonian government made concessionary compromises and adjustments during the implementation phases of several pieces of contentious legislation. The language requirement for citizenship was relaxed. Travel documents and residency permits were made available for noncitizens. Russian-language high schools delayed their transition to Estonian-language instruction. Estonian language classes were increased in response to Russian concerns that there were inadequate opportunities to learn the Estonian language in predominantly Russian communities.

Economic and social improvement. The improving Estonian economy brought more and better jobs to both the Estonian and Russian-speaking populations. Estonia's post-Soviet civil society also continued to develop, helping to meet more local community needs.

Inclusive electoral system. The Estonian electoral system, which requires parties to receive 5 percent of the national vote to participate in second round voting, was one factor supportive of compromise and moderation toward ethnic relations.[53] In that system, parties were rewarded by attracting interethnic support.

Lack of coherence of Russian population. Arguably, the diversity within the Russian population of Estonia, and the lack of unifying institutions bringing Russians together, left a fragmented Russian community that was unable to mobilize a sustained campaign for the human rights of the Russian-speaking population.[54]

Other contextual factors that may have influenced the success of the dialogues were geopolitical forces external to Estonia:

Western security support. NATO welcomed Estonia to the Partnership for Peace framework in February 1994, thus helping to alleviate Estonian security concerns about Russian troops and interest in Estonia. The US and Western European governments made clear to Russia their insistence on respect for Estonian sovereignty.

Russian cooperation. The Russian military completed its full withdrawal from Estonia in September 1995 (with the decommissioning of the Paldiski nuclear base), further alleviating Estonian sovereignty concerns. Taken together, Western pressure and internal Russian political preoccupations prevented Russia from effective support of the Russian community in Estonia.[55]

Summary and Implications

The CSMHI-TCC dialogues contributed to the short- and long-term resolution of Estonian-Russian conflict in Estonia through (1) *attitude* impacts on dialogue participants, (2) *process* impacts on the intermediate processes of conflict resolution in Estonia, and (3) *substantive* impacts on issues central to the conflict. In the context of facilitating internal and external factors, these dialogue contributions were complementary to the preventive diplomacy interventions by the CSCE and other official governmental bodies, which focused on substantive issues such as language and citizenship laws and troop withdrawals. In contrast, the dialogues considered underlying motivations that influenced attitudes toward these issues and toward key developments in Estonian-Russian relations. As participants reflected on their own understandings of the Estonians and Russians in Estonia, and on their underlying psychological approaches to these groups and their pasts and futures, participants came to understand the issues and their significance to both groups in new ways. These psychopolitical dialogues not only generated deeper insights and new approaches, but also helped establish relationships and networks that encouraged participants to continue processes of interethnic discussions between dialogue sessions and into the future. The dialogues further enabled participants to approach their future discussions with new dialogue process skills. Finally, the three community projects supported by the dialogue group—the community center in Klooga, the kindergarten in Mustamäe, and the cultural and tourism promotion NGO in Mustvee—gave concrete expression to the new understandings and relationships that emerged through the dialogue project and thereby reinforced the practical import of the initiative.

Implications

Although the Estonian case cannot be generalized to other cases, the experience of psychopolitical dialogues in Estonia has implications for the potential application of this mode of intervention to other conflict settings.

WHEN AND WHERE TO USE PSYCHOPOLITICAL DIALOGUES

The Estonian dialogues indicate that there is an appropriate milieu and timing for a psychopolitical approach:

- Psychopolitical dialogues may be particularly useful in conflicts that have the potential for significant intercommunal violence. Where distinct identity groups find themselves in conflict, psychopolitical dialogues can help reveal the underlying dynamics that shape the conflict. These dialogues can offer insights in all contexts of intergroup conflict, but this technique may be especially relevant in highly emotive situations (i.e., a straightforward business dispute over a breach of contract would not require the in-depth analysis offered by psychopolitical dialogue).

- For psychopolitical dialogues to be useful, the parties to a conflict must be willing to talk together about the issues that divide them.

- Although psychopolitical dialogues contribute to substantive negotiations by generating new insights and approaches to the issues, they are not a substitute for political settlement of the issues. Other processes, such as track-one negotiations and international mediation, are still required to advance the political resolution of substantive issues.

HOW TO IMPLEMENT PSYCHOPOLITICAL DIALOGUES

The Estonian psychopolitical dialogues illustrate some of the best practices generally endorsed within the conflict resolution field:

- A strong facilitation team was essential to the success of psychopolitical dialogues. By all accounts, the implementation by the CSMHI-TCC team was excellent. Participants were most impressed with Volkan's leadership and psychoanalytic insight, as well as with the strength of the team overall and the inclusion in the team of several senior former diplomats. The multidisciplinary backgrounds of the personnel and the inclusion of area experts allowed the team to provide more expert leadership than any one of the facilitators could have offered alone.

- The CSMHI-TCC team could not have worked well without invaluable input from local Estonian partners and extensive preparatory consultations. Visits to Estonia prior to dialogue sessions, travel to "hot spots" relevant to the conflict, and one-on-one meetings with many key players prepared the facilitation team for the dialogue sessions and ensured that appropriate participants could be identified and relevant agendas could be developed.

- The long-term nature of the dialogue series also appears to have been crucial to its overall success. The quality of discussions developed and matured as participants gained experience and built trust over time. Thus, there was real "value added" in holding additional sessions to build on the initial ones. This case study no doubt would have been very different, perhaps not a study of success at all, if the dialogues had ceased after one or two sessions.

- Interestingly, unlike many interactive conflict resolution initiatives, the dialogues were not held far away in "neutral" territory. Rather, the psychopolitical Estonia dialogues were held most often in Tallinn, the population of which is split almost evenly between Estonians and Russians. Even though many participants were close to home, they still ate lunch and dinner together and enjoyed informal time, which is often an important component of conflict resolution workshops.

Realizing the Potential of Psychopolitical Dialogues

This analysis suggests that psychopolitical dialogues have much to offer in areas of intergroup conflict, and that these intensive dialogues are particularly warranted where there is the potential for violence or where violence has recently erupted. However, such dialogues are too rarely implemented. The barriers to implementation are partially structural. There is little funding, particularly sustainable funding over a period of years, dedicated to implementing such dialogue initiatives. Moreover, few people are trained and experienced in facilitating such dialogues.

At this point, another series of psychopolitical dialogues could contribute to the further development of interethnic understanding in Estonia. Bringing together a new group of participants, today's influential leaders, would beneficially expand the circle of people exposed to reflective insight into the psychological aspects of intergroup relations in Estonia. Indeed, given the lessening of intercommunal tensions that have already occurred, these dialogue techniques might be applied directly to immediately pressing concerns. A primary barrier to a renewal of this work, however, may be the lack of information about the approach and the demonstrable successes of psychopolitical dialogue. Where people have heard about interactive conflict resolution techniques, the techniques may be misunderstood or their objectives and measures of success exaggerated. Spreading the knowledge gained from this and other cases involving interactive conflict resolution methods, such as psychopolitical dialogue, might encourage their wider use in the most suitable situations.

Appendix: Chronology of Events

Time	Event
February 2, 1920–June 17, 1940	Estonia internationally recognized as an independent sovereign state.
August 1940	The Soviet Union formally incorporates the Estonian Soviet Socialist Republic, following the Soviet occupation of the Baltic states.
1940–1991	Russian speakers move to Estonia, give birth there, grow up there.
August 1991	Estonia reasserts independence from the Soviet Union.
February 1992	Estonia reaffirms Law on Citizenship of 1938, granting citizenship only to individuals (and descendants) in Estonia prior to 1940.
June–July 1993	Estonian Law on Aliens passed, suspended in the wake of Russian protests and cutoff of natural gas supply from Russia, revised with input from the CSCE, and passed in revised form.
July 1993	Narva and Sillamäe (Estonian cities with majority Russian populations) hold referenda on autonomy.
1994	Periodic delays in the withdrawal of Russian troops from Estonia, linked to Russian concerns for the Russian minority in Estonia, followed by complete Russian military withdrawal in August 1994 and closing of the Paldiski nuclear base in September 1995.
1995–1999	Legislation requires Estonian language skills for government workers and later for workers in service industries. Shortages of Estonian-speaking and citizen policemen in many predominantly Russian-speaking areas show complications of enforcing laws requiring citizenship and Estonian language skills for all governmental workers.
2000–2006	Remaining challenges to meet educational goals in Estonian language for Russian-speaking children.
April 2007	Two days of riots, with 1 death, 150 injuries and 1,200 arrests, follow the Estonian government's decision to relocate from central Tallinn to a graveyard a Bronze Soldier statue honoring Soviet soldiers killed in World War II.
2014	Russian annexation of Crimea prompts renewed efforts by Estonian officials to reach out and address issues affecting Russian-speaking Estonians.

Notes

1. "Human and Civil Rights in the Framework of Estonia's Political Status," Info-Press, Ministry of Foreign Affairs of the Republic of Estonia, n.d.

2. Paul Gould, "Russian Autonomy Referendum Continues in Estonia," United Press International, July 17, 1993.

3. "Human and Civil Rights in the Framework of Estonia's Political Status."

4. Samuel P. Huntington, "The Clash of Civilizations?" *Foreign Affairs* 72, no. 3 (Summer 1993): 22–49.

5. This study was informed by extensive interviews with dialogue facilitators, participants, and observers, as well as published accounts. Some interviews took place during the heightened tensions of 1993–94, and others occurred up to a decade after the dialogues. The author was not directly involved in the dialogues.

6. United Baltic Appeal to the United Nations, "The Law on Aliens Controversy in the Republic of Estonia," second ed. (September 1, 1993), 13.

7. Secretariat of the Conference on Security and Co-operation in Europe, *Report of the CSCE ODIHR Mission on the Study of Estonian Legislation Invited by The Republic of Estonia* (Prague: CSCE, February 1993).

8. Ignar Fjuk and Aarend-Mihkel Rõuk, eds., *Estonia: Free and Independent* (Tallinn: Estonia Encyclopedia Publishers, 1994).

9. See, e.g., an author interview with Sasha (an ethnic Russian adult) at Camp Kotka, Loksa, July 26, 1993.

10. Fred Hiatt, "Narva, Estonia: Spark in an Ethnic Tinderbox," *Washington Post*, October 9, 1993, A21.

11. "Russia Cuts Off Natural Gas to Estonia, Says It Has Created Type of 'Apartheid,'" *Deseret News*, June 25, 1993.

12. Konrad J. Huber, "Averting Inter-Ethnic Conflict: An Analysis of the CSCE High Commissioner on National Minorities in Estonia" (Working Paper Series 16, Conflict Resolution Program, The Carter Center, Atlanta, April 1994), 17.

13. Hiatt, "Narva, Estonia," A21.

14. "The 'Law on Aliens' Controversy in the Republic of Estonia."

15. Sonni Efron, "Estonia Plans Apartheid for Russians, Yeltsin Says," *Los Angeles Times*, June 23, 1993.

16. Author interview with US Ambassador Robert Frasure, Loksa, Estonia, July 30, 1993.

17. Hiatt, "Narva, Estonia," A21.

18. Author interview with US Ambassador Robert Frasure, Loksa, Estonia, July 30, 1993.

19. Author interview with Andre Kamenshikov, Fairfax, VA, November 23, 1993.

20. Author interview with Timo Lahelma, Tallinn, July 15, 1994.

21. Author interview with John Erath, Tallinn, July 15, 1994.

22. Ibid.

23. Ibid.

24. A more detailed chronology can be found through the Minorities at Risk Chronology for Russians in Estonia. See Minorities at Risk Project, "Assessment for Russians in Estonia," Minorities at Risk Project, University of Maryland, accessed October 2006, http://www.cidcm.umd.edu/mar/assessment.asp?groupId=36601.

25. David D. Laitin, "Three Models of Integration and the Estonian/Russian Reality," *Journal of Baltic Studies* 34, no. 2 (2003): 197–222.

26. The Center for the Study of Mind and Human Interaction disbanded in 2005.

27. Vamik D. Volkan, *The Need to Have Enemies and Allies: From Clinical Practice to International Relations* (Northvale, NJ: Jason Aronson, 1988).

28. Author interview with Vamik Volkan, Charlottesville, VA, December 5, 1994.

29. Robert Cullen, "Cleansing Ethnic Hatred," *Atlantic Monthly* 272 (August 1993): 32.

30. Joyce Neu and Vamik Volkan, *Developing a Methodology for Conflict Prevention: The Case of Estonia*, Carter Center Special Report Series (Atlanta: The Carter Center, Winter 1999), 20.

31. Ibid., 21.

32. Author interview with Vamik Volkan, Charlottesville, VA, December 5, 1994.

33. Neu and Volkan, *Developing a Methodology for Conflict Prevention*, 21.

34. Vamik Volkan and Max Harris, "Negotiating a Peaceful Separation: A Psycho-political Analysis of Current Relationships Between Russia and the Baltic Republics," *Mind and Human Interaction* 4, no. 1 (December 1992): 20.

35. Neu and Volkan, *Developing a Methodology for Conflict Prevention*, 11.

36. Author interview with Vamik Volkan, Charlottesville, VA, December 5, 1994.

37. Deborah and Jonathan Kolb note this basic similarity between some psychoanalysts and conflict resolution interveners. "Mediators, like psychiatrists, must loan some of their problem-solving capacities to their clients on the spot." Deborah M. Kolb and Jonathan E. Kolb, "All the Mediators in the Garden," *Negotiation Journal* 9, no. 4 (October 1993): 337. But mediators, like psychiatrists, can only open up directions of movement for the parties of a conflict, not cause the parties to move in those directions. The intervener's skills enable the parties themselves to move toward resolution.

38. Neu and Volkan, *Developing a Methodology for Conflict Prevention*, 28–31.

39. Endel Talvik, telephone interview with author, January 16, 2006.

40. Neu and Volkan, *Developing a Methodology for Conflict Prevention*, 28.

41. Ibid., 29.

42. Alexei Semjonov, telephone interview with author, March 30, 2006; Jaan Kaplinski, telephone interview with author, April 2, 2006; and Klara Hallik, telephone interview with author, March 31, 2006.

43. Endel Talvik, telephone interview with author, January 16, 2006.

44. Endel Talvik, telephone interview with author, April 3, 2006.

45. Endel Talvik, telephone interview with author, January 16, 2006.

46. Neu and Volkan, *Developing a Methodology for Conflict Prevention*, 30.

47. Endel Talvik, telephone interview with author, January 16, 2006.

48. Secretariat of the Conference on Security and Co-operation in Europe, *Report of the CSCE ODIHR Mission on the Study of Estonian Legislation*.

49. Author interview with Timo Lahelma, Tallinn, July 15, 1994.

50. Author interview with John Erath, Tallinn, July 15, 1994.

51. Ibid.

52. Ann Sheehy, "The Estonian Law on Aliens," *RFE/RL Research Report* 2, no. 38 (September 1993).

53. Sergey Khrychikov and Hugh Miall, "Conflict Prevention in Estonia: The Role of the Electoral System," *Security Dialogue* 33, no. 2 (2002): 193–208.

54. Ibid.

55. Ibid.

Chapter 4

Can Dialogues Change the Course of a Small Nation? The Social Cohesion Program in Guyana

Michael Lund

Introduction

From May 2003 until December 2006, the United Nations Development Programme (UNDP) in Guyana, in collaboration with other international donors and the government of Guyana, implemented the Social Cohesion Program (SCP), a multifaceted effort to address ethnic and political tensions that were impeding Guyana's development and threatening interethnic peace. The program's strategy engaged numerous actors from many levels and sectors in Guyanese politics and society, including national and regional government and local communities; the Guyanese Parliament; political parties; police services; businesses and trade unions; youth, women's, religious, and cultural organizations; and the media. The SCP scrupulously endeavored to achieve local ownership of a conflict prevention process, employing facilitation techniques to impart skills and motivation to program participants in order to help them identify needed actions largely on their own and then undertake those activities.

Guyana lies between Venezuela and Suriname on the northeast coast of South America, and it is the only country on the continent in which English is the official language. Although geographically it is almost as large as the United Kingdom, nearly all of Guyana's multiethnic population of around 780,000 lives close to its coast and in the capital, Georgetown. Slightly more than 50 percent are Indo-Guyanese and about 38 percent are Afro-Guyanese, with the rest being of European, Chinese, Amerindian, and mixed descent. In view of Guyana's small, concentrated population and the SCP's extensive and multifaceted activities, the SCP offers an excellent opportunity to test the assumption that nonofficial conflict transformation workshops can have a significant impact in reducing a nation's intergroup tensions and building peace.

This five-part chapter will assess the ways and the extent to which the three years of SCP activities reduced the sources of Guyana's ethnicized political conflicts and strengthened its capacity for peaceful development. The first part recounts the country's situation up to the early 2000s and the milieu that prompted the adoption of the SCP. The next part presents the reasoning and process through which the SCP's designers formulated its key features, and briefly characterizes its major components. The analysis then turns to the evident impacts of the SCP's activities on its participants and on the wider political and societal environment, but also discusses missed opportunities. The final two sections identify the most important design, implementation, and contextual factors that help to explain *why* the program achieved what it did, and provide a concluding assessment of the SCP.[1]

Nature of the Conflict

To understand the origins and shape of the SCP, one must be aware of the main events and issues that gave rise to Guyana's political conflict. Although Guyana has never broken out into armed conflict such as a civil war, interethnic violence and frequent strikes and other labor unrest have punctuated its political history, starting before its independence from the United Kingdom in 1966 and continuing ever since, often around elections. After decades of mainly socialist policies and authoritarian rule under the People's National Congress (PNC) party, the end of the Cold War and domestic and international pressures led to deeper market reforms and the inauguration of free and fair elections in 1992. The former opposition, the People's Progressive Party (PPP), won the 1992 elections, but its victory did not end the ethnic confrontation that typified Guyanese politics.[2] Nor did the economic reforms of the late 1980s and early 1990s produce the expected levels of economic growth, as the late 1990s and early 2000s saw continued low growth rates, averaging only 0.60 percent annually from 1998 through 2003.[3] From 2000 to 2005, Guyana's real gross domestic product declined at an average annual rate of 2.2 percent. Over this period, international market prices for Guyana's main exports of sugar, gold, bauxite, and rice were dropping and international investment was declining. Emigration of skilled people was draining Guyana of valuable human resources and reducing productivity. Although poverty was slowly declining and improvements were made in education, job training, infrastructure, and social services, Guyana remained one of the poorest countries in the Western Hemisphere.

Economists have attributed Guyana's slow growth not only to years of fiscal mismanagement and inward-looking economic policies but also to weaknesses in public institutions that arose from its internal political and social divisions, which limited the country's ability to cope with external shocks and crises.[4] Guyana's failure to overcome its economic problems stemmed in large part from the lack of sufficient cooperation between the PPP and PNC, which drew the bulk of their electoral support, respectively, from the Indo-Guyanese and Afro-Guyanese portions of the population. Political harmony was frustrated by interparty disputes over constitutional issues and by PNC allegations that the governing PPP favored its supporters in allocating resources.

Following protests and violence over the disputed 1997 election results, a series of formal negotiations between the parties was mediated by international organizations, including the Caribbean Community (CARICOM), the Commonwealth of Nations, and the nongovernmental Carter Center. These negotiations were intended to overcome Guyana's stagnation by arranging discussions among leaders at the highest levels of government and in the political parties in the hopes of arriving at specific agreements. In 1998, CARICOM brokered the Herdmanston Accords and St. Lucia Statement, which agreed on a review of the 1997 election results, a three-year term for the government taking office, and interparty dialogues.

To follow up on these agreements, in 1999 CARICOM made efforts to mediate policy differences between the parties on a number of constitutional and other issues, including land distribution and police practices. The PPP government tended to view the issues that had been addressed and for which implementation mechanisms were in place as best handled through the existing formal governmental machinery. For its part, the PNC opposition expressed frustration with the dominance of the ruling party in those decision-making processes, and it expressed the view that policies were actually formulated outside those channels. It sought to push for power-sharing arrangements that could be used to consider both policy implementation and less-considered issues. These talks soon fell apart and the differences remained unresolved.[5]

Responding to the heightened sense of national crisis that arose in 2001, international donors and the Guyanese government launched the SCP and its related activities in 2002 and 2003. Even though the Guyanese Parliament had made changes to the electoral system in 2000 to address demands for direct representation and reduce the status of regional councils, the feeling that something special was needed to address Guyana's condition began to emerge after the March 2001 elections, which the PPP won again. Although the elections were certified as fair by international observers, they were followed by violent protests. Concerns were rising that, after thirty-five years of independence, Guyana's continuing ethnic and political polarization was not only thwarting the country's ability to make significant strides economically but also posing a threat to its survival as an integral society. It was recognized that the next elections, which were due within five years, could be as troublesome as the recent ones. In an attempt to quell the unrest and violence following the 2001 elections, the Commonwealth Secretariat facilitated a dialogue between Guyanese president Bharrat Jagdeo (of the PPP) and former president Desmond Hoyte (of the PNC). But progress toward implementation of agreements was slow, and in 2002 the dialogue between Jagdeo and Hoyte reached a stalemate. In March 2002, the PNC boycotted Parliament.

Concurrently, a jailbreak and a wave of violent crime, including highly publicized kidnappings, increased drug trafficking, and harsh responses and charges of extrajudicial killings by security forces, added to the growing sense of insecurity and unraveling. Progress was impeded by a legacy of charges and countercharges regarding abuses of power and alleged crimes, the basic facts of which often differed in media reports. Alarm was spreading that public policy issues were increasingly being addressed in the street, rather than through the established representative channels and government institutions designed to manage contentious public disputes and make policy decisions through democratic processes. This troubled climate was epitomized by an incident in July 2002 when the presidential offices were stormed and two persons were killed.

A brief period of goodwill followed Desmond Hoyte's death in December 2002, as newly elected PNC opposition leader Robert Corbin committed his party to talks with the incumbent PPP government. This commitment resulted in a round of dialogue between President Jagdeo and Corbin, the PNC's decision to rejoin Parliament, and the signing of a Joint Communiqué in May 2003. The communiqué pledged the leaders to "constructive engagement" between the two major parties and spelled out agreements to implement parliamentary and constitutional reforms. Although one of the agreements—to set up an Ethnic Relations Commission—was implemented a few months later, the communiqué had been agreed to in the presence of only two other people, and when implementation issues arose the two leaders gave conflicting versions of what was to be carried out. By the end of 2003, most of the steps pledged toward the other agreements—including the creation of a National Development Strategy—still had not been taken, which compounded the sense of stalemate. Although the Herdmanston Accords had produced agreement on a constitutional commission to review the 1980 Constitution, the limited amendments made in 2003 were met again by parliamentary boycotts.

A deepening mood of estrangement, cynicism, and intransigence, borne of a sense of mutually broken commitments, pervaded the political class. Although the government took some steps, such as setting up a Disciplined Forces Commission to address charges of extrajudicial killings by police and including opposition members on various state boards, many observers believed that the major parties and leaders were failing to make progress on salient policy, institutional, and procedural issues. By 2004, consultations to address ongoing constitutional disputes were faltering. The general lack of progress gave credence to a perception that the official level of politics on its own was unable to move Guyana out of its crisis and that some sort of new initiative might help to break the pattern of political stalemate.

The growing perception that more players were needed led at first to initiatives on the part of certain groups in civil society. In 2002, invoking Article 13 of the Constitution (which emphasizes citizen participation in policymaking), prominent private sector individuals, the Bar Association, trade unions, and churches organized a Social Partners Initiative. The initiative voiced the view that unless steps were taken, the country would descend inevitably into violent conflict. It sought to play a role in breaking the impasse on public issues by involving civil society to ensure some checks on partisan politics so as to make meaningful progress. It believed that the country's inability to get back to a functioning formal policy process stemmed from the lack of a public environment in which policy issues could be discussed in order to identify and weigh various options on their merits. To set the priorities of reconciliation and reducing local violence, the initiative engaged in discussions with the government and opposition on issues such as the security situation and police procedures.[6] Ultimately, however, criticism arose about the initiative's neutrality and questions were raised about its legitimacy (as it was neither an elected body nor representative of all civil society groups), and it soon crumbled.

Despite the growing concerns, there was still wide hope that Guyana as "one land of six peoples" could draw on a reservoir of unifying patriotism, common sense and basic goodwill, and its largely untapped natural resources. Efforts to address the crisis were hopeful that even though Guyana risked being sucked into a vortex of violent conflict, it could avoid that turn by drawing upon its existing capacities for peace such as a common language, high levels of education, economic interdependence, and a general yearning for economic development.

The Social Cohesion Program

Genesis of the Program

The impetus for the SCP grew out of an assessment by an unusual multiagency United Nations (UN) mission to Guyana in December 2002, under the auspices of UNDP headquarters in New York and the UN multiagency Framework for Coordination and its Executive Committee for Peace and Security.[7] The purpose of the mission was to consult with the government, civil society organizations, and other donors on possible initiatives to deal more deliberately with Guyana's political crisis. After a week of interviews, the UN mission concluded that Guyana's tensions could escalate into violent conflict if they were not addressed and that the process of dealing with the reforms could benefit from outside attention and support. The mission defined four principal problems:

- Impasses in the official political and policy approval process arising from political deadlock between the two main political parties, owing to their disengagement from agreed-on dialogues.

- The rapid rise in drug-related crime and the intersection of political discontent and criminal activity in severely economically depressed communities, leading to excessive use of force and illegal police practices in pursuing suspected criminals.
- Weakened government capacity to provide basic services, suggesting possible state failure.
- Increasingly divisive and acrimonious public discourse, suggesting racial stereotyping and diverging versions and interpretations of events by the media.

The UN mission proposed a panoply of multisectoral activities that ranged from institutional strengthening of government agencies to media training, all under an integrated strategy.[8] The UN delegation judged that no obvious Guyanese organization was in a strong enough position to run such an initiative, and that the existing governance programs of other international organizations did not have the needed conflict prevention, resolution, or transformation thrust. The usual sectoral programs and externally driven agendas were not making progress in dealing with Guyana's fundamental problems of political process. Yet the mission judged that with a little help, internal change for the good was possible in Guyana. It was felt that the most value-added contribution that the UNDP might make was not to try to answer questions about the causes or remedies of the issues, but rather to provide the space and skills for Guyanese nationals themselves to identify and grapple with those issues.

After the UN mission completed its visit and analysis, the SCP was designed and developed from December 2002 to May 2003. This program was one of the first examples of an integrated UN approach developed under the interagency Framework for Coordination.[9] The program was to be implemented by a Program Management Unit set up under the UNDP country office and headed by the UN resident representative. The management unit consulted with a number of people in Guyana's government and civil society to discuss specific program options and write a proposal. After lengthy consultations, and with the UN Core Group's assistance, management unit staff crafted a strategy that was brought to the government and donors for reactions and support. The staff interpreted the mission's report and subsequent discussions to mean that Guyana needed help to (1) implement the constitutional reforms that were ratified in Parliament; (2) address the abridgements of judicial due process in 2002–3, which had arisen in response to the recent crime wave but also had caused tensions and insecurity; and (3) increase the capacity of civil society to do strategic planning and facilitate community fora to defuse tensions.[10] The plan identified thirteen initial action areas and called for the program to hire a peace and development adviser. The program's adviser arrived in September 2003 and served until November 2006.[11]

The SCP's Theory of Change

The SCP's approach to its activities was shaped by an unusually specific diagnosis of the basic sources of Guyana's political and governance problems and the ways in which Guyana could use certain methods to ameliorate these problems. The SCP believed that the basic problem that Guyana faced was a pervasive animosity and lack of trust between its several ethnic groups.[12] The most urgent concern was the depth of distrust, disrespectful communications, and lack of constructive interaction that were believed to primarily characterize the political leadership. Although there was some sense that these problems correlated with distrust at other levels of society, such as between the members of ethnic groups and between security forces and citizens, the brunt of the problem was "animosity in the realm of national political organization, particularly at the time of elections" for "[i]ronically, racial and social relations tend to be far more civil at the grassroots level and in day-to-day life."[13] A "zero-sum" mentality had made Guyanese politics a constant competitive pursuit of the spoils of power. At any rate, a major weak spot that revealed the country's capacity gap was "at the micro-level of human interactions."[14]

Based on the above assumption, the SCP concluded that Guyana's political leaders "needed to find new ways to talk," and planned to facilitate more effective dialogue among them. It was judged that the most productive way that Guyana could get past the political differences holding up its development was by applying a conflict transformation paradigm that stressed increasing mutual understanding and removing impediments to communication. The first step toward wider social and political harmony and problem-solving in Guyanese society, politics, and policymaking was to increase trust by building capacities for communication and mutual problem-solving. In short, "shifting relationships"—in a sociopsychological sense of addressing dysfunctional interpersonal relationships—was an essential element in achieving social cohesion.[15]

At the same time, the program designers recognized that Guyana was already a "dialogue-fatigued" country, as one UNDP staff member put it. To take into account the several failed previous attempts by third parties to mediate agreements through high-level diplomacy among Guyana's political leaders, the design took a deliberately different approach from that of those dialogues. The view was that even though the official mediation efforts undertaken by CARICOM and other official mediators had produced agreements like the Herdmanston Accords, these efforts had failed to result in the implementation of the agreements because the mediation approach ("talk to each other because you have to") pressured the parties to reach agreements before sufficient trust existed between them. In a classic formulation of conflict transformation theory, the SCP approach would start more modestly—but, in its view, more realistically—by deliberately avoiding any such pressure for closure. Instead, it sought to create venues in which the parties could explore their bases for potential cooperation in a relaxed and informal atmosphere. It was expected that giving the parties a sense of ownership of the process itself would lead to more effective and lasting progress, because any agreements would be based on the parties discovering that they actually wanted to work together ("talk to each other because you want to").[16]

From the SCP perspective, an interactive process that would help people in Guyana to recognize their own unproductive patterns of interaction was the necessary prerequisite for efforts to resolve the substantive policy and other issues that caused such public and vocal confrontation between Guyanese politicians and citizens.[17] Moreover, this kind of intervention needed to be introduced at not only the political level but also several other systemic and societal levels.[18] Accordingly, the SCP did not set the actual achievement of political agreements as an explicit and necessary goal. It was hoped that the SCP could encourage this outcome indirectly, but it would wait for the Guyanese to attain it, once the program improved their capacities for doing so.[19] The SCP-initiated dialogue was regarded as only a beginning. The program designers did not assume that enhanced dialogue and improved interactions alone would address and resolve the substantive policy and social issues that divided the politicians, which both worsened and were worsened by the destructive patterns of interaction. Nor would the program reduce the underlying structural sources of Guyana's problems.[20] The SCP would plant seeds, but whether they sprouted and plants grew and proliferated would depend on the individual participants and partnering organizations.[21]

Consequently, the objectives the SCP set for its initial phase up to September 2005 were stated in open-ended, indeterminate forms:

1. *Progress toward* social cohesion and effective mediation;
2. *Enhanced* security, safety, and access to justice for citizens; and
3. *Progress toward* implementation of agreed constitutional reforms.

With these objectives, the SCP provides a fitting test of the effectiveness of a conflict prevention and peacebuilding approach that relies mainly on improving communications and interactions, with an emphasis on mutual respect and listening, rather than on power-driven negotiations or muscular third-party mediation using "carrots" and "sticks"; fostering understanding rather than immediate agreements; and broader inclusion rather than mainly elite-level, two-sided participation.

Program Components and Activities

The multisectoral, multileveled SCP was not a single project, but an umbrella initiative composed of fourteen projects, which eventually engaged an impressive number of actors:

- Political leaders and parties
- Youths and local communities
- Business community
- Trade unions
- Law enforcement officials (e.g., police, judiciary, magistrates)
- Election processes and procedures (e.g., Guyana Elections Commission)
- Ethnic Relations Commission
- Multistakeholder Fora and the National Conversation
- Local authorities
- Peacebuilding process facilitators
- Media
- The Ministry of Foreign Affairs
- Parliament
- The prime minister's and president's offices.

All fourteen projects were intended to serve the three main objectives under the overall rubric of social cohesion.

To achieve local ownership of the process from the start, the SCP sought to gain buy-in for the first step of setting the agenda. It assiduously applied principles and methods for engaging with a range of Guyanese actors that reflected an open participatory approach and complete transparency in setting priorities and defining activities. Although the SCP tentatively identified a number of program components intended to engage institutions, groups, and sectors such as civil society groups, the media, constitutional bodies, government officials, political parties, and local government bodies, the program's values called for an initial and continuing process of probing for windows of opportunity for activities in which their Guyanese potential partners expressed interest. Because of the need to determine the Guyanese political and social groups that would be the most receptive to the idea of achieving greater social cohesion, the SCP did not presume to prejudge where social cohesion was most lacking and in need of attention. The content of the strategy was deliberately not fixed during the first years, and the project funding was allocated only notionally, moving to commitments only after a certain amount of progress had been achieved.

The activities in each SCP component were inaugurated through the Program Management Unit, which organized initial events or provided other technical, personnel, or financial assistance. In most cases, these events involved workshops that imparted certain values of cooperation and provided training in process-related skill sets such as conflict transformation, strategic planning, organizational development, process design, and policy development. The workshops used small-group interactive techniques and exercises to sensitize and empower the participants. A few other meeting formats, as well as study tours and trips abroad to places such as Eastern Mennonite University in Harrisonburg, Virginia, were organized to provide technical education on substantive topics such as conflict early warning frameworks, ethnic relations, and human rights.[22] The following general list of SCP activities indicates the main levels of society at which they operated.[23]

NATIONAL OFFICIAL LEVEL

- Several SCP events brought "key political role-players"[24] in Guyana together to introduce them to conflict concepts, dialogue and communication skills, and envisioning exercises that encouraged the participants to define what kind of society they would like Guyana to become. Also, in July 2003 the general secretaries of the two major parties (PPP and PNC) attended a UN training workshop in Curaçao to introduce them to conflict early warning and encourage them to discuss how they might set up collaborative procedures to recognize, monitor, and address social tensions.

- In October–November 2003 and April 2005, three-day workshops were held in a retreat outside Georgetown for leaders of the youth arms of the two major parties.[25]
- In late 2004, the UNDP arranged with the Ethnic Relations Commission to facilitate a conflict transformation workshop with political party members and civil society organizations. The following April, the commission convened a two-day workshop with sixty-eight participants from more than thirty religious and cultural organizations, nongovernmental organizations (NGOs), parliamentary political parties, and the government. The workshop was led by Roelf Meyer, a former South African government official who had played a central role in negotiating the end of apartheid.
- The SCP provided several kinds of assistance to Parliament for the implementation of political agreements and constitutional reforms.[26]
- In response to a mid-program review in September 2005, the SCP took on a more short-term focus on potential problems during the general and regional elections scheduled for 2006. In the run-up to the election date (which was held in late August), donors, the government, and political parties focused efforts on achieving credible elections, mainly addressing problems in the Guyana Elections Commission.

MIDLEVEL GOVERNMENTAL AND CIVIL SOCIETY ORGANIZATIONS

- The Private Sector Commission (PSC) was a nongovernmental, cross-ethnic umbrella organization whose membership included twelve business associations (including the Georgetown Chamber of Commerce) and nineteen corporations (such as Guyana Telephone and Telegraph). Although the PSC was officially nonpolitical in a partisan sense, some individuals or member organizations were perceived as being too close to the government or susceptible to pressures from politicians.[27] The SCP engaged the PSC in strategic planning and organizational development to clarify its identity and improve its functioning, thereby helping to resolve its internal disputes.

- In October 2004, the SCP held meetings with the Guyana Trade Union Congress to explore what the SCP, in cooperation with the International Labour Organization, might do to help the congress reunify Guyana's trade union movement (which had splintered along sectoral and ethnic lines), restructure its organization, and improve its partnerships and networks with the government and private sector.

- Alarmed that several police officers had been killed, and faced with complaints that the police were using excessive force during arrests, the SCP responded to a request from the police commissioner, who sought to remedy the police force's serious public image problem. Extensive training and guidelines were provided to supplement the law and strengthen police procedures.[28]

- In response to the weak judicial system, the Guyana Law Association arranged for a team from the United Kingdom to provide training for magistrates to increase their awareness of human rights standards.[29]

- A joint partnership between the Ethnic Relations Commission and the SCP sought to improve the ability of commissioners and staff to carry out the commission's mandate,[30] improve its program management, mediate implementation of the constitutional reform agreement on ethnic relations, and enhance social cohesion in all sectors of society.[31] Based on an Ethnic Relations Commission needs assessment from July 2004, the program conducted strategic planning, ethnic relations, and conflict transformation workshops with commissioners and staff. The commission's most ambitious undertaking was the Multistakeholder Forum, a countrywide series of local and regional consultative meetings to involve citizens in articulating priority needs, which culminated in a two-day National Conversation in Georgetown.

- The SCP worked with the media and NGOs to increase Guyanese civil society's capacity to contribute to national social cohesion. As Guyana's media was essential in any conflict prevention strategy but was especially prone to partisan reporting, the SCP engaged the media immediately after the program was launched. The SCP also helped create a conglomerate of NGOs by supporting several public fora under the themes "Forum on Solidarity and Effectiveness" and "Improving Race Relations."

- In February 2004, the SCP collaborated with the University of Guyana on an international conference on "Governance, Conflict Analysis, and Conflict Resolution."

- In August 2006, the SCP provided technical expertise and logistical support for convening a Guyana Peace Builders Network, attracting ninety-five people from various peacebuilding programs. The program also supported a motorcycle rally for peace and harmony and the signing of a peace pledge to refrain from violence.
- SCP engagement with civil society included capacity building, technical assistance, and financial support to religious groups, cultural groups, and an eclectic group of individuals from which the Spirit of Guyana, a conflict resolution and peacebuilding network, emerged.[32] In May 2005, the program also helped organize the Inter-Religious Organisation, a group of religious leaders that emerged to address barriers to peace among differing faiths.[33]

LOCAL GOVERNMENTS AND COMMUNITIES

- Conflict transformation workshops for regional democratic council officials and staff in three administrative regions were the impetus for youth-based community projects and for a more interactive relationship between regional authorities and local communities.[34]
- Youth-Focused Community-Based Initiatives were set up in three regions to encourage unattached youth to participate in community development. Four four-day training workshops with youths and local government officials introduced conflict transformation and community engagement concepts such as civic education, leadership development, human rights, conflict transformation, proposal writing, and project development. The youth participants were required to exercise democratic decision-making by engaging their communities and local authorities in planning a common project, supported by small grants.

Most of the abovementioned activities were concluded during the three-year life of the SCP ending in December 2006, except for the youth initiatives, whose continuation was approved by the government. In total, these activities involved approximately 164 distinct meetings or other events that involved about 1,650 participants, in addition to numerous face-to-face meetings and conversations for preliminary planning. In addition, at least 23,000 people were reached by media products such as 122 screenings of films and many sponsored media messages. By a rough estimate, about 35,000 people—or almost 7 percent of the adult population of Guyana at that time, with some double counting—experienced some facet of the SCP activities. Overall, the SCP succeeded in stimulating a number of activities that brought Guyanans together to identify and address common problems on a scale probably unprecedented in Guyanese history.

Impacts

The Program Management Unit was able to keep track of the multiple meetings and other activities that occurred directly or indirectly through SCP initiation and support. However, the documentation of which groups had taken what actions was largely descriptive and did not provide a basis for judging the significance of those activities in reducing the social incohesion problem in Guyana. No way was devised to measure whether those "outputs" were resulting in changes that were desired in Guyanese politics and society. Such an assessment needs to probe for credible evidence of meaningful effects of those activities on the participants and their wider environment. This assessment is complicated by the number and diversity of the SCP's activities, which undoubtedly had many unknown effects on the numerous Guyanese people, organizations, and institutions involved. Still, some SCP goals (such as enhanced security, safety, and access to justice) lend themselves to specific indicators, and progress toward the less tangible objectives of social cohesion and effective mediation, implementation of agreed constitutional reforms, and increased capacity for social cohesion and peace can have specific benchmarks. For this purpose, the following section presents evidence collected from interviews and other sources with regard to five kinds of impacts that the SCP may have had in making progress toward greater overall social and political cohesion in Guyanese organizations, society, politics, and government:

- Attitudes, perceptions, and skills of individual participants in SCP workshops/activities ("in hearts and minds")
- Relationships or procedures that a SCP workshop/activity stimulated among the participants ("in the office")
- Actions jointly undertaken by the participants to address problems affecting other actors ("on the street")
- Effects on the general public and civil society ("in the public square")
- Agreements on contested public policies and their implementation ("in government")

Changes "In Hearts and Minds"

Virtually all those interviewed about the SCP felt that they had gained new outlooks and skills from the program's workshops and related activities. To illustrate, the participants in the high-level conflict transformation workshop generally valued the experience. The first session broke down some stereotypes and established contacts among wider circles of both civil society and government leaders than had normally been in touch with each other. It engendered expressions of hope. One year later, top party leaders were still talking about how the workshop had influenced them, with one party leader saying that it "changed the way I think." The early warning trip for top party officials was unprecedented in exposing them to conflict analysis and making them aware of the UN commitment to conflict prevention worldwide. For these officials, the trip conveyed the idea that they were responsible for avoiding violence and that there were conflict prevention systems available for them to use, and they became more aware that others such as the UN were expecting them to be more vigilant and proactive. The events for young party leaders raised their consciousness about their mutual responsibility as fellow future leaders. These events apparently broadened the youth leaders' horizons and increased their leadership skills and credentials. Evaluations from the first event expressed deep appreciation for the experience and acknowledged the need for the training by virtue of the team-building, conflict resolution content, and collaborative skills imparted. The subsequent party youth activities opened up new contacts, relationships, and communications that increased comfort and dispelled false images of the others and their positions, showing that the other participants were serious and respectable. The events also brought to light that the future party leaders shared a common overall *national policy* outlook that was distinct from other sector-oriented, "donor-driven" youth organizations.

Other public and private sector participants gave similarly favorable responses. In the Private Sector Commission, the executive director and a board member were pleased with the process they had experienced. Something "clicked in their minds." At least one especially active member reported being deeply influenced personally by the social-psychological exercises and listening skills training, making him realize that the group could reach valuable "win-win" solutions through compromises that achieve a greater good. The trade unions facilitations reportedly encouraged positive thinking about how the unions could work together for mutual gain, helping to extricate them from the negative tendency to simply blame others. The police officers interviewed said that they recognized more clearly how the daily incidents they dealt with, such as intergroup mistrust, mistrust of the police, and inequalities, often reflected wider dynamics both in society and within the police force. Participants in the judiciary and magistrates training said that they gained sharper and more sensitive listening skills and greater patience and empathy. By reflecting together, they also became more self-conscious of their roles as public officials and of their personal responsibility.

Likewise, the ethnic relations commissioners were convinced that the capacity-building workshops and strategic planning sessions served as team building and engendered a better understanding about the issues confronting the commission, the commissioners' capabilities, and unmet needs. The peacebuilding process facilitators and the Spirit of Guyana gained more skills to facilitate community dialogues and to work with women, youth, and organizational conflicts. These individuals felt more confident about their ability to serve as resource persons in any activity intended to be inclusive and proactive about peace and development. The Youth-Focused Community-Based Initiatives participants displayed new levels of consciousness about balancing the competing needs and interests of diverse communities, whether such diversity was based on ethnicity, political persuasion, age, or gender.

In sum, all the interviewed participants from various workshops reported distinct improvements in their attitudes and motivation.

Change "In the Office"

Because the SCP scrupulously cultivated the participating groups as partners in order to engender local ownership, the impetus and amount of any follow-up activities—beyond participating in a workshop or other activity at the outset and extending into some further activity—depended on the involved organizations and their members. Consequently, after the initial SCP event or other support, much of the actual implementation of the program's activities was carried out not by the Program Management Unit but by other actors. These subsequent activities deserve to be counted as SCP achievements, for it explicitly sought to have multiplier effects.

At the outset, the participating groups generally expressed keen interest in building on the experience gained from their initial encounters. All these workshops progressed from the skills and outlooks developed in their respective initial sessions to various degrees of resolve to take action through their own further dealings with one another and joint actions outside the group.

For example, at the PSC, the initiative improved intraorganizational harmony. Reflecting the flagging growth of Guyana's economy, the PSC had experienced a decline in membership. It had widened its membership in 1997 to include corporate members, but the corporations' larger sizes and higher membership fees led to concerns that the corporations were beginning to dominate the organization. The problem was generating tensions over internal governance, such as who within the association had the prerogative for speaking publicly on behalf of the private sector. The respondents deemed the facilitation sessions "successful," as the sessions helped them formulate new rules regarding the respective domains of the locally based chambers of commerce and the national body, and about procedures for speaking officially on behalf of the membership as a whole.

Similarly, the strategic planning sessions with the Ethnic Relations Commission helped devise ways to enhance its ability to deal with complaints, provide scaled-up training and national public education, establish a research and documentation center, and acquire office equipment to improve its daily functioning. The Peace Builders Network also helped to consolidate the peacebuilding expertise in Guyana so it could provide potential support for any peacebuilding subgroup engaged in a community, regional, or national activity.

The judiciary and magistrates training helped to improve their institutionalized procedures and rules. Participants reported that following the training, they approached conflicts without using coercive legal methods, not only within their own homes and communities but also in their official capacities on the job. The judiciary workshops may have contributed to reduced court loads because minor cases such as marital disputes and other disturbances and grievances could be mediated instead of automatically prosecuted, so they did not have to go to court. The followup group forwarded recommendations to extend the training to more participants and to change police policies so as to institutionalize the methods being learned. These ideas included preparing a mediation manual for police stations and writing its use into standard operating procedures, having a designated place for mediation in local police stations, allowing mediation accomplishments to figure in performance ratings, and establishing local mediation boards. Also, the national commissioner and local police commanders held an "open day" to invite ideas and raise issues for improved policing. Some of these ideas, such as requiring human rights training for all police recruits, have been adopted, although it is unclear whether conflict mediation training of recruits has been consistent.

Regional democratic councilors shared the knowledge gained at their training workshops with their colleagues and attempted to facilitate better decision-making processes in their daily encounters, with varying degrees of success. An elected office, some councilors reported that they had begun to engage in more productive working relationships with each other for the good of their communities, and not as opponents caught up in unproductive competition for community resources. Reports from the Region 4 Council highlighted that its statutory meetings committed time to discussions about social cohesion and working for community development and social justice regardless of ethnicity. The Region 10 councilors, formerly embroiled in social tensions, were able to sit with each other and talk about shared challenges in a respectful manner and to allow for consensus building in decision-making rather than resort to the usual majoritarianism. Region 10 stakeholders in the community who were interviewed felt encouraged that a regional strategy was developed after the workshops. The relationship between the regional democratic council and a new development initiative was deemed "good and fruitful." All promises and commitments to support the strategy development were honored.

However, as noted, some workshops convened the participants from a single organization such as the PSC (with its related member organizations), while other workshops brought together members of more than one separate organization, such as for the political parties and trade unions. As might be expected, more concrete follow-up appears to have occurred among the members of a single organization than between members of several separate organizations. In cases where members of more than one organization were initially convened, more contact, communication, and interaction was made possible than would otherwise have occurred. However, in some of these discussions disagreements arose as to how to proceed further and the proposed actions did not always materialize. For example, the participants in the key leaders' high-level meeting agreed on broad goals and directions needed for Guyana to move forward, and that it was up to them and Guyana to make things happen. They also "accidentally" began to agree on the nature of Guyana's core problems and on the need for more efforts to build national cohesion. This led to a consensus that something should be done to take the consultative process to the ground level through conducting a national conversation. However, one observer who praised the workshop doubted that it had had enough impact for the participants to want its efforts to be continued. Further meetings were planned, but did not happen.

The workshops with political party leaders revived old connections and opened some new channels for discussion. Though the older party officials had always been more or less in touch with each other and were not always rancorous, even during crises, the added personal contact from the early warning trip encouraged more frequent cross-communication and more inclination to give the benefit of the doubt to the motives and actions of their counterparts. This reduced the reflex to retaliate harshly or unilaterally, which tempered provocations or escalating rhetoric. In their workshops, the party youth leaders pledged to commit themselves to applying the skills and attitudes learned, and urged that more sessions be held for them and their colleagues. Their enthusiasm led to considerable sustained contact through training workshops, camps, a world youth conference, and group dinners. Interestingly, when asked to define the needs of Guyana's youth, the two party youth groups arrived at some priorities in common (such as curbing drug abuse) but differed on assessments of other problems. The opposition party youth tended to emphasize unemployment, poor facilities, and lack of participation and access to educational and economic opportunities, whereas the government party youth tended to focus on violence and threats to the state and property and development, the distortions of the media, and prejudice and misperceptions. But although the participants were unable to agree on a common vision statement for Guyana, their subsequent workshops produced a greater commitment to working together on specific problems, came up with concrete ideas to address national problems, and agreed to a joint calendar of activities and a working group to decide on subsequent joint activities. They also committed to dialogue as their first response to emerging differences.

Trade union respondents reported that their SCP sessions created the unusual opportunity to sit back and look together at the bigger picture of their overall policies, and to air differing views in a nonthreatening way about the issues they faced, thus breaking down everyday barriers to communication. The Guyana Trade Union Congress acknowledged the need for internal reforms. The SCP engagement spurred further communications in the following months among the leaders of the three participating organizations about issues that existed between them. The trade union congress executive decided to talk further with individual unions, including some that had split off from the congress, about opportunities for reconciliation, modernization, and capacity-building. The idea of reunification was introduced, along with possibilities for the unions to play a neutral role in politics, give greater attention to labor standards and employee interests, and work more effectively with the government and employers' federation, such as in conjunction with the National Competitiveness Strategy. However, despite opportunities for further engagement, including offers of mediation, disagreements arose over the methods for doing so and no further discussions occurred. The workshop experience did not heal the rifts that were preventing greater labor movement unity, and major issues still stood between these organizations.

Change "On the Street"

Participants in the high-level leaders' workshop went back to their respective constituencies to report the news about the new impetus that had started. They also gave general support for the idea of holding a national conversation across the country at the community level to replicate the workshop in a similar process on the ground. This eventually became the Multistakeholder Forum under the Ethnic Relations Commission. But the initial workshop's breakout groups had reflected differences as to what the forum process meant and what to do with the ideas that would result from it. Disagreement arose about whether the commission should be the Guyanese vehicle to carry forward the forums and whether the process should focus its recommendations directly on the National Assembly. One view was that such a forum process could only be meaningful if the ideas it generated were fed into the National Assembly for its consideration. Another view saw the process as a distinct forum in which the participants should engage seriously to produce views in the national interest and carry ideas forward in several ways, only one of which might include motions to the legislature. A third group felt that the existing consultative process on national development was adequate, so a new forum was not needed. Rather, it thought that other ways could be found to use political processes to engage a wider circle of leaders and civil society.

The party general secretaries and youth leaders involved in the early warning and trips abroad agreed to debrief their respective colleagues and to consider organizing local activities to address conflicts. Reporting back to their parties, including the potentially more radical members, may have helped to temper or "mellow" the rank and file, thus enabling leaders to take more moderate positions on public issues. The youth contacts and trips to the United States resulted in some envisioning of joint youth party units' activities, such as development projects that could boost the agenda of a national plan for youth. But it is unclear whether any such external projects materialized after the trip.

The SCP training spurred the PSC internal planning to go beyond strengthening its governance; the PSC was emboldened to see itself as having more of a public role by influencing public policy and to take deliberate steps to fulfill that role. The facilitation sensitized PSC members to the unproductive communication traits typically exhibited by other actors in the public sphere. This greater awareness led the PSC to realize more deeply that it had a serious stake in political stability as it affected the prospects for economic growth. The PSC's increased cohesion helped it to become a more unified and disciplined bargaining group in representing business interests with regard to policy issues affecting the enabling environment for business, such as crime and debt write-off. Business persons existed in all the ethnic communities, so it was an area that potentially could move Guyana forward on issues shared by many Guyanese.

Beginning in mid-2004, the PSC met with the president; parties and parliamentarians; other businessmen; labor, cultural, and religious organizations; and NGOs to encourage discussion of "ways to move forward by accepting each other and talking with each other." As the 2006 election period approached, PSC members met with the Guyana Elections Commission and lent their support to a media code of conduct. For the first time, PSC members noted that opportunities were opening up to express their views on policy issues, even though the PSC was an outsider to the political process. In view of the weak and divided nature of Guyanese civil society, where there was little middle ground, the respondents felt that the PSC was "the singular NGO that stepped out in this direction." But although it earned the trust of many politicians as an honest broker, it "felt and still feels the wrath of politicians."

The greater internal cohesion of this prominent organization had powerful symbolic value. Although the changed PSC did not directly build bridges in the wider Guyanese society between the major contending ethnic and party-based cleavages, it presented to the public a salient embodiment of interethnic cooperation in pursuit of functional purposes. If the PSC was able to change the way it operated, the obvious signal was that government and the rest of Guyana could follow the PSC example. The PSC not only had a significant effect on relations between the business sector and government, but also provided an example of how civil society could move into collaborative spaces with government, rather than remain confrontational or competitive.

On their part, the trade unions asked the SCP for guidance in promoting dialogue and national unity as the election period approached. Relations with the government became somewhat better, as reflected in a post-election visit to the union organizations by the Minister of Labor. The Ethnic Relations Commission/SCP–sponsored conflict transformation training workshops led to other opportunities for diverse cultural and religious groups to discuss and reduce ethnic tensions. For example, it seized the opportunity to host a public forum after the UN Special Rapporteur on Racism and Discrimination had visited and issued a report on Guyana. By prioritizing the commission's work both internally and in terms of community outreach, the SCP also contributed to an enabling environment for a peace campaign. Activities with the media, trade unions, the University of Guyana, party youth leaders, women, and the police force also led to steps to engage groups that had not participated. In one instance, the Spirit of Guyana's Region 3 subgroup engaged in mediating disputes in a local school and market.

Change "In the Public Square"

Although the SCP initially approached each component as a discrete activity, it witnessed considerable spontaneous interaction and interdependence in how these activities unfolded. Unexpected symbiotic and mutually enforcing linkages emerged both among civil society groups and between them and governmental actors. One of the SCP's accomplishments was spawning complementary activities across several components, which achieved some of the hoped-for multiplier effect. The PSC's involvement, for instance, was triggered when an executive PSC committee member witnessed the SCP at work in another context and took the initiative to get in touch with the SCP organizers. After asking for guidance from the SCP, several trade unions contributed elections observers. A subgroup of the Spirit of Guyana network was invited by the Region 3 Council to conduct four one-day workshops on inclusive decision-making for chairpersons of Neighbourhood Democratic Councils and head teachers from nursery, primary, and secondary schools. Ninety-two people participated. The University of Guyana conference in February 2004 on conflict analysis and governance helped to give impetus to activities such as the media roundtable discussions and NGOs taking on board the issue of peace education. Community facilitators trained by the Ethnic Relations Commission were encouraged to participate in the UN Volunteer program to increase community participation and improve social relations across groups and regions.

By far the most significant impact of this wider nature resulted from the numerous SCP activities on reducing violence before and after the 2006 general and regional elections. In view of Guyana's past experience, the elections were anticipated months ahead as a possible flashpoint. The SCP took on the task of fostering an atmosphere of peaceful competition, with reduced election violence as a possible indicator. In fact, the SCP's activities demonstrably contributed to such a result through several efforts to delegitimize the use of violence for political goals.

Among these SCP-supported efforts during the election campaign, respondents believed that the program's law enforcement training prepared the police to act more effectively to avoid violence. When standing by during political meetings, for example, the police were better able to talk with abusive persons, hecklers, and other potential troublemakers, and learned how and when to draw the line on provocations so as to avoid escalating the situation. The Ethnic Relations Commission proactively engaged the media, parliamentarians, and general public in the run-up to the elections through media training, wide dissemination of the Racial Hostility Act, and activities on its mandate to monitor and sanction incitement to ethnic discrimination. In one instance, the commission quietly gave some private, friendly counsel to a candidate who was engaged in provocative behavior. Also, by supporting multimedia, broadly disseminated peace-promoting messages through CDs, news articles, and television coverage, the SCP helped obtain wide support from many key actors to the norm of peaceful political competition, discrediting the notion that violence was a legitimate response to political disputes.[35] The SCP collaborated with the Inter-Religious Organisation in supporting a peace pledge signed by the political parties that were competing in the elections. The SCP also supported the drafting of a media code of conduct and the procurement of 11,000 peace buttons, which resulted in obtaining almost 10,000 signatures in support of the peace pledge. A fifteen-minute documentary on the Bikers Uniting Guyana's Motorcycle Rally for Peace and Harmony was produced and broadcast on five television stations, and DVD copies of the documentary were widely distributed across Guyana. Spirit of Guyana also produced 500 CDs with popular "peace" songs and messages that were distributed widely to taxi drivers and other role-players in forming public opinion. The Guyana Peace Builders Network met and developed several peace initiatives for the upcoming elections, including peace vigils across Guyana and a forum on "Uniting Guyana During and After Elections." Members of the Guyanese public met with leaders of all the participating parties to discuss how these parties planned to work toward peace and unity before and after the polls.[36] All in all, as one respondent expressed it, the message of avoiding provocation and encouraging peaceful elections "bombarded the psyche" via these many channels.

The 2006 elections were notable as the first in Guyanese history to be conducted without violence. The activities supported by the SCP—directly through media messages and indirectly through its influence on the security and justice institutions—contributed greatly to the overall climate of restraint and helped to deter electoral violence. In addition to mobilizing many nongovernmental actors behind the cause of peaceful elections, the SCP-initiated workshops helped to cultivate a civil society through its catalytic work in lending support to the Ethnic Relations Commission as it carried out the Multistakeholder Forum and National Conversation.

After the high-level conflict transformation workshop, the SCP seized on the momentum of the political leaders' support for a national dialogue among Guyanese about ethnic and other differences and their collective future. The aim of a National Conversation was to enhance social cohesion by stimulating participatory democracy through broad-based dialogue. The results were intended to inform the priorities of the National Assembly. Although the Ethnic Relations Commission's decision to undertake the Multistakeholder Forum came relatively late in 2005, the responsibility to manage this process fell under its auspices, as the aims of the national dialogue were consistent with its mandate.

In holding the Multistakeholder Forum, the commission assumed that the opportunity for dialogue would help Guyanese to overcome their differences and that communities would devise collective solutions for improving their own lives and consequently contribute to national peace and development. The process, managed entirely by the commission, had three phases: (1) launch of the forum; (2) conferences in local neighborhoods, municipalities, and Amerindian communities; and (3) regional conferences and the National Conversation.[37] The SCP supported a national advertising campaign on the Multistakeholder Forum through brochures and flyers in local communities; face-to-face meetings with community leaders; and personal and written invitations to encourage participation by national groups. A national committee was established to provide oversight and guard against politically partisan interests. Communities were involved to ensure that appropriate persons would participate. The two-day national-level National Conversation in Georgetown was the culmination of group fora involving sixty-five

Neighbourhood Democratic Councils; six municipalities and a number of Amerindian village councils; and separate conversations with 750 women, youth, and religious leaders covering Guyana's ten administrative regions.

About 300 people participated in the National Conversation, including Ethnic Relations Commissioners; observers from the international community and government representatives; and representatives from the parliamentary parties, security services, regional and local governments, labor unions, women's and youth organizations, the private sector, and other NGOs. The small group and plenary discussions were facilitated by Guyanese trained by the SCP and the SCP-instigated Spirit of Guyana. During the concluding session attended by the program evaluators, discussions were constructive and participants appeared open to talking as a first response to problems arising in their communities. It became a process of exchange, analysis, and learning that familiarized participants with concepts of "talking to," "speaking for," and "talking with," and promoted tolerance by reinforcing the skills necessary for democratic community dialogues.[38]

In effect, the Multistakeholder Forum and National Conversation created Guyana's first major safe and accepted space outside of official channels for large numbers of Guyanese to discuss and agree on actions to overcome ethnic and other differences, and to articulate their own role in the development of their communities and country. In ways not done before, ordinary Guyanese were able to sit and talk with each other in a respectful and highly interactive manner about national challenges. The Multistakeholder Forum and National Conversation raised to high public visibility and importance the notion that Guyana's continuing ethnopolitical polarization required urgent and concerted action. As a result of these and other activities, Guyana's civil society groups seemed to find a greater sense of mutual dependence and cooperation. For example, the inclusion of the regional and neighborhood democratic councils in the National Conversation process was hailed as an advance in regional planning, one that could improve how development strategies might be implemented. The Region 10 consultations in particular had the unanticipated impact of connecting residents with the agencies and organizations that could respond to local problems almost immediately.

All in all, the SCP helped to catalyze the beginnings of a largely independent, broad-based citizens' process that operated outside Guyana's partisan, often stalemated official political channels. Although Guyana was still a diffuse and fragmented civil society, the SCP helped to create a latent constituency of awakened citizens that cut across party lines. A "new dynamic" seems to have been spurred in Guyanese politics, through which actors outside the political parties and government had more visibility and carried more weight in pressing for greater political accountability by the political class to address the weaknesses in service delivery and persisting problems such as land distribution.

Changes "In Government"

Less evident are the effects of the SCP's skill- and trust-building activities on the adoption of official agreements and government policies that could overcome the country's political polarization.[39]

An encouraging sign was the transformation in the lexicon of the body politic. Officials could be heard using terms like "cohesion," "working together," "living together," and "inclusion," none of which had been prominent in Guyana's political vocabulary. At various levels of religious, cultural, trade union, business, media, and political society, the initiation into the conflict transformation paradigm diluted the high-octane political rhetoric of the past.

More tangibly, some progress may have been made with regard to policies at the street level, especially concerning violence. The abovementioned increased efficiency and other changes in the court system, and possible crime reduction, may have helped achieve the SCP objective of "increasing access to justice for citizens." In part because SCP-related training helped the police to recognize that suspected criminals have rights, after the training there was marked decline in reported instances of police brutality and police shootings, and thus complaints against the police. The SCP created more community-level trust for the police, which encouraged more community help in identifying criminals, such as by alerting the police to the locations of criminal hideouts. A possible program effect was reduced crime and violence in some communities, although the evaluation could not obtain comparative data for areas where trained police worked and did not work.

In spite of these promising results, there was little evidence that any of the "hot button" national-level policy issues that animated the escalating political tensions, such as the electoral lists, had been resolved. Even though the party leaders had considered setting up a local early warning mechanism, this project was not implemented. A few steps were taken toward addressing disputes concerning the formal processes of government, but these efforts did not produce the visible results that could avoid further destructive controversies. Most important, the SCP was not able to make much headway in its goal of making progress toward resolving the outstanding constitutional issues. Regarding the SCP's objective of achieving "progress toward implementation of agreed Constitutional reforms," the SCP stimulated interest in making constructive progress on these reforms, yet this interest produced little follow-through. As the appointment of further commissions remained unfulfilled, that track became confined to the Ethnic Relations Commission as the only one of five envisioned bodies to become duly constituted.

This lack of progress at the policy level was reflected in the mixed views of participants in the National Conversation regarding the likely impact on public policy of the elaborate Multistakeholder Forum participatory process. On the one hand, Region 10, for example, was cited as having completed its consultations with members of local communities and finishing the first draft of a development strategy, which included key inputs, suggestions, ideas, and perspectives from the Multistakeholder Forum. Some local projects developed and funded by SCP also were implemented. Some forum participants also expressed optimism that the local government elections expected in the next year would provide an appropriate mechanism to remedy unresponsive or nonexistent community administrative structures. As the Constitution required that elections for municipal and neighborhood authorities be held every three years, and yet none had been held since 1994, many Guyanese understandably felt they were long overdue. On the other hand, other National Conversation participants expressed doubts about the likelihood of timely, suitable responses from incumbent political leaders to the voiced concerns of local communities. In fact, regarding the especially germane issue of reforming local government structures, in the following years interparty disputes continued to block the holding of any elections at the local level. Proposed local government reform legislation was brought before a National Assembly select committee, but the differences between the political parties over the authority of the Minister of Local Government and over control of fiscal transfers were apparently unbridgeable.

In sum, although the SCP began to weave a web of greater mutual interdependency and sense of common responsibility among the political class, it was not able to actually move the political debate to the point of addressing major national policy issues, overcoming blockages in the representative and policy institutions, and putting new policies in place. The SCP added lubricant and coolant to Guyana's overheating, potentially destructive political machinery, but it could not rebuild the engine needed to move Guyana's political system forward.

Missed Opportunities

Staff openness and flexibility, as well as staff members' iterative dealings with so many people in so many circles, reduced the risk that the SCP would miss major opportunities because information about ongoing political and institutional dynamics was being tacitly gathered. Indeed, the SCP was unusually prepared to seize opportunities because of its wide network of contacts. In the case of the Private Sector Commission, for example, the SCP jumped into action in response to the commission's request for help in strategic planning and organizational development, and in the words of one respondent "got 90 percent result from 10 percent of effort." Nevertheless, some opportunities were missed:

- There seems to have been a lack of basic information circulated widely about the SCP's activities and achievements. The plethora of program activities also seems not to have been inventoried in easily grasped forms. The Program Management Unit might have compiled and disseminated regularly an ongoing record of activities such as through a newsletter, so that both donors and program participants would know more about what the various initiatives were doing. A related criticism from a donor partner was that points raised in the interdonor discussions were not always recorded fully, circulated, and built upon in subsequent discussions. The absence of a broad awareness of the overall forward movement may have reduced the SCP's multiplier effect.

- Some capacity-building initiatives might have borne more fruit if the SCP had pushed a little harder on groups, such as the University of Guyana project groups, that showed interest and were willing to pursue further activities but for some reason were hesitant or distracted and needed more coaxing or prodding. A few party youth participants were disappointed that more progress was not made and that the SCP did not press for it. In instances such as the interparty activities, ownership and responsibility for taking next steps, as well as the steps themselves, also seemed to be unclear. Rather than remain disappointed with groups that demonstrated a relative lack of subsequent progress, the Program Management Unit might have pressed these groups further.

- Notwithstanding the importance of local ownership, the wide discretion that the SCP left to the Guyanese participants in determining which activities to pursue meant that some needs for increasing social and political cohesion were arguably less fruitful or direct routes than others. Because some partners exert greater leverage on critical dimensions of social cohesion (e.g., security, parliamentary debate) than others, the extent to which different partners implemented activities does not by itself determine a component's relative effectiveness in achieving the SCP's overall objectives. As worthwhile as any individual activity could be deemed in its own terms, in several instances the social cohesion agenda was diverted into appealing activities that nonetheless did not directly address the most serious manifestations of social incohesion. The SCP might have focused its energies more selectively on entry points that, although more resistant, might have had greater payoffs because of their inherently greater influence in Guyana's politics, economy, or society. Evidently, some empirically grounded theory of change and analysis needs to discipline such elasticity, or an initiative could pursue almost any direction that seems to hold promise.

This last shortcoming pertains to the activities with the party leaders, Parliament, and trade unions. Instead of picking up on the party leaders' interest in continuing the leaders' workshop, for example, the SCP focused on other activities that may have been less productive. The leaders' workshop initiative thus "got lost," according to one participant. The leaders' lack of momentum raises the question of whether the SCP should have been deepened in some directions instead of widened, such as by prioritizing a sustained dialogue within certain key groups rather than moving on to engage yet more groups.

Although any intergovernmental organization that works at the invitation of sovereign governments must heed the incumbent government's interests, some observers thought that the SCP was unduly hesitant to move down some avenues because of government preferences. The SCP did encounter some government reactions that reflected the highly sensitive political environment, such as when a former UN in-country official who had made a public statement about a particular human rights incident was asked to leave Guyana. On the justice issue, the Program Management Unit felt that the Guyanese government did not really allow the SCP to seriously tackle it. (Of course, observers who were not present in the conversations cannot second-guess how much pressure was too much or too little.)

Less understandably, there may have been insufficient attention to keeping the respective government authorities informed about the Multistakeholder Forum process as it moved up the levels from the local communities to the National Conversation. As a result, government officials tended to see the National Conversation's long list of final demands as too general and unfocused, and in some instances uninformed, where the recommendations were not cognizant of existing laws or steps that the government was already taking. One approach that could have prevented such government criticism would have been to tie the relevant sectoral officials and programs into each step of the Forum process more deliberately. A more targeted and useful document could have been produced by winnowing the issues through consultations with governing bodies at various levels.

Helpful but Insufficient

All things considered, did the SCP's efforts to foster a culture of dialogue change the course of this small nation? To what extent did the SCP activities reverse Guyana's political deterioration and restore its ability to develop? Clearly, this ambitious initiative set in motion an impressive range of activities under the new theme of social cohesion, achieving in multiple small ways its declared objective of enhancing Guyana's capacity for social cohesion and peace at the national, regional, and local levels. The program was a catalyst for potential progress away from Guyana's degenerating partisan political conflict. In addition to specific impacts of particular components on their respective targeted organizations and arenas, the SCP provided a national focal point for acknowledging the country's frustrations and mobilizing untapped energies to begin to manage them. By sensitizing a large number of people at multiple levels and in many sectors to common interests that were threatened by Guyana's crisis, it made these people more self-aware of their roles in both contributing to and reversing the crisis, and it provided alternative, more productive aspirations and skills. It not only held out the vision of a new way to pursue public problems, but also provided dialogue and other tools to address the issues, and it helped organize mechanisms such as the Ethnic Relations Commission and the National Conversation to help galvanize collective action. The commission's Multistakeholder Forum and outreach aggressively took advantage of Guyana's small population to activate a broadly inclusive consultation process and public awareness campaign that achieved an impressive degree of penetration into the society. Moreover, although Guyanese society possessed an abstract desire for change, it is highly unlikely that the breadth and scale of this effort would have emerged without an outside stimulus and external support. Even government spokespersons suggested that Guyana's actors would not have accomplished the amount of impetus toward productive engagement simply by themselves.

Nevertheless, despite the new dynamism among civil society organizations, the SCP activities were unable to create a cohesive social movement that could hold the competing parties and politicians to a higher standard of conduct in politics and policymaking. A review of the post-2006 situation sheds some light on the extent to which the SCP's efforts produced lasting changes. This picture appears to be mixed, particularly regarding the possible gap between formal changes made on paper and realities on the ground.

Certain developments in Guyanese politics indicate that the tight grip of the ethnicized bipolar competition between the two largest political parties is loosening. In 2005, a new third party, the Alliance for Change (AFC), was formed by leaders who had defected from the two major parties and from another opposition party. These leaders hoped that the creation of the AFC would act as a symbol of interethnic unity through a campaign that focused on the theme of ending ethnic strife, and that this would pressure the two largest parties to cooperate. The AFC increased its proportion of votes from 8 percent in the 2006 elections to 11 percent in the 2011 elections. Although the 2011 election tally allowed the ruling PPP to form the government and decide the presidency for the fifth successive time, the PPP failed narrowly to win a majority in Parliament. This unprecedented turn of events was due in part to the votes for the AFC and for a new coalition, called the Partnership for National Unity (PNU), led by the PNC but composed of several smaller parties. The nonviolent 2006 elections also apparently had set a standard for the 2011 elections, for these elections were also peaceful as well as better administered.[40] The trend away from ethnicized party competition and election-related violence seemed to continue into the 2015 elections, as a multiracial coalition of the PNU and AFC narrowly won full control of the government without violent incidents, ending twenty-three years of PPP rule.

Another notable post-2006 trend was the apparent reversal of Guyana's economic and social decline. One international study declared dramatically that 2001 to 2011 had ended up as a "decade of economic and social transformation" for Guyana.[41] Although annual economic growth rates in the first half of the decade averaged only about 1.3 percent, and devastating floods wracked the country in 2005, from 2006 to 2010 the growth rate averaged 4.4 percent, dipping slightly in 2011. In addition to economic growth, progress was noted in education, health, housing, social services, and poverty reduction. Differences in the poverty rates of the three largest ethnic groups also were narrowing, though Amerindians continued to be the worst off.[42]

In this assessment, the optimism created by the peaceful elections of 2006 may have helped make this socioeconomic progress possible. The momentum was attributed not only to more effective economic policies but also to improved administrative efficiency, national cohesion and stability, rule of law, and civil norms, brought about by a number of new laws and administrative changes that made the various ministries more effective and accountable to Parliament and strengthened judicial administration and local governments.[43] Other economists also attributed Guyana's turnaround not solely to better economic policies but also to the burst of activities aimed at increasing social cohesion, public trust, and inclusivity in national politics, which seem to have reduced Guyana's political and ethnic tensions.[44] However, it remains unclear how much of this improved socioeconomic and political climate can be attributed to the SCP in particular, or whether it arose independently from smarter economic management, global factors, and broader changes in politics. Also, several threats—including Guyana's vulnerability to natural disasters, poor infrastructure, crime and violence, weakened national consensus, and uncertain investment climate—were still thwarting the country's progress.[45] Indeed, not long after the 2006 elections, political and ethnic tensions and politically influenced violent crime resurfaced. An Afro-Guyanese gang attacked two Indo-Guyanese villages in January 2008 and twenty-three people were killed. In early 2011, a grenade explosion in a market and discovery of homemade bombs added to tensions. The new police procedures apparently had not improved overall police effectiveness in deterring violent crime in Guyana, as its rates remained high, and police harassment continued. Drug trafficking has been enabled by high levels of corruption in the Guyana Police Force, due to continued understaffing and low pay, as well as the country's overall size. The weak judicial system continues to suffer from poor training of justices.[46] Moreover, despite much study and debate, interparty agreement to move ahead with the constitutionally mandated but long-delayed elections for town, village, and neighborhood officials still had not been achieved.

Judging also from news reports and commentary from Guyana from 2010 to 2014, inflammatory rhetoric and racially charged language still often surface in the media and political discourse. In anticipation of the elections scheduled for 2011, media representatives met with the Guyana Elections Commission and agreed that a new media code of conduct was needed.[47] A litany of allegations and counter-allegations have been made, although with little documentation, regarding the incidents of violent crime; extrajudicial killings by politically connected death squads and gangs; arbitrary treatment by the police, especially of the Indo-Guyanese population; politicians' collusion in drug-running and gang violence; executive usurpations of authority; government corruption and bribery; use of government contracts, privatization, and other benefits as patronage to selected localities and interests; parliamentary deadlocks due to legislative obstinacy by the opposition in control of the National Assembly; political cooptation of the Ethnic Relations Commission and specific civil society groups; illegal seizure of Amerindian land; deteriorating schools; and stifling of media by the government as well as media bias in favor of opposition parties.

All in all, despite several years of economic growth, social improvement, and greater dispersion of power, it is unclear whether Guyana's chronic political wrangling and confrontation, typified by aborted interparty talks and parliamentary boycotts, have abated. These continuing problems have led some observers to worry that Guyana's improved political situation is slipping, and once again they have called for a government of national unity, "dialogue," and cooperative engagement among the parties.[48] Guyana may not have yet reached the tipping point when, faced with contentious issues, politics can transcend debilitating confrontations.[49]

Contributing Factors

Program Design and Implementation Factors

A partial explanation for the SCP's impacts and its limits arises from aspects of the program's design and implementation.

STRATEGIC THOUGHT

The UN was unusually proactive in anticipating possible further escalation of tensions and declining governability and in acting to reverse those trends by initiating the SCP. It therefore took advantage of the opportunity to engage in conflict prevention, rather than wait for the eruption of violent conflict and its more difficult obstacles. The SCP was also exceptionally conflict-sensitive in assessing the sources and dynamics of the political situation that were inhibiting Guyana's development and explicitly seeking to improve these problems through more effective decision-making and governance processes. Before starting the program, the UN Core Group and the Program Management Unit invested much thought and deliberation in crafting a contextualized response to the situation. The SCP's multisectoral scope also showed that it was influenced by emerging international findings about effective conflict prevention that had been tried in the 1990s, such as in Macedonia, the Baltic countries, and South Africa.

UNITED NATIONS STATURE

UN sponsorship was key to the SCP's ability to obtain Guyanese governmental approval and in-country partners for this unusual external initiative, as the UN's standing freed the program of suspicions that it served some other country's agenda. As one party leader put it, the participants were "guinea pigs" for a UN experiment but apparently willing ones. Also critical was the prestige and support of the widely respected UN resident representative, Youssef Mahmoud, who was praised for being a fair-minded advocate for the SCP. He represented a diplomatic presence, a "UN Ambassador" who gave higher visibility to the SCP and encouraged the government and donors to keep its efforts moving.

PARTICIPATORY APPROACH

The SCP's deliberately broad and open agenda lent itself to local commitment and creativity in deciding what directions to pursue under the overall theme of "social cohesion." The constructive ambiguity afforded by this apolitical euphemism had definite practical value by providing a positive, nonjudgmental banner under which to introduce and run the program. Its potential connotations left room for many participants to define what was worth pursuing and to undertake a variety of activities. To engender maximum local ownership, the SCP's small Program Management Unit team also expended considerable effort to probe for the kinds of activities of greatest interest to the Guyanese organizations. Led by the peace and development adviser, the team members received universally positive marks for their sincerity, dedication, hard work, and collaborative spirit. By engaging as honest brokers through an elicitive approach to potential partners, they achieved buy-in and legitimacy for the SCP. The overall nondirective philosophy of neutral facilitation tapped into a pent-up desire for wider civic involvement and elicited a wide range of activities.

In addition to this local participatory approach, the SCP used periodic, iterative consultations with the UN Core Group in New York, a steering committee of the contributing donors within Guyana, and the Guyanese government in order to respond to the need for a shared understanding and cooperation among the program's main supporters, which maintained solidarity behind the program. This contact also ensured a flexible but strategic approach regarding whether and how new activities were added to the program, thus avoiding duplication. In particular, the program's interaction with an interdonor Thematic Working Group on Governance kept its own programs, partnerships, and support grounded in an ongoing analysis of Guyana's political environment, its needs, and the resources available for promising activities. The information sharing among donors improved bilateral and multidonor support to critical sectors, enabling the SCP to focus its work in areas where it had comparative advantage.[50]

APPEALING PRODUCT

The training workshops conducted by high-quality facilitators were well received by the participants as providing valuable ideas and useful skills. Participants requested more training and wanted to expand their training to other members of the same groups. The trust the SCP engendered and its attractive products enabled the Program Management Unit to act on emerging opportunities so as to carry them forward and to be approached by prospective partners with requests for SCP engagement. For example, the SCP was able to step forward to capitalize on the momentum of the conflict transformation workshop by supporting the Ethnic Relations Commission's idea of a national dialogue among Guyanese about ethnic issues and their collective future. It then fulfilled a funding request from the commission for the Multistakeholder Forum's nationwide conversations, including direct support to the commission and help in strengthening skills for facilitating the meetings. The SCP's financial support and skill-building also enabled the commission to publicize its purpose and work.

Because of its inspiring dynamism, the Program Management Unit also received requests for support in initiatives that were not envisioned in the initial plans. As mentioned, the PSC had not been engaged initially by the SCP, but it took the initiative to get in touch with the program. The success of the initial human rights workshop for police led the police commissioner to request SCP assistance in improving the police forces' mediation and anger management skills. As this request was seen to be in line with the program's aims, the SCP responded. By shifting its focus in mid-term to possible electoral violence in 2006, it showed adaptability to emerging needs in the country.

NURTURING

In addition to demonstrating its expertise in the initial facilitations, the Program Management Unit's hands-on follow-through was crucial for the SCP's subsequent activities to take place and to spawn further activities. Although most activities were initiated by the SCP while others were undertaken without its assistance, most of the subsequent implementation activity resulted directly or indirectly from the energies of the management unit team. The team spent an extraordinary amount of work and time to inform stakeholders of potential SCP project opportunities, assess their interest and commitment, organize and manage events, conduct the sessions, and follow up on their efforts.

In one example, to buttress the initial training and capacity building provided to the Ethnic Relations Commission, the SCP obtained the services of an experienced specialist in ethnic conflict. A human rights specialist was recruited for three months from the Office of the UN High Commissioner for Human Rights to familiarize the commission with standard operating procedures and guidelines for processing individual allegations or complaints.[51] While running the program, the peace and development adviser's behind-the-scenes nurturing included sharing articles, stories, and poems about peacebuilding experiences in other countries, sending weekly emails of encouragement, and holding occasional team-building meetings. The peace and development adviser and other management unit staff also wrote and distributed analytical articles that described to other audiences how to do what was being done in Guyana.

VOLUNTARY STRATEGY

Notwithstanding the value of its elicitive, participatory approach, the SCP's strategy contained inherent drawbacks that partially explain its limited impact on Guyana's public policies and divisive political discourse. The participatory method was key to obtaining local buy-in and inspiring many of the activities that the Guyanese took on, but the purely voluntary basis of participation also meant that roadblocks could prevent the program from going in particular directions. The program's assumption that the basic source of Guyana's social incohesion was a widespread lack of trust and cooperative relationships, and its main remedy of engendering Guyanese-led solutions through skill-building, lacked sufficient inducements to overcome persisting divisions or disputes among the involved parties actively or passively, such as in the cases of the trade unions and political party leaders. Because of its principled commitment to local ownership and participant prerogatives in determining the focus and pace of activities, the SCP lacked incentives or disincentives to break through instances of inaction or deadlock. Even though activities such as the early warning workshops for the party leaders and trips abroad for the party youth leaders "sprinkled" insights and skills among various individuals, little effort was made to ensure that these experiences would lead to concrete collective application.

One source of this weakness lay in the program's procedures. Some donor interviewees suggested that the SCP's multipronged thrust may have led to insufficient effort to try to measure program results in terms of their impact and gather evidence of results. Other than seeking to reduce general distrust through capacity-building, the SCP seems not to have conceptualized the intermediate, bridging qualities that would be needed to achieve its ultimate objectives, such as social cohesion. Two years into the program, a key SCP document referred only to values engendered during its processes of engagement but did not define any expected effects outside the process on its environment, or distinguish between short-term and long-term effects.[52] The SCP lacked a way to operationalize its stated objectives by defining concrete indicators of social cohesion, security, and similar factors that would reflect plausible expectations for what the activities could produce.

To be sure, the SCP deliberately chose building trust and relationships as its initial entry points for definite reasons. Introducing elements of a more "muscular" form of mediation, such as conditioning economic aid on political progress, would have violated the basic SCP philosophy. The lack of these more robust approaches, however, left a critical gap between the process of changing attitudes and communication patterns on the one hand and official or nonofficial political and policy processes and issues on the other. Any changes in overall public policies and further implementation of constitutional agreements would have to be made at the level of political and policy negotiations, and by engaging the government and political parties in an intensive manner. But the SCP strategy did not differentiate within the range of its activities at multiple levels in society in terms of their differing potentials for achieving social cohesion and political change.

The SCP had disavowed a more power-based approach because previous official mediations along those lines had seemed to fail. However, no provision was made for a distinct channel through which international actors could exert leverage to translate the progress that the SCP was making at the grassroots and middle levels into changes at the political level, such as an official diplomatic negotiation or mediation process that would address outstanding policy and political issues, with actors that might now find it easier to resolve some of the difficult high-level issues. A separate but parallel process that engaged government and opposition leaders more deliberately, with specific inducements, could have provided a separate but complementary channel through which Guyana's leaders could apply their intensified relationships and newfound communication and other skills (instilled by the SCP) to substantive policies.[53]

Contextual Factors

The SCP's impacts were also shaped by opportunities and constraints in the program's international and domestic environment that lay outside of its influence.

Guyana's nature as a small, poor, and highly aid-dependent nation with an avowedly democratic polity was crucial. This fundamental status explains in part why the PPP-led Guyana government was receptive to the UNDP initiative. The SCP would not have been accepted or implemented but for its endorsement and support by top-level, executive government officials. According to a highly placed government respondent, the Guyanese government itself recognized that there was a problem of potential worsening conflict and national reconciliation, and accepted that it needed to draw on expertise in conflict resolution to deal with the situation. This acquiescence allowed access to directly assist many political and government officials, agencies, and operating processes. However, once the SCP began, the relative amount of distance and discretion that particular activities had in relation to official political and government levels seems to have been a major reason why some of its initial workshops led to more significant activities than others. The more that the activities sought to achieve agreement on concrete public policies, the fewer results were obtained. The participants in SCP-supported events who followed through enthusiastically with other activities were most often the ones who did not have high-level decision-making roles in established organizations with close ties to political parties or the government. The degree to which participants' functions were shaped by the inherent constraints of operating in political bodies in a high-stakes, partisan national-level political competition helps to explain the extent to which the SCP's initial events resulted in subsequent substantial actions.

Consequently, some respondents regarded the existing constitutional structures as more than simply institutional barriers to cross-party cooperation on policy issues. Patronage patterns had made major nongovernmental interest organizations and professional associations—such as the trade unions, the teachers, and the bar association—subordinate to the political parties and government agencies. These long-standing corporatist arrangements made these organizations less inclined to take independent positions on policy issues. The rationale was that the parties, with their ability to control the state, would adequately serve these organizations' interests. However, because Guyanese elections traditionally are akin to ethnic censuses, the parties were not held accountable to those specific functional interests. One example was the trade unions' lack of progress in securing and protecting workers' rights. A program-specific illustration of this pattern was the lack of traction for the SCP's plans to contribute to "access to justice"; the justice sector in particular was a source of political contention. Although the SCP addressed many levels in political and civil society, the program's thrust was predominantly nongovernmental at the middle and local levels. The one exception in the official realm was the activities led by the Ethnic Relations Commission. In this case, the constitutional creation of the commission was propitious, for it provided one anchor in Guyana's officialdom for SCP-stimulated activities such as the Multistakeholder Forum, although these activities mainly engaged civil society.

This overarching political obstacle was compounded by the classic challenges of changing the routines of any large, hierarchical organization, not to mention stimulating collective action that requires coordination among separate interests and organizations. Thus, some trainees reported experiencing a "ceiling" within their respective organizations, above which their new individual outlooks could not bring about change. Extraordinary changes are especially difficult for formal organizations, for they lie outside their normal routines. Efforts to shift attention and energies from prior agendas and obligations to new ones require time investment, consensus-building, and approvals. Although experiences with conflict resolution training may deeply influence the individuals who work at various levels within such organizations, it cannot change the overall policies of the organizations that the trained individuals subsequently reenter, unless such changes are mandated at the executive level.

By contrast, progress was easier where the participants had more autonomy over their own operations and thus were outside the activities that involved higher-level players in official or quasiofficial organizations. Generally, lower levels of government and civil society had considerably fewer hurdles to overcome. The following lower-level groups made much more progress in the sense of engaging in more activities: community youth leaders, station-level police officers, the Private Sector Commission, regional democratic councils, and peacebuilding process facilitators.

Certain broad social trends in Guyana also helped to contain instability. Emigration and remittances provided a safety valve for violent conflict, even as emigration bled the country of valuable human resources. As suggested earlier, improved economic growth and services may have had an independent effect on social stability, even though political interactions did not noticeably change. Finally, at bottom, opposition leaders and government officials shared a common interest in avoiding complete deterioration in Guyana, for this could make it easier for more radical "outbidders" to take their place.

Conclusion

The distinctive features of the SCP experiment and its modeling of conflict-sensitive peacebuilding have significance outside Guyana and have been examined by the UN and others for potential lessons from the experiences of this carefully designed, multifaceted initiative.[54] This chapter's assessment of its actual results verifies the promise of this kind of initiative, but also drives home a sobering reality: the mainly dialogue-fostering, social-psychological, interactive methods through which the SCP sought to engender more productive interpersonal relationships in many small groups had only indirect and limited impacts on official, national-level politics. Even in a small nation such as Guyana, it is difficult and takes a long time to discipline political and governmental behavior, especially in a context of lagging development and strong temptations to exploit social divisions for political gain. The pursuit of a bigger "piece of a small pie" can continue to drive people apart, frustrating the achievement of public goods. Competitive elections are far from a panacea, for they introduce temptations to resort to any but the most obviously offensive tactics to achieve political advantage over one's opponents.

Evidently, continuing long-term efforts are required to achieve slow progress toward building institutionalized, authoritative, rule-governed political and policymaking relations. It remains untested whether more powerful international inducements on a complementary track could have intensified political cooperation and thus enabled Guyana's political leaders to build on the SCP's skills and civic achievements by reaching concrete, enforceable agreements to improve Guyana's prospects for investors and the everyday welfare of Guyana's people.

Notes

1. This chapter is based mainly on an external evaluation of the SCP that the author and Roxanne Myers conducted for UNDP in 2006–7. Roxanne Myers is an independent consultant in public and social policy with many years' experience as a researcher, lecturer, academic administrator, evaluator, facilitator, and advocate in conflict resolution, peacebuilding, and governance. The evidence in this chapter is derived from off-the-record interviews and group conversations in Guyana in December 2006 with seventy-four SCP participants and other informed observers, direct observation of the culminating national conversation of the Multistakeholder Forum, and a document review. Direct statements from respondents are given in quotation marks without individual attributions. A shortened version of the evaluation is UNDP-Guyana, *Can Fostering a Culture of Dialogue Change the Course of a Nation? An Evaluation of the Social Cohesion Programme: Key Findings and Summary of Recommendations* (New York: UNDP, August 2007). Conclusions drawn from the evidence are this author's.

2. The two largest political parties, the People's National Congress and the People's Progressive Party, changed their names slightly over this period, but will be referred to here as the PNC and the PPP.

3. International Monetary Fund, *World Economic Outlook Database*, Report for Selected Countries and Subjects (Washington, DC: International Monetary Fund, September 2004).

4. Kari Grenade and Denny Lewis-Bynoe, "Reflecting on Development Outcomes: A Comparative Analysis of Barbados and Guyana," *Journal of Eastern Caribbean Studies* 36, no. 1 (2011): 20, 25.

5. Office of CARICOM Facilitator, "Guyana: Dialogue between Main Political Parties Resume," Press Release 7/1999, September 4, 1999, 2–3.

6. "Civil Society Moves to Get Involved in Decision-Making, Seeks People's Views on the Way Forward," *Stabroek News*, July 14, 2002; and "Measures Recommended in 2002 After the Social Partners Initiative," *Stabroek News*, February 16, 2008, 16.

7. Besides staff from the UNDP and its Bureau of Crisis Prevention and Recovery, the mission included representatives from the UN Department of Economic and Social Affairs, Department of Political Affairs, Office of the Coordinator for Humanitarian

Affairs, Office of the High Commissioner for Human Rights, and Regional Bureau for Latin America and the Caribbean, as well as three donors: the UK Department for International Development (DFID), the Canadian International Development Agency (CIDA), and the European Commission.

8. UN Inter-Agency Framework for Coordination on Preventive Action, *Inter-Agency Technical Mission to Guyana* Report (New York: United Nations, December 2002), 9–14.

9. The UN's motivation to address the tensions in Guyana through supporting a proactive initiative was animated by trends in UNDP headquarters in New York and in the international development community generally. The Guyana initiative was among the first of several UN initiatives explicitly intended for conflict prevention and peacebuilding, and to which they assigned one of the first designated Peace and Development Advisers. Through these initiatives, the UNDP's Bureau of Conflict Prevention and Recovery was seeking to mainstream "conflict sensitivity" in UN programs. Another motivation behind the SCP was the desire of donors to ensure favorable outcomes for democracy promotion activities that had been conducted throughout South America since the 1990s. In addition, especially after September 11, 2001, the international development community had become concerned about "fragile" or "failed states" as possible sources of transnational problems such as drug and human trafficking and terrorism, and was beginning to promote interagency approaches and multidonor harmonization, as development agencies increasingly saw development and security as interlinked problems. Aware of the damage that intrastate political crises and violent conflicts have caused to societies and to development goals and programs, and committed to using development programs wherever appropriate to mitigate the sources and drivers of such conflicts, most major development agencies and the World Bank had been sponsoring assessments of the potential for conflict in particular countries. By 2004, the UN Secretary-General sought to encourage multilateral approaches to conflicts and related problems through the High-Level Panel on Threats to Security.

10. UNDP Guyana Mission, "Improving Social Cohesion, Security and Governance in Guyana," Multidonor Proposal: Version 5, June 2005.

11. The execution of the SCP was assisted and guided by the Guyana "Core Group" at UN headquarters. In the first instance of support for a UNDP country office through the Department of Political Affairs–administered UN Trust Fund for Preventive Action, an initial grant of some US$450,000 was invested at the start of the program. The Trust Fund contributed additional project funding in subsequent years, and the CIDA and DFID also funded SCP projects.

12. "At the root of Guyana's current crisis lay worsening political and social relations; this consistently had failed to transcend the country's history of racial polarization. Economic liberalization and impressive economic growth at the beginning of the 1990's have come to a grinding halt as attempts at political and institutional reform have foundered on the pervasive mistrust that still characterizes much of Guyana's public life." UN Inter-Agency Framework for Coordination on Preventive Action, *Inter-Agency Technical Mission to Guyana*, 7.

13. Ibid.

14. Youssef Mahmoud, "Dialogue as a Conflict Prevention Strategy: The Case of Guyana" (PowerPoint presentation, Folke Bernadotte Academy, Stockholm, Sweden, n.d.).

15. "The inability of the political parties to consistently work together, whether in parliament, in policy making, in implementing needed reforms, has been characterized by mistrust, negativity, harsh public rhetoric and gridlock. As such, there is a need for greater attention to improving relationships among political stakeholders." UNDP Guyana Mission, Social Cohesion Programme, "Final Evaluation of the Social Cohesion Programme," Terms of Reference, October 2006, 1. The view that stimulating dialogue was needed was also fed by the view that fragile states were often characterized by "silent crises" in which weak governments are unable to respond adequately to public needs and instead tend to react to national stress by adopting authoritarian methods that discourage wider participation. Thus, because representative institutions are weak or not trusted, the population increasingly seeks solutions outside these institutions. Mahmoud, "Dialogue as a Conflict Prevention Strategy."

16. Chris Spies, "Guyana: A Case Study Prepared for the Social Cohesion Programme (UNDP Guyana) for the UNDESA Expert Meeting on Dialogue" (New York: United Nations, November 21–23, 2005), 9–10, http://www.un.org/esa/socdev/sib/egm/paper/Chris%20Spies.pdf. As expressed in the Terms of Reference, "It was intended that stakeholders, based on a new set of skills, aptitudes, and processes, would build their own solution to a difficult crisis, and in doing so develop a lasting capacity for the peaceful resolution of future crises. The building of this important national capacity was seen as providing the most sustainable way of enhancing Guyana's prospects of achieving social cohesion and development." UNDP Guyana, "Final Evaluation," 2.

17. "The capacity being built was geared towards the peaceful resolution of disputes, increased human security and the implementation of political agreements." UNDP Guyana, "Final Evaluation," 2.

18. The strategy of the SCP was focused "not only on reviving the stalled process of political dialogue and reform but also providing assistance for the building of a political and civic culture." Ibid.

19. "The critical international role was not . . . to intervene to resolve the immediate conflict, but to support stakeholders in acquiring the skills and building the processes wherein they could resolve their own conflicts. The international role was meant to focus, facilitate and encourage process rather than be wholly outcome oriented." Ibid.

20. The SCP's choice of entry point—the improving of relationships—sidestepped but did not reject the prevailing academic analysis of Guyana's political problems. Research literature had located the problem in the design of Guyana's basic political institutions. Several analyses argued that the crisis came from ongoing institutional impediments that perpetuated the public's chronic racial voting and political mobilization. These structures created incentives that did not stem solely or directly from the fact that Guyana's population comprises two major ethnic communities that were divided historically by differing livelihoods and cultures, and reinforced by physically separated communities. Instead, the difficulty arose from the conjunction of those divisions and the country's parliamentary and unitary system of government. Despite an element of proportional representation, the Westminster model first established under the autonomous government during the British colonial period had allowed the party that won a general election to both control the unicameral parliament and form the government. Moreover, political power often has been wielded in a highly centralized form, especially in the past. See, e.g., Perry Mars, "The Security-Development Crisis in Guyana" in *Security and Development: Searching for Critical Connections*, ed. Neclâ Tschirgi,

Michael S. Lund, and Francesco Marini (Boulder, CO: Lynne Rienner, 2010), 258. This structure has created strong pressures on the parties to continually appeal to the two largest ethnic bases in order to win and stay in office. The "winner take all" competition exacerbates these intergroup differences by keeping the communities in competition for political power and its concomitant economic perquisites, which politicizes many particular policy issues, local social problems, and violent episodes in ethnic terms. Thus, the underlying problem is not deep-seated, abiding ethnic discrimination or interracial socioeconomic inequalities (as measured by objective indicators of income, jobs, educational opportunities, and the distribution of social services), but rather the perpetuation by political leaders and activists of a belief in systemically conflicting interests. In short, political power competition, not lack of trust, is the main behavioral driver at high governing levels, and progress in reaching actual binding political agreements requires common political and policy positions, not simply more civil communications. Acknowledging this view, the SCP stated that it "simultaneously recognised that underpinning causal factors, such as the formal political and electoral structures, and ethnic divisions, were fuelling the immediate tensions. This destructive reinforcement of current issues with root causes of tensions was addressed in the design of the SCP." UNDP Guyana, "Final Evaluation," 2.

21. A few persons interviewed and commentaries reviewed for this study provided a third diagnosis of the sources of Guyana's malaise and the appropriate remedies. In this view, the basic failure has not been that of reaching political accords but of enforcing existing laws. Established procedures were needed for such basic matters as the legal standards for a valid electoral list and proper court procedures in cases arising over arms caches. Thus, the basic problem was not the lack of intercommunal or interparty trust, but rather the deterioration of governing institutions that once may have been stronger. In this view, this problem was worsened by the willingness of some parts of the international community to go along with these breaches of laws and procedures, on the premise that these were symptoms, not causes, of the present impasse. The problem should be attacked not principally through strengthening relationships but through support for strengthening faulty agencies and more strenuous efforts to abide by existing laws. What is needed was more vigorous support for institution-building and legal enforcement, such as efforts to inform people of their rights and responsibilities. However, while these alternative perspectives point to entry points that would change formal institutional structures and actual practices rather than people's attitudes and relationships, they were not clear about the source of the political will to make such changes.

22. In addition, direct funding went to certain written or visual products, personnel, and events.

23. Based loosely on John Paul Lederach's levels of program focus in John Paul Lederach, *Building Peace: Sustainable Reconciliation in Divided Societies* (Washington, DC: United States Institute of Peace Press, 1997), 39; and Mary Anderson and Lara Olson's distinctions between "key" and "many" persons whom programs might address and between individual and social/political targets for change. See Mary B. Anderson and Lara Olson, *Confronting War: Critical Lessons for Peace Practitioners* (Cambridge, MA: The Collaborative for Development Action, 2003), 48–49.

24. UNDP Guyana, "Improving Social Cohesion, Security and Governance in Guyana," 5.

25. Fifteen PNC representatives and eight PPP representatives participated in these youth meetings.

26. The assistance included a needs assessment of capital works, a documentation center, renovation of a committee room, an information technology area, and technical support to the Constitutional Rights Commissions.

27. The PSC was set up in 1992 after the Hoyte government initiated a dialogue with a few business representatives but found that it needed to consult with a body that could speak for a wider range of business interests.

28. In September 2005, a South African specialist in police training facilitated a training-of-trainers course on human rights, in conjunction with the Guyana Human Rights Association. The course produced a human rights manual that was used in in-service training for superior officers and middle management. Three training events were held on conflict transformation and mediation. In December 2005, a specialist in mediation and police training from Zimbabwe was brought in for a facilitated workshop in mediation skills for twenty-four police officers at the station commander level. The SCP facilitated two more courses for junior officers and station commanders in March and April 2006, respectively. Two further workshops prepared a "core group" of police trainer-of-trainers who were expected to coach other policemen.

29. A magistrates' training seminar took place from August 12 to 14, 2005, facilitated by the Guyana Law Association UK and the Guyana Human Rights Association.

30. The Ethnic Relations Commission's constitutional mandate was principally to "(1) provide equality of opportunity between persons of different ethnic groups and promote harmony and good relations between such persons; (2) promote the elimination of all forms of discrimination on the basis of ethnicity; (3) discourage and prohibit persons, institutions, political parties, and associations from indulging in, advocating, or promoting discriminatory practices on the grounds of ethnicity; and (4) foster a sense of security among all ethnic groups by encouraging and promoting the understanding, acceptance, and tolerance of diversity in national life and promoting full participation by all ethnic groups in the social, economic, cultural, and political life of the people." See Ethnic Relations Commission, *About Us*, retrieved April 2015 from http://www .ethnicrelations.org.gy.

31. "Memorandum of Understanding between Ethnic Relations Commission and the UNDP/Multi-Donor Social Cohesion Program," November 10, 2004.

32. Twenty-four participants from different sectors of society, including women's groups, unions, the University of Guyana, the religious community, and political parties, attended two five-day training-of-trainers workshops in August and October 2005 to build capacity for "process design and facilitation."

33. Discussions to develop conflict management projects initially involved groups from the Abrahamic traditions of Judaism, Christianity and Islam, but later included Hindu and other faith-based groups.

34. SCP intervention in the underdeveloped Region 10 focused largely on social and economic development as a key factor in social cohesion. The regional council staff stated that it needed "a good guide to help stymie lopsided development activities among communities," i.e., a regional development strategy.

35. Terrence Simmons and Roxanne Myers, *From Violent to Peaceful Elections: A Preliminary Look at Peace Building Initiatives in Guyana* (Georgetown: Guyana Peacebuilders Network, 2006), 10–12.

36. Ibid.

37. Memorandum of Understanding and National Conversation Proposal, Guyana, 2006, cited in Roxanne Myers and Jason Calder, *Toward Ethnic Conflict Transformation: A Case Study of Citizen Peacebuilding Initiatives on the 2006 Guyana Elections*, Occasional Papers: Peacebuilding Series No. 4 (Franklin, WV: Future Generations Graduate School, November 2011), 47.

38. Although the conversation aimed to establish lines of communication across racial and other divides, from ordinary Guyanese who participated in the National Conversation to politicians we interviewed, many said that the assumption that there was no communication across these divides was actually flawed. "We always talk to each other," they said. The difference the National Conversation made was in the quality and purpose of the conversation. Interviews with Guyanese participants, November 16, 2006.

39. This includes: "New processes, institutions or entities constituted, where relevant skills have been employed or alternative forms of dispute resolution used." UNDP Guyana, Social Cohesion Programme, "Final Evaluation," 3.

40. Commonwealth Secretariat, *Guyana National and Regional Elections: Report of the Commonwealth Observer Group* (London: Commonwealth Secretariat, November 28, 2011), 30.

41. European External Action Service, *Guyana Poverty Reduction Strategy Paper, 2011–15* (Brussels: European External Action Service, July 2011), i.

42. Ibid., i.

43. Ibid., ii, 18–23.

44. Grenade and Lewis-Bynoe, "Reflecting on Development Outcomes," 23–25.

45. European External Action Service, *Guyana Poverty Reduction Strategy Paper*, iii.

46. Taylor Owen and Alexandre Grigsby, *In Transit: Gangs and Criminal Networks in Guyana*, Working Paper (Geneva, Switzerland: Small Arms Survey, Graduate Institute of International and Development Studies, 2012), 35–39.

47. Varany Chaubey, Amy Mawson, and Gabriel Kuris, *Cooling Ethnic Conflict over a Heated Election: Guyana, 2001–2006* (Princeton, NJ: Innovations for Successful Societies, Princeton University, September 2011).

48. See, e.g., Vanda Radzik et al., "We support Fr. Rodrigues's call for dialogue," letter to the editor, *Stabroek News*, February 15, 2008; "Granger rejects dialogue for Guyana," *Guyana Times*, December 2, 2014.

49. See, e.g., Thomas C. Schelling, *Micromotives and Macrobehavior*, rev. ed. (New York: W. W. Norton, 2006).

50. Via the Program Management Unit, the UNDP first offered secretarial help to the Thematic Working Group on Governance. Although the group became defunct in 2004, the SCP supported its reactivation a year later through engagement with the government and the donors. This allowed the Program Management Unit to share its experiences and sharpen the SCP's focus with regard to issue papers on governance, such as local government reform and implementation of constitutional reforms.

51. The SCP also procured office equipment and provided support for a reference library through the technical services of a United Nations Volunteer librarian.

52. Chris Spies, "Guyana: A Case Study Prepared by the Social Cohesion Programme."

53. This separate process might have required other sponsorship than that of the SCP, although it could be linked implicitly to the program. More powerful external incentives provided by the international community also would likely be required.

In cases of successful conflict prevention where the UN or multilateral bodies played important roles, such as in Macedonia and Slovakia, powerful actors such as the European Union and the United States directly and vigorously applied economic and other positive incentives and negative pressures to leaders, along with ideas for diplomatic solutions, not only training in conflict transformation and civic values.

54. The SCP figures prominently in one of the cases gathered together by an international project interested in "innovations for successful societies." The case study focuses on the efforts to avoid violence in the 2006 elections; Chaubey, Mawson, and Kuris, *Cooling Ethnic Conflict over a Heated Election*. See also Myers and Calder, *Toward Ethnic Conflict Transformation*.

Ending Active Conflicts

Chapter 5

Tajikistan: Peace Secured, but the State of Our Dreams?

Anna Matveeva

At the Commonwealth of Independent States summit, the president of Tajikistan, Emomali Rahmon, promoted the positive example of the Tajik peace process and the way his government settled with the opposition. President Alexander Lukashenko of Belarus responded: "I wish we had such an opposition as you do!"

—Anecdote from field research in Tajikistan

Introduction

Tajikistan is one of the Soviet successor states of Central Asia, with a population of about 8.5 million. Located on the borders of Afghanistan and China, it is the poorest state of the former Soviet Union. The conflict in Tajikistan that arose soon after its independence in 1991 is unique in the post-Soviet space, as it is the only one that has been resolved successfully. After ten years of instability, security was restored in the early 2000s and the peace has held. At present, a relapse into violence is highly unlikely.

When the Inter-Tajik Dialogue (ITD) described in this chapter took place, Tajikistan had minimal significance for the United States and the international community. This factor arguably worked in favor of the peace dialogue. This attitude changed after September 11, 2001, and the beginning of the US-led intervention into Afghanistan, when Tajikistan emerged as a front-line state in the global war on terror. Moreover, drug cultivation in Afghanistan—the world's largest heroin producer—turned Tajikistan into an important route for narcotics trafficking, mainly to Europe. Currently, the United States and its allies in the antiterrorism coalition provide significant security assistance and development aid to Tajikistan.[1]

This study traces the process of peacemaking through informal dialogue with the aim of extracting lessons for peacebuilding *know-how* and advancing the professionalization of the conflict transformation field. It identifies the unique factors that contributed to the dialogue's success as well as the more general lessons that can be applied in other situations. It attempts, first, to discern how this interactive process-type intervention was carried out and, second, to determine the contextual circumstances in which interactive process interventions have a reasonable chance for success. Toward this end, it explores both content issues (i.e., the causes and dynamics of conflict, the actors involved and how they related to each other) and process matters (i.e., how the dialogue was designed and conducted). The study concentrates on the decade of the main dialogue (1993–2003), the period in which the country moved from acute civil strife to the establishment of a stable peace. It then briefly looks at the transformation of the main dialogue into a number of different spinoff projects.

The chapter first outlines the nature of the Tajikistan conflict and describes the ITD process.[2] It then analyzes the effects of the peace intervention on the sources and manifestations of conflict in Tajikistan, on the process of its resolution, on channels for influencing the conflict, and on the participants as individuals and as a group. It assesses the factors responsible for these effects—both those arising from the intervention in question and from the wider domestic and regional context—and concludes with some reflections on general lessons for policymakers.[3]

The Nature and Course of the Conflict in Tajikistan

The collapse of the Soviet Union in December 1991 threw Tajikistan into an acute crisis of decolonization.[4] From the onset of its independence in

1991, the country rapidly disintegrated into violent conflict. Casualties are reported as 157,000 dead,[5] but unofficial estimates put the death toll up to 300,000, out of the prewar population of 5.1 million. This makes the Tajik civil war perhaps the bloodiest conflict emerging from the end of the communist era. Remarkably, Tajikistan managed to recover and build a viable state in a relatively short time, and is unique among the post-Soviet states in that its conflict was resolved through a peace settlement.

The conflict in Tajikistan was rooted in the history of its creation as a Soviet constituent republic and in developments during the Soviet era. Tajiks are Persian-speaking people living alongside Turkic ethnic groups of Central Asia. Turkic-speaking Uzbeks constitute a minority group in Tajikistan, but are a majority in neighboring Uzbekistan, the largest country in Central Asia. During the ethno-territorial delineation of Central Asia in the 1920s, the territory of the modern Tajikistan was separated from Uzbekistan and upgraded to full Union Republic status in 1929. This division left Tajikistan without its major centers of urban civilization, namely Samarqand and Bukhara. As "compensation" for this loss of national history, land, and population, as well as economic development purposes, the southwestern part of the Ferghana Valley (Soughd province), heavily populated by Uzbeks, was incorporated into Tajikistan. This northern region is the most developed part of the country. Under Soviet rule, ethnic Tajiks from the mountain regions were moved to this area, which made the population of the northern region more diverse. At present, Uzbeks live in the areas bordering Uzbekistan and in Dushanbe, the capital.[6]

The Soviet system pursued population resettlement, motivated by development projects that required a larger labor force and the difficulties of sustaining a growing population in the mountain regions. Tensions and rivalries between lowlanders and highlanders within a larger Tajik group persisted throughout the post–World War II era. Mountainous terrain and difficulties in communication kept communities apart and militated against the formation of a Tajik national identity. Certain highland areas on the borders with Afghanistan and China had particular significance in the Soviet defense doctrine and were privileged accordingly, including support for their cultural and educational facilities.

In fact, in the run-up to independence there was an acute sense throughout the republic that economic and social benefits were distributed unfairly and that some regions benefited disproportionally and unfairly. The underlying grievances were related to how power was distributed in the republic. Throughout the Soviet period, the more developed north, in which the Uzbek presence was most felt, dominated Tajikistan's politics. In the 1970s, more Kulyabis (people from a region in the south) and Hissaris (from the center of the country) joined the ruling establishment, while Pamiris (from the eastern Pamir mountain region) were heavily represented in cultural circles. By contrast, poorer and mostly rural areas of Kurgan-Tyube (a southwestern region) and Gharm (a mountainous eastern region) had little standing, and these regions became opposition strongholds during the postindependence civil war.

During the late 1980s, rapid democratization accentuated these divisions, as Mikhail Gorbachev's reforms weakened the communist system. The greater freedom under perestroika (the "restructuring" reforms of the Soviet political and economic system) unleashed many suppressed grievances in Tajikistan's society. The intelligentsia was concerned with the assertion of Tajik culture and identity, while a proreligious constituency sought a greater role for Islam. Corruption, low living standards, extensive cotton cultivation, and environmental degradation all constituted popular grievances. Violence first erupted in 1990, prompted by antioutsider riots in Dushanbe, the republic's capital.

Reinforcing these divisions was a disagreement over the place of Islam in politics and society. Tajiks are Sunni Muslims of the Hanafi school, and the republic was a socially conservative society in the Soviet days. Religion occupied a significant space in daily life and family rituals. Following the suppression of Islam in the 1920s and 1930s, more religious freedoms were allowed during World War II. However, the political expression of Islam was suppressed and the state maintained tight control over religious affairs. Consequently, during perestroika, Islam became associated with the revival of the Tajik identity, asserting itself against Soviet secularism, and entered the political domain. The Islamic constituency grew more prominent and its activists united around the Islamic Renaissance Party (IRP), which was officially registered in 1991.

The immediate manifestations of the conflict were triggered by perestroika, attempts at democratization, and the dissolution of the Soviet Union. In the late 1980s, a rapid political mobilization occurred, leading to the creation of parties of democratic orientation, such as the Rastakhez, Democratic Party, Lal-e Badakhshan, and other political groupings of the intelligentsia.[7] The overarching goal of these parties was essentially the same—democratization of Tajikistan—but they became bitterly divided over the role of Islam in politics, splitting the democratic intelligentsia into Islamophobes and Islamophiles.

The escalating instability in Afghanistan and the demise of Soviet power also contributed to the conflict in Tajikistan. The situation in Afghanistan became volatile following the withdrawal of Soviet troops in February 1989 and mounting pressure by mujahideen on Soviet-backed Najibullah government in Kabul, which eventually fell in April 1992. As the communist system in Soviet Tajikistan weakened, the border with Afghanistan became more porous. This enabled the forging of connections between field commanders, such as Ahmad-Shah Massoud, a prominent ethnic Tajik warlord in northern Afghanistan, and Islamic political groupings in Tajikistan. Such alliances led to the penetration of weapons and ideas from across the border.[8]

These factors culminated in the jostling for power and resources among the people from different regions. The Supreme Soviet of Tajikistan elected Qakhar Mahkamov, the first secretary of the Communist Party of Tajikistan, as president on November 30, 1990. Mahkamov supported the August 18–19, 1991, coup attempt in Moscow that attempted to restore communist hard-liners to power; after it failed, he lost credibility. Rahmon Nabiev, the previous first secretary of the Communist Party of Tajikistan, who had been removed from office following a corruption scandal in 1985, began to endorse some opposition demands in exchange for support against Mahkamov. At the end of August, Mahkamov was forced to resign after the Supreme Soviet voted no confidence in him, and Kadriddin Aslonov, a Gharmi, became chairman. In September 1991, Tajikistan declared its independence, as several other Soviet republics had done, and it was expected that a new Union Treaty would be signed that would give more real power to the republics. In Tajikistan, there was no real desire to leave the Union, but the Tajiks did not want Moscow to interfere with their internal politics. In November 1991, presidential elections took place in Tajikistan. Then, in December 1991, the Soviet Union was suddenly dissolved.

The presidential elections split the country into supporters of Rahmon Nabiev (a northerner) and opposition candidate Davlat Khudonazarov (from Gorno-Badakhshan in the east), backed by the IRP and the Democratic Party. Nabiev won the elections, though the opposition refused to accept the result, and a government was formed that was dominated by representatives of the northern Soughd and southern Kulyabi regions, to the exclusion of others. Half-hearted attempts to form a government of national reconciliation yielded little result, but led to a tense standoff between pro-government and opposition supporters in Dushanbe in the spring of 1992. Both sides were arming themselves, but Nabiev reportedly refused to open fire to disperse the opposition.[9]

Violence did erupt in May 1992, with the pro-government and opposition sides quickly mobilizing supporters from their respective regions and forming rogue armies. The opposition forces seized most of the capital and forced President Nabiev to resign at gunpoint. Fierce fighting erupted in the south between Kulyabi (pro-government) and Kurgan-Tyube (opposition) forces. The situation was complicated by the fact that ethnic Uzbeks in the Kurgan-Tyube area sided with the government. An estimated 700,000 refugees fled across the border to Afghanistan.

A relatively unknown Emomali Rahmon[10] was elected president at an extraordinary session of the Supreme Soviet in November 1991 that was dominated by northerners and Kulyabis. Since his election, he has demonstrated personal courage, survived several assassination attempts, and mastered the art of politics, surprising his opponents. The new government disbanded the Kulyab and Kurgan-Tyube provinces and appealed to Russia to intervene to restore peace. Russian (formerly Soviet) forces, including the 201st Motor Rifle Division of the Ministry of Defense and the Border Troops, were then stationed in Tajikistan. Throughout most of 1992, the 201st Division remained broadly neutral.[11] A formal Commonwealth of Independent States (CIS) peacekeeping operation involving contingents from Russia, Uzbekistan, Kazakhstan, and Kyrgyzstan was created in September 1993. Uzbekistan closed its borders to fleeing refugees, even though many were their own ethnic kin, and it is believed in Tajikistan that Uzbekistan's warplanes bombed opposition strongholds, causing civilian deaths.

The opposition, having suffered a defeat in the lowlands, held positions in its mountain-area strongholds. Its command structure, dominated by Islamic forces, fled to Afghanistan and employed guerrilla tactics from across the border. More moderate political figures found refuge in Tehran and Moscow. In July 1995, the various groups forming the opposition created the United Tajik Opposition (UTO), headed by Sayed Abdullo Nuri, an Islamist.

Taliban advances in the mid-1990s made a contribution to the Tajiks' willingness to negotiate, since both sides became frightened at the prospect of being steamrollered by the advancing Pushtun Islamist warriors. The desire for Tajikistan to emerge as an independent and integrated country was the ultimate value that united the warring factions. The Taliban pressure also indirectly increased Russia's commitment to the ethnic Tajiks in Afghanistan, as Moscow regarded this group as the only buffer between the CIS borders and the advancing Taliban.

United Nations (UN) involvement in conflict management in Tajikistan started in 1993 with the appointment of the UN Secretary-General special envoy Ismat Kittani. Then, in April 1994, official negotiations were launched in Moscow.[12] Russia and Iran participated as observers and played important roles at critical junctures by persuading their allies to compromise. Eight rounds of negotiations were conducted. In December 1994, the UN Mission of Observers to Tajikistan (UNMOT) was established to monitor the implementation of a cease-fire. In June 1997, the General Agreement on the Establishment of Peace and National Accord in Tajikistan was signed, formally ending the civil war. The agreement provided for 30 percent UTO representation in government executive bodies, the safe return of refugees, the disarmament and reintegration of opposition forces into government power structures, constitutional and electoral amendments, the adoption of an amnesty law for those who took part in the civil war between 1992 and 1997, and government reform. The Commission on National Reconciliation was the chief mechanism for implementing the agreement.

The parties have largely adhered to the provisions of the agreement. Before the next election, the opposition was incorporated into the government according to an agreed-upon quota. When in government, however, opposition politicians started to capitalize on the lucrative opportunities offered by the positions they acquired and began to compromise their ideological credentials, which weakened their appeal among their former constituents. At the time, the opposition had a real chance to make a decisive impact on Tajikistan's postwar development, but this opportunity was squandered.

Gradually, most power gravitated to Kulyabis, while northerners and the Uzbeks who supported the government received few tangible benefits. The UN and Russia effectively endorsed the deal, notwithstanding the exclusion of sizable constituencies.[13] The northerners' loss of power and influence was not without consequence. Following the defeat of a northern candidate in a presidential race in November 1994, tensions in the north mounted. A series of violent episodes erupted in 1996–97 in the Khujand region and culminated in 1998 in the armed seizure of Khujand, Tajikistan's second-largest city, by the rebel colonel Mahmud Khudaiberdiev, who attacked from Uzbekistan. This armed violence presented a serious military challenge for the government. The attack was repelled, but fear of Khudaiberdiev's forces, believed to be in hiding in Uzbekistan, persists to this day.[14]

The regional neighborhood continued to present challenges. Tajikistan's relationship with Uzbekistan remained a sore point, as the latter closed and mined its border with Tajikistan, introduced a visa regime for Tajikistan's citizens, and accused Dushanbe of harboring Islamic militants. A sharp increase in drug cultivation in Afghanistan led to rampant trafficking through Tajikistan to the European markets. Some of the former field commanders in the Tajik civil war managed to capitalize on this trade.

At present, the state has reinstated itself and is expanding its power, leaning toward full-scale authoritarianism. President Rahmon can rule legally until 2020 and has won all post-1994 elections without credible challenge. The most lucrative positions in the government and state-related businesses are dominated by the representatives of his native Dangara clan of Kulyab region. The northerners retain largely technical posts. This process of power-grabbing unfolded in the midst of widespread popular passivity, as peace dividends outweighed any desire for demands which may risk violence.[15] War fatigue acted as a powerful brake on further protest, however legitimate grievances might be. Thus, provision of security became a trump card of the ruling Kulyabi establishment and of the president himself.

Nature of the Intervention: Inter-Tajik Dialogue

Initiating the Process

The Inter-Tajik Dialogue process emerged from the Dartmouth Conference, a bilateral US-Soviet dialogue on an expert level that dates back to 1960. Within the framework of the Dartmouth Conference, the Regional Conflicts Task Force was formed in 1982 to probe into the dynamics of US-Soviet interaction in such regional conflicts as Southern Africa and the Middle East. With the dissolution of the Soviet Union in the early 1990s, the successor Russian–US task force set two goals: (1) to conceptualize the process of dialogue which it had developed through the 1980s and (2) to apply this process to one of the conflicts that had broken out following the Soviet collapse. The task force selected Tajikistan because of three factors:

- The dangers of the civil war in Tajikistan spilling over to the wider region of Afghanistan and Central Asia;
- The lack of international attention to the conflict and the lack of informal diplomatic initiatives; and
- The considerable regional expertise of the Russian members of the task force, and the good personal relationships they enjoyed with significant citizens of Tajikistan.

The facilitators' team included three American and three Russian members. One US team member, Ambassador Harold Saunders, was a former senior member of the US diplomatic service with considerable negotiating experience in the Middle East and other areas of conflict. The Russian members were senior academics from the Institute of Oriental Studies of the Russian Academy of Sciences. The joint team brought together different assets: vast experience in negotiation and conflict resolution processes on the one hand and in-depth expertise of the region on the other.

The process began in 1993 with the visit of two Russian team members to Dushanbe to negotiate the dialogue initiative with the government side. They met with the Foreign Minister Andrei Kozyrev and secured the necessary approval of Emomali Rahmon, then the chairman of the Supreme Soviet (at the time, the highest executive in the country and a would-be president). Some participants from the government side were recommended. It was far more difficult to find and secure participation of members from the opposition side, as many were in hiding or in exile. Some of these opposition participants lived in fear for their own security if they admitted that they were in contact with opposition forces and were seen as still engaged in fighting. At one point, the Russian team was shot at in Dushanbe.

The first meeting took place in Moscow in March 1993 when seven participants sat together at a negotiating table. Meetings were held in March, May, August, and October of 1993. The facilitators intended to conduct dialogue meetings every two to three months during the most acute stage of the peace process, and later at six-month intervals. The meetings were held mainly in Moscow and in St. Petersburg, but were relocated to Dushanbe in 1996 when the security situation permitted. A combined group from the Kettering Foundation and the University of Nebraska at Omaha visited the Dushanbe area in May-June 1994. A number of participants also benefited from traveling to the United States, using opportunities created by the members of the US team.

Participants

When the idea of the ITD was conceived, its intent was to see whether a group could be formed from within the conflict to design strategies for its resolution. In other words, the initiators did not seek to convene people for peace negotiations—at that stage, it was unknown whether a peaceful resolution was possible—but rather invited them into their own space to talk about the conflict.[16] The selection of participants was handled by the Russian team members, who took advantage of their large network of contacts.

About a hundred prospective participants were interviewed, and the facilitators explained the essence of the Dartmouth Conference and the function of the Task Force, including its role during the Cold War era in building a relationship between American and Soviet citizens. Out of the hundred prospective participants, about ten were initially selected; a sizable number of those who had been approached declined on the grounds that the enterprise seemed too risky. Understandably, in the initial stage the participants frequently rotated in and out of the dialogue, until a group of five or six committed people crystallized.

As the old Soviet state had collapsed and the new state of Tajikistan was yet to emerge, there is little point in identifying participants according to the positions they held at the time. They were representatives of the intelligentsia with some political credentials of their own and access to the decision-making level, but were not decision-makers themselves. In their professional backgrounds, they were lawyers, academics, teachers, and administrators. Some later went on to take up political appointments. Several participants were involved in the delegations at the official talks, and a few received government positions under the power-sharing agreement. Overall, throughout the 1990s the distance between a ruling elite and the ordinary people was not so great. The old Soviet, largely northern elite had been pushed out of power, the new one was only emerging, and Russians and other Europeans had for the most part departed. Everybody suffered equally from the devastation of the civil war. The president himself was a former head of a state farm from a poor and little-known area.

Between thirty-five and forty people in total participated in the dialogue; about seventeen became "regulars" and eventually formed a core group. At first, the sides themselves were not completely aware who they would encounter at the meetings, and delegations had no right of veto over the composition of the other group.[17] Since the engagement was risky, participation required courage, and many who were selected were too frightened to attend or tried to back out at the last moment. (The Russian team members, when interviewed in Moscow in May 2006, recalled an occasion when one participant—a leader of one of the opposition parties—had to be "actively encouraged" to board a plane to Moscow.)

Participants were selected from intellectual and expert communities, and some had direct access to power-holders but were not executives. In practice, some of the participants had frequently changed jobs, as several had held government posts at one time or another. A few participants from each side were included in their respective delegations at the UN negotiations. One critical remark expressed was that the dialogue did not involve representatives of the military.[18] The participants were almost all ethnic Tajiks with origins from different regions of the country. However, although there were northerners among the group, they did not represent the political interests of the north. Although particular effort was made to involve representatives of the pro-government and opposition camps, several participants were not affiliated with either side; these included a prominent representative of the Uzbek community and several civil society members. Some were well-known public figures in their own right—academics, lawyers, and a renowned constitutional expert—with ties to wider society. This ingredient was important, as at times these neutral figures provided unbiased input and could draw attention to issues such as minority rights that the pro-government and opposition participants were not eager to discuss.

The main challenge in engaging with the opposition side arose from its very nature, as the opposition presented an uneasy mix of Democrats and Islamists. The latter had fighters, weapons, and money, and were leading the war on the pro-government forces. The key Islamist figures stayed in Afghanistan, from where attacks on government positions were organized. Some of the more moderate Islamic and Democratic figures were living in Iran, while the Democrats and intellectuals were mainly living in exile in Moscow. At the time, the Islamists' main problem was that they did not have people of appropriate caliber in their ranks who could articulate political positions and engage in negotiations with the opposite side. Thus, they needed the Democrats to be their voice. At first, mainly Democrats (Gharmis from the Moscow diaspora) were represented, but moderate Islamic figures also joined later. Still, as some participants noted, the "real bearded Islamists"—hard-line radicals and spoilers of the peace process—were not included. However, those Islamists who took part in the dialogue process maintained contact with the Islamist leadership in exile in Afghanistan, who in turn worked with their hard-liners.

From the outset, the participants did not have specific objectives for participating in the dialogue and were not sure what to expect, given that the war was still being waged and an interactive peace dialogue was a novel experience. Consequently, the personalities of the facilitators played an important role in getting the process off the ground. The principal shared aspiration of the participants was to end violence, but they had little idea of how that could be done, since the shock of ongoing violence and the atrocities committed had made political discourse difficult. As President Emomali

Rahmon stated in 1993, "We cannot negotiate with people with blood on their hands."[19] When the official negotiations started in April 1994 and the situation became clearer, participants sought to use the dialogue meetings to find out about each other's positions, to learn and practice negotiation skills, and to explore points of prospective agreement in order to be better prepared for the official talks.

The participants formulated shared objectives gradually, as the dialogue progressed through the following three stages:

- To start negotiations between the government and the opposition so that the refugees can go back home.
- To develop a political process of reconciliation and create a Commission for National Reconciliation under the authority of the Peace Agreement.
- To identify the obstacles to democracy and ways of overcoming them—that is, to make democracy in Tajikistan work.

At the early stages of the dialogue, the moderators had to deal with the "reentry" problem—how the participants would be treated upon their return to their own constituency after talking to the other side. The problem was more acute for the people from the opposition side who were based in Tajikistan: two participants from the opposition were unable to return to their homes for two years, since they learned that they were on a hit list. After the peace agreement was signed in June 1997, four dialogue participants became members of the Commission on National Reconciliation and some were given government positions, including opposition participant Abdunabi Sattarzoda, who became deputy foreign minister. This development presented a dilemma for the dialogue: which side did the former opposition-turned-government figures represent, and how they should be identified after they received posts in the government?

Altogether, thirty-five rounds of dialogue were held. The initial meetings were held in Moscow at the Institute of Oriental Studies, and participants stayed in town in different locations. They thus stayed with their own groups, and there was little social mixing. The organizers, mindful of the danger that the group would split into two camps, made efforts to promote interaction. The meetings were moved to venues outside Moscow and St. Petersburg where people had no choice but to start to engage with each other. Now, the former participants fondly recall the ideological battles they fought over dinner encounters that at times lasted until the early hours of the morning.

Methodology

The dialogue used the methodology developed by the task force[20] that reflected ten years of conceptualizing and experimenting by the US-Soviet team. The ITD was the first test of the methodology. It consisted of the following five conceptual stages, although in practice the second and third stages merged:

1. *Deciding to engage.* This stage involved exploring openness to talk across the lines of conflict, deciding whether to use a third party, obtaining political permission or support among contending politicians for informal talks, finding dialogue partners, and defining the projected agenda. The initiators' primary purpose was to "see whether a group can be formed from within the civil conflict to design a peace process for their own country."[21]

2. *Exploring the conflict and issues together.* This stage involved developing the ability to think and talk in an analytical manner—through ground rules, time limits, curbs on posturing and speechmaking, and agreement on the characteristics of civil discourse—about the dynamics of relationships in the conflict (including problems, capacities, and potentials), and developing strategies for organizing the discussion of issues.

3. *Talking and listening more deeply together.* This stage involved learning to explain perspectives; questioning assumptions; acknowledging motivations, needs, and fears; probing concrete problems in depth; working to address the underlying emotional agenda within all discussions of substantive issues; and maintaining an ongoing civil dialogue where people can make substantive progress and practice procedural skills.

4. *Thinking together and experiencing the relationship.* This stage involved transforming the dialogue group into a microcosm of the national relationship that would be required to move problems to resolution, developing scenarios that described how current problems might unfold and impact various actors, developing a political scenario of steps to move the situation toward a conclusion, and exploring these

scenarios together to build an attitude of "what we can do" rather than "what you must do."

5. *Acting together.* This final stage involved developing strategies and actions that would have concrete impacts on the situation and course of events, exploring potential governmental and nongovernmental strategies, and taking individual and joint action.

Format

Initially, the dialogue explored the general political vision: "What kind of country are we seeking to build?" This approach was stimulating for the participants, but at the same time it risked making the debate too open-ended. With some direction from the facilitators, it was decided to concentrate on some concrete issues at hand, such as the return of refugees and internally displaced persons.

The meetings lasted for three days. Gradually, a dialogue structure emerged. First, participants spoke about the developments since the previous meeting. This allowed them to let off some steam and identify the key challenges of the moment. Facilitators would then distill the two or three most important issues out of what had been said, and ask the group whether it agreed that these should be discussed. The participants would thus decide the agenda for each meeting, although the facilitators suggested ideas that they had prepared beforehand. Some participants observed that it seemed odd not to begin with a clearly defined agenda, and newcomers to the group were puzzled and initially requested an agenda. However, the participants came to appreciate such a creative method of working and easily entered into its spirit. The use of such a methodology requires great skill and close rapport between the facilitators and the participants; such an approach is not easily replicable, and it is extremely hard to train others to work in the same fashion.

Toward the end of the second day, a small group of participants, typically including both pro-government and opposition representatives and a neutral intellectual, would jointly prepare a "memorandum"—a summary of the main conclusions and recommendations of the meeting—to be shared with the decision-makers. Such documents started to be written from the sixth meeting in March 1994, at first at the initiative of the facilitating team, which helped to identify the themes and posed relevant questions. Time was allowed for individual participants to comment on the draft, after which there would be a group discussion on the memo. The facilitators did not provide guidance on the substantive content of the memorandum, but when the participants were deadlocked, the facilitators would offer an example from a conflict elsewhere or give an illustration designed to encourage the participants to think outside the box.

Outreach

The memoranda that the participants produced were shared with the government and opposition leaderships in Tajikistan. Initially, the documents had limited distribution and were not shared with the wider public. After the peace agreement was signed, greater efforts were made to publicize the content of discussions through academic publications, in analytical journalism and in university courses. The memoranda were also shared with the US and Russian governments, the UN special envoy, and the Vienna and Warsaw offices of the Conference on Security and Co-operation in Europe (later the Organization for Security and Co-operation in Europe, OSCE). During Dialogue 19, in May 1997, the participants decided to publish a number of their memoranda in Tajik, Russian, and English, with an introduction telling about the history of the dialogue.[22]

The dialogue also kept the international community informed about the situation in Tajikistan and the peace process in order to generate increased international engagement. For example, the eighth round of the dialogue in June 1994 took place in the United States (Washington and New York) and the group of Tajikistanis held a session at the United States Institute of Peace. Throughout the following decade, Harold Saunders and Randa Slim made great efforts to publicize the ITD in numerous publications. In addition to the UN, the dialogue cooperated positively with the OSCE representatives who were monitoring Tajikistan's 1999 presidential and 2000 parliamentary elections.

Capacity-Building in Civil Society

From the onset, the ITD made deliberate efforts outside of its meetings to build the capacity of Tajikistan's intellectuals and nongovernmental organizations (NGOs). The management team built into its program budget funds to develop the capacity of individuals to work at NGOs and universities. To name a few of these efforts, in 1995 and 1997 the Kettering Foundation in Washington, DC, brought two associates of the Tajikistan Center for Civic Education as international fellows to study at the foundation. In 1999, the University of Nebraska at Omaha established a program of cooperation with the Technological University of Tajikistan, and hosted two Tajikistani groups of fifteen participants each for courses on public administration, civil society, and conflict resolution.

In 1995, the US part of the team was approached by the academics among the dialogue participants with a request to help to develop courses in conflict resolution. For a year, after each meeting of the dialogue, separate sessions were organized for interested participants to review the range of subjects to be covered and to compile a reading list. Some key texts were translated into Russian and Tajik. A five-day workshop with a wider group of academics (only a few of whom were ITD participants) was held on the topic of conflict resolution and building civil society. These efforts resulted in a collaborative program with Tajikistan's Ministry of Education to design a curriculum for an undergraduate-level course in conflict and peace studies as part of a larger politics course, and to train twenty-four university lecturers from eight universities across the country to present such a course.

The dialogue had no formal end, but gradually started to scale down after the 2000 parliamentary elections. The Russian members of the facilitating team became less engaged after 2001. At this stage, the second track of the intervention strategy—development of civil society—became more prominent. One of the aims of this strategy was to establish boundary-spanning organizations.

Impacts of the Intervention

Overall, the ITD had significant positive direct effects on cross-lines communication, on the attitude and behavior of the participants, on the process of conflict resolution, and on the political channels that emerged to influence this process. It also had an indirect impact on the sources of conflict and the mechanisms for postwar transition. It is always difficult to prove beyond any doubt the impacts of "process" interventions, but there is evidence that directly links the interactive process of the dialogue with wider political developments in Tajikistan.

On Cross-Lines Communication

Most fundamentally, the ITD performed a convening function at a time when such discussion fora did not exist. The intervention opened the first channel of communication through which the parties to the conflict could come together for a meaningful exchange. Its most crucial period was its initial stage in 1993–94, when, in the absence of other initiatives or projects, it established a link between the two sides. Before this, the sides used to learn about positions of each other through the foreign, mainly Russian, media. The dialogue was a catalyst for a process of engagement which otherwise would have taken a long time to develop and perhaps would not have happened in quite the same form.

On Participant Attitudes and Behavior

Changes in the participants' attitudes and behavior were a clear achievement of the dialogue. Slim and Saunders describe three type of impacts: analytical, substantive, and informational.[23] The section below offers a slightly different breakdown of these impacts.

Some participants observed that the dialogue provided stress relief for them. They could share their thoughts and grievances in a kind of group therapy process, and felt better afterward, even if they could not see progress in their real lives. In the words of one participant, who had suffered from restrictions on free speech in the mid-2000s: "If I come to a dialogue meeting and get a load off my chest, I will not have a heart attack later."

More significantly, from its outset the ITD created a sense that a negotiated peace settlement was possible despite ongoing severe violence. Reflecting now on the value of the initiative, participants are unanimous in stressing that it provided inspiration for peace, which in the midst of the conflict was difficult to imagine. This was an important spiritual value. Although the participants were not sure what to expect from the process in concrete terms, they were all motivated by the desire to stop the war. Otherwise, the sides would have continued to think exclusively in terms of a military victory. The dialogue conveyed hope even in the worst period of 1993–94, when reports of government troops killing civilians in pro-opposition areas became public.

In addition, there was a significant change in dialogue participants' attitudes toward and tolerance of each other. Initially, personal resentment was considerable; several participants could barely stand one another. At times, the exchanges became personal and emotional. One long-standing participant confessed that during the initial rounds, he hated the other side so much that he wished he had a Kalashnikov machine gun with him; eventually, he came to see his former adversaries as friends and colleagues. Participants learned to respect one another, to be tolerant of the opinions of others, and to present their views in concise and acceptable ways. A few participants noted that at first it was difficult for them to listen to their leaders being criticized by the other side and they therefore reacted emotionally. Later, they became accustomed to such criticism and could react more calmly. One participant (then an adviser to the president) noted that it was hard for him not to react against the "in your face" criticism of the president, but eventually he managed to keep his feelings under control.

The participants learned new debate, problem-solving, and consensus-building skills. Those who were involved in drafting memoranda noted that the process was challenging, but was a great learning experience. In the subsequent dialogues implemented by others, there was a marked difference in the behavior of those participants who were ITD alumni, compared to the newcomers, who tended to be more radical and intolerant in their expression.[24] Participants who were included in both the dialogue and the official talks came away with insights into the interaction between the official and nonofficial spheres, helping to reduce the gap between the government and the public.

Although training was not a stand-alone component in the dialogue, it was provided to the opposition side at its request. When the formal talks started in April 1994, the opposition participants realized that they had few skills for articulating their positions or conducting negotiation, which put them at a disadvantage compared to the pro-government side, and they requested training to improve their capabilities. This kind of training has not been standard fare in many peace interventions, and as a supplementary effort it may be better described as "coaching" rather than "training." (The moderators offered the same opportunity to the pro-government side, but the offer was declined.) Later, this type of training was also extended to participants who initiated their own dialogue interventions. However, the moderators have noted that only about two out of ten dialogue initiators became accomplished facilitators. Moreover, when some of the participants facilitated their own "dialogues" in followup projects to the ITD, they have found it difficult to replicate the facilitation method used by the US-Russian team. Based on the interviews conducted, the methods used by facilitators from Tajikistan tend to be more directive; the chairs express their own opinions—sometimes quite strongly—and discourage expression of uncomfortable views, and facilitators are not sure how to get around difficult issues. In addition, the drafting of memoranda is no longer practiced.

On the whole, it may be feasible to develop analytical skills and introduce new debate and consensus-building techniques to dialogue participants, but it is difficult for people who have fixed views and have represented sides to a conflict to switch to the mentality and attitude of a neutral third party. Participants have their own dearly held convictions. This was not a problem and rather an advantage during the main dialogue, but it became a liability when these participants tried to become moderators.[25]

Over time, the core participants developed a sense of group identity, fostering a shared, coherent outlook. Even though they represented opposite sides and initially had been virtually unable to talk and listen to each other—let alone extend an invitation to the other side to begin negotiations—the participants started to act as a group and acquired a sense of confidence in each other, to the extent that they were able to develop joint political statements. After the official negotiations started, the group began to feel a collective ownership of "their" process. One dramatic manifestation of this evolution was that the participants who had access to the power holders took joint responsibility to ensure that the conclusions and recommendations of the dialogue meetings would reach their target audience. The group identity was further strengthened when some participants from the opposition side, whom others had come to know and respect as human beings, faced threats and were fired from their jobs. An indication of the increasingly strong group identity took place at the May 1996 meeting in Tajikistan, when the participants publicly presented themselves as a group. On the personal level, the dialogue had an emboldening effect, for the participants from both sides had to take risky steps together, such as signing an agreed memorandum that would be shared with their respective leaderships.

The participants' common work led them to build relationships that have survived to the present day. In one outstanding example, the two persons responsible for drafting memoranda from the pro-government and the opposition sides achieved a strong bond as they went about securing agreement on their drafts with each participant individually and then with the group as a whole. Their relationship remains close, as both used to work in the same research institute following their retirement from government jobs.[26]

In sum, relationship-building was one of the dialogue's major achievements. It may have been healthy that the debate was so heated at the beginning and that it was so difficult for the participants to contain their emotions.[27] These initial difficulties had a cathartic effect. The intensity of the dialogue also indicated the seriousness of the stakes involved and the depth of the participants' feelings about the issues they were tackling.[28]

On the Official Negotiations of the Conflict

The ITD preceded the UN-chaired negotiations by more than a year; six dialogue meetings occurred before the start of the official talks. When the formal peace talks began in April 1994, the moderating team was mindful of the danger of mounting conflicting initiatives and sought to create synergy with the official process. Thus, the moderators defined the objective of their dialogue initiative as designing a political process of national reconciliation for the country. The dialogue then helped to advance the official negotiations in several specific ways.

From the outset, the participants' own solidarity helped to build trust between the parties to the conflict. Initially, their relationships were characterized by deep mistrust on both practical and deeper existential levels. Even when participants could agree in principle on the acceptability of certain measures, such as disarmament, a great deal of suspicion still prevailed that the other side might not stick to its commitments. On a wider political scale, there was a tendency to deny the opposition legitimacy and to question its very existence. Dealing with such mistrust occupied much time. However, gradually the participants came to terms with the presence of the other side and came to acknowledge that their adversaries could not simply be expelled for "bad behavior" but would remain a part of the same country. This meant that an acceptable relationship needed to be restored.

By facilitating a rapprochement between the elite representatives of the two sides, the dialogue slowly started to generate the necessary trust that enabled the negotiators to begin to communicate with their respective hard-liners. The initial mistrust had been extreme. The opposition negotiators at first viewed the government side as incapable of implementing any agreement, and when the opposition wanted to talk about power-sharing, the government interpreted this topic as part of an attempt of the opposition to unseat it. The opposition made a concession of agreeing to work within the present governmental framework for the time being. Therefore, a less charged subject—the return of refugees—was introduced and agreed upon, and a degree of confidence was built around it. From this point, the sides could move step by step toward more sensitive issues, such as power-sharing.

Another contribution that the dialogue made to the negotiations was to bring to the surface the issues at stake in the conflict. At the beginning, both sides felt an enormous need to be heard and to be able to express grievances, and the ITD provided an opportunity to do so. It brought into the debate a number of unflattering facts and developments that the two sides were reluctant to admit and discuss openly.[29] For instance, at the beginning of the dialogue, the opposition sought to focus attention on the plight of refugees (claimed as between 700,000 and 1.5 million) and the absence of security guarantees for their return. The government side initially was reluctant to take up this subject, arguing that the real number of refugees was actually much smaller and that those who really wanted to return had already done so. The government's general attitude was an extreme unwillingness to discuss political and power-sharing questions with the opposition, whom it regarded as "bandits with arms in blood up to the elbow."[30] The dialogue process enabled the opposition to express its political agenda in a way that would be heard.

Indeed, the dialogue also was a catalyst for organizing the opposition. Its impact may in fact have been greater on the opposition side, as it helped the opposition put its own house in order so as to be better able to contribute to the resolution of the conflict. One of the reasons the government side had given for its prior failure to negotiate with the opposition was that it was unclear who would be able to speak on behalf of various forces contesting the government. This was an early theme in the ITD discourse. For example, at the fourth meeting in October 1993, when the participants discussed how to start a negotiation, they stumbled over the dilemma of who would represent an ideologically diverse, geographically dispersed opposition. The government maintained that it could not possibly negotiate with each field commander individually, nor could it comprehend the opposition's political demands beyond its general claim that the government was illegitimate. President Rahmon was under pressure from his own hard-liners, who maintained that the opposition consisted only of field commanders with no political agenda and no opinions that merited serious discussion.

Engagement in the dialogue demonstrated to the opposition that without a coherent political organization, the government would not take it seriously as a negotiating partner. Initially, the dialogue promoted internal debate within opposition circles on what it was seeking to achieve and how this could be accomplished. Starting in 1994, the Democrats started to influence the Islamists, as the Islamists' standing was boosted through their participation in the dialogue. Despite practical difficulties, the opposition participants communicated messages from the dialogue to the Islamist leadership based in Afghanistan and in Tehran. Within two months of the fourth meeting in October 1993, the leaders of different opposition factions had met in Tehran, developed a common platform, and formed the Moscow-based Coordination Center of Democratic Forces of Tajikistan in the CIS. Two ITD participants signed the document that established the Coordination Center, and four became members of the center's steering committee. After the meeting in Tehran, a Coordination Center based in Moscow was established. Shuttle diplomacy began in 1994 when emissaries from the opposition in Afghanistan and Iran began to frequent Moscow. (Some of these emissaries were visiting Moscow for medical treatment and for a break from the war.) At the fifth meeting in January 1994, participants from the opposition groups presented this new common platform, which was to become the basis for the UTO alliance. The dialogue also helped the opposition groups to start formulating their positions for the negotiations. This assistance contributed greatly to the government's decision to open formal talks with the opposition.[31] The dialogue helped to convey a message to the highest level of Tajikistan's government that important changes on the opposition side had now made engagement feasible.

The ITD also acted as an informal channel for the opposition leadership to test ideas and convey messages to the government. Gradually, the Islamist leadership started to use the channel of the dialogue to formulate its own positions, to test the government's receptivity to its ideas ("if we suggest so and so, what would your reaction be?"),[32] and to pass on messages and signals to the government. One such idea, for instance, was the creation of a State Council, adopted by the opposition at a meeting in Tehran in December 1993. During the fifth dialogue meeting, in January 1994, the government participants scrutinized at length the opposition's proposals to negotiate and its newly established unity. When the opposition participants provided satisfactory answers, a pro-government participant concluded that the proposals were acceptable as a starting point and a basis for negotiations.

As a result, the dialogue enabled the opposition to consolidate its political demands, such as power-sharing and the return of refugees, and provided arguments for those on the pro-government side who supported the idea of negotiations, which elevated the quality of the political debate. A participant in both the dialogue and the official negotiations noted that the intellectual quality of the ITD meetings was superior to that of the official negotiations, although the latter carried a greater sense of completion and the finality of the negotiations.

On the whole, the ITD not only enabled the official talks to move forward but also expedited their consideration of difficult issues. It did not take the place of the formal talks, but rather made the formal process more productive, more efficient, and less frustrating. The sides came to the negotiating table more politically and psychologically prepared. Crucial questions such as "what is the purpose of the negotiations?" and "where should we start?" already had been debated.[33] The meetings provided an opportunity to debate the contentious issues in depth and to explore varied options, obstacles, and perspectives. In this way, the participants developed a clearer view of how to formulate their positions and what they could realistically expect from the opposite side.

The ITD deliberately took up difficult issues that had caused deep mistrust between the parties and had brought the negotiations to an impasse. Observing the course of the official talks, participants concentrated on identifying particular obstacles. For example, the debate after the seventh meeting in 1994 revolved around how to design a process of national reconciliation, and resulted in agreement on a "step-by-step approach" and a "transition period," as the participants later described. In their memorandum of the sixteenth round in May 1996, the participants stated that "the primary obstacle to peace in Tajikistan is the absence of an adequate understanding on sharing power among the regions, political parties and movements, and nationalities in Tajikistan."[34]

The dialogue also helped to make the negotiations more efficient by formulating certain specific political ideas and designs and preparing concrete recommendations for decision-makers. An essential part of the dialogue involved the drafting of memoranda with recommendations to the leadership groups. The memoranda not only crystallized the issues and challenges, but also presented possible paths forward that could be conveyed to the decision-makers. For example, the first memorandum recommended the creation of four working groups for the negotiating process to start dealing with issues such as refugee return, political change, disarmament, and economic regeneration. The closest presidential adviser, Saidmurad Fattoyev, confirmed to one participant that President Rahmon read the memoranda and took them seriously. The then chairman of the Democratic Party and a ITD participant recalled that IRP leaders Ali Akbar Turanjonzoda and Sayed Abdullo Nuri read and debated the memoranda, and discussed them over the phone with other opposition Islamist and Democratic members scattered in different countries.

A number of important proposals elaborated through the dialogue were subsequently adopted at the official negotiations and found their way into the final peace settlement. Although some of these were modified, the spirit remained unchanged. President Rahmon discussed with his entourage many of the issues raised in the memoranda, and some ideas from the dialogue were included in his presidential speeches, since a few dialogue participants served him as advisers. The most notable idea accepted was for a Coordination Council for National Reconciliation, which, after the signing of the Peace Agreement in June 1997, came into being as a Commission on National Reconciliation (CNR).

The commission was created through a series of ITD-related events. In June 1995, the dialogue considered a proposal from UTO supporters for a supragovernmental coordination council that would be responsible for implementing agreements. The memorandum was adopted, and recommended that the council be positioned under the authority of the negotiating parties to address the government's concern that the council would have greater authority than the government. The memorandum described the need for the council "to develop broad participation in the functioning of the political system and the affairs of the civil society on the basis of ensuring equal participation in power among all regions, political parties and movements, and national communities."[35] The CNR later became a mechanism similar to the Council model developed in the dialogue. Moreover, the commission organized its work through four subcommissions, echoing the model proposed in the first ITD memorandum in 1994. The proposed subcommissions were on public security and refugee return, constitution and political reform, political process and national reconciliation, and economic rehabilitation and development. The idea originated with the opposition participants, was shaped by the moderating team, and found its way into a joint memorandum.

Another, more traditional initiative was to create a consultative council of citizens to convey the voices from society to the president and the members of Parliament. The idea of a Consultative Forum of the Peoples of Tajikistan was discussed, adopted in a memorandum, and proposed to the government and the opposition leaderships. In July 1995, Emomali Rahmon and Sayed Abdullo Nuri instructed their respective negotiating teams to establish such a consultative forum, while the UN envoy incorporated that agreement in a protocol signed by the two leaders. In the end, the forum was not established in that exact form, but it provided impetus to other smaller-scale initiatives with a similar spirit.

The dialogue also introduced to Tajikistan the critical concept of power-sharing and the related notions of compromise, alliance-building, and coalition forming. These discussions took place at the ninth and tenth meetings, when the participants moved backward and forward between the third stage (probing problems and relationships to choose a direction) and fourth stage (scenario-building). Sharp debates took place on the nature and organization of power-sharing, and various options were explored. One option was to divide power equally between the government (who were mainly Kulyabis) and the opposition, as they represented the two warring factions. However, this option was rejected because it was inconceivable that half of the population could be supporting the opposition. A second option was to divide the main share of power between the government and the opposition, and give a smaller share to other forces that were not immediate actors in the civil war, for example, the northern region, minorities, and the capital city of Dushanbe. Various quotas were suggested, for example, that government and opposition would each get 40 percent of the posts, with the remaining 20 percent reserved for these others. Other options were put on the table as well. Overall, the debate over percentages reflected deeper political perspectives on inclusion and exclusion, and how different interests could be accommodated. The peace agreement eventually stipulated a 30 percent quota for the opposition, with the rest to remain in the government's hands.

The dialogue standing as a body whose ideas were respected by key political leaders is suggested by the fact that both President Rahmon and opposition leader Sayed Abdullo Nuri cited the ITD in their respective books, while the then Foreign Minister Talbak Nazarov dedicated a chapter to it in his own book. Ashurboy Imomov, a constitutional expert and one of the intellectual leaders of the dialogue, has authored a few publications on the process, in which he further developed ideas debated during the meetings.[36]

In addition to the dialogue's influence on the macro-political level of the official negotiations, it was able to engage with issues and manifestations of the conflict that transpired at the local level. In July 1996, one dialogue participant became a member of a joint government/opposition commission to negotiate local cease-fires. His involvement in getting the commanders on the ground to talk to each other opened a critical east-west road and demonstrated to the rest of the group the importance of drawing local people directly into the work of the larger peace process. In Dialogue 17 in October 1996, participants came to realize that a multilevel peace process was needed. During one of the meetings, a participant from the government side tried to initiate contacts between the field commanders in the southern Kulyab area and the paramilitaries from the other side who operated in the same territory. He challenged an opposition participant to bring the groups to the table. An intense discussion followed between the two, but in the end a face-to-face meeting between the commanders was deemed too sensitive to organize.

On Postsettlement Policies

Beyond the peace negotiations, the dialogue also contributed to defining Tajikistan's postwar political system. Even as the civil war continued, the sides participated in meetings that began to consider potential postwar design. As early as March 1995, those involved in the dialogue began to discuss the concept of a "transition period." The 1995 parliamentary elections were deeply flawed and unfair to the opposition, which could not compete in them. The danger was that the opposition would react disruptively to such an adverse turn of events. Rather than endorsing the UTO's inclination to overturn the results of the elections that had excluded them, however, the dialogue recommended a process of transition to a more inclusive political system. This concept, included in peace agreements elsewhere, was later incorporated into the June 1997 Peace Agreement to describe the postsettlement phase.

Meanwhile, a political vision for the country started to develop. According to the memorandum from the October 1996 meeting, "Participants believe that one of the main obstacles to peace is lack of a common vision about what kind of country the Tajikistani people want their country to be."[37] This statement gave impetus to thoughts concerning the nature of the country that its citizens would want to emerge after the end of the war. In the postsettlement phase, the dialogue also contributed to the development of political parties. Some of these parties were undergoing revival from the perestroika days, although most were newly established. A number of participants became heavily involved in political party activism (IRP, Social Democrats). Although this activity to an extent proceeds to this day, at present the parties play only a limited role in Tajikistan's increasingly authoritarian state.

The value of the dialogue did not expire with the signing of the 1997 peace agreement. In the postsettlement period, peace remained fragile. Manifestations of conflict, such as the refusal to disarm, hostile actions by rogue field commanders, and retaliation by government troops were still in evidence. There was no certainty about the future; a slide back into violence could not be excluded. In these circumstances, as one observer put it, the dialogue acted "as a holding net" that smoothed the edges, provided a safe place to raise issues, and maintained a sense of hope.

Some observers have argued that when the CNR started to function—from September 1997 to February 2000, when the new Parliament took office—it provided an open space for debate and expression of grievances, so there was less need for the ITD.[38] It seems plausible that the dialogue's relevance as a bipolar structure began to diminish after the peace agreement was signed, especially since the opposition no longer presented an armed force with which to be reckoned. However, as the CNR dealt mainly with the government/opposition dichotomy, other issues of contention tended to be relatively neglected. The value of the dialogue in that period may have been to provide a platform for debating new problems, such as the role of emerging political parties that were not part of the war.

Another opinion is that the dialogue cushioned the northern elite's gradual loss of power and influence. This is based on the fact that at a later stage, the dialogue came to include many representatives of the former intellectual elite, who were overwhelmingly from the north. By participating in the dialogue, they still could retain a sense of participating in the making of history, even though their political standing had greatly diminished. An additional view in Tajikistan is that it was useful to involve the country's intelligentsia in an interactive peace process because of the need that emerged later for somebody to explain to ordinary people the causes, events, and outcomes of the civil war. The participants' function in this area is unclear, however, as discussion of the recent past is increasingly a prohibited subject; the government does not encourage such discussion, and society does not know how to handle such sensitive topics. The political history of Tajikistan is being rewritten, and its interpretation is still evolving as a by-product of the unfolding political process.

On Fostering Public Political Space

More broadly, through its various contributions to the peace process over the years, the ITD also contributed significantly to the formation of a self-conscious postindependence political elite in Tajikistan, what Harold Saunders calls "a mind at work in the midst of a country making itself."[39] In addition to concentrating on the government/opposition divide, the dialogue acted as a school for Tajikistan's political class as a whole. Its intellectually stimulating meetings strengthened the analytical capacities of the participants. In the context of Tajikistan, where for a decade intellectual life had been all but suspended, this was a singular achievement. Although Soviet Tajikistan had had an intellectual elite, in which the northerners and Pamiris were disproportionally represented, a political class outside of the Soviet ruling elite—the nomenklatura—was largely absent. The civil war pushed the Soviet elite out of power, but the new Kulyabi ruling group did not have its own political elite. A number of ITD participants moved into this new elite class, creating an informal nucleus of advisors at the decision-making level. After the June 1997 peace agreement was signed, a number of participants received government posts, such as that of deputy foreign minister or deputy chairman of the main opposition party.

Moreover, the dialogue created a platform for the expression of opinions other than those of the government or opposition. Those who were not involved in the official talks, or did not represent sides and were not actors in the peace process, used the dialogue as an opportunity to make their views heard. This became especially important following the peace agreement as authoritarian tendencies in the state gained momentum. For example, a Congress of People's Unity of Tajikistan found its audience there and was able to express its views freely.[40] The ITD also gave impetus to other dialogue interventions by different international actors, such as the UN Tajikistan Office for Peacebuilding (UNTOP) Dialogue Club; a German-Swiss project on "Religion, State and Society," held between 2000 and 2004; and a project on implementing practical confidence-building projects in Tajikistan through a cooperative mechanism within the framework of an Islamic/secular dialogue, facilitated and financed by the Swiss foreign ministry.

The existence of the ITD platform also encouraged the wider civil society in Tajikistan to voice its views. When the peace process was gaining momentum, the participants started to think about how to translate their personal relationships to the wider society. They sought to share their ideas and insights with the general public, as many of them held positions at universities, in the media, and at NGOs. They also saw themselves as representatives of the larger social forces, and worked to ensure that they were bringing the views of the wider society into the dialogue rather than merely expressing their personal perspectives. Thus, in preparation for their dialogue sessions, the participants typically would ask their constituents for their views on current important political, economic, and security problems. This input would then form the basis for discussions on the first day of the dialogue meeting.

Several new organizations were formed from this spillover to civil society. For example, in 1994 an ITD member founded the Tajikistan Center for Civic Education. Another member initiated a research foundation to probe Tajik culture for ideas that would contribute to building a democratic system contextualized in Tajik traditions, and organized a series of educational seminars on the rule of law. When the CNR was drawing to a close, several dialogue members created an organization known as the Public Committee for Promoting Democratic Processes, which was registered as an NGO in February 2000.

The ITD process also gave impetus for additional civil society dialogue projects aimed at creating public spaces to discuss the issues facing Tajikistan and enhancing the culture of political debate. These have been implemented on both national and local levels. A number of former participants from a core group serve on the board of the committee and are actively involved as facilitators and in determining the intellectual content of the new dialogues. The national Intra-Tajik (as opposed to Inter-Tajik) Dialogue, called the Tajikistani National Issues Fora, was established in Dushanbe, while a series of local "Regional Dialogues on Religion, State, and Society" were held in seven different regions of the country. This regional project, which was undertaken from January 1, 2003, to April 30, 2005,established a "sustained dialogue network" of regional fora in Dushanbe, Kulyab, Kurgan-Tyube, Soughd, Panjikent/Aini, Khorough, and Gharm/Nourobod. Two Tajik moderators organized and facilitated each dialogue group, and more than one hundred people participated in this network in different parts of the country.[41]

In summary, the added value of the ITD was not in stopping a civil war, but in the multiple contributions it made toward the conclusion of a peace settlement and the shaping of the postsettlement political process. The cornerstones of the peace agreement—the CNR, the four working subcommittees, and the concepts of power-sharing and of a transition period—had been major elements of several ITD memoranda. If the dialogue had not taken place, it is unclear how long it would have taken before the sides decided to negotiate, how slow and painful the formal talks would have been, how much time would have been wasted, and how the peace agreement would have been designed. The ITD also played a role in political education for a group of people who formed a nucleus for the emerging elite and fostered relationships of trust among key individuals.

Missed Opportunities

Although the ITD and the peace agreement contributed to a successful resolution of the conflict, the ensuing peace has had its flaws. This section explores two adverse tendencies in the postwar period: the situation of the Uzbek minority, who became the net losers in the postwar settlement; and the nature of the authoritarian regime that evolved in the aftermath of the civil war. To the question of whether the dialogue could have influenced these developments, in the case of the Uzbek minority the answer is "yes, maybe," and in the case of the nature of the regime it is "not really."

THE UZBEK ISSUE

The Tajik/Uzbek issue is important in understanding the dynamic of war and peace in Tajikistan, as it reflects a deep-seated divide. The Uzbek minority[42] sided with the government (Kulyabi) side during the war. Given their significant contribution to the military victory, the Uzbeks expected to benefit more and to receive the economic portfolio—their traditional strength—in the new administration. Instead, they received next to nothing. Gradually, ethnic Uzbeks were moved away from positions of political power and influence on all levels. Those who were determined to remain in power were required to Tajikisize their names. Few concessions have been made to the Uzbek language in public,[43] and Uzbek culture is often denied a place in the country (a widespread sentiment is that "Tajikistan is a country of Aryans"). As Tajikistan's relations with Uzbekistan have deteriorated, the loyalty of the Uzbek minority on the border with their kin state has become suspect. Apart from agriculture, Uzbeks currently are engaged mainly in trade, in high-tech businesses such as telecommunications, at international agencies and foreign embassies. The Uzbek community's lack of access to power and resources is becoming a structural factor with future conflict potential.

One ITD participant represented the interests of the Uzbek community, and later became a member of the government negotiating team at the formal talks. He was quite vocal about the plight of his people, but he subsequently left the country and settled in Ukraine. He was replaced by an Uzbek journalist whose style was calmer. Heated debates on power-sharing and the place of the Uzbeks in the political system unfolded in the run-up to the signing of the peace agreement in 1997. Should a share of posts be reserved for the Uzbeks, in the same way that the opposition had received a 30 percent quota? Should special provisions in the Constitution guarantee Uzbek rights and access to power? Yet the ITD participants from both the government and opposition sides were united in rejecting the Uzbek demands, stating that the state should protect the rights of all citizens irrespective of their ethnic origins and should govern in the interests of all. No preferential treatment or affirmative action would be allowed.

A factor that united both the pro-government and opposition forces was their resentment of the Uzbek community and a fear that a state of Tajikistan could become only quasi-independent if it were to be dominated by a heavily Uzbekisized north, with ethnic Uzbeks or Tajiks loyal to Uzbekistan in key positions. It was also feared that Uzbekistan would impose a puppet president in Dushanbe who would take orders from Tashkent. When the opposition realized that the Rahmon government was determined to avoid such a scenario, it became easier to recognize the common goals of a sovereign and united Tajikistan. The road to peace was thereby opened, but at the expense of the Uzbek minority.

The Uzbek issue was one of the substantive issues discussed at the beginning of the ITD, but somehow the subject lost its prominence over time and as other problems came to the top of the political agenda after the peace agreement was signed in 1997. One dialogue discussion that was most relevant to the situation of the Uzbeks took place at the twenty-third dialogue meeting (November 13–15, 1998), in the aftermath of the November revolt in Khujand region led by an armed incursion by Mahmud Khudaiberdiev's troops. This landmark event brought into the limelight the alienation of the north and its marginalized role in the political process. Still, the debate focused more on the northern dimension than on the overall position of the Uzbeks in the country. It identified three issues: (1) how to respond to the north's grievances; (2) how to reform the nominating process so as to be broadly inclusive rather than narrowly exclusive, as it had been in the 1994–95 elections; and (3) how to add the civic or citizens' dimension to the political process. Consequently, the overall group dynamics in the dialogue did not work in the Uzbek participants' favor. As an Uzbek participant would have been one person confronting the whole Tajik group, it was difficult to push issues of Uzbek concern into the debate; consequently, these issues were excluded from the various ITD memoranda.[44]

During the author's field research, a number of former participants were adamant that the Uzbek issues and voices should not have been a subject matter for the dialogue: the process was for the Tajiks and was intended to make peace among them. It would have been counterproductive to dwell upon the Uzbek issue, as it would have deflected energies from the main political questions. However, even though it was natural for Tajik majority participants to feel this way, the content of the debate might have been different if more Uzbeks had been present in the dialogue from the time of the 1997 peace agreement onward.

US co-chair Harold Saunders offers two possible perspectives on how to evaluate the ITD: to consider its contributions to the peace agreement (which, as outlined above, have been considerable) or to look at the ways in which the dialogue transformed the relationship among participants and what it taught them about a long-term peace process. In taking the second perspective, Saunders' own evaluation stresses how participants came to respect those with different views and how they became capable of working effectively together. They also developed the capacity to consider a range of interests beyond their own in designing solutions to the problems they confronted.[45] However, even though this assessment may have been true while the dialogue was active, with the passage of time this judgment must be qualified, as the failure to address the "Uzbek issue" has had serious consequences on Tajikistan's politics and society. It is certainly true that the dialogue contributed to the emergence of a Tajik national identity: destructive regionalism and the lack of sense of a common identity were frequent subjects of discourse during the meetings, and ITD participants clearly emerged with a stronger sense of a Tajik national identity. However, for some this "Tajikness" became the other side of an "anti-Uzbekness." Although the participants are likely to act as a coherent group across the regionalist divide if the old conflict fault lines reemerge, it cannot be taken for granted that they would be able to take other interests into account should new ethnic fault lines appear. For instance, at a discussion held between December 2005 and January 2006 at the Dushanbe meeting of the regional dialogue track organized by the Public Committee for Promoting Democratic Processes, on the subject of "Political Parties in the Parliament," the Social-Democratic Party led by Rahmatullo Zoirov was accused of having a "non-Tajik orientation."[46]

Perhaps at some point after the ITD had achieved its main purpose (from 1997 onward), it could have supplemented the main sessions with regionally focused meetings that would have included representatives from Iran and Uzbekistan. For a small and landlocked country such as Tajikistan, the regional neighborhood is of crucial importance; neighboring countries had played an active role in Tajikistan's civil war. The challenging issue for a regional program would have been the involvement of Uzbekistan, but bringing Iran into the process as well would have softened the edge of the discussion and strengthened the Tajiks' hand, since Iranians and Tajiks are ethnically closely related.

Some former participants note that, in hindsight, a dialogue with academics and the expert community from Uzbekistan may have been helpful. Still, not everyone in Tajikistan would embrace the idea of talking to people from Uzbekistan. According to some ITD participants, a citizen-level dialogue with representatives of Uzbekistan is not possible because there are no unifying political goals for such a dialogue, and the ideologies that have developed on both sides are mutually exclusive. Moreover, in 1998–99, the government of Tajikistan was apprehensive about any contacts on the level of citizens' diplomacy with Uzbekistan. It was alarmed by the cross-border attack of Colonel Khudaiberdiev and expected further hostilities. Thus, government officials expressed no interest in the idea of citizen diplomacy. The ITD heard some thoughts on this issue in 1996 and returned to the subject in 1997–98, but the initiative has not been rigorously pursued.[47]

There are pros and cons involved in taking a regional approach. The drawbacks include a dilution of focus and a divergence from the main conflict issues (which had to do with internal issues and pressures), encouraging the tendency to blame the civil war on outsiders, and the risk of overloading the political system by taking too many challenges simultaneously and addressing none of them properly. However, the regional approach would have benefits as well, as a regional initiative could reduce bilateral sparring and involve a larger group of stakeholders, whose relevance may not have been obvious from the start. In the case of the ITD, a regional initiative would not have substituted for the existing working process, but it could have been a useful supplement, enriching the dialogue once the peace agreement was signed.

AUTHORITARIANISM

In the view of the author, even though the ITD process addressed the subject of Tajikistan's evolving authoritarianism and the underlying causal factors, it could not have made a significant impact on this tendency. After the peace agreement was signed in 1997, ITD participants did consider issues such as the government's failure to fulfill the 30 percent opposition quota and the existence of political prisoners (those opposition supporters who had not been covered by the Amnesty Law and were jailed). Letters to President Rahmon and lists of detainees were put forward, but there was little response.

The problem was rooted in the behavior of members of the opposition leadership group, who became seduced by the lucrative opportunities opened by government jobs. To keep these jobs, they made many concessions to the presidential entourage, and in doing so they seriously compromised their credibility within their own constituencies.[48] The IRP leaders thereby lost the ability to mount any large-scale mobilization and gradually stopped being a force to be taken seriously by their opponents in the government. No longer presenting a collective threat, several former opposition-turned-government figures were gradually sidelined. Those who managed to hold on to official posts came to share the government's position and became its loyalists. Although the Communists, Democrats, and Social Democrats raised concerns about job-buying and about the opposition becoming corrupted, it would have been hard for an interactive intervention facilitated by outsiders to affect the concrete material interests of powerful individuals. The only thing that might have made some difference would have been pressure from the international community, including Russia, on Tajikistan's government to follow agreed-upon political procedures such as fair elections and to be more transparent.

Still, some participants felt that after the peace agreement was signed, the ITD tended to shy away from difficult political issues such as the emerging authoritarianism. Even though some hot topics, such as electoral violations, were raised, they were not included on meeting agendas. Memoranda were drafted so as to be acceptable to officialdom,[49] which led to a degree of self-censorship. Thus, one 2003 letter from the participants to President Rahmon lauded his achievements in the peace process, even though the analytical reports of the meetings (compiled by Harold Saunders) and minutes of the discussions referred to the "negative tendencies" that had started to emerge.

The basic problem was that the participants did not see what they could do about these trends, other than debate them. This may have marked a stage in the ITD when the participants started to move away from directly affecting the political process to serving as less-engaged observers. As time passed, several of the key participants lost their standing and access to the ruling group. The dialogue's impact started to diminish. Then, in 2003, President Rahmon conveyed the message that he did not see any value in continuing the dialogue, and stated in a message to Parliament that the time for dialogue among the Tajiks was up and that Tajikistan should henceforth become a platform for regional dialogue.

A larger question whose relevance goes beyond the ITD is what should replace the conflict resolution process, or constitute its focus, after a peace agreement is signed and the immediate postconflict phase has concluded. In the view of the author, state-building should follow conflict resolution. The emerging state of Tajikistan has been and to an extent still is struggling with the basic problems of governance, getting things done professionally and efficiently, building a functioning civil service, and providing social services to the population. Instead, in the post-Soviet context, external interveners have put much emphasis on the development of civil society. This has been largely successful in Eastern Europe, as it had functioning states which reorganized themselves fairly quickly. However, in Central Asia, where there is no tradition of an independent modern state, civil society became an alternative to a state rather than its building block. This does not mean that engagement with civil society is not worthwhile. However, there is a real danger of expecting civil society to do much more than it can realistically deliver.[50]

The ITD did discuss issues of state-building, although this was not articulated as a coherent approach. Between 1998 and 2000, dialogue participants began to explore how democracy could be made to work in Tajikistan, and debated subjects such as the roles of the Parliament and the political parties. While discussing the poor performance of the parties (apart from the one associated with the president), an opposition party representative noted that the parties themselves had failed to get their act together and had not seized the opportunities available to them. Moreover, it was noted, many parties lacked real constituencies, and this strategic gap could not be filled by developing the skills of their leadership.

Former ITD participants have other reflections on missed opportunities. First, some have noted that the dialogue did not include the real hard-liners. As a consequence, such persons still harbor resentments and grievances which they keep to themselves but which could be activated if the overall political situation were to deteriorate.[51] Second, it did not include representatives of the military, who are still a powerful player in politics in Tajikistan. Another idea (which the author finds problematic) was to use the dialogue technique to start a citizens' peace initiative with Afghanistan. One participant argued that "the way into Afghanistan lies via Tajikistan" and that a dialogue process should have been tried instead of the US-led military intervention of 2001. It should be noted that the US-led operations in Afghanistan met with a mixed response in Tajikistan. The author's reservation is that Afghanistan at the time had too many troubles of its own to become involved with Tajiks from across the border. Moreover, Tajikistan never recognized the Taliban and only maintained relations with the deposed Afghan president Burhanuddin Rabbani, so it would have been unclear how and with whom to engage.[52]

Factors Responsible for the Impacts

Intervention Factors

OBJECTIVES

The ITD was built on a healthy foundation: both sides actually wanted to resolve the conflict. The parties, however, did not know how this could be done, and emotions were too strong and relationships too damaged to make compromise possible. The dialogue set itself to address the polarization and the mistrust between the parties. According to Slim and Saunders, "the Dialogue was designed with a dual agenda: to discuss specific problems at length and to increase understanding of the dynamics in the relationships that cause the problems."[53]

The dialogue did not intend to resolve the concrete issues in contention, leaving them to be decided at the official negotiations; rather, it concentrated on rebuilding and redefining relationships. However, a review of the documents and the written reflections of the US facilitating team show that much time, energy, and creativity were actually spent discussing and framing the issues, such as the return of refugees and internally displaced persons, disarmament, constitutional change, political representation, and social and economic rehabilitation.

The aspirations of the participants may have been similar, but they themselves did not realize this until after a period of time spent in the dialogue. In the late 1980s and early 1990s, everybody in the Tajikistani political class believed in democracy, but as polarization increased, many democratic parties were overtaken by Islamists (in the words of one participant, "Democrats have grown Islamic ears"). However, when the dialogue helped participants to work through their grievances and emotions, they began to see that they had much in common in terms of political fundamentals.[54] Thus, the focus was on transforming relationships so that the participants could work together constructively. The simple but compelling measure of the strength of the emerging relationships was that senior people felt that the process was important enough to attend and participate regularly in the dialogue.

Nevertheless, while relationship-building may be essential, it is not a sufficient part of an interactive peace process. There needs to be progress on issues of conflict over time. Relationships and mutual confidence are critical when the parties turn to a discussion of solutions and must reach agreement on the concrete, practical steps to be taken to resolve their conflict ("If I disarm, would you treat me decently?" "If refugees start to return, would they be safe?"). Relationships also matter when the sides launch political initiatives, such as the development of a joint memorandum. Trust was especially important immediately after the signing of the peace agreement and in the amnesty period when the situation was fragile and the negotiated settlement could have been easily disrupted.

STATURE, SKILLS, AND PERSONALITIES OF THE TEAM

Other key factors also contributed to the success of the ITD process. Among these was the dialogue's third-party facilitation. A third party was essential, because the sides could not talk and listen to each other directly.[55] It was also important for Tajikistanis that the invitation came from an "international movement": the Dartmouth Conference. Participants took pride in referring to their initiative as "The Inter-Tajik Dialogue within the Framework of the Dartmouth Conference."[56] To this day, the dialogue is known in Tajikistan as the "Dartmouth Process."

The concerted efforts of the US-Russian facilitating team demonstrated that the US and Russian experts could work together in a constructive spirit and for the benefit of peace. Both parts of the facilitating team had good access to their respective governments. The US chair regularly updated the US State Department on the ITD's achievements, while the Russian team maintained communication with the Russian foreign ministry, which had shown an active interest in the process. By virtue of his previous official position, the US chair had good access to the UN bodies (Department of Peace-Keeping Operations and Department of Political Affairs), which were regularly informed about the content of the discussions. However, around 2000–2001, the Russian team, which had been committed, started to withdraw and the dialogue began to lose its cutting edge.[57]

The facilitating team was strong and combined different assets. The US and Russian chairs (Hal Saunders and Gennady Chufrin) had sound expertise in negotiations and conflict resolution processes, and have been commended by former participants for their expertise. The US chair also brought vast experience from other contexts and the qualities of a good politician. Another Russian team member (Vitaly Naumkin) was a renowned expert in Islamic studies, and the Russian team brought regional expertise into the process. The facilitators were extremely skilled in moderating the meetings: the moderators did not impose their opinions, but provided expertise and advice. When debates became heated, the moderators could switch attention to a more neutral topic, and then return to the issue in question when passions had calmed. The attitude of the facilitating team was positive. The moderators never appeared depressed. They were consistently upbeat, and always helped to create a dynamic mood.

TECHNIQUES

The team had a methodology, and it proved viable. Stage one was important—to find people of the right caliber to take part and convince them of the value of the initiative. Relevant participants were successfully identified, due largely to the efforts of the Russian team members and their good connections within the Tajik intellectual elite. At stage two, when the participants were mapping problems and building relationships, open-ended questions were asked, such as "What do participants see as the causes of the civil strife?" "What do they see as 'ways out'"? At the second meeting, these initial questions were followed by further questions, such as "What are the interests of the group with which you identify?" "What kind of Tajikistan would you like to see develop over the long term?"[58] When the participants started probing problems and relationships to choose a direction, the facilitators led them to focus on issues. One such issue was the return of refugees, after which the group proceeded to discuss disarmament and security guarantees.

By stage three, the facilitators' team attempted to document some outputs, using various approaches. The co-moderators produced two working papers in the fifth dialogue session in January 1994. Each moderator put in writing what participants had said so they could reflect on the moderators' observations. One paper described principles that should guide the launch of negotiations. The second paper recorded the fears on each side that had blocked their capacity to work together.

Another technique employed was the drafting of memoranda. These came in a variety of forms, with the participants gradually assuming more responsibility for their preparation. For the first eleven memos, a "negotiation text" (a method used during the 1978 Egyptian-Israeli summit at Camp David, moderated by US president Jimmy Carter and his facilitating team) was employed. With this methodology, the facilitating team prepares a text that captures the points of agreement among the participants that emerged during their discussion; this draft text is then presented to the group for review and discussion. The group debates the draft and suggests improvements, after which the facilitators rework the text. This process is repeated a second time, after which all of the participants formally agree to and sign the text. For one memorandum, a different methodology was attempted: each side was asked to draft a text of a proposed memorandum, attempting to summarize the discussions in a way that it would be possible for both sides to sign, and then the facilitators combined the two texts into one. This approach largely worked, although in the end the participants did not sign the above memorandum, as they were reluctant to be seen to agree on something before an official round of negotiations. From the twelfth memorandum onward, the participants did their own drafting and approved their work product with relatively little input from the moderators.

Other techniques employed by the facilitators included "homework assignments," in which participants were asked to think overnight about such questions as, "What are the obstacles to negotiations/peace?" "How can they be overcome?" "What can I personally do to help to overcome them?" At times, small group work was utilized. The facilitators would split the group into two (for instance, those representing the government and the opposition), while a few unaffiliated participants joined either of the groups. The groups were given special tasks, such as preparing a document on a concrete issue (e.g., refugee return) from the other group's perspective. Sometimes this task was too difficult, and the documents generated were not really usable as working papers. However, the participants learned a great deal by trying to appreciate how the other party thought. Such exercises created an ability to explore problems from different angles and to appreciate other's perspectives. Still another technique involved dividing the whole group randomly (or according to their interest in a certain topic) into three smaller subgroups, each of which would debate an issue or question during the evening and report back to the plenary in the morning. These small groups worked on their own, without external facilitation.

Participants also were introduced to the logic and mechanics of negotiations, a process that was new to them. In the run-up to the official talks, the US facilitator asked the group to clearly define the purpose of negotiations in a way that would be acceptable for both parties. Another assigned task was to structure the work of the negotiating teams; that is, to develop the agenda for negotiations.[59] The difference between acting on issues and addressing the underlying psychological dynamics was especially interesting when official negotiations began. The group was encouraged to think through the fears that might block progress in the negotiations—the mistrust and fear between the two sides—a subject that did not appear on the official agenda.

Participants did not realize how much the discussions were framed by the facilitators and how much thought and preparation had gone into the conduct of the meetings. During interviews, participants shared their perception that all of the dialogue's substantive content had come from them, and believed that the moderators were there only to preserve a sense of calm and to manage the emotions. In effect, the facilitation guided the process in such a subtle way that the participants had no sense that they had been led.

A constant feature of the ITD was a sense of progress, of everyone moving toward a positive destination. Despite the ongoing war and the heated verbal battles during some of the meetings, the participants retained a sense that what they were doing was not just empty talk and that their efforts would result in concrete action. Notwithstanding occasional setbacks and some difficult moments, the overall progression toward a peace settlement was clear. Certainly, this outcome cannot be attributed to the dialogue exclusively, as there were concurrent changes in the overall political context. However, the participants felt that the ideas and initiatives they elaborated together were having an impact, and this sense of progress sustained the dialogue. Nonetheless, participants who also took part in the official UN-chaired negotiations noted that they would have liked to have had more frequent meetings during the most intense negotiations phase.[60]

TIMING

The intervention was timely. The ITD started when the worst hostilities were already over, but the situation was fluid and the opposition still presented a credible security threat. Politically, the sides had not yet been entrenched in their positions, nor had an accommodation to the status quo been established. Although both parties acted assertively in public, deep down they realized that the war could not be won militarily and that some compromise would have to be reached.

A related factor was the sustained nature of the initiative. Dialogue meetings were held as often as needed. This gave time and space to explore issues in depth and to build relationships. The US team made commendable efforts to secure funds for such a long endeavor. It was also useful for the participants to know that the meetings would be held at regular intervals, that in between meetings they would undertake certain preparations or actions, and that the facilitation team would not suddenly abandon them. The facilitators wished that the participants had interacted among themselves more actively between meetings, but this may not have been possible in the initial period.

VENUE

The meetings mostly took place in Russia at venues outside Moscow and St. Petersburg. Participants appreciated this consideration, because these venues were seen as neutral and Tajiks had no reservations about traveling to Russia. (Some were based there already.) Being in Russia enabled participants to maintain contacts with a wider policy and academic community, and to purchase books and other resources. The Russian location also had the advantage of removing the participants from the daily experience of conflict; at the same time, the venue was sufficiently familiar that they could feel comfortable socially and linguistically. One round of negotiations took place in the United States, where most of the participants had never previously visited, as they generally had traveled little outside of the former Soviet Union. This was an eye-opening experience, but it may have been too overwhelming for productive talks. In May 1996, it became possible to organize an ITD meeting in Tajikistan itself.

The dialogue strategy contrasted with conventional international practice, whereby organizers of dialogue interventions often take the participants to Western countries. The argument is sometimes made that this will have a "civilizing effect," as one of the participants described it, through the power of example, and that there will be no doubts about the neutrality of a venue. But the experience shows that a successful process can be achieved in a regional venue combined with in-country meetings, provided that appropriate facilities have been allocated. This localization of the dialogue process enables the participants to avoid accusations of "conflict tourism"; moreover, it made more difficult for those who saw no value in such a process to doubt the seriousness of the participants. The more important requirement is that the members of the group be together—they should stay in the same hotel, meet at mealtimes, and travel as a body to encourage the building of social ties and relationships.

LINKING MEETINGS TO ACTIONS

Saunders and Chufrin define as stage five of a dialogue process, "Acting Together to Make Change Happen." The empirical evidence suggests that the participants in fact took concrete action to follow up on the discussions and agreements reached during their meetings. Some examples of these efforts include creating a unifying political structure for the opposition (UTO), conveying messages to the president and key government figures on the opposition's willingness to negotiate, bringing the various joint memoranda to the attention of the leaderships, and making a joint presentation in Dushanbe in May 1996 (at the sixteenth dialogue meeting) when the civil war had not been concluded. Individual members took the ITD's ideas into their workplaces—government, opposition circles, the negotiating forum, citizen discussions, and the media.

This followup action does not always happen in interactive-type dialogue projects. More commonly, talk generates little walk. What explains the willingness of the dialogue participants to move from talk to action? Several factors appear to have been at work. First, the participants were motivated to take action, since both sides were dissatisfied with the status quo of civil strife. Second, the sides challenged and influenced each other, demanding that they each live up to their verbal claims ("If you say you are willing to negotiate, where are you based? How do we find you? What is your phone number?"). Third, the moderating team led the participants to take up realistic tasks (Is it possible to solicit consent of the Islamists to negotiate with a secular government? Will you commit yourself to explore that?). The joint US-Russian team helped to establish what was "doable," both from the viewpoint of the negotiation process and from that of the country political context. Fourth, the US moderator at a number of meetings gave individual assignments to the group with a personalized message: "What can you personally do to overcome these obstacles?" Fifth, as time passed, a natural activist group crystallized, composed of people with political ambitions such as party leaders, top lawyers, and academics. They wanted to make democracy in Tajikistan work, and their activist orientation needed little prompting.

COMPLEMENTARITY WITH THE OFFICIAL NEGOTIATIONS

As Slim and Saunders reflect, the ITD was a factor in the context that shaped the parties' willingness to engage in official talks, yet it is difficult to determine the extent and nature of its influence on government decision-making.

The government's decision to negotiate was taken against the backdrop of sustained diplomatic pressure and its awareness of the escalating costs of war. Still, according to a high Tajikistani official who was involved in the government's decision to negotiate, "After six meetings of the Dialogue, it was no longer possible to argue credibly that negotiation between the government and the opposition was impossible."[61]

The clearly defined framework of the dialogue ensured that it would complement and not compete with the official talks. The dialogue process could generate ideas and stimulate creativity, for which there was no time and space during the official talks. It allowed issues to be explored in more depth and options and scenarios to be developed. Consequently, it was easier to reach decisions at the official negotiations, which presented few surprises.

Also, when the dialogue began, there were no other competing initiatives. When the conflict erupted in 1991, prominent Russian Democrats (academician Yevgeny Velikhov and Anatoly Sobchak, later mayor of St. Petersburg) conducted a successful mediation, but this was more of a one-off effort than an ongoing process. When the official negotiations began in 1994, the participants were asked if they saw value in continuing the dialogue. The overwhelming answer was in the affirmative. The dialogue was mindful of the ongoing UN-chaired official negotiations in which several participants from both sides took part. At this point, the facilitation team decided to bring new people into the dialogue to broaden the debate, and to have substitutes available in case the participants included in the official delegations were unable to attend.

In the view of the facilitation team, the UN-sponsored process and the ITD interacted very well. The US chair approached UN Assistant Secretary-General Marrack Goulding to explain the purpose of the interactive process and to highlight the clear line that was drawn between the dialogue process and the official talks. Senior UN officials took the US leader seriously because he was a renowned former diplomat. In addition, analytical memoranda were sent to the UN Assistant Secretary-General to inform the UN about the substance of the dialogue discussions. The UN, in turn, recognized the value of the informal dialogue process. According to Vladimir Goryaev of the UN Department of Political Affairs: "In addition to facilitating the official inter-Tajik negotiations, UN mediators also maintained liaison with the 'second track' dialogue initiated by Ambassador Saunders of the Kettering Foundation. Despite the apparent complexity of international interventions in the Tajik conflict, clear mandates and effective coordination prevented duplication and 'competition of initiatives.'"[62]

Such links were also secured by the continuing interaction between the US chair and the UN officials, by the dialogue preparation of memoranda in support of the formal talks, and by the fact that several dialogue participants were included in the official delegations, while a number of others provided advice to the decision-makers.

Nonintervention Factors

DOMESTIC FACTORS

As mentioned, a crucial factor contributing to the ITD's success was the broad political consensus among the warring parties. They all wanted to see an independent and united Tajikistan emerge out of the civil war, and no region sought to secede. The IRP did not seriously pursue the creation of an Islamic state and never really defined what its Islamic agenda meant for state-building. In the end, the Islamists found the idea of a secular state acceptable in principle, provided that religion occupied a pride of place and that the political representation of an Islamic constituency was ensured. The debate turned not on deep-seated historical grievances, but on more immediate concerns regarding the perceived power imbalances of the old system.

The domestic security context was also conducive to a peace settlement. The fighting had produced a stalemate around 1996–97, when the government troops were in control of the lowlands, including the Karategin Valley, but could not eliminate the opposition from the mountainous areas from which they threatened the government's positions. The opposition, in its turn, had made advances in Gharm and in the central region, at some point reaching as far as a hundred kilometers from Dushanbe and threatening the city. At the same time, the opposition forces realized that they could not maintain control of a sizable lowland sector (such as the Gharm Valley) or conquer a full province. Thus, the prospect was for either a protracted, decades-long guerrilla war or a negotiated compromise.

One of the core factors behind the civil war was disagreement over power-sharing. The 1997 peace agreement, which both leadership groups accepted, resolved the power-sharing dispute, as each side realized that the other had a sizable constituency. Moreover, President Rahmon and his advisers were astute enough to comprehend that the real interests of the key opposition figures, concealed behind their public positions, lay in satisfaction of their material appetites. If satisfied, the opposition would rather work to support the status quo than seek to rock the boat.

The stance of some military and guerrilla groups toward peace continued to be a liability even after the peace agreement was signed. In 1997, radical elements of the UTO that did not recognize the agreement established the Islamic Movement of Uzbekistan (IMU),[63] a militant organization determined to pursue a holy war against the secular regime in Uzbekistan, and that maintained ties with the Taliban in Afghanistan. The IMU continued to launch raids from their bases in Tavildara in the eastern mountainous part of the country, but was persuaded to leave in 2000. With the assistance of the Russian military, the IMU was relocated to Afghanistan, where it suffered a severe blow as a result of the US-led intervention into Afghanistan in 2001.

In the initial civil war period, rogue armies on both sides were involved in the fighting. The main such force on the government side was the Popular Front. Some of these militias were incorporated into the Tajik regular forces, which were trained and equipped by the Russian troops. The opposition, operating in smaller units, employed guerrilla, hit-and-run tactics. Each field commander had its own regiment whose members were loyal to him. Following the peace agreement, the ex-combatants were disarmed and integrated into the regular armed forces or into peaceful structures. However, some second- and third-tier commanders bent on criminality refused to disband and continued to terrorize the population. The government gained full control of the territory of the Republic of Tajikistan only in 2001, when the last major bandit group of Rahmon Sanginov (known under the nom de guerre "Rahmon Hitler") was eliminated.

Since the country was coming out of state socialism and the civil war, there were no independent businesses. Economic assets and lucrative niches were associated with state positions. Thus, in order to get rich quickly, one had to either resort to overt criminality such as drug smuggling, kidnapping, and robbery, or obtain a good job in the state system, because positions gave access to assets. The government was in control of appointments and could offer tangible economic opportunities to the opposition elite in exchange for the latter's laying down their arms.

Another source of the sustainable peace was that while the war had weakened the state capacity to enforce law and order and provide public services, this capacity was not lost altogether. As soon as basic security was ensured, state authority started to gradually reassert itself. Parts of the country were not touched by the civil war, but had suffered from isolation and a law-and-order vacuum; these areas were positioned to shift to economic development fairly quickly. On the other hand, the emigration of the professional and managerial—mainly urban—classes during the years of instability created severe human resource limitations that reduced the effectiveness of the state bureaucracy.

Tajikistan's society also manifested a substantial will for peace. This capacity was rooted largely in their recent experience of a functioning state, to which the citizens were accustomed and sought to return. There was a general belief that a reconstituted state would accelerate the process of normalization and regeneration. Ordinary people had not yet lost the habits associated with peaceful life, such as functioning schools and hospitals, and looked forward to their restoration. The host population on the whole demonstrated tolerance toward returning refugees. Score-settling and revenge killings did take place, but many of those who feared reprisals for murder, rape, intimidation, beatings, looting, and other forms of brutality fled to Russia.

The factor of presidential leadership also played a role. President Rahmon demonstrated good political instincts, a capacity to learn quickly, and personal courage. Starting in 1995, for example, he traveled three times to Afghanistan, meeting with President Rabbani and UTO leader Sayed Abdullo Nuri.

REGIONAL AND GLOBAL FACTORS

The Tajikistan peace benefitted from the conjunction of a number of favorable external factors. The proximity of Afghanistan served both as a trigger for the fighting in Tajikistan and as a negative demonstration effect which contributed to the desire for peace. The Tajik refugees who had fled to Afghanistan from Tajikistan during the civil war found themselves in unbearable conditions in a country much poorer and less developed than their own, and were horrified by what they saw. Tajiks who remained in the country realized that they would come to live like people in Afghanistan if the war continued and their state was devastated. As for the refugees, they were keen to return and were prepared to accept government rule if only their basic security could be guaranteed. Remarkably, as compared to other conflicts, most refugees returned from Afghanistan within a relatively short time.

The geopolitical setting was also favorable for reaching a compromise. The absence of rivalry between Russia and the United States, and a historical opportunity for the two to work together to advance peace, created a sense of common purpose. Although Russia supported the pro-government side, it also was reaching out to the opposition, as many key opposition figures had found refuge in Moscow. The geopolitical interests of Russia and

Iran also proved to be complementary. Iran had stronger ties with the moderate part of the Islamic opposition, yet its overall goal was not to facilitate the creation of an Islamic state in Tajikistan, but rather to help in the establishment of an independent country of its ethnic kin. Moreover, Iran sought to overcome its pariah status in the international arena and to be regarded as capable of playing a constructive role in regional affairs.[64] As a result, Russia, Iran, and ethnic Tajik warlord Ahmad-Shah Massoud in Afghanistan pulled generally in the same direction.

Neighboring Uzbekistan, which officially participated in the CIS peacekeeping operation, pursued its own political agenda. Uzbekistan's president Islam Karimov, for example, proposed the formation of a Tajik State Council with equal representation from all parties and regions after a total amnesty.[65] To the dismay of President Rahmon, he invited Sayed Abdullo Nuri for talks in Tashkent on two occasions in 1995. It was widely believed in Tajikistan that Uzbek troops were in fact engaged in armed combat and bomb raids in the Gharm region,[66] although Tashkent had denied such involvement. As noted above, the fear of Uzbekistan and the "Uzbek factor," shared by the government and opposition, was an important driver for peace. Some ITD participants noted that, in retrospect, had Russia not supported the Rahmon government and provided peacekeeping support, the way would have been opened for Uzbekistan to enforce peace on its own terms and in a fashion detrimental to the Tajik state.

Russia's involvement was crucial in facilitating the peace talks. At the July 1993 meeting of Russia's Security Council, President Boris Yeltsin established a division of labor: the Ministry of Foreign Affairs was to promote conflict resolution, while the Ministry of Defense and the Border Service were to ensure the protection of the border with Afghanistan. After 1993, the Ministry of Foreign Affairs exerted pressure on Rahmon to negotiate with the UTO. The ministry included other Central Asian countries and Afghanistan, Iran, and Pakistan in the negotiating process, and conducted a meeting with Sayed Abdullo Nuri in November 1993 in Tehran. On these foundations, the first round of inter-Tajik talks took place in April 1994 in Moscow. In June 1994, the ministry of Foreign Affairs secured a four-month cease-fire, and the third round of talks in Islamabad in October 1994 negotiated an extension of this cease-fire monitored by the joint commission. In February 1996, the two parties agreed to create an All-Tajik Consultative Forum.

Russia played a major role in peacekeeping.[67] In September 1993, the CIS Council of Ministers of Foreign Affairs and Defense established the

Collective Peacekeeping Forces in Tajikistan (CIS/PKF), composed of contingents from the Russian Federation—based on the 201st Division stationed in Tajikistan—and battalions from Kazakhstan, Kyrgyzstan and Uzbekistan. The CIS/PKF was the only force capable of protecting humanitarian convoys and strategic installations. Its presence had a stabilizing effect and helped to ensure that heavy weapons did not fall into the hands of the combatants, thereby helping to prevent further destruction and casualties. The CIS/PKF, together with the Russian Border Forces, also helped to control the transshipments of massive quantities of arms, ammunition, and drugs from neighboring Afghanistan.[68]

The interaction between Russia and the UN throughout the official peace process was also constructive. The special envoys and UNMOT military observers maintained regular contact with CIS/PKF commanders to discuss the military situation and options to secure a cease-fire. The Protocol on Military Issues, signed in March 1997, gave CIS/PKF forces the delicate role of accompanying UTO units from Afghanistan to the assembly areas under UNMOT supervision.[69] Still, the UN disagreed with Russia on how to certify the 1994 presidential elections and the 1995 parliamentary elections.

Despite security challenges, international economic and humanitarian assistance to Tajikistan commenced in 1993, with both food and non-food aid. Tajikistan's first UN Consolidated Interagency Appeal was prepared for 1994 and some $225 million was mobilized through this mechanism. International financial institutions started to fund development even before the Peace Agreement was signed. For instance, since 1996, the World Bank Group has approved seventeen projects for a total of $302.1 million.[70] In addition, $1.4 million in grants has been made available to Tajikistan for institution-building and postconflict assistance.

UNMOT (later the UNTOP) and the UN Development Programme (UNDP) worked to demobilize and reintegrate ex-combatants into civilian life. In 1996, the UNDP in Tajikistan developed the Rehabilitation, Reconstruction, and Development Program to support the stabilization of areas damaged by the war. Although the ex-combatants were formally integrated into the national army and law-enforcement agencies, in reality little changed in their lives when they returned to their villages with no money and no jobs. To address this problem, Special Reintegration Committees were established, including representatives of the local authorities, field commanders, communities, and the UNDP. The committees identified community needs and designed projects, on the condition that they would employ ex-combatants as much as possible. By early 2000, more than 1,100 ex-combatants were actively involved in labor-intensive rehabilitation projects. Between 2000 and 2002, 127 projects were implemented, employing 4,141 persons in irrigation; health and sanitation; energy; agriculture; and the rehabilitation of schools, roads, and bridges.[71]

Since 2001, donor attention to Tajikistan has greatly increased, triggered by the September 11 attacks and the subsequent US-led intervention into Afghanistan. In parallel with the local government, the international community started to deliver services to the population in many parts of the country via donor-funded community-based organizations. Such organizations come in many forms and operate on different levels: *mahalla* (neighborhood), village, or *jamoat* (municipality), depending on how a development agency interprets the meaning of "community." They have been established across the country, but had a heavy concentration in the Rasht valley, a former opposition stronghold, where the international presence was strongly felt. Many of these activities focused on conflict prevention: for example, the Community Action Investment Program—the Peaceful Communities' Initiative of the US Agency for International Development (USAID)—financed a program in conflict mitigation at the community level.[72]

As the disparity in resource distribution between different regions of the country was one of the causes of the civil war, the donor community has targeted areas neglected by the government to provide counterbalance and to prevent exclusion. The World Bank Country Assistance Strategy for Tajikistan emphasizes the inequitable distribution of resources regionally, and identifies weak institutions and governance as a particular problem, especially at the local government level where officials exploit the rent-seeking opportunities that their positions provide. However, municipal government capacities are limited at best; they have no budgets of their own, and their functions are restricted by the legal framework.[73]

The role of the Tajik diaspora in fostering cooperation has been constructive, unlike in other conflict situations where diasporas tend to be more radical than the people in the country who have endured the pain of the war. (One example of this concern is the Armenian diaspora in the Nagorno-Karabakh conflict.) The Tajik diaspora in Moscow—some of whom were ITD participants—helped to politically unify the various strands among the opposition based both within Tajikistan and in Iran and Afghanistan. Later, the ITD members who came from the diaspora were instrumental in engaging with the Russian official mediators and pro-government Tajiks in Moscow.

Conclusion

Interactive dialogue-type processes can work well when the parties' over-arching objectives are similar or comparable, and in circumstances when they do not run counter to the unfolding political process on the ground. Saunders and Stewart reflect on the lessons learned and the transferability of the ITD experience:

1. Compromise may be more possible on the issues of power and economic advantage characteristic of the Tajik conflict than on those involving inter-ethnic and religious differences (such as the conflict between Armenians and Azerbaijanis over Nagorno-Karabakh).
2. The Inter-Tajik Dialogue was launched even before the lines of conflict were clearly defined, let alone the demands of the opposing sides.
3. The obstacles to engagement in resolution had to do with anger and injustice done during the course of the ongoing war and with the sides blaming each other for unleashing the violence in the first place. As a result, they shouted and screamed at each other, because each felt that the other was responsible for the atrocities. This was quite different from cases such as Kosovo or Karabakh where the obstacles to peace lay not in immediate reaction to war, violence and human rights abuses, but in mutually exclusive visions of common or separate futures. Once they got over their anger towards each other, they moved with relative ease into serious dialogue. There was none of the deeply entrenched resistance to dialogue that the facilitators encountered a decade later among the participants from Armenia and Azerbaijan.[74]

The dialogue was successful because it set a realistic task for itself and did not attempt to impose a political outcome that would have been incompatible with the interests of one or both parties. The facilitation team did not pursue its own political design, which would have run counter to the aspirations of the participants. As Hal Saunders noted, "The initiators of the Inter-Tajik Dialogue determined that their task was to generate analysis from within the conflict itself, not to impose their own analytical framework on the conflict."[75] Openness to emergent opportunities was critical to success, since when the intervention commenced, the issues of conflict and the state itself were in such turmoil that almost any outcome seemed possible. The realization that neither side could win a military victory created a ripe opportunity. Moreover, the absence of geopolitical regional rivalry meant that the parties knew that they could not strengthen their hand by exploiting differences between outside powers.

This assessment raises the basic question of how far interactive process-type interventions can go, what they can and cannot achieve, and how decisions to conclude them are made. Typically, at the initial period of a third-party engagement, it is not clear how events on the ground might unfold. At times, the situation may seem so hopeless that peace is impossible. At some point, there must be a reality check to determine if a second-track intervention can make a contribution to stabilizing the situation. Second-track interactive interventions can only go so far; they cannot substitute for the social and political foundations needed for a settlement. Fortunately, in the case of the ITD, after the first year it was already clear that its process was achieving something. But the question of the possible limitations of process interventions is important to pose and requires certain courage to answer.

After peace became a reality and the state's power had expanded far beyond what was envisaged at the time of the peace agreement, the dialogue emerged as a platform for interaction between the two sides. In the view of some former participants, the "Dialogue within the Framework of the Dartmouth Conference," if it were to continue, needs to be reformulated and its entire content rethought. For instance, a continuation of the dialogue would need to focus on such issues as personnel appointments, since the current recruitment base for positions of real power is being reduced to the presidential clan. Although the past record of the ITD is held in high esteem, at present the impact of follow-on civil society projects on the political situation is not as clear.

Although stability in Tajikistan has become firmly entrenched, the issues engendering conflict have not withered away, but have acquired a new meaning. On a national level, the most painful and controversial issue is that of the Uzbek minority and, by default, relations with Uzbekistan. Although the subject is hardly mentioned in public, majority-minority tensions are much in evidence. This issue was not prominent in the dialogue because of its mix of participants, but it remains a driver of potential conflict.

On the country's periphery, it is essential to strengthen local government capacities. The community-based approach to development has become popular with donors, but this emphasis may have gone too far. Parallel structures to the local government, propped up with donor funds, only undermine the struggling authorities. It may be better to begin by stressing simple ideas that are based not on the unsustainable development of alternative community-based organizations, but on the need to help local governments in practical ways. For example, relevant officials in the district administrations (*hukumat*) that have departments to deal with social tensions could be empowered to resolve problems in a constructive way. The transfer of practical conflict analysis and mitigation skills would be helpful to both district and provincial authorities.

It also must be noted that each interactive intervention, however well designed and implemented, has a natural life span. At some point, the government and the people of a country must assume responsibility for their own destiny. Interveners must know when it is time to cease their work and to move on to other situations where their assistance may be more needed.

It seems possible to conclude that process-type peace interventions work best when the status of a territory is not at stake, as opposed to the case when it is, such as whether territories such as Abkhazia or Northern Cyprus can be persuaded to join the states from which they broke away. It is similarly difficult when the issue is whether independence, as in the case of Kosovo's forceful separation from Federal Republic of Yugoslavia, should be internationally recognized. When one identity or ethnic group separates from an internationally recognized state and establishes a de facto state (e.g., Kosovo, Nagorno-Karabakh, Abkhazia), an interactive dialogue process cannot avoid a serious debate on different options, which would include possible recognition for de facto states and formation of a new type of relationship with the states from which they originally broke away. If one side (e.g., Serbian, Azerbaijani, Georgian) resists any discussion of such an option, progress is impossible and the restoration of relations between influential individuals cannot overcome a massive political impasse. But when there has not been an overwhelming military victory, and when people can refer to a tradition of a functioning state—both factors that were present in Tajikistan—process intervention may have a better chance.

Notes

1. Statistics for Tajikistan in 2013 were as follows: population below poverty line: 47.2 percent; gross national income per capita: US$990; gross domestic product: $8.508 billion. See the World Bank's Tajikistan data at http://data.worldbank.org/country/tajikistan.

2. Given that the ITD facilitators and conveners (Hal Saunders and Randa Slim) have written extensively on the process, the chapter provides only an essential outline, drawing upon both authors' work.

3. The research for this chapter is based on the methodology provided by the Working Group on Preventing and Rebuilding Failed States of the Project on Leadership and Building State Capacity, Woodrow Wilson International Center for Scholars. In addition to scrutinizing documents generously provided by Hal Saunders, the author benefited from field research undertaken in May 2006 in Tajikistan, where interviews with the ten dialogue participants and engaged local and international observers were conducted, and in Moscow where a meeting with the Russian members of the facilitating team was held. The participants largely demonstrated unanimity of views in their reflections on the dialogue; specific opinions that stand out are credited individually. The specific research was supplemented by observations during the author's work as a UNDP regional peace and development (conflict prevention) adviser for Central Asia (2003–4).

4. Muriel Atkin, "Thwarted Democratization in Tajikistan," in *Conflict, Cleavage, and Change in Central Asia and the Caucasus*, ed. Karen Dawisha and Bruce Parrott (Cambridge: Cambridge University Press, 1997), 277–311, at 304.

5. Randa Slim and Faredun Hodizoda, "Tajikistan: From Civil War to Peacebuilding," in *Searching for Peace in Europe and Eurasia*, ed. Paul van Tongeren, Hans van der Veen, and Juliette Verhoeven (Boulder, CO: Lynne Rienner, 2001), 516–35, at 517.

6. More on the situation of Uzbeks can be found in Shirin Akiner, *Central Asia: Conflict or Stability and Development?* (London: Minority Rights Group, 1997), 29–30.

7. On the earlier period of democratization, see Atkin, "Thwarted Democratization in Tajikistan."

8. Relatively little is written on the role of Afghanistan in the war in Tajikistan. But see, e.g., Mohammad-Reza Djalili and Frédéric Grare, "Regional Ambitions and Interests in Tajikistan: the Role of Afghanistan, Pakistan and Iran," *Tajikistan: the Trials of Independence*, ed. Mohammad-Reza Djalili, Frédéric Grare, and Shirin Akiner (Richmond, UK: Curzon Press, 1998), 119–31.

9. Munira Inoyatova (former Minister of Education), interview with author, Dushanbe, February 2004.

10. In 2007, Emomali Rahmon changed his surname from "Rahmonov" to "Rahmon," dropping the Russified ending. For consistency, he will be referred to as "Rahmon" throughout this chapter.

11. Dov Lynch, *Russian Peacekeeping Strategies in the CIS: The Cases of Moldova, Georgia and Tajikistan* (Basingstoke, UK: Macmillan, in association with the Royal Institute of International Affairs, London, 2000), 154.

12. On the outline of the official conflict management and civil society/multitrack diplomacy, see Slim and Hodizoda, "Tajikistan," 522–28.

13. Kathleen Collins discusses this argument in "Tajikistan: Bad Peace Agreements and Prolonged Civil Conflict," in *From Promise to Practice: Strengthening UN Capacities for the Prevention of Violent Conflict*, ed. Chandra Lekha Sriram and Karin Wermester (Boulder, CO: Lynne Rienner, 2003), 292–93.

14. Author interviews with local observers, Dushanbe, May 2006.

15. The Swisspeace FAST International early warning system, which was operational from 1998 to 2008, recorded a consistently high level of Country Stability in Tajikistan. For more information on FAST's monitoring of Tajikistan, see Swisspeace,

"Tajikistan," http://www.swisspeace.ch/etc/archive/previous-projects/fast-international /countries.html#c1590.

16. Harold Saunders, interview during Wilson Center workshop on the Tajikistan case study, Washington, DC, June 6, 2006.

17. In the dialogue between the Georgians and the Abkhaz, which the author facilitated in 1996–97, such right of veto existed and was in fact used to ban unacceptable figures.

18. Abdurahmon Mahmadov (ITD participant), interview with author, Dushanbe, May 2006.

19. This is a widely publicized quotation. See, e.g., in Anatoly Adamishin, "Uroki primireniya v Tajikistane. Opyt rossiiskoi diplomatii devyanostykh" [Lessons of reconciliation in Tajikistan: The experience of Russian diplomacy in the nineties], *Global Affairs*, September 5, 2012, http://www.globalaffairs.ru/number /Uroki-primireniya-v-Tadzhikistane-15647.

20. See Gennady I. Chufrin and Harold H. Saunders, "A Public Peace Process," *Negotiation Journal* 9, no. 2 (April 1993): 155–77.

21. Harold Saunders, interview during Wilson Center workshop on the Tajikistan case study, Washington, DC, June 6, 2006.

22. A number of memoranda were published in 1997 in Moscow by the facilitators: the Russian Center of Strategic and International Studies and the Kettering Foundation.

23. Randa Slim and Harold Saunders, "The Inter-Tajik Dialogue: From Civil War towards Civil Society," in *Politics of Compromise: The Tajikistan Peace Process*, ed. Kamoludin Abdullaev and Catherine Barnes (London: Conciliation Resources, 2001), 44–47.

24. An example given was the Swiss-funded project on confidence-building between secular and religious politicians. This dialogue project consisted of three thematic working groups; ITD alumni took part in two of them. The facilitator observed that the two groups with former ITD participants functioned differently than the group without. Faredun Hodizoda, submission to the Wilson Center workshop on the Tajikistan case study, Washington, DC, June 2006.

25. In the author's own experience of providing training in other post-Soviet contexts, it is questionable that a few days' training would produce ambitious results. Generational differences may also be a factor: a younger generation less affected by the Soviet experience might be more receptive.

26. Saifullo Safiyev and Abdunabi Sattarzoda (government and opposition dialogue participants), interview with author, Dushanbe, May 2006.

27. One participant recalled an occasion when participants were flinging bottles at one another.

28. In the Georgian-Abkhaz process, by contrast, the meetings have been polite, with passions contained. Contributing to the less emotional tone was the fact that the Abkhaz participants have refused to meet the Georgians who fled Abkhazia, and agreed to talk only to intelligentsia from the capital who had not directly experienced the conflict and therefore could rise above the feelings of their community to see a broader picture.

29. Musso Asazoda (ITD participant), interview with author, Dushanbe, May 2006.

30. Adamishin, "Uroki primireniya v Tajikistane."

31. For a detailed account of the official peace process and Inter-Tajik Dialogue, see the chapter by one of the ITD facilitators; Irina Zviagelskaya, "The Tajik Conflict: Problems of Regulation," in Djalili, Grare, and Akiner, *Tajikistan*, 161–79.

32. Abdunabi Sattarzoda (most senior opposition participant), interview with author, Dushanbe, May 2006.

33. Of crucial importance was the first "Memorandum on the Negotiation Process in Tajikistan, March 4, 1994," in Gennady I. Chufrin, Ashurboi Imamov, and Harold H. Saunders, eds., *Memoranda and Appeals of the Inter-Tajik Dialogue within the Framework of the Dartmouth Conference (1993–97)* (Moscow: Center for Strategic Research and International Studies, 1997), 83–85.

34. Chufrin, Imamov, and Saunders, *Memoranda and Appeals*, 96.

35. "Memorandum adopted at the 12th Dialogue round on June 22, 1995," in Chufrin, Imamov, and Saunders, *Memoranda and Appeals*, 86.

36. See, e.g., "Strengthening of Statehood and Development of Civil Society in Tajikistan: UNDP project on the Creation of a Legal Education Centre" (Dushanbe: TGNU, 2003), 69–80.

37. Memorandum from the October 1996 Dialogue round.

38. See, e.g., author's interview with Saodat Olimova, Sharq Center, Dushanbe, May 2006.

39. Harold H. Saunders, "Evaluating Sustained Dialogue," chap. 10 in *A Public Peace Process: Sustained Dialogue to Transform Racial and Ethnic Conflicts* (New York: Palgrave Macmillan, 2001).

40. Shokirjon Hakimov (former ITD participant not affiliated with either side), interview with author, Dushanbe, May 2006.

41. The project was funded by the Political Division IV, Human Security, of the Swiss Federal Department of Foreign Affairs.

42. The Uzbek minority was 23.5 percent of the prewar population, but possibly may be larger at present following the emigration of nonindigenous minorities such as Slavs, Germans, and Jews.

43. Uzbek schools have survived in the Uzbek-populated rural areas as a legacy of the Soviet system.

44. The first memorandum raised the issue of "national minorities," but made no specific reference to the Uzbeks.

45. Saunders, "Evaluating Sustained Dialogue," 230.

46. Author's notes from field research in Tajikistan.

47. A Russian team member went to Uzbekistan to explore options in the late 1990s, and US team members later traveled to the Ferghana Valley of Uzbekistan in connection with another assignment. However, no involvement of representatives from Uzbekistan followed. At the beginning of the 2000s, another project (the Ambassadors-of-Goodwill Network, facilitated and funded by the Swiss foreign ministry) attempted to initiate such a dialogue process through informal channels; arguably, the efforts came too late, as the situation had become entrenched.

48. It is believed that a division of quotas in drug trafficking was an unwritten part of the peace agreement. Author's prior research in Dushanbe, 2004.

49. Author interviews with dialogue participants, Dushanbe, May 2006.

50. Anna Matveeva, "Exporting Civil Society: The Post-Communist Experience," *Problems of Post-Communism* 55, no. 2 (March–April 2008): 3–13.

51. Muso Asazoda (ITD participant), interview with author, Dushanbe, May 2006.

52. In addition, it appears that insufficient safeguards were put in place to prevent the rewriting of history.

53. Slim and Saunders, "The Inter-Tajik Dialogue," 44.

54. The situation might have been different if, say, the Islamists were determined to establish an Iranian style of Islamic state in Tajikistan and actively had been encouraged to do so by Iran. In that case, the process would have come up against deep convictions that the secularist majority held dear and would have been unlikely to seriously compromise, thus likely reaching a stalemate over a clash of values.

55. Saifullo Safarov (dialogue participant), interview with author, Dushanbe, May 2006.

56. Cited in Harold H. Saunders, "The Inter-Tajik Dialogue," chap. 7 in Saunders, *A Public Peace Process*, 152.

57. Author interviews with ITD participants, Dushanbe, May 2006.

58. Saunders, "The Inter-Tajik Dialogue," 153.

59. Ibid., 155–56.

60. Author's interviews with ITD participants, Dushanbe, May 2006.

61. Slim and Saunders, "The Inter-Tajik Dialogue," 45.

62. Vladimir Goryaev, "Architecture of International Involvement in the Tajik Peace Process," in *Politics of Compromise: The Tajikistan Peace Process*, ed. Kamoludin Abdullaev and Catherine Barnes (London: Conciliation Resources, 2001), 32–37, at 32.

63. On the Islamic Movement of Uzbekistan, see the book by ITD facilitator Vitaly V. Naumkin; *Between Pen and Rifle: Radical Islam in Central Asia* (Lanham, MD: Rowman & Littlefield, 2005), 37–126.

64. Edmund Herzig, "Regionalism, Iran and Central Asia," *International Affairs* 80, no. 3 (May 2004): 503–18, at 517.

65. ITAR-TASS news agency, April 4, 1995, SU/2272, G/2-3, quoted in Lynch, *Russian Peacekeeping Strategies in the CIS*, 164.

66. Author's interviews in Dushanbe and in Gharm, 2004

67. For an analysis of Russia's role in peacekeeping in Tajikistan, see Lynch, "Russian Strategy towards Tajikistan," chap. 7 in *Russian Peacekeeping Strategies in the CIS*, 150–72.

68. Goryaev, "Architecture of International Involvement in the Tajik Peace Process," 36.

69. Ibid.

70. These are concessional credits: a forty-year repayment period, a ten-year grace period, and a zero interest rate (with a service fee of 0.75 percent).

71. The program was funded by USAID, the Canadian International Development Agency, and the Norwegian government (and later by a grant from the European Community). See UNDP Reconstruction, Rehabilitation and Development Program, *Reintegration of Ex-combatants in Tajikistan*, Internet Forum on Conflict Prevention, United Nations Office for the Coordination of Humanitarian Affairs, 2004, http://ochaonline .un.org/DocView.asp?DocID=2379.

72. According to USAID, it "has long been addressing sources of conflict through its ongoing sectoral programs that help to equalize access to health care, water and energy resources, and economic opportunity; as well as to open healthy avenues for political grievances." See USAID/Central Asian Republics, "Conflict Prevention," USAID, 2006, last accessed December 27, 2006, http://www.usaid.gov/locations/europe _eurasia/car/caip_pci.html.

73. UNDP/World Bank, *Summary of the Community-Linked Development Workshop* (Varzob, Tajikistan, May 21–22 2004), available at www.undp.tj.org.

74. Harold H. Saunders and Philip D. Stewart, "Nature of Conflict in Tajikistan and the Transferability of Sustained Dialogue," internal paper, n.d.

75. Saunders, "Evaluating Sustained Dialogue," 226.

Chapter 6

Sri Lanka: When Negotiations Fail—Talks for the Sake of Talks; War for the Sake of Peace

Hannes Siebert with Chanya Charles

Introduction

The dramatic end to Sri Lanka's civil war at the end of 2009 brought to a violent close a long-running and brutal chapter in the political struggle that has divided the island's Sinhalese and Tamil ethnic groups for decades. In the final weeks of the campaign, an estimated 150,000 Tamil civilians were trapped in a postage-stamp-sized piece of land on Sri Lanka's northeastern coast between the remnants of the once-feared Liberation Tigers of Tamil Eelam (LTTE) and the army of the government of Sri Lanka. The international humanitarian outcry over the condition of these Tamil civilians in the final months and weeks of the war, and the government's total rejection of this international concern, presaged the heavy-handed policy against its perceived opponents that the government pursued until the end of the Rajapaksa reign in early 2015. Although the bloodiest chapter in Sri Lanka's conflict has concluded, the government's subsequent policies, such as its internment of 300,000 Tamil civilians,[1] its failure to address Tamil and Muslim concerns, and its arrest of key opposition leaders (including former army chief Sarath Fonseka) raised serious questions as to whether the Rajapaksa government would eventually snatch defeat from the jaws of victory.

"Democratic" Sri Lanka has a history of popular elections, and in 1931 it was one of the first countries in the world to enjoy universal suffrage. But the instrument of majoritarian electoral representation has failed to provide an equitable power-sharing framework acceptable to the political leadership of the different ethnic groups. This has led to a series of broken agreements and acute mistrust between the communities. Sri Lanka's political history illustrates the challenges of protecting minority interests in a parliamentary system in which majority-minority relations are strained by competing ethnic nationalist agendas.

Sri Lanka has earned increasing international attention owing to its growing trade relations with Iran and China, the US-India strategic South Asia partnership, and the designation of the LTTE as a terrorist organization. Beyond strategic interests, the international community became heavily involved in attempting to address the civil war in Sri Lanka. There was a well-resourced international monitoring mission; facilitation support from Norway as a committed international actor; and active engagement by the United States, Japan, India, China, and many European countries. In addition to international efforts, Sri Lanka developed three Peace Secretariats, approximately 150 local peace forums, more than 6,000 mediation boards across the country, an active and trained civil society, and an elaborate stakeholder-owned negotiations forum known as the One-Text Initiative (OTI).

After the breakdown in 2003 of the track-one formal negotiations brokered by the Norwegian government, the OTI was established as a confidential dialogue space. Its initiators hoped to create a stakeholder-owned safety net for the formal negotiations, rebuild confidence between the parties, and jointly generate more realistic options for the parties to consider through a "single text" methodology. Most of the key parties joined, including the LTTE as stakeholder-observer. In its first two years, despite the absence of formal talks, the OTI produced more than eighty-nine "consensus" documents. However, even with all of these national and international peace initiatives, the conflict in Sri Lanka escalated dramatically after November 2005. As the Sinhalese government of President Mahinda Rajapaksa came to power with a strong nationalist agenda, Tamil demands for independence grew stronger and their willingness to compromise diminished. Violence in Sri Lanka reached unprecedented levels; from January 2006 to April 2008, more than 12,000 people were killed.[2]

The OTI represents an example of a "good process" that had little or no impact on the prevention of a renewed outbreak of war in 2005–6 between the participating parties. Still, its confidential dialogue forum continued working quietly throughout the war, providing a space for the parties to jointly focus and search for solutions on issues such as internally displaced persons, fundamental rights, humanitarian support to victims of the war, and exploration of ways to end the war, while maintaining key relationships.

This chapter examines the OTI's impact on Sri Lanka's peace and negotiations process and why it was unable to prevent the gradual breakdown of the agreed-on cease-fire of 2002. The authors argue that lack of trust between the parties, the nonimplementation of agreements, competing ethnic nationalist agendas, and each group's unrealistic expectations and demands of each other dominated and undermined both the track-one negotiations and the One-Text process.[3] The absence of workable links and mechanisms between the track-one (official diplomatic) and track-one-and-a-half (OTI) processes robbed each process of mutual benefits and left the OTI unable to act as an effective safety net. The Norway process became the dominant focus for negotiations, but as the conflict reemerged it unfortunately also became a substitute for broken relationships and a punching bag for the parties. When negotiations failed at the top, the overall peace process was left with the symbolic track-one-and-a-half OTI process in the middle of an unfolding war, where it had little influence on the political leaders who were bent on pursuing a military outcome. The chapter explores the mistakes of the past, and concludes with ways in which the OTI dialogue or other processes still can contribute in the postwar period to political accommodation and reconciliation among the island's diverse communities.

The Nature and Course of the Conflict and Peace Talks

Background

The conflict between Sri Lanka's two primary ethnic groups, the Sinhalese majority and the Tamil minority, can be traced back centuries—beginning with an era of separate kingdoms, to the 1500s when colonization first began, to the start of a parliamentary democracy in 1948 when the British withdrew and Sri Lanka (then called Ceylon) gained independence. At the beginning of British colonial rule in the early 1800s, the island still had functioning governance systems based on semi-independent kingdoms that closely resembled what today we would call a confederation. Following the independence of Ceylon in 1948, ethnic conflict between the Tamils and Sinhalese was characterized at first by nonviolent resistance and action by the Tamil population. Over the past three decades, the conflict evolved into a violent struggle for independence and a Tamil "homeland" (Tamil Eelam).

The 1956 Sinhalese "national revolution" initiated a series of discriminatory policies against the Tamil minority. The newly elected Sri Lanka Freedom Party (SLFP) government declared Sinhalese the sole official language, which restricted Tamil access to public services and education. Tensions increased between the Tamil and Sinhalese communities, leading to ethnic riots in the late 1950s. The government refusal to intervene and control the riots resulted in widespread killing and rape of Sri Lankan Tamils.

The Sinhalese government continued to institutionalize its discriminatory policies throughout the 1970s. University entrance exams became Sinhalese-based, placing Tamil students at a disadvantage. The 1972 Constitution established Sinhalese as the country's only official language and Buddhism as the state religion (whereas Tamils follow Hinduism). Differences over devolution of power and acceptable forms of self-governance proved to be the most contentious issue between Tamils and Sinhalese. Tamils demanded greater devolution of power for the Tamil-dominated provinces in the north and east, while the Sinhalese insisted on a strong centralized government under Sinhalese majority control. Tamil groups such as the LTTE began to campaign for an independent Tamil state: Tamil Eelam.

Protagonists and Positions

The central protagonists in Sri Lanka's conflict are the political parties and groups representing the country's major ethnic and religious groups. In 2004, the US State Department's Bureau of South and Central Asian Affairs reported that Sinhalese constituted 74 percent of the country's 20.1 million population, Tamils 18 percent, and Muslims approximately 8 percent. The majority of people are Buddhist (70 percent), 15 percent are Hindu, 8 percent are Christian, and 7 percent are Muslim. The conflict's major fault line runs between the Tamil and Sinhalese. The Muslims have been trapped in the cross fire.

The LTTE and the Tamil National Alliance (TNA) emerged to advocate the interests of the Tamil people. The LTTE's position was that of a liberation struggle, whether on the battlefield, at the negotiations table, or in the international arena. The systematic discrimination against the Tamil minority and a lack of trust of the Sinhalese majority government led the LTTE to take up arms against the state. After successive failed negotiations beginning in 1985, the LTTE did not believe that there could be a constitutional solution to its grievances or that a majority Sinhalese government would protect Tamil rights. The military tactics of the LTTE, known for the "invention" of the suicide bomber and the use of child soldiers, provided the Sinhalese governments with continued reason and excuse not to acknowledge Sinhalese discrimination or the legitimate rights of the Tamils. In contrast to the militarized LTTE, the TNA is the largest Tamil party in the Sri Lankan Parliament and works within the country's constitutional and legal framework to represent Tamil interests. Although the TNA had strong political ties to the LTTE, its support base is broader than only the Tamils living in the north and east. In 2002, the TNA agreed that the LTTE represented the interest of the Tamils in the formal negotiations with the Government of Sri Lanka (GOSL). In addition to these two groups, several smaller Tamil splinter groups and parties have worked with the Sinhalese government or supported a liberal democratic model not based on ethnic considerations. LTTE splinter groups also have been actors in the conflict.

Observers describe the Sinhalese community's position as a majority people living like a minority in their own country. With more than 72 million Tamil people living as neighbors in southern India (as of the 2011 census) and an ancient history of Indian invasion, fear of Tamil domination often drives Sinhalese nationalist sentiments. The Sinhalese majority is represented politically by four parties: the main United National Party (UNP) and Sri Lanka Freedom Party (SLFP) and the smaller Jathika Hela Urumaya (JHU) and Janatha Vimukthi Peramuna (JVP). Divided by their degree and intensity of Sinhalese nationalist and religious positions, the Sinhalese parties have consistently failed to reach consensus on even reasonable power-sharing proposals that might be acceptable to the Tamil parties. The extreme nationalist JVP and JHU have derailed and undermined any agreement with the Tamils. As no single party in Parliament is able to secure a two-thirds majority under the current electoral dispensation, neither UNP nor SLFP governments have been able to implement the constitutional changes required by negotiated agreements with the Tamil parties.

According to most public surveys conducted after 2002, the majority of Sinhalese people want a peaceful political settlement within a framework of one country. Extreme forms of ethnonationalism, however, resurfaced in 2005. Mobilizing the JVP and JHU to help him win the 2005 elections, President Mahinda Rajapaksa allowed extreme Sinhalese-Buddhist nationalist sentiments to drive the political agenda of the SLFP government. In the name of Sinhalese Buddhist nationalism and patriotism, the nation witnessed the radicalization of Sinhalese youth, with the JVP in the forefront. Observers have also pointed to the rise of a "third force" in the conflict. It is now an open secret that some of the political parties have had underworld thugs carry out their dirty work, including the killing of intelligence officers, judges, political opponents, journalists or anyone who speaks out against atrocities, or those who "get in the way."[4] The security and survival of the Muslim community, located principally in the east and southeast, have depended on whoever controlled the territory they live in—sometimes the GOSL and sometimes the LTTE. The Muslim community speaks predominantly Tamil (though English and Sinhalese are also common languages), and is politically represented by the Sri Lanka Muslim Congress (SLMC) and the National Unity Alliance (NUA). Because Muslims have been excluded from the cease-fire and other peace agreements, the Muslim community has felt increasingly insecure. Many observers have anticipated an increase in strength and numbers of Muslim militant groups that would act to protect Muslims trapped in the cross fire between the GOSL and the LTTE.[5]

Onset of War

The rise of Tamil militancy can be traced to the early 1970s. In 1972, the Tamil United Front was formed. This group called for federalism and Tamil self-determination, but stopped short of calls for secession. The government's discriminatory policies and constant reneging on pacts with the Tamil opposition deepened the minority's distrust of Sinhalese politicians. Claiming that all attempts to negotiate with the Sinhalese government had failed, the Tamil opposition established the Tamil United Liberation Front (TULF) in 1976, with the formation of a Tamil state as its central demand. The TULF won decisive victories in the 1977 general election in the north and the east, confirming popular support for secessionism in these areas.

The 1977 election brought a new United National Party (UNP) government to power, with a significant Sinhalese majority in Parliament. Although President J. R. Jayewardene implemented a number of measures to protect and advance minority rights, these did not meet the minimum demands of the Tamil parties. As Tamil frustrations grew and militancy continued to rise, the government increased the strength of its security forces in the north and suspended constitutional safeguards against human rights abuses. The situation deteriorated after the LTTE killed a police inspector in Jaffna in 1978. Shortly afterward, the government banned the LTTE, passed the Prevention of Terrorism Act, and declared a state of emergency in the north. These measures led to intensified activity by security forces and, in turn, fueled Tamil militancy and popular support for their cause.

The LTTE assassination of thirteen soldiers in 1983 marked a critical escalation of the Sri Lankan conflict. Anti-Tamil violence erupted in the south, with hundreds of people killed and thousands of homes and businesses destroyed. The government sided with the perpetrators of the violence, rationalizing the riots as an inevitable response to growing Tamil militancy. Moreover, the GOSL passed a constitutional amendment that banned the advocacy of secessionism, even by peaceful political means. This pushed the TULF parliamentarians—the official opposition, which had been elected on a secessionist platform—out of Parliament, and ended the constitutional drive to Tamil self-determination.

From 1983 on, the Tamil military and the Sri Lankan security forces became locked in a spiral of armed attacks, with high civilian casualties. By the mid-1980s, Tamil militants had gained control of the Jaffna peninsula in the north, and the LTTE had become the dominant militant Tamil group.

Peace Talks

The Sri Lankan conflict was also characterized by numerous efforts to end and resolve it, followed by failure and renewed fighting. Many international and domestic actors became involved in attempting to reach a peaceful solution. But trust among the Tamil, Sinhalese, and Muslim communities and political establishments was eroded by a chronicle of breakdowns in talks and the nonimplementation of agreements.

The first peace talks between the Tamil groups and the GOSL were brokered by India in 1985, but no agreement was reached. The Indo-Lanka Accord of July 1987, signed by the governments of India and Sri Lanka, made some attempt to deal with Tamil claims. However, the LTTE rejected the agreement, regarding it as a betrayal of Tamil aspirations, which led to the failure of the accord and to direct confrontation between the LTTE and the deployed Indian Peacekeeping Force. In the south, the Sinhalese viewed the accord as India's attempt to expand its influence in Sri Lanka.

In April 1989, negotiations were restarted between the new UNP president, Ranasinghe Premadasa, and the LTTE, with the withdrawal of Indian troops from Sri Lankan as the priority. When the Indian troops left Sri Lanka in March 1990, the LTTE took control of the northeast and thousands of non-LTTE supporters were forced to move. Not surprisingly, negotiations between the GOSL and the LTTE collapsed.

After years of war, it was not until 2002, after devastating LTTE attacks on the Central Bank of Sri Lanka in 1996 and national airport in 2001, that the parties were able to reestablish a peace negotiation process. Brokered by Norwegian facilitators, a cease-fire between the UNP government and the LTTE was signed in May 2002, and Peace Secretariats were established for each of the negotiating parties.[6] The Scandinavian countries were invited to monitor the cease-fire, and several joint mechanisms were created to implement shared agreements and normalize the political environment. However, despite six rounds of negotiations in Japan, Thailand, Germany, and Norway, in which the parties made substantial progress in addressing the military, political, economic and constitutional challenges that had divided them over decades, the talks broke down in April 2003. Their ultimate collapse was due to disagreements with the LTTE's proposal for an Interim Self-Governing Authority for the North and East. The UNP government viewed the LTTE's proposal as a threat to the country's sovereignty, and the Tamil demands provoked deep-rooted anger and fear among Sinhala nationalists. The LTTE questioned the intentions of the UNP government in excluding them from donor conferences in the United States and Japan in support of the peace process, and in not engaging directly with them on their proposal. Although the LTTE demands were reasonable and based on minimum expectations, the UNP was unable to manage the reaction of the nationalists and to adequately prepare the south for the outcome of the negotiations. The UNP was unseated in national elections ten months later.

Although the six rounds of formal talks failed to deliver a permanent solution, they marked a turning point in Sri Lanka's peace process, and formed several joint mechanisms and semipermanent formal peace structures. Following the breakdown of the official talks, the main parliamentary parties representing the different ethnic groups (UNP, SLFP, SLMC, and TNA) started to meet confidentially to break the deadlock and to create a safety net for the national negotiations. These meetings led to the establishment of the OTI in 2003 as an effort to create and strengthen an enabling environment for dialogue on process and substantive issues among the parties. The motivation of the parties in establishing the OTI was that the formal peace talks had failed because negotiations had occurred only at the track-one level between the two opposing sides and excluded the other major parties whose support was essential to enable long-term constitutional changes.

When the Indian Ocean tsunami hit Sri Lanka in December 2004, taking 34,000 lives, there was a brief hope that the parties in the conflict could put their differences aside to rebuild their devastated nation. The GOSL and the LTTE agreed to establish the Post-Tsunami Operational Management Structure (P-TOMS) to provide relief funds and services. However, the Sinhalese nationalist lobby led by Mahinda Rajapaksa (who at the time was prime minister) declared the agreement unconstitutional and ousted President Chandrika Kumaratunga. In a controversial Supreme Court decision, her term was ended a year early. Today, the P-TOMS agreement remains a symbol of the potential ability of the parties to negotiate and reach agreements that serve the interests of Sinhalese, Tamils, and Muslims.

The stakes were raised when the hard-line government of President Rajapaksa took over in November 2005. Most of the parties in his alliance questioned the validity and need of the 2002 cease-fire agreement, and positions toughened against Tamil calls for self-determination. But under pressure from the international community, Rajapaksa agreed to two rounds of talks in 2006 with the LTTE in Geneva, Switzerland. From the outset, however, it was obvious that the parties were "talking for the sake of talking" and had no intention of addressing the other side's concerns and demands. On January 16, 2008, the GOSL unilaterally terminated the cease-fire agreement of 2002, claiming that it was "flawed from inception"[7] and that the LTTE had launched attacks and illegal activities during the period of the cease-fire. The LTTE called for the continuation of the Norwegian facilitation and for the Donor Co-Chairs—a group composed of the United States, European Union, Norway and Japan, which began meeting in Tokyo in 2003—to have a greater role in ending the conflict. Although the LTTE agreed to negotiate a new cease-fire agreement, the GOSL refused and continued the war to eliminate the LTTE. Following the collapse of the cease-fire agreement in 2008, Norway's formal role as facilitator ended, although it continued as "informal" facilitator together with the Co-Chairs.

Despite the persistence of the conflict, domestic and international efforts were made to mitigate its consequences. Both the Tamil parties and the GOSL have had functioning human rights agencies (the North East Secretariat of Human Rights and the National Human Rights Commission, respectively) that subscribe to fundamental human rights principles. Both bodies were respected and regarded as capable of defending a human rights framework for the peace process, preparing the way for the United Nations to assist with monitoring and investigating human rights violations. In 2007, UN High Commissioner for Human Rights Louise Arbour called for an international human rights monitoring mission for Sri Lanka, similar to the one sent to Nepal in 2005 to help protect civilians from its escalating violence. The GOSL refused to give permission for the establishment of such a mission, pointing to the existence of its own National Human Rights Commission. In spite of this resistance, each of the main political groupings established Peace Secretariats to coordinate their peace efforts. The 2005 P-TOMS agreement suggested that the parties might be capable of achieving some degree of cooperation. However, after the 2006 Geneva talks broke down, little coordination occurred between the secretariats. The Peace Secretariat for Muslims (PSM) often functioned as a bridge between the GOSL Secretariat for Coordinating the Peace Process (SCOPP) and the Liberation Tigers of Tamil Eelam Peace Secretariat (LTTE PS).

As a result of these many consultations and other efforts, a number of accords and agreements were reached and certain principles and norms were adopted in an effort to limit the scope and effects of the conflict. But these gains were constantly undermined by the assassination of moderate leaders on both sides. By not tolerating dissension, and ruling by fear, each side undermined its own gains and the possibility for agreement with the other.

The toll of the Sri Lankan conflict has been devastating. Most estimates suggest that more than 100,000 were killed, with almost two-thirds of these casualties in the north and the east. From 2001 to 2006, the numbers fluctuated, depending in part on the cease-fire and the status of the negotiations. In the final months of the war in 2009, estimates placed the number of deaths at between 15,000 and 20,000.[8] These estimates are hotly disputed by the Sri Lankan government, which insists that minimal loss of life took place even though it refused to grant full access to the conflict zone or provide evidence to back up its claims. The conflict also had a huge impact on internal displacement and refugees.[9]

The One-Text Initiative: Design and Implementation

Origins and Rationale

A fundamental characteristic of all the Sri Lankan peace processes has been the tendency of the two main protagonists (GOSL and LTTE) to bargain with each other to achieve their strategic interests, but to exclude the other main political stakeholders and opposition parties. Inclusive processes and visible problem-solving were absent from most of their dealings. Within this limited arena, these parties tended to play a zero-sum negotiations game, in which the bargaining and discourse focused on "solutions" and "winning." Few attempts were made to create enabling processes that could provide a roadmap to reach agreed, fair, and just outcomes that would meet the expectations of all parties and provide the foundations for a sustainable peace. Other key peacebuilding elements that were lacking were the building of trust among stakeholders, responding to human rights violations, providing reparations for people affected by the war, and establishing transparent and accountable mechanisms to inform and involve ordinary people in core issues affecting their lives.

Despite the breakdown in April 2003 of the formal negotiations facilitated by Norway, the GOSL and the LTTE had continued to communicate through a series of written exchanges. Based on these communications and the joint achievements since the signing of the cease-fire agreement in 2002, it seemed that there was still some goodwill and opportunity to explore ways to resolve the conflict peacefully. Although the ruling UNP's slim parliamentary majority prevented it from offering further concessions to the LTTE without committing political suicide, the UNP government entered into agreements without the consent of President Chandrika Kumaratunga, the leader of the SLFP opposition. However, the exclusion of the Sinhalese opposition and Muslim parties from the negotiations and peace processes caused the parliamentary parties to suspect the government's intentions. This lack of trust led to a deadlock and internal uproar in the south, and the 2004 general election saw the defeat of the UNP.

Frustrated by the political stalemate, but hopeful that a negotiated solution could be found, the office of the government's chief negotiator—Professor G. L. Peiris of the Ministry of Constitutional Affairs—initiated confidential conversations between the confidants of the top leadership of the key parties to explore the possibility of a One-Text Dialogue process at a track-one-and-a-half level. At the same time, the former foreign minister and chief strategist of the president, Lakshman Kadirgamar, considered a similar low-key secret negotiations approach through the Bandaranaike Centre for International Studies. Both efforts explored with the lead author options and possibilities for the creation of an inclusive confidential dialogue among the main Sinhalese, Tamil, and Muslim parties.

Inspired by the success of the One-Text negotiations approach used by the South African multistakeholder negotiations forum, the Convention for a Democratic South Africa; the 1978 Camp David negotiations between the Israelis and Palestinians; and former US senator George J. Mitchell's use of the "single text" methodology during the Northern Ireland negotiations since 1995, the parties wanted to create a more structured "Sri Lankan One-Text" methodology to move the peace process forward. Although the parties had engaged in six rounds of negotiations, each of these negotiations lasted only a few days, and usually ended prematurely because of the exclusion of Muslim and opposition parties and a lack of confidence in the process. Using the One-Text process concept and framework, the parties met confidentially to discuss, plan, and design a track-one-and-a-half dialogue process that could sustain and support track-one negotiations and inform track-three processes.[10]

This initial dialogue group consisted of members of the two major Sinhalese political parties and the main Tamil and Muslim parliamentary parties. Key members from leading civil society groups with access to all political groupings joined the initiative as knowledge resource experts and partners. After testing the concept and developing a Sri Lankan version of One-Text for more than eight months, in January 2004 the four main political parties decided to institutionalize this informal dialogue process by formally establishing the Sri Lanka One-Text Initiative, intended as an inclusive, stakeholder-driven initiative to support the formal track-one negotiations and the peace process in general.

Basic Design

The process of creating the OTI began with building trust between the individual stakeholders and the facilitators and then increasing the trust among the stakeholders themselves. Collaboration on the OTI's design, guiding principles, and mechanisms provided an initial context within which to build trust and confidence. The design process was driven by the parties' need to create an authentic negotiations structure that could serve as a safety net for future track-one negotiations, and also generate consensus options systematically—a safe space to facilitate dialogue and exchange ideas between Sri Lanka's political stakeholders in an inclusive forum. The overriding goal was to enable stakeholders to develop common ground among their opposing positions through problem-solving interventions and information sharing.

Rather than being a method of conflict pedagogy that uses specific interpersonal and interactive techniques or exercises to impart the desired skills, knowledge, interactions, and values, the OTI created a mechanism and working space for stakeholders to collectively explore and discover common ground and ways to constructively propose and deal with critical issues without having to take formal positions on issues. The process was called "One-Text" because one literal text is drawn from the different narratives and positions of the political stakeholders as well as from various citizens' groups. After eliciting the issues and interests of all the parties, jointly appointed party researchers and technical committees draft proposals and present them to the parties for their input and criticism. The parties continue to provide additional options and criticize drafts until all parties feel that they have an inclusive and representative concept paper. The content developed is confidential and is the intellectual property of the parties involved.

This process provided an opportunity for second-tier leadership to explore major issues and offer multiple and consensus options to top leadership for consideration. Once the parties reached a consensus on issues, such agreements and recommendations could then be offered to the top leadership, the Peace Secretariats, and the Norwegian facilitators.

Accordingly, the stakeholders developed and jointly agreed to a fourteen-step negotiations process framework to achieve the objectives and thus to produce a paradigm shift in Sri Lanka's negotiations culture. Implementing and modeling these principles were seen to be the main way to alter the usual bargaining process and, at the same time, to increase the pressure on the bargaining parties to reach a more expeditious and ultimately more sustainable settlement.

Apart from engaging the political parties and civil society stakeholders in the process, the OTI provided links and mechanisms among tracks one, two and three. In reaction to past peace processes that lacked transparency and were detached from the lives of ordinary people, the initiative's stakeholders believed it essential to engage regular citizens in the national processes that would affect them. Although supporters of the different parties would never literally sit at the negotiations table, the OTI assumed that by keeping track-three stakeholders informed as negotiations progressed, and by building their conflict resolution capacity, it was less likely that regular citizens would reject the final negotiation outcomes and solutions. The OTI also decided to provide concrete support to several of Sri Lanka's main civil society organizations, helping them to contain violence at local levels, prevent incidents from impacting national negotiations, and engage ordinary people in the peace process. With the approval of the One Text Stakeholder Council, five influential civil society groups (the Center for Policy Alternatives, the Bandaranaike Centre for International Studies,

Sarvodaya, the Anti-War Front, and the Foundation for Co-Existence) were engaged. A standing committee on people's participation created a program to engage citizens at the district level. Through the development of national, community-based People's Forums, OTI stakeholders increased the local capacity for peacebuilding and conflict resolution.

Participating Stakeholders

All OTI operational, content, and policy matters were determined by the participating political parties and organizations. Authorized party members from each of the six major political parties, local and international technical experts (appointed by the parties), policy advisors and party researchers, technology support consultants, nominated members from civil society, and other individuals associated with the major political stakeholders or parties all participated in the consultation process. The six major parties engaged in the process represented 80 percent of the seats in Parliament, as well as the nonparliamentary LTTE. Each of the main parliamentary parties appointed two members of Parliament or senior party representatives (as "stakeholders"), a senior policy advisor, and a full-time party researcher to the process. The LTTE was represented through its Peace Secretariat, which was part of the LTTE political wing. In addition to LTTE Peace Secretariat representation, both the SCOPP and the PSM (the government and Muslim Peace Secretariats) were represented through the stakeholder and management councils and several technical committees. By 2006, the OTI included twenty-two party appointees, five civil society appointees, and twelve full-time staff. More than 65 percent of main stakeholder groups, including 72 percent of targeted political stakeholders, were participating in the process. The level of representation increased with several senior cabinet members joining the process, including the Minister of Constitutional Affairs and the chairman of the president's "All-Party Forum."

The only parties that did not participate in the OTI were the two right-wing Sinhalese nationalist parties—the JHU and the JVP—and several smaller Tamil parties. The process was obviously incomplete in the absence of both the JVP (the main Sinhalese nationalist party) and the LTTE. Concerted attempts were made to engage the JHU, JVP, and the Ceylon Workers' Congress (one of the smaller Tamil parties), but initially they remained uncommitted. In the latter part of 2004, the JVP, JHU, and LTTE agreed in principle to join the OTI, and in January 2005 the LTTE and JVP appointed representatives to the process. However, although the JVP nominated a representative, it never actively joined the forum. The LTTE designated its representative as an "observer stakeholder," as its official position was not to engage in "parallel" negotiations. Though the LTTE did not attend the ongoing meetings, its members continued contact with its representative.

Objectives, Values, and Procedures

The broad goal of the OTI was to help develop, implement, and maintain a stakeholder-driven, stakeholder-owned peace process that would enable Sri Lanka's main political actors to collectively find common ground on critical issues. Third-party facilitation and principled negotiations were to be central. The specific OTI objectives, core values, and standard procedures were elaborated and explicitly articulated in a mission statement and "Shared Values and Operating Principles" document formulated by the stakeholders.

The document proclaimed certain core values as a way to set an example for those who were negotiating the country's future at all levels. These principles included popular sovereignty in Sri Lanka, respect for the stakeholders' equality of interests, co-ownership and equal partnership in the peace process, equal opportunity at common forums to share concerns and aspirations, and strengthened capacities in the general population for peacebuilding and conflict resolution.

To apply these values, the documents defined the following objectives:

- Provide a sustainable, inclusive process with political and civil society participation;
- Develop rapport between the OTI parties through systematic interactions and empathetic communication, and build their trust and confidence in the negotiation process;
- Infuse a problem-solving, conflict resolution attitude and behavior among the negotiating parties;
- Identify mutually interdependent interests and seek to develop multiple policy options for contested issues;
- Develop needed capacities of the parties for engaging with the negotiation process; and
- Empower nonelite peace activities by deepening and widening the peace process throughout all sectors of Sri Lankan society.

To pursue the OTI's objectives, the documents committed the stakeholders to specific methods and operating procedures:

- Using the collective, inclusive nature of the OTI as a key process for generating informed options and proposals that contribute toward a sustained track-one negotiation process and a negotiated settlement;
- Applying the "single text" methodology in particular, including problem-solving techniques and formulation of multiple-option solutions;
- Ensuring transparency in all OTI transactions and interactions;
- Exercising the right of dissent to advance the consensual aspirations of the process, rather than to dilute any emerging consensus or collective momentum;
- Respecting the confidentiality of the negotiations according to Chatham House rules;[11] and
- Creating concrete mechanisms to link the track-one, -two, and -three processes, such as by working with civil society partners to mobilize the mass of the people in support of a negotiated settlement and to help contain violence at the local level.

Further, to provide specific guidance for managing and facilitating the stakeholder forum, the task group outlined rules or "negotiations steps" for deciding on such matters as agenda-setting; proposing and tabling issues; establishing and operating committees; doing research and data collection, including determining credible sources; drafting terms of reference for technical committees; choosing mediation techniques; and defining criteria such as "consensus" and "sufficient consensus." As a "living document," these negotiations steps were intended to bring discipline and transparency to the process. Many stakeholders felt that a strict set of procedural rules would provide safety and protect their positions if the majority did not agree with them. Others saw the steps as a means to "obstruct" the process. But as the proposed steps responded to the procedural challenges that members had faced in past negotiations, all parties finally agreed to them. Much of the initial OTI effort was devoted to formulating and reaching agreement on these foundational elements and setting up ways to pursue them. If the stakeholders were expected to actually apply all these values, objectives, methods, and procedures, then they would have to change and adapt some of their own behavioral culture. Consequently, it took almost eighteen months for the parties to agree to these various commitments. A joint task group continuously revised the documents until all parties were satisfied and agreed with the content. The joint task group completed this body of work in September 2005, and it was approved by the Stakeholder Council later that year.

DIALOGUE ACTIVITIES

At the business end of the design, the OTI organized six formats to provide stakeholders and public participants with venucs for engaging in dialogue to share information and discuss key topics of concern:

1. *Stakeholder dialogues.* Each month, representatives from the main parliamentary parties and political groups met to discuss critical issues of the peace and negotiations process. To increase their mutual knowledge of each other's positions and views, these stakeholders had their research teams provide relevant data and information to a shared OTI library and write position and analysis papers.

2. *Electronic workspace.* The ongoing exchange of information and dialogue was made possible by using electronic formats to allow the political stakeholders, OTI staff, and party-nominated researchers to connect with each other. New positions and proposals were incorporated into a virtual document to which all the political parties, civil society organizations, and local and international experts and advisors had access.

3. *Problem-solving workshops.* Regular problem-solving workshops were conducted with the assistance of experienced facilitators to enable parties to discuss issues at length, resolve specific disputes, and get beyond deadlocks. The workshops took the form of weekend retreats; one-day, closed-door meetings; or any form agreed upon by the stakeholders, and ranged from interventions between two parties to collective meetings of all stakeholders.

4. *Confidential roundtables.* At the request of stakeholders, or in response to the needs of the negotiations process, confidential roundtable forums that incorporated all sides of the political spectrum were held regularly. These meetings were structured to use common resource persons who were shared with all the stakeholders.[12]

5. *Public forums.* Large gatherings of stakeholders, civil society members, students, and other interested parties were organized in which critical issues and components of the peace process were discussed in a panel format. Most forums were planned around the visits of international experts who could enrich the dialogues and enhance public education.[13]

6. *People's Forums.* To link tracks one, two and three, a People's Participation Standing Committee created People's Forums to enable villagers and community leaders to discuss issues that affected their lives and to "negotiate" the same issues being discussed by the main political stakeholders.

In its first year of operation, the four civil society implementing partners held forty-two of these forums throughout the country. The initiative grew to more than 150 forums, and the implementing partners created a People's Forum Federation and similar structures.

Five domestic and international civil society organizations collaborated with the OTI to facilitate dialogue among all the parties, track-one-and-a-half interventions that could inform track-one negotiations, and track-three processes to link the national process with districts around the country.[14]

STRUCTURE

With the increasing participation of many participants at the different levels, the OTI expanded into a complex set of operations and governance structure. Figure 6.1 below portrays the initiative's main operating entities and formal relationships.

To maintain these activities, the OTI was overseen by a Stakeholder Council, Management Council, and Board. The Stakeholder Council consisted of all party and civil society representatives, chairs of standing committees, and management staff, and was the final decision-making body, meeting once a month to set policy. The Management Council oversaw day-to-day operations and implementation. The Board represented the OTI as a legal registered entity and ensured that administrative, financial, and legal obligations and regulations were met. The OTI structure included four types of technical committees—standing committees, thematic groups, task groups, and subcommittees—that brought together local and international experts on specific topics with the editorial and research departments. Standing committees were permanent and met monthly on subjects such as human rights, people's participation, and the cease-fire. Thematic groups were experts on complex issues that required technical advisors. Task groups, such as the Facilitation and Process Support Committee, arranged for support to sustain the OTI and its outreach. Subcommittees were temporary committees for specific tasks, such as the United National Party and Sri Lanka Freedom Party Committee working on southern consensus. Finally, the initiative had several crucial support units: an independent in-house research department with senior researchers; an editorial staff for drafting core OTI documents and developing knowledge resources;[15] local advisors and experts to help reach agreement on important, credible data and

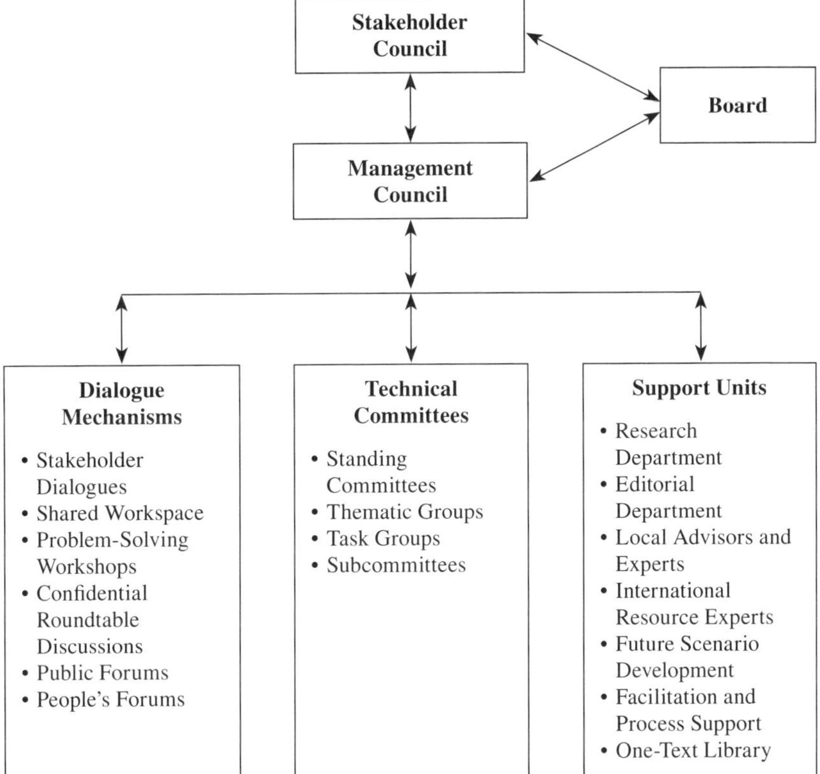

Figure 6.1.   OTI Structure and Entities

to recommend external third-party experts; international resource experts who visited to reflect with OTI stakeholders on lessons learned from India, Kenya, Nepal, Palestine, South Africa, and other conflict transformation processes; a future scenario unit to address issues in postconflict peacebuilding and perform quarterly internal evaluations of the OTI process; a facilitation and process support unit that managed and facilitated the Stakeholder Council meetings; and OTI's physical and virtual library.

All of the initiative's national meetings and regular activities were held at its office in the capital city, Colombo. The parties' researchers and advisors worked there together, protected by private guards and additional security for monthly stakeholder meetings.

FINANCIAL SUPPORT

The OTI received support from many government and nongovernmental Sri Lankan and international actors. Initial funding was provided by the US Agency for International Development (USAID) through the Academy for Educational Development (AED). When the LTTE Peace Secretariat joined the initiative, the funding was restructured and the governments of Norway, Switzerland, Denmark, and the United Kingdom joined the United States as core funders from 2004 through 2009.[16] Norway regarded OTI as complementary to the track-one process, for it included most of the major parties needed to achieve eventual constitutional change and thus secure a sustainable peace. To link the OTI to its international supporters, in 2005 a standing committee of representatives from the contributing agencies and governments was established.[17] The committee met monthly after each Stakeholder Council meeting and was given an update, and its members provided strategic, political, material, and process support.

Impacts of the One-Text Initiative

Initially, as part of a deliberate strategy to build confidence and trust, the stakeholders often focused on "process and technical issues" to assist in dealing with more complex political challenges. When the conflict grew more intense in 2005, the members' mandate became more limited and much of the dialogue got stuck on technical or "soft issues," thereby diverting the focus from the more intractable issues. During the height of the crisis, the relationships between members strengthened, and process procedures and the dialogue "rituals" stayed intact. Some of its members were imprisoned and others received death threats, but all continued their efforts to resolve the national conflict.

Effects on Participants

One of the most important effects of the OTI process in Sri Lanka was the fostering and strengthening of interpersonal relationships across the divide. Through their engagement in the process, participants from different political and ethnic groups were able to interact constructively and to develop significant rapport. Their efforts to come to agreement on shared values and other founding principles of the initiative was itself a significant breakthrough and boosted members' morale and confidence. The rapport was also demonstrated through ongoing informal conversations among stakeholders and their commitment to the process, even at difficult political moments.

The initiative did not escape the hard political realities of assassinations, imprisonment and torture, and death threats, which occurred both between the protagonists and within their respective ranks. In late 2004, an extreme Sinhalese nationalist militant group started to send death threats to the Sinhalese OTI members. Although many of the members ignored these threats, it was evident that pro-peace Sinhalese were being identified and intimidated. One of the initiative's first major setbacks was the assassination of Lakshman Kadrigamar, the OTI's, cofounder and Sri Lanka's esteemed former foreign minister, by an unknown assassin in 2005. The assassination sent shockwaves through OTI, as it took place a few weeks after Kadrigamar's first meeting with the LTTE's One-Text representative. Nevertheless, this event eventually strengthened the relationships between the members and helped them to implement security measures for all members. Yet following Kadirgamar's death, the initiative witnessed the assassinations of three other key people on both sides of the peace process: the deputy head of the government's Peace Secretariat, the head of the Tamil Human Rights Secretariat, and the LTTE's chief negotiator. The latter was killed in the same week as a proposal was presented, on behalf of the chief negotiator to the United States and Italy, to resume talks under the auspices of the Sri Lanka Co-Chairs (the United States, European Union, Norway, and Japan).

Although overall participation at meetings declined in the period leading up to the elections (February to April 2005), parallel bilateral and multilateral meetings increased among stakeholders that addressed various key issues, including a memorandum of understanding between the majority Sinhalese parties, the UNP and SLFP. Strengthened relationships and personal commitments, in turn, helped move the process along at difficult moments.

Personal threats to members became common as the war unfolded in 2005. From 2005 to 2009, the members participated at great personal risk. One of the senior Tamil advisors had to withdraw following an attempted attack on himself and threats to his daughter. "Peace" became a dirty word during the war. Ironically, the level, number, and seniority of the OTI members increased. The One-Text office became a meeting place for the leaders from each party who stayed committed to finding a peaceful and negotiated solution to the country's conflict. The arrest and torture of TNA member

J. S. Tissainayagam in 2008 had a special impact on the relationships among members. Members of all parties appealed for his release; several tried to visit him in jail; and a civil society partner institution, the Center for Policy Alternatives, assisted with his legal proceedings. Several donors questioned the stakeholders' real commitment to the process and to each other, arguing that participants were only interested in compensation. But after April 2005, the stakeholders did not receive any fees or reimbursements, yet they continued to meet monthly and expressed their intention to continue the process even if no funding was obtained for their efforts.

Effects on Interparty Collaboration

The initiative's first major achievement in the overall peace process was the facilitation and support of the establishment of the PSM in 2005. For several months, the OTI hosted and facilitated talks between the two main Muslim parties, the SLMC and NUA, that resulted in the establishment of the PSM. This new secretariat provided the Muslim parties with a recognized mechanism to engage in direct negotiations with the other peace secretariats and the international community on critical issues such as post-tsunami reconstruction, strengthening of the cease-fire agreement (from which the Muslim parties had been excluded), and future representation at the track-one negotiations. Together with the government's Peace Secretariat and the LTTE Peace Secretariat, the PSM became a full OTI member.

Another OTI accomplishment was the stakeholders' increased ability to reach consensus on principles, procedures, and actions. The most significant collective achievement was the adoption of the mission statement, operational principles, shared values, and negotiation steps. In fact, many stakeholders commented that the mission statement and shared values document could form the preamble and framework for a final agreement between the GOSL and LTTE.

As the safeguards were established to protect their fundamental shared values and interests, and agreed procedures and steps were put in place, the parties showed increasingly noticeable confidence in addressing substantive issues. These issues included the post-tsunami reconstruction and the P-TOMS agreement, challenges to the 2002 cease-fire accord, implications of the 2005 national elections, ongoing local conflicts between different ethnic and religious groups, deadlock-breaking mechanisms, and efforts to develop a human rights accord/understanding. From January 2004 to December 2005, the parties reached 132 consensus decisions in the following areas: on human rights (25); on matters related to strengthening the cease-fire (29); on bilateral relations (5); on people's participation and local forums (2); on conflict management and intervention issues (9); on issues relating to the Muslim community (9); on joint mechanisms, organizational, procedural, and process matters (34); and on internal household issues (19). The Stakeholder Council approved and adopted seven One-Text documents and drafts produced by technical committees, and rejected seven drafts over the same period. The first joint all-party Ceasefire Sub-Committee and Human Rights Standing Committee provided invaluable opportunities to address concerns and full implementation of the cease-fire. The Human Rights Standing Committee was the first of its kind for human rights entities and parties across the political divide (including the national Human Rights Commission in the south, and the Human Rights Secretariat in the northeast) to actively work together. During the conflict in Trincomalee in 2005, the parliamentary leaders of the TNA and SLFP in the OTI agreed to share the same public platforms to call for peace and work with local People's Forums to develop a sustainable solution.

On a more general level, to increase research capacity and to provide all the parties with equal access to knowledge resources and information on the issues discussed at the dialogue table, the OTI partnered with a local IT company, Info-Share, to create the previously mentioned "Peace Library," an online/desktop information resource.[18]

At the track-three level, the success of the People's Forums that grew out of the People's Participation Standing Committee was a significant success. The forums focused on good governance, peace, and civic awareness, building the capacity of communities to take charge of their future. Reaching 150 communities across Sri Lanka, the People's Forums engaged with thousands of people to establish community-based dialogue forums and interfaith dialogues, conduct conflict resolution trainings, address joint environmental and economic challenges, support income-generation activities, and improve legal services.

Effects on the Conflict and Track-One Negotiations

The OTI's role in providing ongoing channels for dialogue and deadlock-breaking mechanisms was viewed as a positive achievement. Clearly, it achieved its goal of opening up dialogue for stakeholders beyond formal negotiations and during the time of active war. At the political party level, it provided space for parties to debrief and informally discuss their public conflicts. In late 2004, for example, the TNA vehemently objected to a proposal that the Sinhalese national parties had put forward in Parliament, declaring it "offensive" and a violation of Tamil rights. All TNA members in Parliament took to the floor and protested in front of the Speaker of the House, and the house postponed further consideration of the proposal. At the One-Text Stakeholder Council meeting that evening, many of the senior parliamentary leaders from each party were present. An in-depth discussion of the controversial proposal was able to explore options that would resolve the parliamentary deadlock.

However, following the election of President Rajapaksa in 2005, the SLFP and UNP OTI representatives were unable to have any effect on the deteriorating relations of the GOSL, the opposition, and the LTTE. The new president's decision to resolve the national conflict through war changed the entire national discourse. Although President Rajapaksa allowed several cabinet ministers to participate in the initiative, their participation did not lead to the reestablishment of formal negotiations. Despite the commitment that the OTI members displayed in the face of personal threats, the peace process was paralyzed by the lack of willingness on the part of the parties as a whole to come to an agreement.

The initiative's biggest achievement was that it managed to maintain a safe space for senior members of Sri Lanka's main parties to continue their work for peace and a sustainable solution to the national crisis. For many stakeholders, the OTI's existence was a symbol of their hope, path, and desire for peace.

Missed Opportunities

Despite the encouraging collaboration among initiative stakeholders at the track-one-and-a-half level, only limited progress was made in broadening and deepening stakeholder links to the top leadership. Additional representation and active participation from existing stakeholders were needed to ensure progress on the multiple issues which the OTI's numerous committees were structured to address. But the initiative often overstretched its efforts to bring JVP and JHU representatives into the process, rather than focusing on critical issues confronting the country. Although both the JVP and JHU indicated their interest and willingness to participate in the process, neither of them made a firm commitment to do so.

Although Norway participated in the OTI international resource committee and cofunded the initiative, the links between the track-one and track-one-and-a-half processes were never formally established. This lack of constructive links robbed the track-one process of a sustainable support mechanism and the track-one-and-a-half process of sufficient recognition to enhance the urgency and seriousness of its dialogues. Sri Lanka's three Peace Secretariats had only minimal communication and collaboration. The OTI was the only formal structure where the three secretariats were officially jointly represented and collaborating. OTI stakeholders considered it a priority to establish constructive working relationships between these official peace bodies. The three secretariats drafted a joint terms of reference for their participation in the initiative and jointly served on several technical committees. However, each community and party used the secretariats primarily as propaganda vehicles and mailboxes for messages from the others and for the international community. It was only with the initial monitoring coordination of the cease-fire agreement in 2002 and 2003, the negotiations with the P-TOMS agreement in 2005, and the preparations for the negotiations in Geneva in 2006, that their potential for peace was evident.

As the initial OTI funder in 2004 through the AED Sri Lanka Peace Support Program, USAID supported activities that encouraged multistakeholder engagement in the peace process. When the LTTE expressed interest in participating in 2005, however, problems arose. Although including the LTTE in the OTI met the USAID objective of "multistakeholder engagement," it violated the US government policy prohibiting support of organizations with connections to groups on the State Department's list of Designated Foreign Terrorist Organizations. Since relationship building and trust were essential factors in the OTI's operations, the withdrawal of USAID support sent the wrong message. Also, because USAID was a primary donor for the People's Forums, this "antiterrorism" policy also limited the geographic range of the local forums' conflict intervention and reconciliation efforts. Although the United States was a strong supporter, AED could not fund People's Forum activities for communities in LTTE-controlled areas of the north and east, or in areas where LTTE representatives might be present.

At that time, many of the activities conducted through the USAID grant to OTI, such as the International Negotiators Program, Public Forums and lectures, publications, and research, were shifted to an alternate support organization. AED helped to found the South Asia Peace Initiative (SAPI) in 2005 to carry out the activities that did not involve the LTTE. In hindsight, this response may have been a mistake. Building a new organization parallel to the OTI diminished the role that the initiative played and created a difficult dynamic among OTI, SAPI, and the AED project. Fortunately, in the case of the People's Forums, funding from the Canadian International Development Agency and the Peace Appeal Foundation enabled the forums to reach communities in the north and east. The US Embassy's subsequent willingness and commitment in 2008 to again provide US support to the initiative constituted an important signal from an international actor that still had significant influence on the parties.

Favorable and Unfavorable Factors

A number of factors were critical in shaping the initiative's impacts. Some of these factors were related to OTI's own features, and some were largely outside its control. Although the features and the context interacted, several factors are distinguishable.

Implementation Factors

Limited cooperation among peace secretariats. The existence of the three Peace Secretariats for Sri Lanka's main groups (SCOPP, LTTE PS, and PSM) was a core asset and important mechanism to engage each of the communities in the peace process. The secretariats provided access to the process and helped to express each community's fears, perceptions, hopes, and aspirations. However, the limited cooperation among the three secretariats contributed to a lack of linkages to the track-one process and to insufficient integration between peace efforts on all levels. To counteract the absence of sufficient lines of communications or structures for collaboration on the peace process, the three secretariats informally agreed to form a joint committee to explore areas of cooperation and to deal with ongoing technical and logistical matters. This formal cooperation was not consolidated, however, thus preventing the resolution of critical issues.

Poor linkage between the OTI and the track-one negotiations. The absence of effective linkages connecting the OTI with the track-one negotiations and Norwegian facilitators reduced its potential impact on the peace process. Several attempts were made to link the process to Norway's facilitation, but no progress was made. The OTI facilitator did provide regular briefings to the Norwegian Embassy, but there was little effective two-way flow of communication. Consequently, despite innovative options generated by the OTI process, the lack of adequate communication mechanisms prevented these options from reaching the top leadership and the leading international facilitator.

Uneven powers of stakeholder representatives. Also weakening the process were the uneven positions of influence and unequal levels of participation reflected among the representatives of the political stakeholders, particularly for the purpose of effective decision-making. Some parties appointed their top leaders, others selected members of Parliament, and some chose ordinary party members or observers. The process made a distinction between permanent members and observers in terms of responsibilities, but no distinction was made in terms of actual roles, prerogatives, and benefits. An example of this uneven representation was the position of the LTTE representative. Although the representative was only appointed by the LTTE PS as an "Observer Stakeholder," his contribution and role were regarded as at the same level as the members with full participatory status. Because of the importance of the LTTE's role in the overall process and its security concerns that barred the appointment of a full member, the other OTI members allowed this exception. The LTTE's representative co-chaired the Ceasefire Committee with the GOSL representative. However, an unfortunate effect of this uneven representation was the perception that the decisions agreed upon might not be binding or credible. In addition, even though a number of stakeholders demonstrated high levels of participation and commitment to the process, an overall assessment of the initiative revealed that several key stakeholders were noncommittal, hesitant, or only poorly aware of the process, thereby hampering its ability to function as a track-one-and-a-half process.

Lack of engagement by "peace spoilers." To create a sustainable process, all the parties in the initiative, including the LTTE and TNA, agreed to bring in representatives from the extreme Sinhalese nationalist JVP and JHU parties. Since these parties were considered "peace spoilers" and opposed the cease-fire agreement with the LTTE, the OTI stakeholders believed that it was essential to engage them in a confidential negotiations process. Despite both parties' expressed willingness to participate in the process, neither of them made a commitment to do so.

Imbalanced civil society representation. In the absence of a nationwide Tamil institution, the four implementing partners of the People's Forums were southern-based and/or Sinhalese-dominant. This often created tension with the LTTE PS and led to a lack of credibility in conflict areas.

Insufficient conflict resolution capacity. Participants' uneven and sometimes weak conflict resolution abilities limited the initiative's effectiveness and resulted in the reproduction of track-one problems and dynamics in the One-Text process. The four civil society partners were responsible for providing all capacity building, training, and knowledge creation services to stakeholders and to each party's peace unit. But since civil society was just as divided as the political society in Sri Lanka, the result was an unequal distribution of such services. Parties often boycotted valuable services provided by partners that they perceived to be on the other side of the political divide. Some of these concerns were valid, but many were personality-driven and reflected an unwillingness to receive information and knowledge from those they did not trust or with whom they disagreed. Limited capacity also resulted in low quality of outputs and the lack of mechanisms for translating outputs into impact.

"Decisions by full consensus" that blocked progress. Procedural issues also contributed significantly to the OTI's limited impact. The agreed negotiations and decision-making procedure of the initiative was based on the principle of "decisions by full consensus." This principle opened the door for many parties to obstruct the process and hinder progress on critical issues. Parties were able to block processes that were simply intended to explore avenues to break deadlocks or develop bilateral understanding between them. This became such a problem that the process was unable to move forward for several months in the midst of the build-up to the renewed civil war. To address the problem created by the full consensus requirement, the parties agreed to adopt a "sufficient consensus" procedure. This was complemented by an expansion of the agreed negotiations steps that allowed individual parties to explore options and put forward recommendations even before "sufficient consensus" was required or approval was given for the creation of a technical committee. This change allowed for the creation of interim working groups and bilateral committees that could engage and offer options that had not yet obtained the approval of the full forum.

Overly complex structure. To compensate for the severe lack of trust between the parties, the all-party working group designed a structured negotiations process and framework that new members later described as "extremely rigid." According to an external evaluation of the process, stakeholders found the organization and method overly complex, difficult to understand, and nontransparent. The structure of the initiative also contributed to the national leadership's too often being removed from realities at the local level. Securing better linkages could have made the national process more responsive and accountable.

Security issues complicating logistics. Although members from the LTTE Peace Secretariat and Human Rights bodies were willing to participate in national meetings, ensuring their security presented a major challenge. Attempts were made to change the venue of certain meetings to venues in the north or east, but these arrangements created similar problems for participants from the south.

Organizational and funding challenges. Organizational challenges also reduced the initiative's effectiveness. These challenges included an overburdening of the facilitation capacity and poor institutional capacities and infrastructure. Also, as mentioned, when the LTTE requested to join the initiative, funding had to be restructured to include a wider range of donors because the US State Department had classified the LTTE as a terrorist organization.

Contextual Factors

Norwegian facilitation. The commitment of the Norwegian government to its role as the formal track-one facilitator was a great asset to the process. The Norwegian facilitators' selfless and consistent facilitation among top leaders, even when formal talks broke down, provided an umbrella under which national initiatives such as the OTI could bring parties together and work to restore the peace process. Norway often took the blame for the parties' failure to deliver on commitments, but the presence of the Norwegian facilitation kept hope alive that the peace process could succeed.

Active Co-Chairs. The four Co-Chairs' (the European Union, Japan, Norway, and the United States) presence and role provided much-needed backing for the Norwegian facilitation, and also helped to keep most parties in the process. However, their decision to exclude the LTTE from the donor conferences in the United States and Japan in 2002–3, and their inability to influence the GOSL and LTTE in order to prevent the

2005–9 war, were both disappointing. The absence of India and China as the major regional stakeholders from the Co-Chairs group was an unfortunate omission.

Sri Lankan monitoring mission. The monitoring mission's presence on the ground in the north and east and their numerous successful interventions prevented many killings and ensured a level of stability and normalization between 2002 and 2004. Although the international component of the mission worked well, the national component of the GOSL and LTTE was less successful.

Strong civil society. Sri Lanka's strong and diverse civil society was also important because it managed to mobilize people from all ethnic communities and religions in support of the peace process. According to public polls in 2003, more than 85 percent of the country supported the peace and negotiations process. With extraordinary national networks, organizations such as Sarvodaya and the National Anti-War Front were able to reach into more than 20,000 villages. Elders in more than 6,000 villages were trained in mediation skills and were operating active mediation boards.

Lack of political will by leadership. The most important contextual factor affecting the success of the One-Text process was the general lack of interest and political will on the part of the country's political leadership to actually reach a negotiated and peaceful settlement to the conflict. The OTI operated in an environment characterized by an increasingly militaristic approach to the conflict and the legitimization of violence as a solution. Little political capital was available for engagement in the peace process. In fact, a lack of progress in the initiative often reflected the unwillingness of the main parties to engage with or address specific issues or to explore options. This led to an underutilization of this joint resource, increased frustration on the part of its participants, and limited results on substantial matters.

Turning point events. Major events such as the 2004 tsunami, the 2005 national elections, the 2008 collapse of the cease-fire agreement, and the decision of the GOSL to go to war with the LTTE were major events that influenced many OTI operations. The initiative's stakeholder, technical, and subcommittees, as well as the community-level dialogues initiated through the People's Forums, all had to contend with the social, political, and economic effects of these defining events.

Opaque stakeholder decision-making authority. Also problematic was the fact that the major parties had centralized, nondemocratic, nontransparent internal party structures that the initiative found difficult to access. The process assumed that participating members would provide full reports and feedback to their individual parties, and also assumed that the parties had approved documents that were submitted for final adoption and approval of the Stakeholder Council. Although these assumptions were evident in the adoption of most OTI documents and drafts, it was not clear whether party leadership was sufficiently consulted to make the decisions binding. This problem stemmed from the internal practices of the parties themselves. It was difficult to have sustainable and accountable negotiations without decision-making procedures within a party that authorized their negotiators with proper mandates.

Personal risk for voices for peace. Lastly, the very strength of the initiative in building confidence and strengthening relationships across the divide posed the biggest threat to the members themselves. As the process advanced and created increased understanding of each other's positions and interests, it faced the challenge of transferring this knowledge and experience to the respective parties. Against the backdrop of the limitations outlined above, this posed an almost impossible task for members. As the parties entered a period of war from 2005 to 2009, their participation in a "peace process" became less tenable, as neither the governing SLFP nor the LTTE tolerated dissenting voices.

Summary

Sri Lanka's civil war lasted for more than two decades, killing some 100,000 people and displacing hundreds of thousands more. Both the government and the LTTE waged a brutal war. The armed hostilities from 2005 to 2009 caused immeasurable human suffering, displaced hundreds of thousands of people, and took the lives of more than 12,000 people, mostly civilians in the north and east. Neither side was able to claim victory. Although the GOSL most likely feels that it won the battle against the LTTE, new forms of extreme Tamil resistance may haunt Sri Lanka for years to come. Some describe the outcome of the war as deliberate "ethnic cleansing" of Tamils in the north and east. In mid-2008, a major outcry and protest arose from the 60 million Tamils in southern India against their own government for not stopping the war in Sri Lanka. International observers, such as the United Nations and Amnesty International, warned of serious war crimes and gross human rights abuses being committed by all sides. The true cost of the Sri Lankan conflict will never be known. In its final years, the lack of access to LTTE-held areas, as well as the GOSL's media censorship, media intimidation, strong-arm tactics, and limitation of access to affected areas to international officials, humanitarian aid agencies and journalists alike, effectively prohibited an accurate reporting of the conflict's costs. Though the United States and other international governments have called for war crimes investigations into the conduct of both the GOSL and the LTTE, they either do not possess or choose not to use the leverage required to ensure such investigations take place.

It is no small irony that for decades, Sri Lanka's people were considered its greatest asset, allowing the nation to leapfrog other countries with higher per capita gross domestic product in development rankings. But even as its per capita gross domestic product has grown, Sri Lanka's people have been the greatest casualty of the conflict. Sri Lankans have killed each other and silenced their own to feed religious and nationalist aspirations. With the war's brutal conclusion, the parties still have to face each other to find a new set of solutions to restore "normalcy" and provide for those who were affected by the war.

It is beyond the scope of this chapter to assess the prospects for post-conflict dialogue, reconciliation, and political harmony in Sri Lanka. In light of the Rajapaksa government's postwar policies and practices, hopes that its fragile democracy can be the vehicle for reconciling the aspirations of Sri Lanka's diverse peoples were at best uncertain. However, the defeat of the extreme nationalistic and increasingly authoritarian Rajapaksa government at the beginning of 2015 showed that the majority of Sri Lankans want peace and do not tolerate the abuse of power. The Tamil and Muslim voters who felt abandoned by Rajapaksa turned the electoral tide, and a significant percentage of Sinhalese joined this anti-authoritarian outcry. Rajapaksa tried in vain to convince the military to support him in his efforts to hold on to power, but was left with no choice but to accept defeat. The new unity government has showed significant willingness to address the constitutional, justice, and humanitarian needs of the oppressed Tamil community. Thus, real opportunities now exist for reconciliation through building cooperation and productive exchanges in order to rekindle hope between former enemies. In this context, the OTI is still well placed to serve as a mechanism and platform to assist in facilitating such a process, though it is not insulated from real politics and the deep wounds left by the war. Its past experience suggests some clear lessons that are relevant to the current challenges:

- It is essential to strengthen individual relationships between stakeholders and to secure a space and process for ongoing dialogue and exchange.
- To help a national dialogue and reconciliation process to make progress, the parties could build on the foundation of the OTI principles and procedures and the agreed-upon shared values, adapting its agreed-on steps as a framework for a new process.
- Any such process needs to be formally linked to the top leadership, with authoritative mandates from each party.
- To ensure an accountable and people-friendly process that effectively advances reconciliation and healing, strong links need to exist between national processes and grassroots communities. People's Forums could be established in crisis areas in the north and east and focus attention on areas and border villages most affected by the war.
- For a future process to succeed and to ensure a just and sustainable solution, committed international actors, including India and China, must assist all parties fairly and equally, and use their influence to prevent discrimination against minorities. All foreign countries should be sensitive and careful not to further encourage human rights violations under the pretense of fighting "terrorism."
- To prevent peace "spoilers" and extreme nationalist groups from hijacking the process, the main parties must engage them in the process and act strongly against hate speech, gross human rights violations, and corruption.
- Internal democracy in each party needs to be strengthened, and accommodating national democratic and constitutional institutions need to be developed and protected by an independent constitutional court or council.
- A military option was chosen by both sides in the recent war in part because of a lack of trust, but also because of a lack of faith in the dialogue process. The OTI and its civil society partners could encourage and facilitate the development of a strong dialogue process and deadlock-breaking mechanisms.
- Since religion has been exploited by all communities to feed nationalist aspirations, religious leadership from all communities and religions

should be encouraged to actively promote common values for peace, reconciliation, tolerance, and healing.

As the physical destruction and emotional wounds of past war continues to affect every level of Sri Lanka, the responsibility for rebuilding the country lies with the entire nation. All communities and levels of society, including civil society, religious communities, business, security institutions, and political leadership, need to work together on a new collective vision for the country and to chart a new journey that embraces the humanity of all, and restores and protects the dignity and rights of every person on the island.

Notes

1. Robert Templer, "War Without End," *New York Times*, July 21, 2009, http://www.nytimes.com/2009/07/22/opinion/22iht-edtempler.html.

2. South Asia Terrorism Portal, "Fatalities in Terrorist Violence in Sri Lanka 2002–2015," retrieved April 2015, http://www.satp.org/satporgtp/countries/shrilanka/database/annual_casualties.htm.

3. Lead author Hannes Siebert was one of the co-founding members and facilitators of the One-Text process in Sri Lanka from 2003 to 2005. Contributing author Chanya Charles was the program director for the Academy for Educational Development (AED), the original donor implementing agency on behalf of the US Agency for International Development (USAID). The draft chapter was condensed by the volume editor.

4. Nirmala Kannangara, "Mervyn Behind Kelaniya Crimes," *The Sunday Leader* (Colombo), June 6, 2013, http://www.thesundayleader.lk/2013/06/23/mervyn-behind-kelaniya-crimes/; Sunil De Silva, "Religious Leaders call for Stop of Abductions," Caritas Sri Lanka, April 23, 2012, http://www.caritaslk.org/index.php/news-stories/archived/152-religious-leaders-call-for-stop-of-abductions.html; and US Department of State, Bureau of Democracy, Human Rights, and Labor, *Sri Lanka Human Rights Report 2013* (2013 Country Reports on Human Rights Practices), 2013, http://www.state.gov/documents/organization/220616.pdf. In the period after the 2002 cease-fire, many suspicious killings took place that did not seem to be the responsibility of the LTTE or Sri Lankan security forces. In the media, the killers were described as "pistol gangs" on motorbikes or camouflaged gangs in white vans.

5. [Jeffrey Lunstead], "Source Report on Muslim Militancy in Sri Lanka," US State Department, June 9, 2004, available through WikiLeaks, https://www.wikileaks.org/plusd/cables/04COLOMBO950_a.html.

6. A Muslim Peace Secretariat was to come later, in 2004.

7. Foreign Minister Rohitha Bogollagama, quoted in "CFA Was Seriously Flawed from Inception," *Daily News* (Colombo), January 5, 2008, http://archives.dailynews.lk/2008/01/05/pol05.asp.

8. In 2001, the year before the cease-fire was signed, almost 4,500 total combatant and civilian deaths were reported. The number of fatalities dropped dramatically after the signing of the cease-fire agreement to only fifteen combatant and civilian reported

deaths, although no numbers are available from the LTTE. Following 2003, the death toll rose gradually for three years, increasing with rising tensions and the failure of formal negotiations. In 2006, after the pro-Sinhalese nationalist government was established, it rose dramatically, with more than 35,000 deaths estimated between 2006 and 2009. World Watch, South Asia Terrorism Portal, "Fatalities in Terrorist Violence in Sri Lanka 2002–2015," http://www.satp.org/satporgtp/countries/shrilanka/database /annual_casualties.htm. The United Nations stated that the conflict had killed between 80,000 to 100,000 people since 1983; see C. Bryson Hull and Ranga Sirilal, "Last Phase of Sri Lanka War Killed 6,200 Troops: Government," *Reuters*, May 22, 2009, http:// www.reuters.com/article/2009/05/22/us-srilanka-war-idUSTRE54L0YW20090522; and Peter Wonacott, "Sri Lanka Declares Rebel Chief Dead, Ending War," *Wall Street Journal*, May 18, 2009, http://www.wsj.com/articles/SB124263479362029841.

9. The number of Tamil refugees from Sri Lanka in southern India was estimated at 99,600 in 2007, as determined through a worldwide survey of refugees conducted and confirmed by the United Nations High Commissioner for Refugees/US Committee for Refugees and Immigrants (UNHCR/USCRI) report. The dramatic increase of refugees in India was a result of persistent air strikes on LTTE targets and Tamil villages by the Sri Lankan air force and of desperate attempts by civilians to escape the heavy fighting in the north and east. Most of these refugees had to abandon their homes and sell their belongings to pay for the costs of transportation and entry into the camps. Internal displacement was much greater. In April 2008, the total number of internally displaced persons in Sri Lanka was estimated to be between 500,000 and 600,000 (CIA Factbook). With the end of the war, the GOSL placed more than 300,000 Tamil civilians and ex-combatants in so-called "welfare villages": multiple internment camps in the north of the country run by the Sri Lanka military, where access by international humanitarian aid agencies, journalists, and others was severely limited and constrained. By the end of 2010, more than 100,000 people remained in these camps, despite pleas by the United Nations and other international bodies for the camps to be closed and their residents allowed to return to their homes. See USCRI, *World Refugee Survey, 2007* (Washington, DC: USCRI, 2007), http://www.refugees.org/resources/uscri_reports /archived-world-refugee-surveys/2007-world-refugee-survey.html. The CIA Factbook no longer has the cited Sri Lankan displaced persons data: see UNHCR, *UNHCR 2012 Global Report: South Asia* (Geneva, Switzerland, UNHCR, 2012), http://www.unhcr .org/51b1d640a.pdf; and UNHCR, *UNHCR Global Appeal 2009 Update: Sri Lanka* (Geneva, Switzerland: UNHCR, 2009), 292–97, http://www.unhcr.org/4922d42a0.pdf.

10. The strategy recognized that a peace process has multiple levels, or tracks, and multiple stakeholders with constituencies: track one (the official facilitator or mediator), track one-and-a-half (advisors to the negotiating parties and first-tier leaders of stakeholder groups), track two (national level civil society, the private sector, and the media, as well as second-tier leaders of stakeholder groups); and track three (grassroots constituencies and local leaders of stakeholder groups).

11. When a meeting, or part thereof, is held under the Chatham House Rule, participants are free to use the information received, but neither the identity nor the affiliation of the speaker(s), nor that of any other participant, may be revealed. For more information, see http://www.chathamhouse.org/about/chatham-house-rule.

12. To protect the "safe space" for the ongoing stakeholders' dialogue, the only "public" document to which the One-Text stakeholders gave full public access to was their website (www.onetext.org).

13. The public events allowed by the OTI stakeholders were organized by its civil society partners. The stakeholders allowed this public activity to promote shared knowledge creation and public awareness of specific issues. The events were connected to specific experts and issues addressed during the resource persons' visits, and the civil society partners published papers and articles on those issues.

14. These were the Center for Policy Alternatives, the Bandaranaike Center for International Studies (BCIS), Sarvodaya, the Berghof Foundation, and the South Asia Peace Initiative (SAPI). As Sri Lanka's largest community-based organization in the country, with a network in 14,000 villages, Sarvodaya was both a stakeholder and implementing partner for the People's Forums.

15. Examples of papers produced by the research and editorial departments include "Concept Paper on Options for Stakeholder Roundtable Approach to the 2002 Cease-fire Agreement," "Assessment of Minimum Consensus among Stakeholders in the Political Campaign Period of the 2005 November Presidential Elections," and "Comparison of Approach to Negotiations by LTTE and New President Mahinda Rajapaksa after November 2005."

16. The Peace Appeal Foundation and the Berghof Foundation also contributed core funding and support to the facilitation department. The People's Forums were supported by the Canadian International Development Agency, the Peace Appeal Foundation, USAID, AED, and Merck & Co.

17. The committee contained representatives from the Canadian International Development Agency, the European Union, the Norwegian and Swiss embassies, the Friedrich Ebert Stiftung Foundation, USAID, UNDP, the Danish International Development Agency, the Swedish Development Agency, the Peace Appeal Foundation, and the Berghof Foundation.

18. By 2005, all the parties had access to this comprehensive resource with more than 1,000 documents and titles. Parties' peace and research units were able to contribute action research to the library.

Transcending Past Conflicts

Chapter 7

The Harvard Study Group on Cyprus: Contributions to an Unfulfilled Peace Process

Diana Chigas

Introduction

The Cyprus conflict has challenged the international community for nearly fifty years, since the first bout of intercommunal fighting in 1963 brought the United Nations (UN) in to manage the peacekeeping and peacemaking processes. Since then, six UN Secretaries-General and some 20 UN representatives, supported and sometimes supplemented by the United States, the United Kingdom, and more recently the European Union (EU), have tried and so far failed to bridge the differences between Greek Cypriots and Turkish Cypriots and, since 1974, to reunify the island.

From 1999 to 2003, at the same time as the negotiation process managed by Special Representative of the Secretary-General Álvaro de Soto (known as the Annan process) was being formulated and conducted, the Harvard Study Group (HSG) on Cyprus met regularly. Although the HSG acted independent of the UN process, its aim was to facilitate the start of negotiations and, once negotiations started, jointly to develop ideas that could be useful in the process. The ultimate outcome of the UN's Annan process is well-known: on April 24, 2004, the Turkish Cypriots voted overwhelmingly to accept the UN's comprehensive plan for reunification of the island, while the Greek Cypriots voted equally overwhelmingly to reject it. This case study seeks to understand the contributions of this informal dialogue process to the UN efforts to broker an agreement that would end the division of the island and allow a reunified Cyprus to enter the EU.

Did the HSG make a constructive contribution to the negotiations and, more broadly, to the ongoing peace process? To answer this question, this study analyzes the conflict and issues under negotiation and outlines how the study group designed and implemented its initiative. It then analyzes the positive and negative effects of the HSG process, including both the elements of design that helped produce the results and the circumstances and historical precedents that facilitated its impacts. It concludes with lessons about the role of process interventions in peacemaking processes, the conditions that can make these processes a useful complement to official peacemaking, and the elements of design and implementation that enhance the chances of success.[1]

Nature and Course of the Conflict

Cyprus is a small island in the eastern Mediterranean, approximately forty miles off the coast of Turkey, with a population (as of 2011) of approximately 840,000 in the Greek Cypriot–controlled south of the island and approximately 300,000 in the Turkish Cypriot–controlled north.

The seeds of conflict in Cyprus were sown during the British colonial period from 1878 until 1960. Colonial rule gave rise to nationalist movements in the 1930s, and in 1955 Greek Cypriot dissatisfaction developed into guerrilla warfare against the British with the formation of EOKA (National Organization of Cypriot Fighters).[2] Greek Cypriot opposition to British rule did not result in demands for independence, but rather for union with Greece (*enosis*).[3] Turkish Cypriots, opposed to the prospect of becoming a minority in an "enemy" state, called for the island to be divided between Turkey and Greece (*taksim*) and formed their own clandestine organization, the Turkish Resistance Organization, to counter the EOKA threat.[4] British reactions at the time worsened intercommunal relations, as the British formed an Auxiliary Police Force made up entirely of Turkish Cypriots, which engaged regularly with EOKA.

Negotiations between Greece and Turkey led to the 1960 London and Zurich Agreements, which established the basic structure for a new and independent Republic of Cyprus (ROC) and explicitly ruled out both *enosis* and *taksim*. To ensure a balance between Greek Cypriots and Turkish Cypriots, the new Cyprus constitution provided for a Greek Cypriot president and Turkish Cypriot vice president; a national parliament with two communal chambers to deal with issues such as education, culture, and religion; and a cabinet, public service, and police and armed forces in which Turkish Cypriots, who were 18 percent of the population, would be represented at a level of 30 percent to 40 percent. Each community would have a veto over legislation touching on its vital interests. The constitution was backed by a set of treaties that established two sovereign British military bases (a total of ninety-nine square miles of territory); allowed a limited number of Greek and Turkish troops[5] to be stationed on the island; and gave Greece, Turkey, and the United Kingdom the right and responsibility to guarantee the territorial integrity, sovereignty, and independence of the ROC, by military intervention if needed.

From the outset, most Greek Cypriots were dissatisfied with the agreements and regarded them as a betrayal of the cause of *enosis*. They attached little legitimacy to the new independent ROC and hoped that they would eventually be able to unite the island with Greece, while Turkish Cypriots, who broadly accepted the arrangements, nevertheless regretted that the island had not been partitioned between Greece and Turkey. Without the spirit of bicommunal cooperation needed to make the arrangement work, by 1963 the ROC was mired in a constitutional crisis that culminated in a proposal by the Greek Cypriots (despite warnings against such a move by the Greek government) for thirteen constitutional amendments that they hoped would resolve the constitutional deadlock on contentious issues such as the right of veto by the president or vice-president. The Turkish Cypriots and Turkey viewed the amendments as proposals that threatened to alter fundamental arrangements for power-sharing and governance, and rejected them. From then on, Greek and Turkish Cypriots grew increasingly hostile and segregated. Turkish Cypriots left all public offices, and were unable to return. Fighting erupted in the capital city of Nicosia on December 21, 1963, and within days the conflict had spread across the island, causing hundreds of deaths and displacing more than 30,000 Turkish Cypriots from mixed areas to enclaves that could more easily be protected. Turkish military intervention was averted through international diplomatic efforts, and in 1964 the United Nations Peacekeeping Force in Cyprus (UNFICYP) was deployed, mainly to protect Turkish Cypriots. UNFICYP remains in place to this day.

Conflict between Greek and Turkish Cypriots intensified after a military dictatorship took control of Greece in 1967. Greek interference on the island increased with its support of EOKA-B, a pro-*enosis* nationalist movement formed in 1971. On July 15, 1974, the president of Cyprus, Archbishop Makarios III, was overthrown in a Greek-sponsored coup and replaced by Nicos Sampson, a former EOKA gunman known for his anti-Turkish and pro-*enosis* views. Turkish Cypriot villages and enclaves were attacked during fighting between left-wing supporters of Makarios and the EOKA-B forces. This time, after failing to secure support for a joint intervention under the Treaty of Guarantee, Turkey intervened militarily on the island on July 20. When talks to restore constitutional order collapsed on August 14, Turkey resumed its offensive, taking approximately 37 percent of the island. A UN-brokered cease-fire was finally concluded, extending the "Green Line" (buffer zone) from Nicosia, where it originally had been implemented, across the entire length of the island.

The events of 1974 had the effect of creating two ethnically homogeneous zones on the island. The arrival of the Turkish army sparked the exodus of more than 150,000 Greek Cypriots to the south, creating a massive refugee problem. After the UN cease-fire, an agreement on exchange of populations resulted in approximately 40,000 Turkish Cypriots moving from south to north, while another 10,000 Greek Cypriots living in the north were pressured to go south. Thousands were dead or missing, and in the eyes of the Greek Cypriots, the north of Cyprus began to undergo a process of Turkish colonization and Turkification. Turkish settlers from mainland Anatolia (estimated at about 115,000) began to arrive on the island, and Turkish financial support helped to develop closer ties and integrate northern Cyprus with Turkey.[6]

The new state of affairs after 1974 completely changed the parameters of a settlement. *Enosis* was finally dead as an aspiration for Greek Cypriots, and any settlement would have to include a Turkish Cypriot territorial entity, as a unitary state was out of the question for Turkish Cypriots. In 1975, the Turkish Cypriots announced the formation of the Turkish Federated State of Northern Cyprus. Rauf Denktash, a founder of the Turkish Resistance Movement and negotiating representative of the Turkish Cypriot community, was established as the leader of the new state, in part to underscore the Turkish Cypriots' insistence on this demand for a Turkish Cypriot entity, which was now backed by their possession of territory.

Since 1975, there have been at least fifteen official diplomatic interventions, mostly by the UN, to try to settle the Cyprus conflict. None has broken the impasse. At different points, either one side or the other has rejected internationally sponsored proposals, often when the sides seemed close to an agreement. The partial successes included the two High Level Agreements that have formed the basis of all subsequent discussions: the Makarios-Denktash Guidelines of 1977 and the Kyprianou-Denktash Guidelines of 1979, which outlined a broad commitment to "an independent, non-aligned, bi-communal federal republic." The 1977 agreement consisted of four principles on governance and bicommunality to guide negotiations.[7] The 1979 agreements, concluded between Rauf Denktash and Spiros Kyprianou, who was elected president following Makarios' death in 1977, reaffirmed the four guidelines and elaborated further that an agreement would respect human rights and fundamental freedoms, that demilitarization of the island would be foreseen, and that the parties would refrain from destabilizing actions.[8] Although the word "bizonal" does not appear in either agreement, it is implicit and has been accepted internationally as the basis for the bicommunal federation.

From 1979, successive rounds of bicommunal talks under several UN secretaries-general have produced no results, while the parties have taken actions that have made settlement more difficult. In November 1983, the Turkish Cypriots unilaterally declared independence, following a UN General Assembly resolution that had infuriated them with its call for the withdrawal of all occupation forces from Cyprus. The Turkish Republic of Northern Cyprus (TRNC), as the newly declared state was called, was quickly recognized by Turkey, while the rest of the international community condemned the move.[9] As negotiations stalled, the 1990s saw an increase in tension and polarization, primarily owing to the EU acceptance in 1994 of the Greek Cypriot–governed ROC's application for membership and the EU's subsequent decision in 1997 to open negotiations with Cyprus the following year. This move further isolated the Turkish Cypriot community; scuttled the ongoing UN-facilitated talks; and prompted Turkey and the Turkish Cypriots to initiate a policy of integration in the spheres of economy, finance, defense, and foreign affairs.

The climate began to shift in 1999 after the Helsinki European Council decided that "a political settlement will facilitate the accession of Cyprus to the EU." The decision elaborated: "If no settlement has been reached by the completion of accession negotiations, the Council's decision on accession will be made without the above being a precondition. In this the Council will take account of all relevant factors."[10] This decision was intended to provide incentives for the Turkish Cypriot leadership, which was perceived at the time as the main obstacle to settlement, to change its position. At the same time, the caveat that "all relevant factors" would be considered was meant to send a message to the Greek Cypriot side that intransigence on their part would also be frowned upon.

In 1999, veteran peacemaker Álvaro de Soto was appointed to lead a United Nations team to facilitate a resumption of negotiations. The process took place in the shadow of the ROC's EU accession process, and it relied on the EU process to help generate political will for an agreement. After start-and-stop negotiations between Glafkos Clerides and Rauf Denktash from 1999 to 2001, the UN team, in view of the approaching EU accession deadline, presented the first version of the Annan Plan in November 2002. The Plan had 182 pages of main articles and another 9,000 pages of annexes (draft laws).[11] As negotiations stalled throughout 2002 and 2003, a further version of the plan (Annan III) was presented in March 2003 in an effort to settle the conflict before the signing of the Treaty of Accession. The UN Secretary-General called upon Denktash and Tassos Papadopoulos, the newly elected president of the ROC, to put the plan directly to the people in simultaneous referenda. At a meeting in The Hague on March 10 and 11, Papadopoulos accepted the referendum idea grudgingly, while Denktash rejected it.

At the same time, a change of government in Turkey, Denktash's continuing intransigence, disappointment at the economic situation in northern Cyprus, and the fast approaching deadline for EU accession helped to mobilize a prosettlement movement in the north. Under the banner "This Country Is Ours," a coalition of ninety-one nongovernmental organizations (NGOs), opposition political parties, the Chamber of Commerce, and trade unions staged mass demonstrations calling for signing of the Annan Plan and the resignation of Denktash. In late 2003, the prosettlement parties won the parliamentary election. Denktash chose to withdraw from the negotiations and to campaign actively for the rejection of the plan, and Mehmet Ali Talat, leader of the Republican Turkish Party (CTP) took over from him as negotiator. A fifth version of the plan (Annan V) was submitted to a referendum on both sides in April 2004. In the north, nearly 65 percent of the population voted for the plan, while in the south, after last-minute backpedaling by Papadopoulos' coalition partner AKEL (Progressive Party of the Working People) on its support for the plan, more than 75 percent of Greek Cypriots voted to reject it. The solution failed. Greek Cypriots—even those who voted for it—had serious reservations about the plan, and Papadopoulos had waged a very effective media campaign for a "no" vote. After a four-year hiatus, the two sides agreed to resume talks, setting up a number of working groups and technical committees to pave the way to full-fledged negotiations, which began in the fall of 2008. These negotiations have proceeded haltingly. Suspended in 2012 and 2014, they have yet to produce an agreement. However, following the election in April 2015 of a prosettlement leader in the north, talks resumed under UN auspices with heightened intensity. Tangible progress on addressing core issues has been made, and there is optimism that an agreement might finally be reached, despite complicating factors ranging from a fiscal and budget crisis in the south following the larger Eurozone crisis to the discovery of natural gas reserves.[12]

Antecedents of the Harvard Study Group: Political Escalation and Citizen Rapprochement

The strengths and limitations of the Harvard Study Group on Cyprus, along with other politically focused processes, can be understood only in the context of previous (and concurrent) civil society efforts to promote bicommunal rapprochement in the 1990s.

Until the 1990s, dialogue and contact between Greek and Turkish Cypriots were limited and sporadic. Only a handful of people—mainly left-wing trade unions, politicians, and peace activists—crossed into the buffer zone to meet. On the island, restrictions on freedom of movement meant that special arrangements were needed for people to have contact with individuals on the other side of the Green Line.[13] Bicommunal meetings were either held off the island or arranged with the assistance and under the umbrella of international diplomatic missions. In the 1990s, several civil society initiatives coincided to give impetus to the expansion of bicommunal efforts.[14] First, from 1990 to 1993, Ronald Fisher, then at the Canadian Institute for International Peace and Security, organized several problem-solving workshops, some of which focused on the role of education in maintaining the conflict and its potential contribution to peacebuilding on the island. Second, after two years of intensive monocommunal work to bridge divides within each side, in 1993 Louise Diamond, executive director of the Institute for Multi-Track Diplomacy (IMTD), was able to convene a group of ten Greek Cypriots and ten Turkish Cypriots for an intensive workshop on conflict resolution in Oxford, England.[15] This workshop was symbolically significant because it included the children of the leaders of the two communities. At the same time, the US Agency for International Development (USAID), then holding an annual congressional appropriation of $15 million for Cyprus, decided to launch a pilot project, asking for a conflict resolution workshop for Greek and Turkish Cypriot students studying in the United States, which was facilitated by Conflict Management Group (CMG).[16]

The success of the 1993 workshops prompted USAID to release over $700,000 in 1994 to promote coexistence and conflict resolution in Cyprus. CMG and IMTD joined forces as the Cyprus Consortium to launch an intensive effort to bring the two communities together through conflict resolution training.

The workshops brought Greek and Turkish Cypriots together in a neutral space (outside of Cyprus or in the buffer zone) to learn and practice communication, conflict analysis, and cooperative problem-solving skills; build relationships; and create new possibilities for dealing with the conflict. The workshops were directed at a wide range of sectors: ordinary citizens, professionals, youth, women, educators, and others. Significantly, the workshops also targeted political leaders from all the major parties on both sides for the first time, in order to enhance the legitimacy of bicommunal conflict resolution efforts. By the end of 1994, several hundred people had been trained, a corps of thirty Greek Cypriot and Turkish Cypriot trainers was providing introductory conflict resolution training to bicommunal groups, and an office in the buffer zone had been created specifically for these local trainers to manage the expanding bicommunal activities. By 1997, the Cyprus Consortium had trained more than 800 people, and Greek and Turkish Cypriot local trainers and other international facilitators had trained countless more.

These people formed the core of a stronger citizen-based peace movement, which in 1994 began to take shape with the support and facilitation of a strategy for peacebuilding by the first Fulbright Scholar in the field, Benjamin Broome.[17] The Trainers Group (as the local trainers had come to call themselves) initiated followup trainings and dialogues, as did subsequent Fulbright Scholars who were sponsored continuously by the Cyprus Fulbright Commission to support bicommunal rapprochement. It is fair to say that by 1997, a genuine bicommunal peacebuilding movement involving thousands of people from both sides had been formed. Until the opening of the Green Line in 2003, this movement also served as the primary—if not only—channel of meaningful intercommunal communication.

The movement, however, was still fragile. As one evaluator of these efforts remarked, "There is a large gap between the number of people currently involved in reconciliation efforts and the number necessary to represent a significant portion of each community's population. . . . The strong emphasis on bi-communal contact has overshadowed the importance of influencing public opinion, the media and changing negative practices and attitudes within each community."[18] Although some initiatives at the political level did occur,[19] the stature and influence of the bicommunalists in their community were not enough for them to establish themselves as facilitators on the track-one-and-a-half level.[20]

The bicommunal activities, in part the victim of their own success, were politicized by the authorities and media on both sides and repeatedly attacked since the return of the first "Oxford Group" members in 1993. The politicization of the bicommunal movement came to a head at the end of 1997 as the authorities in the north withdrew permission for Turkish Cypriots to participate in bicommunal meetings in response to the EU's decision in Luxembourg to open accession negotiations with the ROC. This "ban" had a devastating effect on the level of contact and marked a crucial turning point in the growth of bicommunal activities.[21] Some activities continued, but the resulting brake on the momentum of the civil society–based movement for bicommunal rapprochement made the need for activities at the political level increasingly apparent.[22] Several efforts were undertaken in the 1997–98 timeframe: a 1997 initiative by the International Peace Research Institute of Oslo (PRIO) to bring together a group of business leaders to promote cooperation between Turkish Cypriot and Greek Cypriot businesses; a civil society group that met in Oslo in 1998 and produced a statement of shared values and substantive proposals for settlement; PRIO's Dialogue Forum, which brought together influential stakeholders from both sides for discussion beginning in 2000; and the Cyprus Consortium's Intractability Working Group, which brought together policy leaders, including parliamentarians with more hardline attitudes, to engage in joint analysis of intractability in Cyprus and examination of both sides' assumptions and strategies.[23]

Nature of the Intervention: The Harvard Study Group

The HSG had its immediate origins in a request by Diego Cordovez, then Special Adviser on Cyprus to the UN Secretary-General, to Robert Rotberg, president of the World Peace Foundation[24] and adjunct professor at Harvard University's Kennedy School of Government (where the foundation was based at the time). Cordovez requested that Rotberg organize an informal conference that would bring together Greek Cypriots, Turkish Cypriots, and representatives of the international community. After the failure of another round of UN-sponsored talks in the summer of 1997, Cordovez had "come to the conclusion . . . that the nature of the structure of the new Cyprus is the key element,"[25] and had asked Rotberg to organize the conference to explore "the contentious issues that divide the island,"[26] and in particular, incentives and options for power-sharing and for the economy. Rotberg had no experience in Cyprus, but had worked with Cordovez previously and had an ongoing relationship with him. Rotberg invited Diana Chigas of CMG and Louise Diamond of the IMTD to be part of the facilitation team, in part because of their long experience of work in Cyprus both with political leaders and with civil society.

This initial two-day conference was hosted in New Hampshire in July 1998 by the World Peace Foundation, in response to the UN special adviser's request. It convened nine Greek Cypriots and nine Turkish Cypriots, many of whom had been part of the Cyprus Consortium's Intractability Working Group, together with Cordovez and ten knowledgeable Americans (including a former US Cyprus Coordinator and several academics). It was a "one-off" event with interesting discussions on a range of issues from federalism to economic development. The conference itself had little sustainable impact, but it opened the door to creation of a longer-term dialogue group—the HSG—that would focus specifically on developing ideas for the negotiation process.

In particular, the conference participants indicated their willingness and interest to continue to develop new ideas to start a process that would deal with the recognition/embargo issue, which had caused significant tension. In January 1999, the US Embassy invited Rotberg to Cyprus explore possibilities for a sustained program of dialogue. During this trip, he consulted with participants from the July 1998 meeting, as well as people recommended by the embassy.

The general parameters of the HSG were developed by Rotberg in consultation with the US Embassy in Cyprus, which was to provide the funding. For the United States, the goal was to "make everyone smarter about the issues,"[27] including identifying possible zones of agreement as well as understanding the underlying reasons for disagreements on particular issues. The stated objectives of the study group reflected this concern:

The key goal of the Harvard Study Group project (HSG) is to enrich people's thinking on the Cyprus issue. By bringing together informed and influential Greek Cypriots and Turkish Cypriots, the project is intended to assist in injecting informed realism into the public debate . . . thereby facilitating progress towards a negotiated settlement. . . .

The overall objective of the HSG is to bring together Greek and Turkish Cypriots so that they can, in a constructive and realistic manner, move away from stalemate towards a vocabulary for solutions that both sides can accept.[28]

In light of these objectives, it was important that the group include people from across the spectrum of opinion on the Cyprus issue. The initial goals of the study group also reflected the interest in diversity of opinion: the dialogue "would be designed to engender candor and respect for opposing views, as well as to inspire new insights into old problems."[29] In 1999, the US embassy, through the UN Office on Project Services (UNOPS), agreed to fund five HSG meetings over twelve months. Two would take place in the United States and the remaining three would take place in Europe or the Middle East. Rotberg again invited Chigas and Diamond of the Cyprus Consortium to join him on the team of facilitators.

Selection of Participants

The HSG was intended to be a "track-one-and-a-half" process in which key individuals from the parties would be brought together in their personal capacities, rather than as representatives of their side, for direct, private interaction in meetings that would be low-key, closed to the public, and nonbinding.[30] The selection of participants was therefore important, as their connections and participation in governance or political processes would be the mechanism through which their efforts would have an impact.[31]

The facilitation team sought a group of participants (no more than sixteen) who were representative of the full spectrum of political views on the Cyprus problem, had connections to "political levers of power," and yet also were "serious thinkers who can exchange views beyond the party line" and would be able to participate in the process in their personal capacities even while maintaining communication with their respective leaders and constituencies.[32] In choosing participants, the facilitators also considered issues of gender balance, and of group "chemistry" and dynamics for problem-solving, and decided to include a few people who were not as politically connected but were creative thinkers. Participants were given the explicit understanding that they were being invited in their personal capacities, and that they would not be asked to make any commitments to any ideas at the meetings.

Approximately twenty people were invited to the study group, in the hope that fourteen to sixteen would attend. The group that arrived in Cambridge, Massachusetts for the first meeting in May 1999 included six Greek Cypriots and seven Turkish Cypriots. The Greek Cypriot participants included several members of Parliament and high-level officers of political parties, a former ambassador to the United Nations, and a former presidential candidate, and the Turkish Cypriot participants included several high-ranking members of the major political parties, businessmen, and a former official in Denktash's government. The initial group unfortunately did not include representatives from two major Greek Cypriot parties, AKEL (the communist Progressive Party of the Working People from the south of the island) and DIKO (the center-right Democratic Party, which eventually came to power in 2003), nor from the Turkish Cypriot DP (Democratic Party), headed by Serdar Denktash, Rauf Denktash's son. They had been invited, but for a variety of reasons they were not able to attend. During the first meeting, the study group decided not to reinvite those who had been unable to attend the initial session, in order to preserve and build on the positive group dynamic that had emerged. However, this decision meant that the DIKO and AKEL perspectives ultimately were not represented in the group.

Structure and Methodology

As the initial proposal stated, the basic approach of the HSG was one of "a sustained and committed discussion of a host of issues identified by the Cypriots themselves as core to any resolution."[33] The substantive agenda reflected the basic issues for negotiation: legitimacy (sovereignty and recognition of the TRNC), constitutional options, territory, return of refugees, economics, and security. The study group focused on joint analysis of issues, emphasizing dialogue on underlying interests, needs, and concerns, and developing new and creative ideas to meet the concerns of both sides. It did not follow any specific methodology, such as the interactive problem-solving workshop, the five-stage public peace process, or "facilitated joint brainstorming" methodologies,[34] but it was consistent with and drew on all of them, and added three elements to an otherwise straightforward problem-solving format:

- *Presentation of "tools" and concepts of conflict resolution.* The facilitators made occasional conceptual interventions, explaining various tools or concepts related to conflict analysis and resolution and introducing some training-type exercises, to enhance the group's capacity to discuss underlying interests, concerns, and needs, as well as address intangible aspects of the conflict.
- *Invitation of outside experts to each meeting.* International experts were also invited to each meeting to provide information and analysis to enhance the range of ideas being considered. Some of these outsiders were substantive experts—for example, on electoral laws in divided societies, on sovereignty and recognition, on federalism, and on banking. Some brought in experience on how similar questions were handled elsewhere, from Israel and Palestine to Northern Ireland to Ecuador and Peru.
- *Formation of working groups and "homework" between meetings.* Some of the deepest and most creative brainstorming was done in groups that were smaller than the plenary groups, both to enhance the intimacy of the conversation and to permit different group members with different interests and expertise to focus on their specialized concerns. Throughout the study group process, participants organized regularly into smaller working groups to develop ideas on specific issues, then reported back to the plenary. The plan was to have these working groups continue work on the island between meetings, by email, phone, or (where possible) in person, so as to consult and draw more knowledge and information into the discussion. This plan worked to some extent, but it was limited by the participants' busy schedules.

The first meeting discussed the issue of what products should emerge from the process. Consistent with the spirit of the brainstorming process, the participants were clear that they did not want to develop joint recommendations, statements, or memos to be submitted to the leaderships on both sides, but preferred to transmit the results of the discussions privately. The risk of this decision, of course, was that different participants would transmit different messages and interpretations of the discussions, and possibly increase rather than decrease tensions. Yet the political sensitivity of issuing a joint document was very real, as were the risks to the participants themselves and to the process of being seen to "supplant" political decision-makers if they made definitive recommendations. As one participant stated: "We cannot suggest solutions, but explore directions to which one can find solutions for problems."[35] The group of the facilitators therefore decided to prepare an "interpretive summary" of the meetings that distilled the ideas and perspectives that emerged in the discussion. It summarized and organized the main ideas that had emerged on the issues in discussion, the different options put forth, and the underlying concerns, interests, and perspectives about the options and issues, as well as any questions or gaps.

The Meetings

Five meetings were held approximately every three months, beginning in May 1999. The first two meetings took place in the United States—the first in Cambridge, Massachusetts, at CMG's offices near Harvard, in order to provide legitimacy to the process and to link it to past Harvard-based efforts. The following three were held in Ireland, Israel, and Jordan. Ireland and Israel had been chosen based on the participants' expressed desire in the first meeting to meet with people there and learn about the strengths and weaknesses of their peace processes. Following the fifth meeting, the World Peace Foundation obtained funding for a sixth meeting in Vienna and a further follow-up meeting in September 2003 at the Kennedy School of Government at Harvard.

The nature and depth of the discussions were influenced by the group's own confidence in the usefulness of dialogue and by the evolution of the "track-one" (official) UN-mediated negotiation process. When participants arrived at the first meeting in May 1999, they were aware that the parties had been growing further apart since the previous summer, and were skeptical of the possibilities for productive negotiation and the potential usefulness of the study group. As the members of the group gained confidence both in the existence of a zone of agreement and in each other, they were able to have productive discussions at a very concrete level and to generate a number of specific options. In the second and third meetings in July and October, participants were able to discuss core issues concretely and in detail. They discovered considerable common ground, and developed a number of different options on a few critical aspects of power-sharing and division of powers, and on a set of principles and guidelines to govern territorial adjustments (regarding the boundary between the Turkish Cypriot and Greek Cypriot entities) and return of refugees, among others.

The depth and specificity with which participants had discussed the issues in the first three meetings led the facilitators to prepare for the fourth meeting a template-framework of the points discussed in the previous three meetings, outlining areas in which consensus had been reached, areas of disagreement, options worthy of further consideration, and gaps in the discussion. This template-framework served as the basis for the fourth meeting in Jerusalem, where it was refined and elaborated.

By the third meeting in October 1999, new developments in the political situation had begun to have implications for the HSG process. By the end of the General Assembly session in New York, a few days before the third meeting began, it was becoming clear that efforts to restart talks were bearing fruit and that the UN Secretary-General would issue invitations to the two leaders in Cyprus as early as the following month. This complicated the study group's functioning, which in the absence of any official process had not been very constrained; participants had felt free to discuss a wide variety of options and perspectives without being concerned that they might prejudice official talks. The prospect of official negotiations, which indeed began in December in proximity format[36] and took place at the same time as the study group's fourth meeting, brought with it concerns that the unofficial study group process might inadvertently prejudice the negotiators' positions and strategies. The relaxed and open group dynamic became slightly more cautious, as the group members became more self-conscious.

Second, as part of the preparation for the resumption of negotiations, ROC president Glafkos Clerides had reshuffled the government, and two of the study group's members had moved into government positions: one as government spokesman, reporting directly to Clerides, and another as minister of communications and works. This turn of events was important, as several Greek Cypriots noted; the reshuffling was intended to send a political message to the Turkish Cypriots and the international community, as the people who entered government were "open-thinking people who have made their approaches to the Cyprus problem public."[37] The two members, however, felt that it was inappropriate for them to continue with the study group now that they had assumed official functions, and at the third meeting they announced that they would withdraw from the process. They feared that it would be difficult to separate their official roles from their unofficial participation in the group, and, more important, they were concerned about possible public reactions and the implications for the official negotiation process, which they were confident would resume by the end of the year. After consultation with the group, President Clerides, and US Embassy staff, their concerns were allayed, and the two remained in the process. The fact that two HSG members were in the government, and one of the two was on the negotiating team, obviously enhanced the potential for the study group's impact. At the same time, it introduced uncertainty, especially for outsiders, as to whether the discussions were truly unofficial and exploratory or whether they represented a position the (Greek Cypriot) government might accept. This uncertainty made the study group vulnerable to attack and risked restricting the group's hitherto-open discussions.

The anxiety within both the study group and the larger political environment as the official talks resumed was manifest in the fifth, and supposedly final, HSG meeting in Jordan in February 2000. Two rounds of proximity talks had been held under UN auspices, and a third round was scheduled to take place at the end of May. A news blackout prohibiting press statements by the parties, imposed by the UN, had generated much speculation and concern about the direction of the talks. It was in this context that the fifth meeting took place. The meeting was tense, and at several points participants returned to their "default" settings: the conventional positions and stories of their respective communities. In the hope of exploring the possibilities of a joint recommendation at the conclusion of the process, Rotberg prepared a document that contained "Headings of Report and Recommendations" as a basis for discussion. Unlike previous frameworks and interpretive summaries, this document did not simply present various options on controversial issues or explain the concerns and views of the different participants. It consciously proposed new material and possible resolutions of disagreements that had remained after the fourth meeting. It mentioned that some suggestions "could be controversial," but that these were simply intended to stimulate discussion and facilitate consensus-building. In the tense political environment that prevailed at that time, however, the opposite occurred. Greek Cypriots in the group viewed the document as biased toward the Turkish Cypriot position, and, as one participant noted, even if the Greek Cypriot participants had accepted the document with changes, it would have been a nonstarter for the Greek Cypriot population in general. The document was withdrawn—indeed, actual return of the document was requested—as the group preferred not to construct a single public set of joint recommendations for a united Cyprus in the shadow of the official negotiation process. Instead, options were discussed at length.

A great deal of time was dedicated to the issue of sovereignty and recognition of the TRNC,[38] the sticking point that participants had explored since the first study group meeting but had not addressed directly since then. The facilitators structured an "interests exercise" to help identify the underlying interests, needs, fears, and concerns driving the positions on this issue, and participants generated a few options for general statements of principles to take all of these considerations into account, but they did not agree on any one statement. The meeting ended with some discussion of issues that the group had not covered in detail previously, such as a reconciliation or historical clarification commission.

Two further study group meetings were held. The last HSG meeting as a group was held outside Vienna in 2001, during which the participants developed in greater detail the idea of a historical clarification commission. The other meeting took place in Cambridge, Massachusetts in 2003, and brought study group members together with representatives of the main international actors responsible for Cyprus (Greece, Turkey, the EU, the UN, the United Kingdom, and the United States) to discuss how the election of Tassos Papadopoulos as ROC president and his assumption of the role of chief negotiator might affect the negotiations. The Cambridge meeting also discussed the obstacles to a settlement and ways to overcome them.[39]

Impacts

It is not easy to assess the impact of NGO interventions in a conflict. It requires determining not only the changes in attitudes, perceptions, and relations that occurred as a result of the intervention,[40] but also the "transfer" effect beyond the group itself—in other words, "how effects (e.g., attitudinal changes, new realizations) and outcomes (e.g., frameworks for negotiation) are moved from the unofficial interventions to the official domain of decision and policy making."[41] In the case of the HSG, this assessment is even more difficult, as no agreement was achieved in the official negotiations. On the contrary, while Turkish Cypriots voted by a clear majority for the product of the negotiations that the study group was intended to influence, the Greek Cypriots overwhelmingly voted against it. Was the informal process then a failure? How, under those circumstances, can one assess the impact on the sources, manifestations, and mitigators of conflict? How, moreover, can one assess the specific contributions of the study group independently from the cumulative impacts of the bicommunal activities and official international initiatives that had been going on for years before the study group began, or from other contextual factors that influenced the behavior of the parties?

This section analyzes the contributions at three levels:[42]

- The *micro* level—individual/personal impacts on study group members.
- The *meso* level—the foundations for transfer, or actions taken by study group members on the basis of their experiences in the study group to further negotiations and rapprochement.
- The *macro* level—contributions to or influence on the peace process, including influence on the substance of one of the most serious negotiation processes on Cyprus to date ("upward" transfer) and contributions to public attitudes and support ("preparing the ground") for negotiation of a settlement ("downward" and "lateral" transfer).[43]

This section also considers negative reactions of authorities to the study group and its activities, and the authorities' effect on the study group impacts.

Micro Level: Individual/Personal Impacts

One of the most commonly observed impacts from NGO conflict management interventions is the breaking down of stereotypes and enemy images.[44] The HSG members did not experience dramatic change in perceptions, in part because many of them had significant previous bicommunal experience. As one participant noted, the study group experience was not as powerful as the "first time," when she had shifted her whole outlook on the problem. Yet although the purpose of the group was to develop new ideas and not specifically to catalyze attitude change or build relationships and trust, it did have some important further effects on participants' attitudes about the conflict and the possibilities and processes for resolution in the course of the six meetings.

CHANGED PERCEPTIONS FROM "WIN-LOSE" TO
"MUTUAL GAINS" POSSIBILITIES

Several participants, even among those with previous experience in bicommunal dialogue, shifted from an adversarial to a more mutual gains-based framing of the process. As one participant noted at the end of the first meeting, the goal had to be to "satisfy, not nullify" the interests of the other side. Another participant commented that the most important learning experience he took away from the process was that one has to consider the voice of the other side, "because if you don't understand the problems of the other side and they don't understand yours, you won't have a solution."[45]

Though not all participants experienced this change in perception equally, the shift to looking at the conflict as a common problem had a palpable effect on the group dynamic, which quickly became one of joint problem-solving rather than simply one of debate and discussion. Participants listened to each other, built on each other's ideas rather than rejecting ideas with which they did not agree, and when there was disagreement they inquired into each other's underlying interests, concerns, and perceptions. Only on a few occasions did the facilitators have to intervene strongly to structure and manage the dialogue. As a result, rather than advocating competing models for government structure, allocation of powers, or issues of refugee return, participants were able to move beyond arguing to both develop new options that might satisfy both sides and explore how to refine these options to address their own and their opponents' fears. In this sense, the process of discussing ideas was as important as the ideas themselves. Many of the options were not strictly speaking *new*, as they were based on other models (e.g., Belgian, Swiss, French government structures) or had been raised in other contexts or previous rounds of negotiation. But the discussion about them was different; participants assessed and refined the options with a view to building "a joint vision that does not destroy what each side has now, but which offers benefits to both sides for a future together."[46]

GREATER ENGAGEMENT OF "HARD-LINERS"

Several people noted that the "hard-liners" in the group had changed by the end of the process, moving away from the more rejectionist stance with which they had arrived; at the end, they were "ready to listen and challenge instead of coming with a closed position."[47]

INCREASED MUTUAL UNDERSTANDING AND
UNDERSTANDING OF THE ISSUES

Participants, even those with deep experience interacting with the "other," reported that they developed a much deeper and more detailed understanding of the other side's concerns and thinking. Several Greek Cypriots, for example, had not fully or accurately been aware of the feelings of Turkish Cypriots (and Turkey) on security. One Greek Cypriot participant realized for the first time how important the issue of security remained for Turkish Cypriots; several others had assumed that because of the Turkish intervention and subsequent consolidation of Turkish Cypriot presence in the north, the security fears of the Turkish Cypriots had been taken care of. A Turkish Cypriot similarly noted that "we found we could put ourselves in the Greeks' shoes." The bicommunal meetings in which many of the participants had already taken part also had helped to clarify misinformation about the other side and helped the participants develop an empathetic understanding of the other side's experiences, perspectives, and needs.[48] The HSG was able to deepen this understanding for those who already were engaged in dialogue, and to help them understand priorities and preferences much more concretely and specifically than previous experiences had done.

Meso Level: Participant Actions and Foundations for Transfer

The larger impact of these kinds of dialogues beyond the individual or personal level depends, at least in the first instance, on what the participants did with the ideas, insights, and experiences they had in the study group. Several things happened as a direct result of the HSG meetings.

First, the study group participants went back and reported to their own authorities, political parties, and in some cases constituents. In later interviews with the author, several Turkish Cypriot participants commented that everything was reported back to and discussed with Rauf Denktash, who until 1999 had refused to engage in negotiations and ultimately opposed the Annan process. After a certain stage, the reporting "went beyond Denktash."[49] These participants reported to (and were invited to report to) the Turkish Embassy; some also had conversations in Ankara. The "message was reaching Ankara as well," one study group member noted.[50] At the same time, the presence of a leader in the opposition party (CTP) ensured that the ideas and results of discussions were carried back to that party as well. The "reporting back" extended even further among the Turkish Cypriots, as several study group members took their insights and ideas to the media, appearing on talk shows and radio call-in shows and talking with newspaper editors. On the Greek Cypriot side, several study group participants were from the government party, Democratic Rally (DISY), and several also assumed leadership positions within their party or in the Clerides government. This connection provided a direct channel into decision-making institutions. Greek Cypriot participants engaged in little, if any, public outreach similar to the Turkish Cypriot members' efforts, possibly because the former had a direct line to the government in power and felt less need to persuade a broad constituency in order to influence the process.

Second, the interpretive summaries prepared by the facilitators at the end of each meeting were transmitted directly to the US Embassy in Nicosia, as well as to the office of the UN Special Representative. Both the embassy and the UN were aware of the ongoing discussions both before and after official talks began, and Rotberg continuously consulted with them.

Finally, the study group appears to have led to expanded joint actions by what were to become the main prosettlement parties on either side of the Green Line—the Greek Cypriot DISY and the Turkish Cypriot CTP. The study group was not the only forum in which the second-level leaders of the parties met, but it was one forum in which three people who were or would become second-level decision-makers in both parties got to know each other and their perspectives over the nearly two-year period. The study group thus served as one mechanism for reinforcing an institutional "coalition across conflict lines."[51]

Macro-Level Impacts on the Negotiation Process: "Upward" Transfer

Did any of these activities by the HSG members make a difference to the broader peace process on Cyprus? They seem to have made contributions in several important areas.

MOMENTUM FOR NEGOTIATIONS

One assessment noted that the HSG "played an important role at a time when the 1998 Turkish Cypriot ban on bi-communal activity posed a major obstacle for dialogue. The initiative helped to restore Cypriot faith in the possibility of bi-communal communication and discussion."[52] The first HSG meeting was held only months after Rauf Denktash had announced he would no longer talk about a federal settlement but would insist on confederation and recognition of two sovereign states on the island.[53] Participants were wary of the possibilities for a solution. It was not clear whether there was a zone of possible agreement,[54] and thus participants were unsure whether it would be worth the effort to try to develop possibilities. At the same time, the United States and the UN were trying to revive the talks, and US support for the study group can be seen as part of this effort to create space for dialogue. By the end of the first study group meeting, participants believed that joint solutions might be found and that dialogue could be useful.

CONTRIBUTIONS TO THE ANNAN PLAN

Many people both inside and outside the HSG see the footprint of the study group discussions in the Annan Plan. One study group member believes that the "basis of the Annan Plan was through us. The principles we developed were elaborated upon, became the roots" of it.[55] Others are less definitive, but can "read the work of the Harvard Group" in the plan.[56] Several ideas developed and discussed in the study group were reflected in the drafts of the plan, even if they did not appear in the form that had been articulated in the group: a United States of Cyprus ("United Cyprus Republic" in the Annan Plan) with "constituent states," ideas about how to address issues of sovereignty and legitimacy and principles and priorities regarding distribution of powers between the federal government and constituent states and return of refugees, among others. The plan also addressed a new idea discussed by the study group: the idea of a reconciliation commission to deal with historical clarification and promote dialogue.

Was transfer to the UN-mediated process direct? It is unlikely that the ideas from the study group transferred directly to the UN-mediated process. The UN began proximity talks after the third study group meeting, and the first draft plan was presented only in 2002, more than a year after the sixth meeting had been held. Moreover, the UN talks were held under strict confidentiality, limiting its ability to reach out to the population at large. There was little direct contact between the UN and civil society initiatives, and what has been described as a "top-heavy" process (i.e., limited to top-level decision-makers on both sides) and top-heavy relationship between political leaders and civil society restricted the negotiations to a "tight-knit circle."[57]

At the same time, the UN staff both in Nicosia and New York, as well as US representatives in the embassy and in Washington, were aware of the study group and other civil society initiatives, and read their proceedings. Although the study group itself was not fully representative of those who would vote on Cyprus, the options it identified reflected deep discussions by a diverse political spectrum, even if the participants were not mandated representatives of their parties. Ideas were developed and tried out, and some appeared acceptable to both sides. In this sense, the products of the study group provided a signal to the mediators about the priorities of the parties and possible balances or trade-offs among issues, the zone of possible agreement, the potential for compromises, and possible sticking points. This outcome was consistent with the US government's initial goals in financing the study group: to "make everyone smarter about the issues" and to identify potential areas of agreement as well as underlying reasons for disagreement on specific issues.[58] The UN team also consulted extensively with people on the island and with other international actors (including the United States) in preparing the drafts. The HSG members were among those consulted. Thus, the understandings and ideas gained in the study group were also transferred indirectly, either through study group members' influence on their leaders or through their own conversation with the UN team; members of the UN team were "sponges," one UN staff member noted, listening to ideas being proposed.[59]

AN ENRICHED PROGRAM FOR AND PERSUASIVENESS
OF PROSETTLEMENT PARTIES

High-level CTP members reported that the study group discussions enriched their own party's platform for a solution to the Cyprus problem.[60] The ideas developed were incorporated into their thinking about possible solutions, including ideas on the Constitution and on granting and regulating the right of return. When Mehmet Ali Talat replaced Rauf Denktash as chief negotiator in 2003, these ideas came directly to the negotiation process.

Beyond the ideas, several prosettlement members of the group commented that the deeper understanding of their counterparts and the specific and concrete nature of the options developed helped them become better advocates for negotiation and settlement. "When we were asked a specific question," one Turkist Cypriot participant noted, "for example, how will the customs work, how the tax system will work, we need [to have] answers." The discussions and the options developed in the study group, they said, helped them provide answers and helped them respond to criticism of their support for the negotiation of a bizonal, bicommunal federal structure; and to answer concretely and in detail how Greek Cypriots would respond and what possibilities might be plausible, thereby increasing their credibility. When they were criticized or questioned, they could respond, "if this happens, this is what the Greeks would say," because they had discussed these issues in the study group. Their ability to offer specific answers to specific questions about how a reunited Cyprus state would operate allowed the Turkish Cypriot participants to paint a more precise picture of what a non-status-quo solution would look like and to deal with people's concerns more concretely.[61]

Macro-Level Impacts on Public Acceptance: "Downward" Transfer

Between 1997, when the EU decided to open accession negotiations with the ROC in the absence of an agreement, and the 2004 majority vote for the Annan Plan, a dramatic change in public attitudes toward negotiations occurred, in particular on the Turkish side of the island.[62] The study group's impacts on this process were limited and difficult to separate from other influences on public opinion. Efforts to reach the population had already begun in the media as early as 1998–99, as opposition members and people involved in bicommunal activities were already engaging in an effort to stimulate discussion of the issues, as well as to help the broader public understand "the other."[63] HSG members were brought into this network and shared their views and experiences, often in interactive media programs. These programs described experiences with the "other side," and presented and discussed core issues that ranged from the implications of EU membership to the options for a solution. At the same time, several HSG members, among others who had been involved in bicommunal activities, assumed leadership in the "This Country Is Ours" platform, a coalition of more than forty political parties, trade unions, chambers of commerce, and NGOs that were in favor of a settlement. Between July 2000 and early 2003, this coalition organized several mass rallies and was critical in mobilizing public opinion in favor of the Annan Plan.[64]

Study group members, again in the north, also played a role in addressing local obstacles to agreement. It was clear before the first Annan Plan was published that some territorial adjustment would be part of a settlement. The plan called for a territorial adjustment that would give the Greek Cypriot "constituent state" control over some of the territory then under Turkish Cypriot control, including areas that previously had been inhabited mostly by Greek Cypriots; this would permit a larger number of refugees to return to their homes and live under Greek Cypriot administration. One such area was the town of Morphou, which since 1974 had gained a significant Turkish Cypriot population. These people would have to move after a settlement. Early on, the local association in Morphou invited HSG members to talk about what they were discussing in the study group concerning territorial adjustment and return of refugees, and these members took the lead in Morphou to convince local people that the settlement's concept and the mechanism would work. Morphou voted overwhelmingly for the Annan Plan.[65]

Negative Impacts

Guidance published in 2012 by the Development Assistance Committee of the Organisation for Economic Co-operation and Development on evaluation of conflict prevention and peacebuilding notes that "[a]ll engagement (including evaluation) in such settings [of conflict and fragility] should be sensitive to conflict and avoid doing harm."[66] An assessment of the study group's impacts therefore requires an examination of any negative impacts, or "the extent to which the intervention aggravates or mitigates grievances, vulnerabilities or tensions."[67]

The HSG initiative had some significant negative impacts that undermined the overall effectiveness of the effort in the longer term. In fairness, some negative impacts of the HSG process stemmed from the very existence of such a group and could not be avoided in the nationalistic context in which it operated. Yet two decisions taken during the course of the study group made it even more vulnerable to criticism: the decision to "freeze" the group's membership after the first meeting, and the decision in the fifth meeting to present a facilitator's discussion draft of possible joint recommendations.

First, the study group's decision not to reinvite people who had not attended the first meeting meant that two important political parties on the Greek Cypriot side, DIKO and AKEL, did not participate in the group. Their omission left the study group vulnerable to nationalist attacks and risked undermining its credibility.[68] As parties, DIKO and AKEL represented 40 to 50 percent of the Greek Cypriot population at the time. On the Turkish Cypriot side, the absence of the DP (led by Serdar Denktash, Rauf Denktash's son) could be covered by study group participants who had good connections to Denktash, but the absence of DIKO and AKEL meant that a significant set of perspectives was missing.[69] Significantly, DIKO and AKEL had formed a coalition that allowed them to form a government in 2003 under the leadership of Tassos Papadopoulos (DIKO), who replaced Glafkos Clerides (DISY) as President. Because the coalition parties had not participated previously in the negotiation of the Annan Plan, they had every incentive to question both the plan and any effort associated with it. More important, no one within the DIKO or AKEL party structures had participated in developing the ideas that had guided the plan's development; the parties therefore lacked the capacity to work effectively with others to refine unacceptable elements.

Second, the close involvement of the United States in the HSG, both as a financial supporter and in decisions regarding the study group's participation and agenda, opened the process to accusations of American manipulation, especially from the traditionally left-wing AKEL. Project director Robert Rotberg had raised this concern directly with the US Embassy, emphasizing the need for the group to be seen as separate from US government policy, yet even these efforts could not eliminate the study group's association with US policy. Thus, when the discussion draft document prepared by Rotberg was handed out to the group in the fifth meeting, the Greek Cypriot reactions to the document's perceived "bias" played into a larger and more difficult dynamic that brought the study group under attack. As the fifth meeting was ending, accusations were leveled in the press that the group, and especially the government spokesman who was participating in the group, was conducting secret negotiations, and criticism intensified as the UN-facilitated negotiations progressed. After the sixth meeting in Vienna in 2001, the controversial document that had been given to participants and then withdrawn by the chair at the fifth meeting was leaked to the Turkish press and published in its entirety in January 2002.[70] The document, the Turkish paper reported, had been "prepared by an American-sponsored bi-communal working group suggesting the creation of a 'United States of Cyprus,'" and "look[ed] like an extended version of the 'confederation' proposal of Turkish Cypriot leader Denktash."[71] Although the Turkish article referred to the HSG as a "nongovernmental study group," it noted that "it was established with the guidance of the former Clinton Administration of the United States and the document was presented to the U.S. State Department in December 2001."[72] This statement was picked up by the Greek Cypriot press and led to accusations that the three Greek Cypriot study group members associated with the government, as well as participants in the 1998 PRIO-sponsored citizen-based "Oslo Group," were traitors, "hand-picked by the Americans," and "betraying the pain inflicted by the Turkish invasion."[73]

Ultimately, this controversy significantly undermined the ongoing impact of the study group. The study group's product—even if the ideas in it were, as some Greek Cypriot members of the group believed, largely acceptable—became discredited because of its association with the United States. The HSG's international supporters and audience pulled back from it as well. As the date for the referendum approached, the United States and UNOPS were accused of having supported the "yes" campaign and thereby had interfered in Cyprus' internal affairs. The United States, fearful that the withdrawn draft that was now circulating publicly would damage the official talks, dissociated itself completely from the HSG effort. UNOPS was more indirectly linked to the study group as the manager and provider of its funds, but it suffered from criticism of bias in other areas, and dissociated itself from the project as well.

Reasons for Impacts: Intervention and Context

Why did the HSG make a positive difference while also having some negative impacts? Its contributions came about through a confluence of factors, some of which came from the initiative itself and some from its timing in relation to the context in which it took place, including previous and parallel bicommunal conflict resolution efforts and their synergies with the study group effort.

Intervention Reasons

A number of characteristics of the HSG organization and process helped it successfully develop the convergence, the range of ideas, and the deep mutual understanding it achieved among its members, and make a larger sociopolitical impact.

Inclusion of a broad spectrum of viewpoints. One of the strengths of the HSG effort was that it included a wide range of political viewpoints, from right to left and from prosettlement to hard-liners, especially on the Turkish Cypriot side. The presence of "hard-liners" was significant. Although people with more rejectionist points of view had engaged in some bicommunal workshops in the past, after 1996 few were so engaged, and the outreach to hard-liners on both sides was weak.[74] Therefore, their reemergence in the study group was an important development. The broad range of perspectives embraced within the study group made it difficult to achieve consensus but ensured a thorough discussion of the issues, a deep understanding of the complexity and diversity of views on each side, and perhaps most significantly a degree of "realism" in the dialogue. The "realism" was useful to facilitate "reentry" to their own communities and ensure that the discussions and the products of the study group would remain relevant.

Inclusion of influentials. The participants were elite members of their own societies with good channels of communication to key actors, such as political parties, the Chamber of Commerce, and government authorities. Several held or came to hold (during the course of the study group or afterward) high-level positions within their political parties—especially DISY and United Democrats on the Greek Cypriot side and CTP, UBP (National Unity Party), and the New Cyprus Party on the Turkish Cypriot side—or in the government itself. At the same time, the study group included members of the business community, including the future president of the Turkish Cypriot Chamber of Commerce, which in 2002–3 played a significant role in the successful mobilization of the opposition to Denktash. The spectrum and the level of participation ensured that there were direct channels of communication and influence to key players on both sides.

Previous experience with bicommunal dialogue. More than half of the group had previous experience, some over many years, in conflict resolution training workshops, which played a critical role in the quality and creativity of the discussion. These participants had attained a high level of skill and mutual understanding through the previous experiences that they brought to the study group. Some of the participants had built this capacity over many years of bicommunal dialogue. It is not clear that, even with a more structured and active facilitation style than the organizers chose to adopt, it would have been possible to both build the necessary skills and achieve the depth and specificity of productive substantive discussion within the study group's timeframe.

Dialogue sustained over time. The study group was not a "one-off" event. The sustained nature and frequency of meetings—approximately every three months—allowed the brainstorming and problem-solving process to maintain momentum and achieve some depth. It also allowed participants to get to know each other over a longer period of time, build greater trust, and consequently tackle more difficult issues productively.

Focus on concrete ideas. The participants appreciated that the group had a goal apart from "getting these guys together and seeing what happens."[75] The goal was to generate concrete and realistic ideas for a settlement, even if it would not necessarily build consensus. Indeed, the ground rule that consensus was *not* being sought, and that participants would not be committed to any of the ideas, facilitated greater specificity in the discussion. This was not the first group to deal with real political issues, but it was among the few to address them in such a detailed and concrete manner.

Good timing. The group also had the good fortune of good timing. Not only did the participants address substantive issues concretely, but they did so at a time when negotiations had broken down and people were discouraged at the possibilities for progress. Because bicommunal activities had been significantly reduced due to the Turkish Cypriot–imposed "ban" and the international community was eager and working to restart negotiations, the HSG provided a channel of communication and dialogue at a propitious moment.

Ownership of the process and product. Although the process was initiated by a third party (albeit in consultation with a wide range of local people), the participants gained and felt ownership over the study group's product. As a group, they developed a set of goals and purposes that drove the process, helped to focus the discussion, and made it concrete. At the same time, until the fifth meeting, the facilitators adopted a minimally interventionist approach—proposing the topics for discussion, and lightly structuring exercises to establish the tone and content based on interests, needs, and concerns, rather than an exchange over positions. This approach helped the participants develop a sense of ownership over the ideas generated in the group, and strengthened their desire and ability to act on the discussions they had had. Indeed, some continue to observe that some of the ideas developed in the group are better than what they characterize as "mishmash" in the Annan Plan.[76]

Bringing in comparative international expertise. The outside expertise brought in—from serious research on electoral laws and sovereignty to sharing of experience in the Northern Ireland and Israeli-Palestinian peace processes—helped participants gain new insights and facilitated development and consideration of a broader set of ideas.

Problem-solving format. Despite the substantive focus of the initiative, study group meetings were conceived not as conferences but as problem-solving workshops. Participants shared their perceptions and concerns, expressed the interests and needs underlying their positions, jointly analyzed the underlying issues, and jointly developed ideas for resolution.

The first two meetings had an emphasis on developing a common set of goals for the process and a definition of a shared problem, which created a solid basis for brainstorming and helped keep the discussion on a "mutual gains" track. Decisions on framing the issues helped avoid positional exchanges. For example, rather than discuss the labels "federation" and "confederation"—both loaded terms for the Cypriots—the group focused on outlining and discussing the details of allocation of powers.

Facilitation team's diversity of skills. Successful problem-solving depends not only on addressing the substance of the problem, but also on getting the process right and on building personal relationships. The facilitation team brought to the study group a valuable mix of skills and backgrounds to deal with all three dimensions. Rotberg brought substantive expertise and focus, especially (but not only) with regard to governance. Chigas brought the expertise and experience of Roger Fisher's interest-based negotiation processes, while Diamond, a former therapist, brought decades of experience dealing with psychological and emotional dimensions of conflict and group life. Attention thus could be paid to all three aspects of the process—even if not simultaneously—and appropriate interventions could be designed when difficulties arose.

Access to achieve complementarity with international third parties. The ideas and conclusions emerging from the study group's discussions were transferred to the mediators—both in the UN and in the United States— even before the actual talks began. The consultations and cooperation with the UN (through Diego Cordovez at first) and with the United States in setting up the study group process set a tone of collegiality and complementarity to official processes that had not existed initially. The structure and ground rules of the study group initiative—the diverse participation and the ground rule of brainstorming with no commitment—along with the ongoing consultations with the international third parties, helped to maintain complementarity during most of the period during which the study group and official talks proceeded simultaneously.

Nonintervention Elements

The advances in the peace process prior to 2004 can also be attributed to a number of factors unrelated to the HSG that nonetheless enhanced the impact of the study group itself.

The process that led to the Annan Plan and the referenda was perhaps the most serious and substantive of all the UN-initiated efforts since the early 1970s. In considering "success" in this context, one needs to look at the dramatic change in the Turkish Cypriot position from 1997 to 2004. The critical factors driving this change stem from the accession of Cyprus to the EU, Turkey's relationship with the EU, and the domestic dynamics in northern Cyprus to which they contributed.

The prospect of EU accession was intended from the start to act as a catalyst for a solution to the Cyprus problem. The expectation was that the carrot of accession would bring economically much poorer Turkish Cypriots to the negotiating table,[77] which would put pressure on noninterested or intransigent parties (i.e., Denktash and his supporters, as well as the Turkish government) to make concessions.[78] The EU's gradual removal of the conditionality of a conflict settlement for accession derived from this logic.

The EU carrot did not work in a straightforward way. Initially, the European Council decided that the division of Cyprus was not an obstacle to accession; this was its position until as late as 2001. This stance elicited a negative reaction by the Turkish Cypriot leadership. The application of the government of Cyprus to join the EU was both illegitimate and illegal to Turkish Cypriots, because they were not involved in the application process.[79] The EU was seen also as blatantly biased toward the Greek Cypriots, and the decision to proceed with accession even without a settlement appeared to confirm that. Opposition to the EU initially had significant public support. Indeed, in the 1998 general election, the pro-*taksim* (division) parties gained a two-thirds majority of the vote, an increase from the 1993 elections.[80] For the Turkish Cypriots, the potential economic benefits of EU membership were not sufficiently powerful to persuade them to change their position on a settlement. On the contrary, in the 1990s, the Turkish Cypriot leadership, which argued that both Cyprus and Turkey should enter the EU at the same time, branded the EU economic carrots as a "bribe." As Tözun Bahcheli has noted, "Turkish Cypriots prefer[red] to have their own state in order to secure their future, even as they realize[d] that lack of recognition and isolation ha[d] impeded economic development."[81] Public hostility was maintained in part by misinformation about the EU; European Commission officials did not adequately share or distribute information, while pro-*taksim* forces were able to misrepresent the costs and benefits of the accession process.[82]

However, a number of socioeconomic and political changes in the north and in Turkey in the late 1990s turned the situation around. Prior to the

Helsinki summit of the European Council in 1999, Turkish Cypriots had hoped that Brussels would be unwilling to admit a divided island. By 2002, both in northern Cyprus and in Turkey, there was a growing realization that Cyprus' accession to the EU was inevitable.[83] Once it became clear that the EU would not tie Cyprus' accession either to the achievement of a settlement or to Turkey's admission, the pressure mounted for a settlement, helping to mobilize the prosettlement forces in the north. As several analysts have noted, it is "hard to imagine the mass demonstrations of early 2003, the massive swing to the opposition in the December [2003] elections, and the referendum result without the prospect of EU membership."[84] The EU, in this sense, created a "fading opportunity"[85]—a realistic deadline, after which the possibilities for getting a better deal would decrease—and thereby provided a powerful incentive to those Turkish Cypriots who desired a deal to negotiate.

Until that point, Rauf Denktash's nationalist position had been supported by the Turkish government. But that support too had eroded, and after 2002 the prosettlement forces had begun to find a silent coalition partner in the Turkish government. After the initiation of Turkey's EU accession process with the Helsinki Decision in 1999, views in Turkey about EU membership had started to shift, and in November 2002 a "genuinely pro-EU" party won the elections[86] and changed the Turkish government's policy rhetoric on Cyprus. This change was not enough to prevent Denktash from coming out against the Annan Plan during the EU summit in Copenhagen in December 2002, where Cyprus was accepted as a future member state. However, it did undermine Denktash's authority, and Turkish support for the UN process helped create a safe space for the mass demonstrations that occurred in 2003 requesting that Denktash either sign the Annan Plan or resign.

The catalyzing influence of the EU accession process was possible in part because of internal changes occurring within the north, as well as the prospect of Turkey's own EU accession. By the early 2000s, the state institutions in northern Cyprus had already lost a great deal of legitimacy. Closer contact with Turks gave rise to a perception of cultural differences between Turkish Cypriots and Turks. At the same time, people who had taken the idea of Turkish Cypriot "sovereignty" seriously—including many civil servants—became disappointed with the experience of real limits on the autonomy of the TRNC's administration, and the feeling grew that they were not governing themselves but were being controlled by Ankara.[87] The Turkish Cypriots' struggle for self-determination became tied increasingly to a solution involving EU membership.

At the same time, the deterioration of the economy helped convert passive discontent with the project of sovereignty and statehood into active opposition, as the state was less and less able to contain it through patronage. The stage was set for a shift in Turkish Cypriot opinion and support for a settlement. A banking crisis in 2000, associated with corruption among Denktash loyalists,[88] wiped out the savings of many Turkish Cypriots and led to the first mass demonstrations.[89] The fallout of the financial crisis in Turkey in 2001 further discredited the political-economic foundations of the Turkish Cypriot "independent" state. Some believe that when Denktash came out against the settlement in Copenhagen in 2002, then rejected the plan at The Hague in March 2003, Turkish Cypriots came to realize that he did not want a settlement—and the scales were tipped to give momentum to the NGO-business-labor-CTP coalition that organized the demonstrations and produced an electoral victory for the prosettlement camp.

In this context of larger forces pushing Turkish Cypriot and Turkish domestic politics toward a prosettlement stance, the HSG and other previous and concurrent civil society–based bicommunal efforts were not dominant factors. However, they did provide valuable resources to the process, both in terms of experiences and perspectives for the leaders of the prosettlement coalition—nearly all of whom had been active in previous bicommunal activities and dialogue—and of ideas and information. Many people in the Turkish Cypriot community believed that the Annan Plan had done a good job at meeting the real interests and priorities of the parties.[90] The study group's contribution to the mediators' understanding of the problem, as well as the public discussion of the group's (and others') work, could have contributed to this favorable perception.

Denouement: Failure and Missed Opportunities

Turkish Cypriot support for the Annan Plan was not matched by the Greek Cypriots, and this lack of support may be the most significant missed opportunity of the overall peace process—for the study group, for Greek Cypriot bicommunal activities, and for the international community in general.

It was common knowledge that from the time the ROC government submitted its application to join the European Community in 1990, the Greek Cypriots' motives were as much political as economic, if not more so.[91] Europeanization of the Cyprus issue, it was hoped, would both put pressure on Turkish Cypriots and Turkey to abandon their positions and, if there was no agreement, provide Greek Cypriots with security against any potential armed intervention by Turkey.[92] In negotiation terms, EU membership was the Greek Cypriots' "best alternative to a negotiated agreement."[93] Thus, to the extent that EU accession would not be conditional on achievement of a settlement, it could never really provide incentives to Greek Cypriots to be flexible in negotiating. Indeed, Greek Cypriots hoped that EU accession would help them negotiate a better deal on the "three freedoms"—freedom of movement, settlement, and property—with the implementation of the EU acquis, or total body of European law.

This strategy was perhaps not an unsound one, if one perceived the problem to be the intransigence of the Denktash regime and Turkey. The EU was sympathetic to this view and failed to push for a settlement as a prerequisite for accession.[94] Greek Cypriots were perceived to be "clearly willing to make concessions";[95] MIT's CASCON System for Analyzing International Conflict went so far as to classify the Turkish Cypriots as the "Status Quo Side" and the Greek Cypriots as the "Non Status Quo Side."[96] However, in focusing almost exclusively on the effort to overcome Turkish Cypriot intransigence, the UN, the EU, the United States, and the NGOs and bicommunal activists overlooked the sources of resistance on the other side of the Green Line. The Greek Cypriots had a more profound and difficult decision to make, and they were less prepared for it. As one UN official noted, the Papadopoulos government had inherited a highly functional and wealthy state. After a solution, the state would be largely dysfunctional, with the hope that EU decision-making in many areas and the high degree of autonomy of the component states would compensate for these problems.[97] There were fears that reunification would be a drag on the Greek Cypriot economy.

Unlike in the north, where the EU and specific options related to power-sharing were being discussed publicly several years before Álvaro de Soto's team prepared the Annan Plan in November 2002, there was little discussion in the south. Even in 2002, polls showed that fully 64 percent of the population in the south would have rejected the plan in November 2002, and that the strength of the opposition was growing.[98] The kind of public information and advocacy work that had helped the Turkish Cypriot prosettlement camp gain adherents came late in the south, and was overwhelmed and marginalized by a well-orchestrated "no" campaign that succeeded in framing people's perception of the UN proposal in negative terms. PRIO's Cyprus Centre initiated a valuable public information project to provide easily understandable and accurate information on the plan in late 2002, but this response was too little and too late to affect the public debate. Neither the government nor the political parties nor the bicommunal activists nor the HSG members held public discussions on ideas for a settlement; on the contrary, the official rhetoric was that every refugee would return home—something nearly everyone admitted, privately, would not happen. The bicommunal activists and supporters of the "yes" vote did not have the resources to promote a settlement, and once they had been attacked and demonized by the more nationalist political establishment,[99] they were marginalized, and the arguments for a "yes" vote were never really heard. As a result, many people have noted, Greek Cypriots did not have a "vision" or "counterproposal of where to go."[100] As one analyst observed, for decades there had been talk of a "bi-zonal, bi-communal federation" but the talk was only general; the first time that Greek Cypriots saw federation was in the Annan Plan, and they did not like it.[101]

Could something have been done differently? Were there missed opportunities that might have changed the Greek Cypriot view of the Annan Plan? It is difficult to assess whether anything would have made a difference to the Greek Cypriot vote at that time. The missed opportunities in this sense extend far back to the beginnings of the bicommunal movement in the mid-1990s and the EU's initial treatment of the ROC's application for membership. Nonetheless, the HSG also missed several opportunities.

Inclusion of DIKO and AKEL

No one expected at the time of the HSG that Tassos Papadopoulos would play such an important role in Greek Cypriot politics. Even when he was elected in 2003 and formed a coalition government with AKEL, people expected that AKEL leader Dimitris Christofias would be the dominant player (given AKEL's electoral strength) and would serve as a damper on Papadopoulos' extremism. This expectation proved to be wrong. In retrospect, greater insistence and effort to include significant AKEL and DIKO participants might have helped bridge the gap between the "yes" and "no" camps on the Greek Cypriot side, or at a minimum introduced more realism into the discussion.

Dissemination and Discussion in the Greek Cypriot community

Preparation of the Greek Cypriot public for negotiations could have begun earlier than 2002, when the basic framework of the Annan Plan was first put forward and the negotiations were moving toward a "closure" rather than option-generating stage. Greater publicity and public discussion of the ideas on which the Annan Plan was based—already well developed by 2000, even if they had not been developed in the same detail as the UN's plan—might have helped encourage thinking and discussion on what Greek Cypriots really wanted, prepared people for what might come out of the negotiations, as well as provided valuable input to those negotiating a settlement about public preferences, priorities, and concerns. Yet as one HSG member noted, "We were in government. . . . We felt less need" to give publicity to the ideas and to the Annan Plan more generally, while the "Turkish Cypriots were in opposition and had to appeal to the people to get beyond Denktash."[102]

But there was more to the failure to bring ideas into the public domain. Throughout the 1990s, communications about bicommunal and conflict resolution work with the larger communities were limited; many of the ideas developed in bicommunal dialogue groups and off-island meetings were never documented or disseminated or, when they were documented (such as in the case of the Oslo group), were given little or no attention by the media.[103] Turkish Cypriots more actively used the media to write about bicommunal activities and to counter contradictory views or misinformation, while the Greek Cypriots seemed more hesitant. As a result, as one Clerides government–linked HSG member noted in retrospect, "We weren't really in touch with what people felt."[104]

Greater linkage between civil society–based bicommunal initiatives and activists and the more "track-one-and-a-half" processes, as well as greater outreach from the bicommunal movement within the Greek Cypriot community, might have facilitated the quality of public dialogue that could affect public attitudes toward a settlement.[105] This would have been a difficult but not impossible task, which third parties might have facilitated by engaging in more continuous follow-up with politicians who had participated in the first bicommunal workshops in 1994, encouraging monocommunal contact and dialogue, and pushing for broader outreach and more systematic participation criteria. The civil society and political efforts proceeded along parallel tracks in the south from the beginning, in part because of political parties' resistance to inclusion of the bicommunalists in decision-making, and in part because of the bicommunalists' own strategy of influence through opposition to the government.[106] The difficulty in coordinating various efforts also made it difficult to build a broad coalition of prorapprochement actors in the south similar to the one that had formed in the north. Adding to this problem were the limited reach of the bicommunal efforts within Greek Cypriot society[107] and the emphasis of international donors on bicommunality as a condition for funding.[108]

International Influence

A final missed opportunity relates to the failure of the international community—from NGOs to the mediators themselves—fully to understand the negative impact of EU accession on the real incentives for Greek Cypriots to conclude a settlement before entering the EU. Greek Cypriot proponents of delaying an agreement argued that the ROC's bargaining power would increase after Cyprus' accession in May 2004, and that derogations provided for under the UN plan would no longer be feasible.[109] But in 2003, attention was still focused on overcoming Denktash's intransigence, although Papadopoulos had voiced concerns with "the issue of balance" in the plan.[110] International officials involved with the negotiations, as well as HSG members, believed that it would be "politically impossible for the Papadopoulos government to renege on its promise [in The Hague] to sign the settlement agreement."[111] This belief, in retrospect, proved to be untrue, and after Cyprus was invited to join the EU at the European Council meeting in Copenhagen in December 2003, there was no incentive to reach an agreement prior to the accession date of May 1, 2004. The deadline was intended to, and initially did, provide an incentive to reach closure on a settlement, with the difficult trade-offs that entailed. After Copenhagen, however, the deadline ceased to perform that function. In this context, there may have been an opportunity to build on informal dialogues begun, for example, at the World Peace Foundation and the Harvard Kennedy School in 2003, or at Oxford in October 2003[112] to improve the Annan Plan in ways that would have dealt with both Greek Cypriot and Turkish Cypriot continuing concerns with the substance of the plan.

Summary and Conclusion

The basic goal of the HSG was to enrich thinking—among the parties and the international third parties—on possible solutions in order to facilitate progress toward a negotiated settlement. The study group accomplished this goal in several ways. It developed some new and revised some existing ideas for resolving the basic issues for negotiation, and perhaps more important it generated ownership among key Cypriots of those ideas. It helped to identify a zone of possible agreement among some key actors on both sides that both helped to revive energy and hope for negotiations and helped third parties identify parameters for a possible agreement. Finally, on the Turkish Cypriot side especially, both before and after an official proposal was presented by the United Nations, it helped prosettlement parties sell the UN-drafted plan to the broader public.

Circumstances in 2004—EU accession, economic challenges in north Cyprus, a favorable Turkish Cypriot government—made the Cyprus conflict more "ripe" than ever for a negotiated solution.[113] They also enhanced the study group's potential to make progress on substantive issues and to contribute to the negotiation process.

Yet the negotiations failed for many reasons the study group could not address. Ironically, EU accession—which was intended to be and indeed ultimately acted as a powerful carrot for reunification—was also perceived by many Greek Cypriots to be their best alternative to a negotiated agreement: the way they could attain their security interests without an agreement. In this sense, accession affected the power dynamics between the parties, simultaneously weakening the Turkish Cypriots (and ultimately helping to overcome their leadership's intransigence) and strengthening the Greek Cypriots. Faced with the challenge of overcoming Turkish Cypriot intransigence for many years, international third parties and Greek Cypriots favoring a federal solution failed to analyze and address Greek Cypriot incentives for a compromise agreement. Coupled with the lack of public discussion within Greek Cypriot society about priorities among interests and about what a "bi-zonal, bi-communal federation" might look like, this made commitment to a perceived second-best solution (after a unitary state) highly unlikely in 2004.

Still, the study group's experience provides useful lessons for future unofficial and official efforts in Cyprus, as well as for interactive problem-solving processes in conflict generally. First, the importance of concrete focus cannot be overstated. The process's ability to address in depth the most important substantive problems was critical to its usefulness in Cyprus. This statement is true more broadly; dialogues eventually need to address concrete issues effectively in order to have sociopolitical impact.[114] At the same time, in Cyprus this degree of focus would not have been possible if many people in the group had not had extensive previous experience and skill-building in interests- and needs-based conflict resolution processes. Some form of prior investment in the development of attitudes and skills for non-zero-sum problem-solving can enhance the depth and contribution of dialogue efforts, and also can have an ongoing influence on the negotiation process as participants take on positions in official talks, which several study group members did, especially once prenegotiations began later and official negotiations restarted in 2008.[115]

Second, the sustained nature of the dialogue made it possible to explore deeply most of the key issues in conflict and develop a range of options for dealing with them. Over six meetings in two years, the study group members were able to develop relationships that allowed them to have difficult conversations constructively and to develop sufficient understanding of the issues and of each other's concerns to enable them to develop joint approaches.

Third, representation of the full range of views, at least on the Turkish Cypriot side, was a key factor in the relatively greater influence of the study group's work in north Cyprus. The inclusion of more hard-line views made it difficult to develop joint recommendations, but the benefits of greater inclusivity both for the quality of discussion and for the greater realism of the ideas generated far outweighed the lack of a joint product around which participants could mobilize. Had DIKO and AKEL perspectives been included in the study group from the start, issues that later became sensitive might have been identified and addressed early on.

Finally, the HSG experience points to the importance of establishing linkages with the official negotiation process *and* with broader, more grassroots constituencies. In the north, the study group took place within a context in which key people—several of whom were in the study group itself—linked with other key people (e.g., in the opposition political parties, in the business community, in trade unions) and with "more people."[116] Key groups formed coalitions, and the leaders of the pro–Annan Plan "This Country Is Ours" platform reached out to NGOs and directly to the people in the villages through the media and visits. In the south, by contrast, the study group's work initially fed directly into the government negotiating team, but this work was parallel to and disconnected from other civil society peace work, and did not reach out to other key actors.[117] Although the establishment of linkages are not the only factors explaining the success of the "yes" campaign for the Annan Plan in the north or its failure in the south, the study group's experience suggests that transfer of the learning and ideas from these interactive problem-solving processes is not always direct, and that systematic followup efforts to link these "key people" efforts to "more people"[118] and to other key people (such as the international community) can enhance their contribution.

Notes

1. As the author was a member of the team that facilitated the Harvard Study Group, much of the description and analysis in this case draw on personal experience and observation as well as personal notes and documentation from the HSG process. In addition, in June 2006, I conducted interviews in Cyprus with all but two of the HSG members, as well as staff at the US embassy and the United Nations, and in the United States with the HSG facilitators, either in person or by telephone. I also had the opportunity to interview Álvaro de Soto and other UN team members, as well as facilitators of other bicommunal activities, in person or by telephone in 2007 in connection with a case study on the cumulative impacts of peacebuilding in Cyprus. The 2007 case study included interviews by a bicommunal team of authors of participants in other bicommunal activities, and also refers to the Study Group's activities, obstacles, and impacts. See Maria Hadjipavlou and Bulent Kanol, *The Impacts of Peacebuilding Work on the Cyprus Conflict* (Cambridge, MA: CDA Collaborative Learning Projects, 2008).

2. The conflict and negotiation history recounted in this section is drawn from several sources: Maria Madjpavlou and Bulent Kanol, *The Impacts of Peacebuilding Work on the Cyprus Conflict* (Cambridge, MA: CDA Collaborative Learning Projects, 2008); International Crisis Group, "The Cyprus Stalemate: What Next?," *Europe Report* No. 171 (Brussels: International Crisis Group, March 8, 2006); James Ker-Lindsay, "From U Thant to Kofi Annan: UN Peacemaking in Cyprus, 1964–2004," South East European Studies at Oxford Occasional Paper No. 5/05 (European Studies Centre, University of Oxford, October 2005); Mensur Akgün, Ayla Gürel, Mete Hatay, and Sylvia Tiryaki, "Quo Vadis Cyprus?" (working paper, TESEV, Istanbul, April 2005); George Christou, "The European Union and Cyprus: The Power of Attraction as a Solution to the Cyprus Issue," *Journal on Ethnopolitics and Minority Issues in Europe*, European Centre for Minority Issues, Issue 2 (2002); Ronald J. Fisher, "Cyprus: The Failure of Mediation and the Escalation of an Identity-Based Conflict to an Adversarial Impasse," *Journal of Peace Research* 38, no. 3 (May 2001): 307–26; Philippos K. Savvides, "Cyprus: The Dynamics of Partition" (paper presented to 2nd Annual Graduate Student Workshop, Kokkalis Program, Kennedy School of Government, Harvard University, 2000), http://www.ksg.harvard.edu/kokkalis/GSW2/Savvides.PDF; Rauf R. Denktaş, "The Crux of the Cyprus Problem," *Perceptions: Journal of International Affairs* 4, no. 3 (September–November 1999), http://sam.gov.tr/wp-content/uploads/2012/02/RaufDenktas.pdf; Ergün Olgun, "Cyprus: A New and Realistic Approach," *Perceptions: Journal of International Affairs* 4, no. 3 (September–November 1999), http://sam.gov.tr/wp-content/uploads/2012/02/ErgunOlgun1.pdf; and Keith Kyle, *Cyprus: In Search of Peace* (London: Minority Rights Group, 1997).

3. For a more complete account of the history of this period, see Zenon Stavrinides, *The Cyprus Conflict: National Identity and Statehood* (Nicosia: Loris Stavrinides Press, 1976).

4. Akgün et al., "Quo Vadis Cyprus?," 16.

5. Greece was allowed 950 troops; Turkey was allowed 650.

6. As of 2003, UNFICYP estimated that 165,000 internally displaced Greek Cypriot persons were living in the south, while 45,000 Turkish Cypriots who fled from their homes during the 1960s and after 1974 were living in the north. Norwegian Refugee Council/Global IDP Project, "Profile of Internal Displacement: Cyprus: Compilation

of the information available in the Global IDP Database of the Norwegian Refugee Council (as of 3 June, 2003)," Norwegian Refugee Council/Global IDP Project, Geneva, June 3, 2003, http://www.internal-displacement.org/assets/library/Europe/Cyprus/pdf /Cyprus+-May+2003.pdf.

7. The four guidelines of the 1977 agreement were: (1) We are seeking an independent, nonaligned, bicommunal federal republic; (2) The territory under the administration of each community should be discussed in the light of economic viability or productivity and land-ownership; (3) Questions of principles like freedom of movement, freedom of settlement, the right of property and other specific matters are open for discussion taking into consideration the fundamental basis of a bicommunal federal system and certain practical difficulties which may arise for the Turkish Cypriot community; and (4) The powers and functions of the central federal government will be such as to safeguard the unity of the country having regard to the bicommunal character of the State.

8. "The 10-Point Agreement of 19 May 1979," The Cyprus Question, Ministry of Foreign Affairs of the Republic of Cyprus, November 3, 2006, http://www.mfa.gov.cy /mfa/mfa2006.nsf/All/028429D5BB7B89F4C225721B0033C262/$file/May%201979 .pdf.

9. This development created a number of deep problems that plagued all negotiations, as well as other attempts to build bridges across the "Green Line," by introducing questions of sovereignty into the issues of the relationship between Greek and Turkish Cypriots. Turkish Cypriots would henceforth demand that any settlement be negotiated between equal states, while Greek Cypriots would insist on having continuity of the Republic of Cyprus in any agreement for a new constitutional order. Moreover, Greek Cypriot characterization of the TRNC as an "illegal" or "so-called" state led to efforts to prevent any implicit recognition of Turkish Cypriot sovereignty. This included a de facto economic embargo on the Turkish Cypriot community, backed by a European Court of Justice decision prohibiting EU member states from accepting agricultural products from northern Cyprus without phytosanitary certificates issued by the Greek Cypriot–controlled Republic. The embargo generated enormous resentment in the north, as it prevented or dramatically increased costs of exports and prevented any cross-community business dealings. For further explanation of the court's ruling, see Stefan Talmon, "The Cyprus Question before the European Court of Justice," *European Journal of International Law* 12, no. 4 (2001): 727–50.

10. Helsinki European Council, "Presidency Conclusions," para. 9, December 10–11, 1999, http://www.consilium.europa.eu/uedocs/cms_data/docs/pressdata/en/ec /ACFA4C.htm.

11. For detailed accounts of the course of negotiations, see David Hannay, *Cyprus: The Search for a Solution* (London: I. B. Tauris, 2005) and United Nations Security Council, "Report of the Secretary-General on his Mission of Good Offices in Cyprus," S/2009/610, November, 30, 2009, http://www.uncyprustalks.org/media/SG%20Reports /Good_Offices_report_S2009610.pdf.

12. For an historical review and information on the current status of the negotiations, see the United Nations Good Offices Mission, "About the Peace Talks," last accessed June 10, 2015, http://www.uncyprustalks.org/nqcontent.cfm?a_id=2467&tt=graphic&lang=ll. Elections in the Greek Cypriot-controlled ROC in 2013 resulted in a change of government, with Nicos Anastasiades of Democratic Rally, one of the only parties to support the Annan Plan in 2004. Talks resumed in February 2014 after an eighteen-month

hiatus, but quickly stalled due to escalation of tensions with Turkey over exploration of natural gas reserves. In April 2015, Mustafa Akinci, former mayor of Nicosia's Turkish Cypriot–controlled section and long-time advocate for a settlement, defeated his conservative rival in elections in the north. With prosettlement leaders in both communities for the first time since the 2004 referendum, talks resumed in June 2015.

13. Until the opening of the Green Line in 2003, Turkish Cypriots were required to obtain permission to exit the north and enter the buffer zone, while anyone (including tourists) going to the north from the Greek Cypriot–controlled south theoretically was not allowed to spend money in the north and was required to return south by 5 p.m. the same day. This policy was designed to guard against implicit "recognition" of the regime in the north, while the requirement by Turkish Cypriot authorities that all visitors obtain a "visa" (and pay £1 for it) was designed to force that "recognition." As a practical matter, this arrangement ensured that very few people from either side visited the other.

14. For fuller descriptions of the evolution of bicommunal dialogue on Cyprus, see Benjamin J. Broome, *Building Bridges Across the Green Line: A Guide to Intercultural Communication in Cyprus* (Nicosia: UNDP, 2005); Oliver Wolleh, *Local Peace Constituencies in Cyprus: Citizen's Rapprochement by the Bi-communal Conflict Resolution Trainer's Group*, Berghof Report No. 8 (Berlin: Berghof Foundation, 2001); and Fisher, "Cyprus."

15. The Institute for Multi-Track Diplomacy was founded in 1992 by Ambassador John McDonald and Dr. Louise Diamond to promote a systems-based approach to peacebuilding and facilitate transformation of deep-rooted social conflict through education, conflict resolution training, and communication. McDonald and Diamond developed the concept of "multitrack diplomacy" to capture the different levels and different efforts, or "tracks" of peacebuilding—from civil society to academia and business, as well as government—needed for sustainable peace. For further information about the institute, see its "About IMTD" page at http://www.imtd.org/index.php/about.

16. The Conflict Management Group is a US-based NGO founded by Roger Fisher, author of the well-known book on interest-based negotiation, *Getting to YES: Negotiating Agreement Without Giving In* (New York, Penguin, 1991). The organization provided negotiation and dialogue training, advice, and facilitation. The group is currently part of Mercy Corps, the US-based humanitarian and development NGO.

17. Broome, *Building Bridges Across the Green Line*, 25.

18. Marion Peters Angelica, "Evaluation of Conflict Resolution Training Efforts Sponsored by the Cyprus Fulbright Commission, 1993–1998" (Nicosia: Cyprus Fulbright Commission, July 1999), 35, 43, http://www.cyprus-conflict.net/angelica%20rpt%20-%201.html.

19. For example, a Bureau of Bi-Communal Reconciliation and Strengthening of Civil Society was organized in Democratic Rally (DISY), the ruling party at the time to which President Clerides belonged. Kate Clerides, a member of the original Oxford Group and long-term participant in bicommunal activities, pushed for this institution, which was a new and significant development in the conservative spectrum of politics in Cyprus. DISY would later become the only prosettlement party in the south of the island when the Annan Plan, the product of several years of UN-facilitated negotiations, was rejected by the Greek Cypriot population.

20. Wolleh, *Local Peace Constituencies in Cyprus*, 45.

21. Angelica, "Evaluation of Conflict Resolution Training Efforts," 35; Broome, *Building Bridges Across the Green Line*, 41.

22. Those who continued to meet and work together went to Pyla, the only bicommunal village on the island, but the hour-long drive from Nicosia and the close police observation made it less convenient, and thus less frequently used, except by the youth groups that continued to work. Others, with the facilitation of Resident Fulbright Scholar Marco Turk, participated in a mediation skills training program that included both bicommunal (prior to December 1997 and off the island) and monocommunal elements and led to the establishment of mediation centers in both communities.

23. For a description of the PRIO-supported business group, see Gina Lende, "The Brussels Business Group: dialogue across the conflict divide in Cyprus," in Jessica Banfield, Canan Gündüz, and Nick Killick, eds., *Local Business, Local Peace: The Peacebuilding Potential of the Domestic Private Sector* (London: International Alert, 2006): 307–14. For a description of the Oslo Group process, see A. Marco Turk, "Cyprus Reunification Is Long Overdue: The Time Is Right for Track III Diplomacy as the Best Approach for Successful Negotiation of This Ethnic Conflict," *Loyola of Los Angeles International and Comparative Law Review* 28, no. 205 (2006): 205–55.

24. The World Peace Foundation is an operating foundation that aims to provide intellectual leadership for peace. It was founded in 1910 by publisher Edwin Ginn to educate a global audience about the ills of war and to promote international peace. The World Peace Foundation was based at Harvard's Kennedy School of Government at the time of the HSG initiative, and since 2011 has been based at the Fletcher School of Law and Diplomacy.

25. Robert I. Rotberg and Ericka Albaugh, *Cyprus 2000: Divided or Federal?*, World Peace Foundation Report 20 (Cambridge, MA: World Peace Foundation, 1998), 22.

26. Rotberg and Albaugh, *Cyprus 2000*, 12.

27. Interview with staff of the Bicommunal Support Program, US Embassy, Nicosia, July 2006.

28. World Peace Foundation, "Proposal to US Embassy," internal document, 1998.

29. Ibid.

30. Diana Chigas, "Negotiating Intractable Conflicts: The Contribution of Unofficial Intermediaries," in Chester A. Crocker, Fen Osler Hampson, and Pamela Aall, eds., *Grasping the Nettle: Analyzing Cases of Intractable Conflict* (Washington, DC: United States Institute of Peace Press, 2005), 123–58.

31. Herbert C. Kelman, "Evaluating the Contributions of Interactive Problem Solving to the Resolution of Ethnonational Conflicts," *Peace and Conflict: Journal of Peace Psychology* 14, no. 1 (2008): 33; Ronald Fisher, ed., *Paving the Way: Contributions of Interactive Conflict Resolution to Peacemaking* (Lanham, MD: Lexington Books, 2005), 211, 224.

32. Ibid.

33. World Peace Foundation, "Proposal to US Embassy," internal document, 1998.

34. See, e.g., Herbert C. Kelman, "The Role of the Scholar-Practitioner in International Conflict," *International Studies Perspectives* 1, no. 3 (2000): 273–88; Harold H. Saunders, "Sustained Dialogue in Tajikistan: Transferring Learning from the Public to the Official Peace Process," in Fisher, *Paving the Way*, 127–41; Randa Slim and Harold Saunders, "The Inter-Tajik Dialogue: From Civil War towards Civil Society," in *Politics of Compromise: The Tajikistan Peace Process*, ed. Kamoludin Abdullaev and Catherine Barnes (London: Conciliation Resources, 2001), 44–47; Keith Fitzgerald, "Georgian-Ossetian Joint Brainstorming," in David Smock, ed., *Private Peacemaking:*

USIP-Assisted Peacemaking Projects of Nonprofit Organizations, Peaceworks no. 20 (Washington, DC: United States Institute of Peace, 1998), 6–9; and Susan Allen Nan, "Track One-and-a-Half Diplomacy: Contributions to Georgian-South Ossetian Peacemaking," in Fisher, *Paving the Way*, 161–73.

35. World Peace Foundation, *First Meeting of Harvard Study Group on Cyprus, Interpretive Summary*, internal document (Cambridge, MA: World Peace Foundation, May 1999).

36. Proximity format refers to an indirect format for a negotiation, in which the parties attending the negotiation sessions (i.e., in the same location) do not meet directly, but communicate through an intermediary.

37. Author interview with Greek Cypriot HSG participant, July 2006.

38. The issue of "recognition" has been a significant obstacle to implementation of all peacebuilding activities, from bicommunal cooperative projects to the negotiation process itself, as Greek Cypriot fears that any collaboration with Turkish Cypriot institutions and any acknowledgement of Turkish Cypriot sovereignty may lead to the recognition of the TRNC and legitimize later Turkish Cypriot secession from a unified state. See Bulent Kanol and Direnc Kanol, "Roadblocks to Peacebuilding Activities in Cyprus: International Peacebuilding Actors' Handling of the Recognition Issue," *Journal of Conflictology* 4, no. 2 (2013): 39–47.

39. For a description of the meeting and the chair's conclusions, see Robert Rotberg, *Cyprus After Annan: Next Steps Toward a Solution*, World Peace Foundation Report 37 (Cambridge, MA: World Peace Foundation, 2003).

40. Tamra Pearson D'Estree, Larissa A. Fast, Joshua N. Weiss, and Monica S. Jakobsen, "Changing the Debate About 'Success' in Conflict Resolution Efforts," *Negotiation Journal* 17, no. 2 (April 2001): 101–13.

41. Ronald Fisher, "Introduction: Analyzing Successful Transfer Effects in Interactive Conflict Resolution," in Fisher, *Paving the Way*, 3.

42. There have been a number of efforts to systematize and identify criteria for evaluating the effectiveness of track-one-and-a-half and track-two efforts. See Pearson d'Estree et al., "Changing the Debate about 'Success'"; Fisher, *Paving the Way*; Kelman, "Evaluating the Contributions of Interactive Problem Solving to the Resolution of Ethnonational Conflicts"; and Esra Cuhadar, "Assessing Transfer from Track Two Diplomacy: The Cases of Water and Jerusalem," *Journal of Peace Research* 46, no. 5 (2009): 641–58. This framework draws on this work in distinguishing different types of "transfer," including effects on public-political constituencies and public attitudes (downward transfer), effects on the leadership and the negotiations (upward transfer) and effects on other initiatives (lateral transfer). It also draws on these analysts in identifying different levels of impacts necessary for effective transfer to occur: changes in participants' thinking, attitudes, and relationships; changes in participants' actions (the foundations for transfer); and achievements outside the workshops that can be linked back to the process.

43. See Cuhadar, "Assessing Transfer from Track Two Diplomacy," 643; and Fisher, *Paving the Way*, 6–7.

44. See Diana Chigas, "The Role and Effectiveness of Non-Governmental Third Parties in Peacebuilding," in *Moving Toward a Just Peace: The Mediation Continuum*, ed. Jan Fritz (Dordrecht: Springer, 2014), 273–315; Fisher, *Paving the Way*, 219; and Diana Chigas, "Capacities and Limitations of NGOs as Conflict Managers," in *Leashing*

the Dogs of War: Conflict Management in a Divided World, ed. Chester A. Crocker, Fen Osler Hampson, and Pamela Aall (Washington, DC: United States Institute of Peace Press, 2007), 553–87.

45. Author interview with HSG participant, July 2006.

46. World Peace Foundation, *Second Meeting of Harvard Study Group on Cyprus, Interpretive Summary*, internal document (Cambridge, MA: World Peace Foundation, July 1999).

47. Author interview with HSG participant, July 2006. This statement was reflected in the comments of many others in the group.

48. *See* Angelica, "Evaluation of Conflict Resolution Training."

49. Author interview with HSG participant, July 2006.

50. Author interview with HSG participant, July 2006.

51. Herbert C. Kelman, "Coalitions Across Conflict Lines: The Interplay of Conflicts Within and Between the Israeli and Palestinian Communities," in Stephen Worchel and Jeffry A. Simpson, eds., *Conflict Between People and Groups: Causes, Processes, and Resolutions* (Chicago: Nelson-Hall, 1993), 236–58.

52. Helen Barnes with Christina Demetriades, "Experiences of Dialogue in Cyprus," Case Study, Democratic Dialogue (Nicosia: UNDP, 2005), http://www.democratic dialoguenetwork.org/files/documents_bk_marzo_7/12/attachment/EXPERIENCES _OF_DIALOGUE_IN_CYPRUS.pdf.

53. Ker-Lindsay, "From U Thant to Kofi Annan," 22; and Akgün et al., "Quo Vadis Cyprus?," 42.

54. David A. Lax and James K. Sebenius, *The Manager as Negotiator: Bargaining for Cooperation and Competitive Gain* (New York: Free Press, 1986). This phrase refers to the existence of potential agreements that would benefit both parties more than the value of their no-negotiation alternatives. The term was coined by Lax and Sebenius, and has alternatively been called the "bargaining range" or "zone of agreement."

55. Author interview with HSG participant, July 2006.

56. Author interview with HSG participant, July 2006.

57. Author interviews with members of UN team, February, April, and May 2007.

58. Author interview with US Embassy staff, July 2006.

59. Author interviews with members of UN team, February, April, and May 2007.

60. Author interview with Turkish Cypriot HSG member and CTP member, July 2006.

61. Author interview with Turkish Cypriot HSG member, July 2006.

62. Pro-*taksim* (division) parties had regularly gained over 60 percent of the vote in elections from 1974. In 1998, following the EU decision at Luxembourg to open negotiations with Cyprus, this percentage increased to two-thirds. But by 2003, Turkish Cypriots were demonstrating in the streets, and the pro-negotiation opposition parties gained about 50 percent of the vote. See Hannes Lacher and Erol Kaymak, "Transforming Identities: Beyond the Politics of Non-Settlement in North Cyprus," *Mediterranean Politics* 10, no. 2 (July 2005): 154.

63. One television show, for example, brought people together to talk about their experiences of meeting Greek Cypriots for the first time, to share what happened to them, and how their interaction had changed their minds. The program ran 55 shows over three years and invited 125 guests. Author interview with director-general of BRT (Turkish Cypriot television station), July 2006.

64. Ali Carkoglu and Ahmet Sözen, "The Turkish Cypriot General Elections of December 2003: Setting the Stage for Resolving the Cyprus Conflict?," *South European Society and Politics* 9, no. 3 (Winter 2004): 135.

65. Author interview with Turkish Cypriot HSG member, July 2006.

66. Development Assistance Committee, *Evaluating Peacebuilding Activities in Settings of Conflict and Fragility: Improving Learning for Results* (Paris: Organization for Economic Cooperation and Development, 2012), 9.

67. Ibid., 36.

68. The absence of AKEL and DIKO stemmed from a group decision at the end of the first meeting not to reinvite those who could not attend that meeting, because the group had already begun to develop a positive problem-solving dynamic and new understandings and did not want to disrupt that momentum.

69. Significant representation from the Greek Cypriot business community was also missing. While this did not increase the study group's vulnerability to attack, it too likely undermined its effectiveness and influence with a key constituency in the peace process.

70. Yusuf Kanli, "Is a 'New Cyprus State' in the Offing?" *Turkish Daily News*, January 27, 2002, http://www.hurriyetdailynews.com/default.aspx?pageid=438&n=is-a-new-cyprus-state-in-the-offing-2002-01-27. See also substantial excerpts from the document presented and withdrawn at fifth HSG meeting in "United States of Cyprus," *Turkish Daily News*, January 23, 2002, http://www.hurriyetdailynews.com/default.aspx?pageid=438&n=united-states-of-cyprus-2002-01-06.

71. Kanli, "Is a 'New Cyprus State' in the Offing?"; see also the summary in Cyprus PIO: Turkish Press and Other Media, January 28, 2002, http://www.hri.org/news/cyprus/tcpr/2002/02-01-28.tcpr.html#05.

72. Ibid.

73. Jennie Matthew, "Conflict Resolution Critics 'Playing a Political Game,'" *Cyprus Mail: News Articles in English*, January 29, 2002, http://www.hri.org/news/cyprus/cmnews/2002/02-01-29.cmnews.html. See also "Spokesman Denies Press Allegations about a Solution Plan," *Athens News Bulletin: Daily News Bulletin in English 02-01-22*, http://www.hri.org/news/greek/ana/2002/02-01-22.ana.html#22. Even in late 2006, UNOPS, its successor UNDP, and the United States were being accused of providing direct financial support to the "yes" campaign for the Annan Plan, which Greek Cypriots perceived as biased. The US Embassy and UNDP made public the financing figures in order to clarify the record. See UNDP, "Bi-communal Development Programme 1998–2005," UNDP Projects Database, http://mirror.undp.org/cyprus/projects/sectorsubsector.pdf. See also the accusations made in the press, described in Makarios Drousiotis, "The Construction of Reality and the Mass Media in Cyprus" (Nicosia: IKME, 2005), http://www.makarios.eu/upload/20051111/1131713084-12865.pdf.

74. See, e.g., Angelica, "Evaluation of Conflict Resolution Training," 35.

75. Author interview with HSG member, July 2006.

76. Author interview with HSG member, July 2006. This sentiment was reflected in the comments of several study group members in interviews with the author in July 2006.

77. It is estimated that the gap in per capita income in 2000 was over 2:1 ($5,966 in the north compared to $13,155 in the south). Ron Ayres, "The Economic Costs of Separation: The North-South Development Gap in Cyprus," *Ekonomia* 6, no. 1 (2003): 39–52.

78. Christou, "The European Union and Cyprus," 6–7; and Natalie Tocci, "EU Intervention in Ethno-political Conflicts: The Cases of Cyprus and Serbia-Montenegro," *European Foreign Affairs Review* 9 (2004): 551–73.

79. Turkish Cypriots claimed that the application was illegal because the 1959 Treaty of Guarantee stated that Cyprus could not become a member of an international organization to which only one motherland (in this case, Greece) belonged. The EU rejected this argument. See Tözun Bahcheli, "The Lure of Economic Prosperity versus Ethno-Nationalism: Turkish Cypriots, the European Union option, and the Resolution of Ethnic Conflict in Cyprus," in *Minority Nationalism and the Changing International Order*, ed. Michael Keating and John McGarry (Oxford: Oxford University Press, 2001), 210.

80. Lacher and Kaymak, "Transforming Identities," 154; and Carkoglu and Sözen, "The Turkish Cypriot General Elections of December 2003," 128.

81. Bahcheli, "The Lure of Economic Prosperity versus Ethno-Nationalism," 211.

82. Tocci, "EU Intervention in Ethno-political Conflicts," 559. Many of the bicommunal activists tried to address the lack of information and misinformation about the EU, such as by bringing speakers to talk about the EU and themselves appearing in the media in radio and television programs. From early on, a bicommunal EU Study Group attempted to look at the implications of EU membership.

83. Nathalie Tocci, "Towards Peace in Cyprus: Incentives and Disincentives," *Brown Journal of World Affairs* 10, no. 1 (Summer–Fall 2003), http://brown.edu/initiatives /journal-world-affairs/101/towards-peace-cyprus-incentives-and-disincentives.

84. Lacher and Kaymak, "Transforming Identities," 154; and Tocci, "EU Intervention in Ethno-political conflicts," 560.

85. Fisher, Ury, and Patton, *Getting to Yes*.

86. Tocci, "Towards Peace in Cyprus," 202.

87. Lacher and Kaymak, "Transforming Identities," 156; and Tocci, "EU Intervention in Ethno-political Conflicts," 560.

88. Serdar Denktash's father-in-law went to prison for his role in creating the crisis. Lacher and Kaymak, "Transforming Identities," 157; and "Denktash Relative Has Property Confiscated," *Cyprus Mail*, September 24, 2000, http://www.hri.org/news/cyprus /cmnews/2000/00-09-24.cmnews.html#05.

89. Lacher and Kaymak, "Transforming Identities," 157.

90. Mustafa Damdelen, the head of the Turkish Cypriot Chamber of Commerce and a bicommunal dialogue veteran, noted: "The recent UN plan was the most comprehensive document that could have satisfied the needs of the two communities at optimum levels." Mustafa Damdelen, "The View of the Turkish Cypriot Business Community on the UN Plan and EU Membership Process" (presentation at the "Cyprus' European Union Accession and the Greek-Turkish Rivalry" conference, April 5–6, 2003, Yale University, New Haven, CT).

91. Christou, "The European Union and Cyprus," 7.

92. Christou, "The European Union and Cyprus," 7; Tocci, "EU Intervention in Ethno-political Conflicts," 557; and David Milne, "One State or Two? Political Realism on the Cyprus Question," *The Round Table: The Commonwealth Journal of International Affairs* 92, issue 368 (2003): 145–62.

93. Fisher, Ury, and Patton, *Getting to Yes*.

94. Saskia Ramming, "Cyprus's Accession Negotiations to the European Union: Conditional Carrots, Good Faith, and Miscalculations," *International Negotiation* 13, no. 3 (2008): 365–86.

95. Christou, "The European Union and Cyprus," 19

96. See Lincoln P. Bloomfield and Allen Moulton, "Cascon Case CYC: Cyprus (communal) 1963–," MIT Cascon System for Analyzing International Conflict, 2000, http://web.mit.edu/cascon/cases/case_cyc.html. CASCON is a computerized history-based conflict analysis and decision-support system designed to serve as an aid to the memory and the imagination. CASCON derives from earlier MIT research under the direction of Professor Lincoln P. Bloomfield on the subject of local conflict and its prevention. The database includes information on eighty-five post–World War II conflict cases. The history of each case is structured using the Bloomfield-Leiss conflict phase model.

97. Author interview with member of UN mediation team, May 2007.

98. For an English summary of the results of a poll conducted by and published in the Greek Cypriot newspaper *Politis* on November 20, 2002, see "Poll Shows Growing Opposition to Peace Plan," *Cyprus Mail*, November 26, 2002, http://www.hri.org/news/cyprus/cmnews/2002/02-11-26.cmnews.html#03.

99. It is interesting to note that the most serious attacks on the HSG process and the earlier Oslo Group civil society brainstorming group came only in early 2002.

100. Author interviews with US Embassy staff and Greek Cypriot politician, July 2006.

101. Author interview with Greek Cypriot academic, July 2006.

102. Author interview with HSG member, July 2006.

103. This conclusion is shared by Marion Angelica, the evaluator of the Fulbright Commission's bicommunal work. See Angelica, "Evaluation of Conflict Resolution Training."

104. Author interview with Greek Cypriot HSG member, July 2006.

105. A 2013 evaluation of UNDP's Action for Cooperation and Trust (ACT) program underlined the challenges of the lack of informed debate on proposals being negotiated and the limited efforts to connect tracks one and three, and outlined UNDP's efforts to broaden engagement with and participation in the peace process. See Meg Kinghorn and Sean McGearty, *UNDP ACT Outcome Evaluation Report* (Nicosia: UNDP, 2013).

106. The exception to the bicommunalists' self-isolation from government and political parties was the efforts of Katie Clerides to establish the Bureau of Bi-Communal Reconciliation and Strengthening of Civil Society within her party (DISY). DISY was and continues to be the only Greek Cypriot party that has come out unequivocally in favor of the Annan Plan as a basis for settlement of the conflict.

107. Angelica comments that the lack of a clear, understandable selection process contributed to a mystique and a feeling of exclusivity that soured people on becoming involved in the training or other bicommunal activities. Angelica, "Evaluation of Conflict Resolution Training."

108. See Barnes and Demetriades, "Dialogue in Cyprus."

109. Tocci, "Towards Peace in Cyprus," 205. See also Philippos Savvides, "The EU as a 'Catalyst' for Peace: The Case of Cyprus" (presentation at the "Cyprus' European Union Accession and the Greek-Turkish Rivalry" conference, April 5–6, 2003, Yale University, New Haven, CT), http://www.yale.edu/eustudies/Cyprus_Conference_Savvides.pdf.

110. Kypros Chrysostomides, quoted in "Spokesman Says Wanted Changes to Annan Plan within Its Framework," *Cyprus News Agency: News in English*, September 24, 2003, http://www.hri.org/news/cyprus/cna/2003/03-09-24.cna.html#08.

111. For a summary of the discussions of HSG members and US, UN, EU, and British officials involved with the negotiation process, see Rotberg, *Cyprus After Annan*, 16.

112. See Rotberg, *Cyprus After Annan*; Othon Anastasakis, Gilles Bertrand, and Kalypso Nicolaïdis, *Getting to Yes: Suggestions for Embellishment of the Annan Plan for Cyprus* (Oxford: South East European Studies Programme, European Studies Centre, St Antony's College, University of Oxford, February 2004).

113. *See* I. William Zartman, "Timing and Ripeness," in *The Negotiator's Fieldbook: The Desk Reference for the Experienced Negotiator*, ed. Andrea Kupfer Schneider and Christopher Honeyman (Washington, DC: American Bar Association, Section of Dispute Resolution, 2006), 143–52; and Richard N. Haass, *Conflicts Unending: The United States and Regional Disputes* (New Haven, CT: Yale University Press, 1991).

114. Mary B. Anderson and Lara Olson, *Confronting War: Critical Lessons for Peace Practitioners* (Cambridge, MA: CDA, 2003), 70.

115. Several HSG members and other long-standing participants in bicommunal activities were asked to take leadership roles in the technical committees and working groups that launched a new round of negotiations in Cyprus in 2008, following the victory of AKEL in elections. The committees and working groups developed more than twenty-five confidence-building measures and had made progress in laying the ground work for talks between the leaders by 2009. See United Nations Security Council, "Report of the Secretary-General on his Mission of Good Offices in Cyprus."

116. Anderson and Olson define "key people" as people or groups that because of their power or influence are critical to the continuation or resolution of the conflict. "More people" refers to broad outreach to people at all levels across sectors. They found that effective peace work links work with key people with work with more people. Anderson and Olson, *Confronting War*, 55.

117. Maria Hadjpavlou and Bulent Kanol, *Cumulative Impact Case Study: The Impacts of Peacebuilding Work on the Cyprus Conflict*, Reflecting on Peace Practice Project (Cambridge, MA: CDA, 2008), http://cdacollaborative.org/media/53258/The -Impacts-of-Peacebuilding-Work-on-the-Cyprus-Conflict.pdf.

118. Anderson and Olson, *Confronting War*, 55–58.

Chapter 8

The Burundi Leadership Training Program
Susanna Campbell and Peter Uvin

Introduction

The Burundi Leadership Training Program (BLTP) was proposed in late 2002 "to increase the ability of the country's ethnically polarized leadership to work together in consolidating its post-war transition and advancing Burundi's post-war economic reconstruction."[1] It was conceived by Howard Wolpe, the former US Special Envoy to the African Great Lakes Region, during his tenure at the Woodrow Wilson International Center for Scholars (WWICS). It was funded for eighteen months by the World Bank's Post-Conflict Fund, with ad-hoc contributions by the US Agency for International Development, the European Union (EU), and the UK Department for International Development. The authors evaluated the BLTP for the World Bank's Post-Conflict Fund in 2004.

The BLTP appeared two years into Burundi's five-year transitional administration, which started with the August 2000 signing of the Arusha Peace and Reconciliation Agreement and formally ended with the August

2005 election of Burundi's current president, Pierre Nkurunziza. During this unstable period, in which international and regional actors pressured Burundi's transitional leadership to implement the Arusha agreement, the BLTP offered a more empowering alternative. Rather than criticizing Burundi's new leadership for failing to implement the complex reforms outlined in the agreement, the BLTP aimed to strengthen its capacity to take on the difficult tasks of peace consolidation and institutional transformation.

The BLTP was broadly successful. It helped former enemies learn how to relate better to one another. In some instances, these improved relationships contributed to important breakthroughs in Burundi's ongoing peace process and supported reforms in key national institutions. The program's experience shows that well-targeted leadership programming can support the transformation of both individual leaders and the institutions that they govern. But the implementation of the BLTP in Burundi also emphasizes the importance of the *fit* between activities and their context. The program's successes were a result of *how* it navigated Burundi's complex and changing political dynamics. It was able to negotiate this difficult environment because of the identities of its staff, their relationship with key players in Burundi, and their specific skill sets. These staff were well placed to take advantage of a key opportunity in Burundi's postwar transition: the existence of a transitional power-sharing government that was both open to and in need of support.

This chapter begins by providing an analysis of the nature and course of Burundi's conflict until the initiation of the BLTP, identifying the primary factors affecting individual and institutional transformation. It then outlines the nature of the BLTP's activities and presents an assessment of the program's impact. Next, it teases out the internal and external factors that contributed to the program's impact, and concludes with an analysis of the program's potential replicability.[2]

Nature and Course of the Conflict

The Years of Conflict

Burundi is a very poor, highly populated, small landlocked country in east-central Africa. Its hilly terrain is home to 7.8 million people: a large Hutu majority, a small Tutsi minority, and an additional 1 percent of Twa. As in neighboring Rwanda, these groups share the same language and culture, having occupied different roles in a complex traditional social hierarchy in which social mobility within and between groups was common. Contrary to common assumptions about the primordial nature of the Burundian conflict, an examination of Burundi's precolonial history does not reveal an ancient ethnic conflict that compelled neighbors to kill one another.

During the three decades between Burundi's independence from Belgium in 1962 and the outbreak of its civil war in 1993, the competition for control of the Burundian state became increasingly ethnic and violent in nature. During most of this time, the country was ruled by a small Tutsi oligarchy from Bururi province.[3] This clique derived its power from control over the higher echelons of the army, the key levers of the state (and, consequently, the fruits of the foreign aid enterprise), and the business sector. Under their rule, Hutu could hold only low-level positions in the state and army. Dissent was held down through acute and structural violence, including the "partial genocide" of 1972, when almost all educated Hutu of any social class were murdered. Over time, the Burundian political scene came to represent what some authors have referred to as the "ethnic security dilemma."[4] The Tutsi population feared that the Hutu masses would develop their own violent discriminatory state in Rwanda's image, while the Hutu masses feared a repeat of the 1972 massacres and were continually reminded of the Tutsi oligarchy's willingness to use violence and oppression.

After taking power in a bloodless coup d'état in 1987, Major Pierre Buyoya began to institute a series of political and economic reforms. He launched these reforms partly in response to international pressure following the massacre of approximately 3,000 Tutsis and 15,000 Hutus in 1988, and partly in response to pressure from within the Burundian elite to enlarge the circle of the state. Buyoya's reforms culminated in the first democratic presidential elections in the summer of 1993, which resulted in a loss for his party, UPRONA (National Party of Union and Progress), which had been the vehicle of Tutsi political control for decades. Melchior Ndadaye, president of the newly formed FRODEBU (Burundian Democratic Front), won the 1993 elections and became Burundi's first democratically elected Hutu president. The elections transferred control of the state, down to the lowest levels, to Hutu, but the army remained in Tutsi hands. Some of those Tutsi frustrated with this sudden loss of power reacted with a coup d'état in October 1993, during which the new president and many in his entourage were killed.

Immediately following the death of President Ndadaye, widespread popular anger and violence, often directed toward ordinary Tutsi in the hills, broke out in many parts of the country. The violence was organized by extremist Hutu counterelites, mostly affiliated with FRODEBU, and claimed the lives of many Tutsi to such an extent that many Tutsi consider this violence to be genocidal. The national army, still controlled by Tutsi, responded as it always had—with great brutality. For thirty years, political competition in Burundi had become increasingly violent and ethnic in nature: now, the floodgates were open and an ethnic civil war had begun. As no side managed to acquire the upper hand, a decade of violence-marred stalemate began. The civil war and ensuing genocide in neighboring Rwanda in 1994 only served to deepen the ethnic dimension of Burundi's civil war.

Hutu rebel groups emerged, split, regrouped, and attacked from locations across the Tanzanian and Democratic Republic of Congo borders, the latter of which was also imploding into violence and lawlessness. Burundi's formal political processes remained deadlocked as presidents came and went, chaos reigned, and violence prevailed everywhere. Hundreds of thousands of Burundians fled their homes, with Tutsi predominantly fleeing to safer havens close to the communal administration and military garrisons; and Hutu fleeing to internally displaced persons camps in the hills or abroad, especially to Tanzania. During the decade of Burundi's civil war, it is estimated that 250,000 to 300,000 died from the violence, not to mention the lives lost to malnutrition and disease.

The Peace Process

International and regional efforts to broker peace in Burundi began immediately after the outbreak of the war in late 1993. These efforts were stepped up after the 1994 Rwandan genocide, with the aim of preventing Burundi from going down the same path. The international and regional response included "a UN [United Nations] and several other special envoys, a UN commission of inquiry, an OAU [Organisation of African Unity] military observer mission, regional summits and negotiations, several high-level fact-finding and jawboning delegations, a number of initiatives by nongovernmental organizations, an ongoing Washington policy forum, and ultimately, regional economic sanctions."[5] According to Michael Lund, Barnett Rubin, and Fabienne Hara, the level of response was "out of proportion to the significance in traditional strategic or economic terms of this Maryland-sized country."[6]

The BLTP was certainly not the first dialogue or training activity in Burundi. Between 1993 and 1998, no fewer than thirty-six governmental and nongovernmental organizations (NGOs) were implementing some type of dialogue, facilitation, or other conflict management program in Burundi.[7] These activities worked with many of the same people that the BLTP later engaged. Unlike the BLTP, however, the peacebuilding programs of the 1990s occurred during a time of conflict escalation, making such efforts more dangerous and challenging for both the facilitators and the participants. As this chapter will show, the effect of the BLTP may have resulted as much from its ability to bring together a particular group of people at a critical and propitious time for peace as from the particular training approach that it employed.

In August 2000, the multitude of peacemaking efforts culminated in the signing of the Arusha Peace and Reconciliation Agreement. This agreement was comprehensive in terms of political and social reforms, but the two principal armed groups were absent from the Arusha process, which meant that the final agreement lacked the crucial element of a cease-fire. In addition, many of the most contentious issues in the peace process—the interim presidency, composition of the military, transitional justice, electoral law, and the constitution—were left for the parties to the agreement to negotiate during the transitional period, which was initially set at three years.

The Implementation Monitoring Committee was given the responsibility for overseeing the implementation of the Arusha agreement. The Special Representative of the Secretary-General to Burundi, Berhanu Dinka, headed the committee, which was composed of signatories of the agreement.[8] Unfortunately, even though the committee held regular meetings and followed key events, it did not have the leadership or leverage necessary to ensure that the agreement was implemented. Even the committee's own executive committee lamented its incompetence: "It is deplorable that the [Implementation Monitoring Committee], which should have been the driving force behind the campaign to educate the population and garner support for the accord, should be reduced to the mere role of spectator."[9]

Building on Nelson Mandela's role as the mediator of the Arusha agreement, South Africa took the lead in pushing forward negotiations with the rebel groups, the National Liberation Front and the Forces for the Defense of Democracy, the largest rebel movement by far. In October 2003, they reached a cease-fire agreement with the Forces for the Defense of Democracy called the Pretoria Protocol on Political, Defense, and Security Power-sharing in Burundi. The Arusha and Pretoria agreements marked the beginning of the transition out of civil war and presented a roadmap for the development of new institutions designed to support and maintain peace, integrate the army, adopt a new constitution, organize elections, and kick-start development—a typical package applied in all postconflict countries. The National Liberation Front, however, remained largely outside of the peace process for several more years, and only joined the state institutions in 2009.

The Beginnings of the BLTP

The BLTP was initiated in March 2003, when Burundi still faced significant military, political, economic, and sociopsychological challenges. Indeed, the most likely outcome of the peace process predicted at that time by knowledgeable observers was that it would not hold. The implementation of the peace agreement and the transformation of Burundi's governing and social institutions faced at least four major challenges. First and foremost, the security situation needed to be stabilized. To move the Arusha and Pretoria agreements from paper to reality, soldiers and rebels had to lay down arms and be integrated into the national army or demobilized and reintegrated in their communities; rebels who had not signed the agreements had to be brought into the fold; and police and army structures needed to be reformed and trained, with their leadership and "rank and file" made more multiethnic.

Second, a viable system of guarantees had to be created to ensure that ethnic exclusion and destruction would not return, neither against Hutu nor Tutsi. While the initial conflict in Burundi was clearly rooted in the competition for political power, in the previous thirty years—and especially the previous decade—ethnicity had taken on a life of its own. The social and physical separation between people had grown. A sense of victimization prevailed, as both sides charged the other with genocide, and fear and distrust along ethnic lines was shared by all. The power-sharing arrangements outlined in the Arusha agreement were a response to this ethnic polarization, but they would not work if they did not have minimal backing of Burundian society.

Third, the old clique controlling power had to retreat from commanding the state, army, and economy, and make space to include new entrants in these spheres of power. In Burundi, as in so many extremely poor African countries with almost no private sector, an individual who ceased being a general, a parliamentarian, or a minister did not often have another interesting and well-paid job waiting in the wings, but risked losing all economic security and falling from social grace.

Fourth, the challenge of Burundi's institutional transformation took place against a system of unimaginable poverty and social exclusion of most ordinary Burundians. The rural poor, whether Hutu, Tutsi, or Twa, were killed and abused by all sides. Their land was stolen. Their food, credit, and aid were skimmed off. Their children died from preventable diseases at a rate that was one of the world's three highest. Few of those in power or vying for it, regardless of their party affiliation, were deeply connected to the poor or seemed to have their interests foremost at heart. There was a real risk that peace in Burundi would be established without improving the conditions of the poor, the rural, the farmers, or the young. In the longer run, this would remain an explosive situation.

In sum, although the Arusha and Pretoria processes culminated in wide-ranging and general agreements, many of the key issues were left unresolved, precisely during the years that the BLTP was active. Although South Africa and several of Burundi's neighbors (Kenya, Rwanda, Tanzania, and Uganda) continued to press for and conduct high-level negotiations, their attention was focused almost exclusively on achieving a cease-fire with the National Liberation Front. The Implementation Monitoring Committee, charged with overseeing the implementation of the Arusha agreement, failed to live up to its responsibility. At the same time, Burundi's transitional leaders seemed reluctant to implement the reforms outlined in the Arusha and Pretoria agreements, in part because they knew these reforms would lead to their removal from office. The international community's main political response to the slow progress was to withhold promised aid disbursements until the transitional government got on with its work.[10]

The BLTP Empowerment Alternative:
Building Trust in Individuals and Institutions

In contrast to the often tense rapport between the transitional government and the international community, the BLTP was designed to add an entirely different dynamic for transitional change, using processes focused on empowering individuals rather than on applying conditionality to the entire government. The program sought to contribute to Burundi's transition (and, after the elections, to its consolidation) by investing in the people in charge of creating the post-transition institutions. It sought to provide key individuals with the attitudes, skills, and relations that it hoped would help them to conduct complex daily negotiations about institutional reform. It also tried to make this process more inclusive by including key civil society leaders. In short, the BLTP sought to create an additional path to solve the Burundian crisis, in combination with the efforts of the UN mission, South African facilitation, pressure from donors, and other unofficial dialogue processes in the past and present.

To empower Burundian leaders to solve their own problems, the BLTP aimed to address several deficits that it identified in the peace process: the zero-sum, winner-take-all wartime mindset; the mistrust between key leaders of different ethnic groups; the lack of consensus on the rules of power-sharing and public decision-making; and the need to reestablish lines of communication and understanding between Burundian elites, which had become broken by years of war.[11] Although all of these factors existed before the war, the conflict had made them more pronounced. The aim of the BLTP was to transform those individuals who were in a position to transform Burundi's institutions.

Burundi presented a stunningly difficult context for institutional and individual transformation. Burundi's leaders were not a group of committed professionals negotiating to solve a difficult problem, but a group of distrustful, hurt, insecure, and often unrepresentative people who had used any tool, under conditions of near-Hobbesian institutional anarchy, to assure themselves of a seat at the table and a piece of an increasingly smaller pie. It is these leaders that the BLTP sought to assist in transforming Burundi. All of the program's efforts occurred against a backdrop of violence, unpredictability, profound institutional weakness, deep poverty and risk, and regional instability.

The BLTP developed three different types of workshops to address these complex dynamics: the Ngozi workshops, the followup workshops, and the targeted workshops. These workshops combined conflict resolution training and third-party–facilitated dialogue tools. Using training tools, the program sought to transmit specific communications and conflict resolution skills to its participants.[12] Using dialogue tools within the workshop exercises, it sought to put select Burundian leaders in a context in which they were likely to develop an increased understanding of and relationship to one another. The dialogue component of the BLTP contained some elements of interactive problem-solving workshops, which, according to Herbert Kelman, aim to "facilitate a kind of interaction that differs from the way parties in conflict usually interact—if they interact at all."[13] Nonetheless, the program's specific combination of training and apolitical dialogue represented a new type of intervention, potentially resulting in different outcomes from other initiatives that focus on training or on dialogue exclusively.

Initial Ngozi Workshops

The signature products of the BLTP were the three Ngozi workshops that took place in 2003 and 2004 and were named for the town in which they were held. The BLTP described these intensive six-day workshops, each of which involved about thirty people, as "interactive workshops in communications, negotiating skills, visioning, group problem-solving, and strategic planning [that] are designed to assist in the restoration of trust and confidence among Burundian leaders and to encourage participatory and collaborative decision-making."[14] The workshops were designed to help participants recognize that their self-interest could be more effectively advanced through collaboration and inclusive political processes; restore trust in one another and rebuild personal relationships; build consensus on the ground rules for sharing state power and making public decisions; increase mutual understanding so that they could stop blaming each other for the war and the political violence; develop a discourse that encourages problem-solving rather than confrontation; and recognize the interdependence among the society's constituent parts.[15]

Over the six days of the workshop, the participants were sequestered in the rather remote northern town of Ngozi. They actively participated in the long workshop sessions and then ate and drank together at night. The structure was designed to create relationships and break down barriers, since part of the BLTP's powerful initial aim was to create an environment in which "participants are able to see each other as 'whole' persons, not simply as stereotypic reflections of their ethnic and political categories." The change in participants' attitudes toward one another was the first crucial step. The BLTP hoped that this new way of thinking would help the participants identify their common interests and build consensus on the new rules of the postwar game, such as power arrangements, decision-making procedures, and other behavior patterns.

To select the initial group of "leaders" for the Ngozi workshops, the BLTP team conducted an informal poll of the most influential people from across the political spectrum in Burundi. They requested lists of influential people from key informants, and from these and other names selected a representative group of individuals, taking into account ethnicity, region, political affiliation, gender, and professional background. This eclectic process of participant selection was necessary to ensure that all parties to the conflict were represented at all of the workshops, which was crucial for the program's credibility and impact.

Followup Workshops

To reinforce the attitude change achieved with the ninety-five leaders trained at the three initial Ngozi workshops, in 2003 and 2004 the BLTP organized nine followup workshops, each of which usually lasted two days. The followup workshops were an important innovation in the BLTP design, which the BLTP had included in response to a common criticism of both training and dialogue programs—namely, that there was no opportunity to reinforce the skills or relationships gained in the initial sessions.

The initial followup workshops after Ngozi I and Ngozi II, both of which took place in 2003, were focused on the design of development projects, proposal writing, and negotiation/mediation skills. By the time of the Ngozi III followup workshop in June 2004, the BLTP had reoriented the workshops' focus away from economic development projects and concentrated on developing the leadership competencies and capacities of the participants, reinforcing the network, and discussing issues of current political importance. From June 2004 on, the BLTP team largely responded to requests of the Ngozi participants themselves when designing followup workshops. In April 2005, the participants decided to create a steering committee composed of the members of the BLTP network, which was made up of participants from all three Ngozi workshops, to help convene and guide the direction of the network.

Targeted Workshops

At the suggestion of some of the high-level military officers who attended the first Ngozi workshop in March 2003, the BLTP began to organize trainings specifically for the security sector. The objective of these targeted workshops was to help unblock negotiations regarding the integration of the rebel and national armies in line with the Arusha and Pretoria agreements. Once the negotiations were unblocked, partly through BLTP efforts, the program continued these security sector trainings with the goal of increasing communication between former rebels and the national army that now together constituted the Burundian Armed Forces. Between November 2003 and the elections in summer 2005, the BLTP organized three training sessions with army and rebel commanders to prepare for the implementation of the cease-fire agreement and to plan the integration of the Burundian Army (the Joint Ceasefire Commission and the Etat-Majeur Général Intégré); two workshops with the Joint Liaison Teams of the UN Office in Burundi (ONUB), composed of the Burundian Army, the rebel groups, and ONUB staff; and two sessions for the newly integrated command of the new Burundian Police Force.

Soon after the August 2005 election of Pierre Nkurunziza, Burundi's post-transitional president, the BLTP trained the entire new Burundian government—including the president, two vice presidents, twenty cabinet ministers, the appointed secretary general of the government, military and civilian chiefs of staff, and several senior advisors to ministries. The willingness of the country's top officials to spend five days in this "training session" testifies to the credibility that the BLTP had acquired. Firmly in power for five years to come, these people hardly needed to have BLTP's seal of approval in order to claim control of the state and interact with the international community. All the same, they both asked for and participated in the full workshop. There was no followup to this workshop (understandable for a new and busy government) but it is probably no exaggeration to state that no leadership training project has ever encompassed such a high political level. The BLTP's primary spin-off project, the Community-Based Leadership Program (CBLP), trained twenty Burundian "master trainers" to do similar but less structured conflict resolution and dialogue work at the grassroots level in two provinces.

Impacts

It is not easy to evaluate projects like the BLTP. As with so many of the most important things in social life, measurement and attribution problems are extremely severe; basic concepts such as social capital, trust, and respect are deeply contested; the dynamics at stake are chaotic, unpredictable, multidimensional, ambiguous, and complicated; and the disjuncture between the long-term objectives and the short-term project cycle is even greater than usual. Peacebuilding and development is a young field, and solidly established methodologies for project evaluation had only begun to be developed when the BLTP project was implemented. Even now, project managers and donors invest too little in baseline data, monitoring, and evaluation systems—and this project was no exception.

Table 8.1. Burundi Leadership Training Program Outputs, Expected Outcomes, and Indicators

	BLTP actions (outputs)	Expected outcomes	Indicators (identified by BLTP team)
Direct impact on individuals	Initial workshops Followup workshops	Changes in relations between participants	Participants lose their fear and speak honestly. Participants understand, and respect, that other participants see the world differently than they do. Participants understand not only how the other feels, but also that if they had been born in different circumstances, they also could be in that situation. Participants come out of their boxes, think and act as individuals, and see others as individuals. Participants build new relationships among themselves.
	Support for participant activities	Changes in relations between participants and others Changes in participants' immediate environment	Participants change their perception of other people/groups. Participants use their new knowledge, perspective, and tools to build relationships with others outside the group.
Indirect impact on social processes	Support for elaboration of development projects Impact on other donors' projects (e.g., CBLP)		Participants have an improved capacity to work collaboratively. Participants create new patterns of relationship and behavior outside of their formal group structure. Participants are able to accept that different views of history are possible, which should allow them to live with their community.
	Selection of participants New, targeted BLTP projects or network activities	Indirect impact on national institutions	No specific criteria mentioned.

This evaluation of the BLTP uses elements of both a "theory-based evaluation" model and an assisted internal evaluation practice. A theory-based evaluation approach breaks down the intervention into its component activity parts, trying to hypothesize the working assumptions that connect each activity to its desired outcome. Within conflict resolution and peacebuilding, the theory that guides the intervention is often referred to as the *theory of change*, or the project's hypothesis about factors that will contribute to building peace or deescalating conflict.[16] The BLTP theory of change was that improved relationships, greater understanding, and the development of a common vision among Burundi's leaders would enable them to collaboratively transform Burundi's institutions into institutions that guarantee peace. In other words, the BLTP was based on the belief that the main stumbling blocks to peace involved personal (vision, understanding) and interpersonal (trust) factors, which inhibit the creation of sustainable institutions for peace.

Following from the overall theory of change, the causal chain of results describes each step in the assumed connection between the project's entry point (i.e., conflict resolution training) and its desired influence on the cause of peace identified in the theory of change (i.e., transforming state institutions into guarantors of sustainable peace). This process resembles a scenario-building exercise in which the project staff describes the predicted causal chain between their entry point and desired outcome(s).[17] The data collected from this process identify how well each step in the chain is borne out. Table 8.1 presents the relationships among the theory of change, outputs, expected outcomes, and indicators identified during discussions with the BLTP team.

To understand the relationship between the program and the evolving context, this evaluation is grounded in the sociopolitical dynamics of Burundi. It assesses both the accuracy of the BLTP's theory of change for the Burundian context and the impacts that the BLTP's activities had on its predicted causal chain of results. By putting the intervention in the context of its long-term social and political dynamics and its specific place and time, the evaluation seeks to understand the BLTP's specific relevance and contribution.[18]

The Ngozi Workshops

POSITIVE EFFECTS

The three Ngozi workshops had noticeable positive effects. At the level of *individual attitude change*, both the authors' observations and interviews with dozens of participants and observers indicate that the BLTP workshops did effect a personal transformation in the way people perceive themselves in relation to the other participants. People humanized and individualized each other in ways they often had not done before. They began questioning their own attitudes and modes of behavior, and broke through some of the stereotypes that they may have carried for years: an "a-ha moment" of initial change.

The degree of attitude change during the workshop depended on the previous experiences and mindset of each individual. Some "extremists"—people who were entirely defined by one single issue from which they could not budge—underwent a real transformation in their capacity to see others as people rather than as categories of "opponents" and "evil." Other participants had spent years fighting in the bush, living in camps, or simply living abroad. They came to the BLTP with prejudices and stereotypes that had been hardened by a long-standing lack of interaction with "different" groups. Having normal conversations with a broad range of people created a new sense of possibility for them and allowed them to break through the fixed categories that had dominated their lives. This change illustrates once again the importance of including people who represented the "tough cases" in dialogue and training processes, rather than working only with the "progressives."

Most participants also cited the *relationships* that they built at the workshops as an important impact. Even though there was more open collaboration and dialogue during the workshops than during the war, making the job of pulling all of these people together easier, there was still a real threat that division and violence would erupt again. The BLTP provided a venue for decision-makers to come together informally and relate relatively openly with one another; however, it is not clear if and how this social capital persisted beyond the workshop (see below).

In general, the participants were pleased with the *skills, tools, and methods* learned in the BLTP training. The workshops were successful at helping to build better communication among participants, but much less successful at bringing the participants to a level that allowed them to use these skills in their professional work. Although there was a clear demand for more such professionally relevant training, the BLTP provided only a minimal degree of conflict resolution training to the participants. The BLTP's aim was *not* to train professional negotiators, mediators, analysts, or trainers (until later on), and therefore it is not surprising that this was not a prime contribution of the program. Subsequently, twenty Burundians involved in the BLTP received in-depth training in running BLTP workshops. It is unclear if a stronger focus on building participants' conflict resolution skills would have been relevant to the program's main aims.

The Ngozi workshops managed to create an environment propitious to attitude change and relationship building by being apolitical—not dealing directly with the political context in Burundi (and certainly not with the difficult issues), remaining closed to the public, being nondirective, and acting as if there was shared goodwill among all participants. All of this occurred in a place outside of most of the participants' normal context of life, helping them to interact as individuals over a six-day period. This approach was a sensible strategic choice on the part of the BLTP team. It helped to create a protective bubble that favored the sort of human interaction and individual change that the program sought to achieve. According to the BLTP team, "Everything is done to establish the workshop as a 'safe' environment in which individuals feel comfortable taking certain risks, opening up to each other, exploring new ways of relating to one another."[19]

Of course, in real life, none of the BLTP workshop conditions prevailed. The great challenge then was to ensure that the gains from the workshop were not temporary (not lasting beyond one's trip home), limited (applying only between those who personally participated in the workshop), or theoretical (creating no concrete engagements under more difficult conditions). To avoid these outcomes, a good followup dynamic was needed, and the participants were aware of this need. Indeed, while they raved about the success of the BLTP methodology in helping them to better understand themselves, their environment, and their interaction with others, they also constantly asked for support in translating this theory into practice, whether through activities, more training, or discussions of Burundi's most pressing issues.

MISSED OPPORTUNITIES

In spite of these successes and impacts, the BLTP missed two primary opportunities: the workshop hardly dealt with the concrete issues in Burundi, and the tools taught in the workshop trainings were not modified for the Burundian context. The program ought to have invested more time, in terms of both methodologies and substance, to focus on the concrete challenges prevailing in Burundi, going beyond the feel-good factor of helping the participants to get along with one another.[20]

When presented with this critique, the BLTP team's main counterargument was that bringing up these complicated and divisive issues too soon risked creating interpersonal conflict and defensiveness that would have undermined the success of the workshop. This was a valid point. Equally clearly, there was no fixed answer to this debate. Even if it is important for discussions to remain apolitical to encourage a de-escalation of tensions during the initial days of the workshop, it also seems important that participants eventually address the tough issues in the same atmosphere of confidence and quiet. Only then might people learn how to begin resolving these same issues outside the workshop, in the real world. The question is the speed with which to introduce such issues, and through which methods.

The Followup Workshops

The followup workshops were intended to increase the impact of the Ngozi workshops: reinforcing the initial attitude change, solidifying relationships among the participants, and increasing their capacity as individuals and as a group to influence national institutions. The proportion of initial participants who attended the followup workshops was high—more than three-quarters came to the first followup workshop immediately after their Ngozi workshop. Although there was a natural decline in attendance, significant numbers continued to attend subsequent ones: even several years later, occasional followup workshops attracted as many as forty participants.

Nonetheless, the development of a group of persons who felt at ease with one another did not easily or directly translate into a cohesive, sustainable network of people who worked across lines of ethnic and political division to create institutional change. The real difficulty facing the BLTP was how to transfer the impact and reach of the workshops beyond the immediate participants—the transfer effect: "If interventions are to make a difference, there needs to be transfer of knowledge, attitude change and resources to people beyond those directly participating in the project."[21] Creating this change, and documenting it, was a crucial challenge.

As the BLTP project progressed, attempts were made to move more toward collective action, away from the initial approach that focused more on the climate of trust and camaraderie between the participants. This shift toward collective action was hard to make: the followup workshops did not manage to go beyond general, noncommittal discussions on issues of contemporary political importance, such as justice and disarmament. Few other concrete actions came out of the Ngozi groups: they produced a development project in one province, and a new training for Muslims. This part of the project had the least impact. Moreover, the absence of concrete commitments or a space to discuss pressing current issues among people from different backgrounds proved to be a major limitation when, in subsequent years, the political space in Burundi started narrowing and polarizing.

The Targeted Workshops

The targeted workshops produced the BLTP's most concrete results. They were different from the Ngozi workshops in that they trained people within the same organization who shared a professional environment and negotiated with one another on a regular basis, rather than a cross-section of Burundian society. Additionally, these organizations faced concrete challenges that people working for them wanted to solve, creating an incentive for them to apply the new conflict resolution and dialogue approaches that the BLTP offered. The transfer effect from the interpersonal effect to the institutional effect was, therefore, immediate.

The targeted workshops represent what John Paul Lederach calls the "conjunctural response capacity," which refers to a project's ability to respond flexibly to emerging opportunities and challenges while still maintaining a long-term vision.[22] Although the targeted workshops were not part of the BLTP's original project proposal, they did fit the BLTP's vision, and the BLTP team was quick to respond when Ngozi participants requested them. They were also flexibly designed, allowing workshop content to be adapted to the new aims, and rapidly implemented, enabling them to respond while the need was still felt. With hindsight, they may well have been the BLTP's most influential activities, although they would not have taken place without the prior occurrence of the Ngozi workshops, which convinced key leaders that the BLTP methods could be useful in other arenas.

The training of the Integrated Military Chiefs of Staff (Etat-Majeur Général Intégré; EMGI) in Gitega in May 2004 delivered the most significant results. Workshop participants and observers unanimously agreed that the breakthrough on one of the questions that blocked the integration of the army—the question of the "status of combatants"—was the direct result of the BLTP training that the EMGI received. However, the success of the BLTP EMGI training cannot be attributed to the training alone. There were clear signals from military leaders that an agreement was desirable. The BLTP increased the trust and communication between the EMGI members and gave them the confidence that they could resolve these difficult problems themselves. Following the BLTP training, they went back to work and reached an agreement.

The success of the EMGI's agreement can be compared to earlier BLTP trainings of the Joint Ceasefire Commission (JCC), which was also charged with negotiating key issues relating to the integration of the army. The JCC received the same training session as the EMGI, and the participants were equally appreciative, but the negotiations still remained deadlocked. What accounts for the difference in outcome? The JCC remained deadlocked because the participants lacked the incentives to reach an agreement. They received high per diems during the training sessions and meetings, and thus were not anxious for these meetings to come to an end. More important, they were instructed by their political leaders not to reach a final agreement. The relationship- and confidence-building provided by the BLTP training could not surpass these institutional and political barriers. The degree of effect of the targeted BLTP workshops was therefore partly determined by the incentives within the target institution or organization to use the BLTP's methods, an aspect referred to as "institutional ripeness."

The targeted workshops, by their nature, overcame three challenges faced by the Ngozi workshop. First, the interpersonal impact automatically translated into an institutional impact, once a critical mass within an institution had been trained. Second, the choice of "leaders" was also much easier: it was predetermined by the targeted institutions. Finally, even though the BLTP might have kept its targeted trainings relatively apolitical, the participants were familiar with the tough substantive issues they would have to deal with in their institutions, and could thus begin addressing them right away.

Beyond the Workshops

It is easy to document the positive impact of the Ngozi and targeted workshops on the participants while the workshops are in process. The much harder task is to document and analyze the impact beyond the workshop: did the social relations developed at the workshop last outside, in the real world? Did the participants apply the tools they learned at the workshop? Even harder: did they behave differently in their professional worlds, or toward nonworkshop participants? Did they change their overall behavior in the political, social, or economic realms? And finally, the hardest question of all: did this all have an impact on the dynamics of peace and transition in Burundi?

Interviews with participants suggest that outside of the follow-up workshops, there were an increased number of occasions in which participants interacted—certainly, there were a number of sometimes heartwarming stories to this effect. But this impact was limited: it was mainly social and was by no means universal. Indeed, some other participants' stories went along the lines of "he is my neighbor, but he never greets me outside of the workshop."

Did participants use the tools learned outside of the workshop? As discussed above, the targeted workshops that focused on a single organization were very different from the Ngozi workshops, which comprised participants from diverse sectors and organizations. Participants and observers widely agreed that the targeted workshops facilitated significant breakthroughs in "ripe" institutions. As for the Ngozi workshops, many participants reported that they had applied their new conflict resolution tools to their immediate family environments. The BLTP staff also cited instances in which participants used tools taught in the workshops in professional spheres—foremost by teachers and professional trainers, sometimes in general workplace management, and a few times in real negotiations. This effect is important, albeit diffuse and difficult to verify.

On the one hand, many of the Ngozi participants were important people in their parties, armies, or organizations during both the transitional and postelection periods. They were not the very top leaders, but rather the ones just below that level. If these people used the attitudes and skills acquired at the workshops in their professional spheres—as they extensively said they did—this outcome is of importance. Given the relative importance of the Ngozi participants, something real must have been happening as a result. On the other hand, it is hard to gauge precisely what this "real" effect would look like. Conflict resolution and dialogue approaches can be used in the service of both good and bad ends. Furthermore, the BLTP's "leaders" were active in so many spheres of life that it is hard to develop a clear understanding of concrete institutional impacts. In addition, these are all self-reported cases (unlike the EMGI), of which no independent confirmation exists.

Contributing Factors: Organization and Context

This section discusses two factors that were essential to the BLTP's contribution: the BLTP's organizational performance—who the team was and how it designed, launched, and implemented the project—and the context in which the BLTP was implemented.

Organizational Structure

The political standing and skills of the BLTP team played a major role in its success. The BLTP was led by Howard Wolpe, the former Special Envoy of the United States to the Great Lakes Region of Africa during the Clinton administration and a former seven-term US congressman. Wolpe, who was still referred to by his former title of "Ambassador" by almost all Burundians, carried great prestige. He had the political connections and diplomatic skills necessary to bring Burundi's leaders to the table, and the contextual knowledge to know who they were and how their game was played. The credibility and political clout of Eugene Nindorera, the former Minister of Human Rights and one of Burundi's most widely respected citizens, was very important as well, as was the networking of the core program administrator, Fabien Nsengimena. Without these people, the BLTP could not have started with such high-level participants or had such a high degree of credibility and access. For this type of politically sensitive project, having the right people on board is absolutely crucial.

That said, there is more to the success of the BLTP than simply having good people: a good startup process is crucial as well. The BLTP was extremely well prepared. Hundreds of preparatory conversations were held with all parties to the conflict, foremost in Burundi, but also in Dar es Salaam, Pretoria, and Brussels. The authors have seldom seen a project for which the preparation was so complete and thorough, the buy-in so widespread, and the understanding of the challenge so nuanced. The BLTP maintained and expanded the buy-in that it received during the preparatory phase by systematically documenting and distributing information on its successes and by continuously giving personal updates to the most important national and international players. This was smart politics.

The process for selecting participants was also crucial to establishing a sense of prestige at the workshops. Many participants and nonparticipants questioned why one "leader" had been chosen over another. Nonetheless, according to most informants, it was a successful process. People who were invited felt honored to be seen by their peers as leaders. As a result, especially after the first workshop, the BLTP had little difficulty getting its invitees to attend.

Contextual Coherence

The impacts of the BLTP should not be seen in isolation from other initiatives and policies but must be understood as a complement and an additional input to them. When the BLTP began its work in 2002, a number of factors had come into play that pushed Burundi in the direction of peace. Most Burundians were sick of the war and knew that no one could win. Burundi was in a "mutually hurting stalemate," and thus, grudgingly but unavoidably, the politics of compromise was taking over from the politics of military victory.[23] Moreover, the economic cost of the war was clear to all. With the exception of the very few who profited from the war and the sanctions, Burundians from all walks of life—poor and nonpoor, urban and rural—had been much better off before the war. All Burundians were eager for a more prosperous life.

The peace process also created considerable support for collaboration and compromise. The internationally mediated Arusha agreement meant that Hutu rebel groups, extremist Tutsi parties, and the most radical people within the bigger parties were all losing their capacity to single-handedly derail the process. The exclusion of certain Hutu rebel groups from the Arusha peace process, the adoption of the Arusha agreement by the majority of Burundi's political parties, and the inclusion of Burundi's largest rebel faction in Burundi's transitional government in 2003 marginalized Burundi's remaining radical political parties and armed groups. It was not certain, of course, that this dynamic of collaboration and compromise would last forever, nor was it the only game in town. Still, it was a central part of the landscape. The BLTP supported this collaborative movement by giving people opportunities, self-understanding, and a few skills to enable them to work more effectively within this new dynamic.

The BLTP came at a crucial and unprecedented time in Burundi's transition, when leaders of different political, ethnic, and socioeconomic groups found themselves running a transitional government together. Leaders were trying to figure out which allegiances would assure them future power and prosperity, and they knew that they were required to make compromises that they might not have been willing to make in the past. The BLTP came in at the right time and helped people to adopt new attitudes and build new relationships that could enable them to more effectively navigate this new terrain.

The alignment between the BLTP's approach and the needs of the Burundian context was not accidental. The BLTP proved to be able to learn from its environment and adapt its approach to new and emerging opportunities. This contextual "coherence"—how well a project fits within the overall political, military, economic, and aid components of the international community's actions—requires organizational flexibility. The degree of coherence of the BLTP was high, for it was explicitly and intelligently designed to complement the already existing approaches of the UN mission, the South African facilitation, and bilateral donors. Thus, an important factor in the BLTP's success was this high "conjunctural" and "transformative capacity responsiveness," referring to its capacity to respond flexibly to opportunities and challenges as they emerged while still maintaining a sense of the longer term—a vision of transformation.[24] The BLTP was a flexible, learning-oriented project, in constant communication with other players, and willing to question and change its own approach. The unplanned but especially relevant targeted military workshops of the EMGI were an important example of this "conjunctural response capacity."

In a broader perspective, the BLTP achieved great relevance, contextual coherence, and flexibility with little in the way of formalized conflict-sensitive systems. Granted, it did not conduct cutting-edge conflict assessments, it did not systematically question and evaluate the relevance of its approach, and it did not produce good monitoring data at all—its written reports are relentlessly upbeat and un-self-critical. And yet its organizational systems clearly worked well, suggesting that a clear vision and a willingness to adapt to reach this vision, rather than highly developed analytical procedures, explain its success. This runs counter to much of the specialized literature on conflict sensitivity, which is characterized by an ever-growing quest for analysis, programming, and monitoring systems.[25]

Two factors may help explain the BLTP's contextual relevance. First, the BLTP team was small and made up of high-caliber people who were willing to learn and make quick changes once better approaches were identified. Second, there was the personality of Howard Wolpe, which had deep imprints on the BLTP's functioning: he acted both as an idealistic believer—to the point of looking almost naïve at times—and as a hard-headed realist, patient and well versed in the games of politics. This demeanor allowed him constantly to remain open to people, take them at their word, welcome them with open arms, and remain enthusiastic, while at the same time avoid being rapidly disappointed or easily tricked. Indeed, Wolpe's combination of trust and knowledge may have substituted for well-developed program design and monitoring systems. The role that the knowledge, approach, and skillset of the BLTP team played in its success questions the value of the conflict analysis and assessment tools that peacebuilding organizations are encouraged to use. The BLTP case shows that these assessment and analysis tools cannot substitute for deep professional experience and political sensitivity.

Policy Implications: Changing People and Institutions

The design and contribution of the BLTP may have significant implications for similar projects in other countries. A full assessment of these policy implications requires a discussion of the complexity of trust-building, the debate as to whether institutional or individual transformation must come first, the importance of contextual ripeness for the success of BLTP-type projects, the positives and negatives of an apolitical approach, and general lessons for other projects that aim to replicate the program's approach and contribution.

Building Trust: No Magic Solution

The BLTP sought to deal with the problem of mistrust during Burundi's transitional period. As table 8.2 (developed in discussion with BLTP staff) shows, there are many causes of mistrust in Burundian society. The BLTP could not and did not address many of these factors, as key variables that condition the changes it sought to promote were outside of its control. The participants may have made progress in overcoming some of the causes of mistrust, but as the other causes could still have been in place, major counter-pressures remained at work. In addition, participants may have built greater trust between themselves, but not toward others outside the workshop. The new incentives for collaboration and compromise during Burundi's transitional phase tried to address some of the other variables affecting trust (especially the "lack of knowledge" and "impunity" causes shown in table 8.2), but neglected the ones that the program directly addressed.

In short, one could argue that the BLTP covered a neglected yet important area in the transitional process of Burundi. It could not control all relevant variables, but neither could other projects or actions. Its contribution was important and necessary, although insufficient by itself—a fact that is also true for most other activities and projects. Since the initial implementation of the BLTP, this type of leadership-dialogue training has been replicated in several other countries that are emerging from war. The BLTP experience suggests that the effectiveness of these BLTP-type projects depends in part

Table 8.2.   Aspects of Mistrust in Burundian Society

Cause of mistrust	Relation to the war	Entry points and possible solutions
Stereotypes and misperceptions	Predate, but significantly worsened by war	Attitude change; education system and reconciliation mechanisms
Lack of interaction	Mainly created by the war	Communication and shared resources
Cultural differences	Long predate war	Long-term and hardly programmable, although education, spirituality, and sensitization are important
Past wrongs	Predate, but significantly worsened by war	The past cannot be undone, but transitional justice may contribute to acceptance
Lack of knowledge	Predates, but significantly worsened by war	Media, improved governance, truth commission
Impunity	Predates, but may be worsened by war	Justice, rule of law, improved governance

on how these new projects address the particular causes of mistrust among individuals in each of these countries.

Institutions and Individuals: Beyond the Chicken and the Egg

The BLTP's approach situates it within an important debate about the relative importance of individuals and institutions in initiating change. In the case of the program's targeted workshops, the willingness of individuals to transform institutions depended on the incentives for change that existed within a particular institution. The BLTP's contribution to organizational or institutional change was much weaker for organizations where the incentives were not stacked to encourage cooperation and compromise (as with the Joint Ceasefire Commission) or where there was not an important organizational platform (the Ngozi I–III followup workshops). The incentives for change may have been particularly evident within Burundi's military institution. Once it was clear that the peace process was progressing, many high-level members of the military saw the integration of the army as a way to secure a seat in power by ensuring that they had a position in Burundi's strongest governmental institution. The same opportunity did not exist under a purely representative system, which could result in a complete reshuffling of the military and the exclusion of many of the Tutsi who had previously dominated this institution. In other transitional institutions, such as the Burundian Parliament and the political parties, the incentives for change were much weaker because progress (such as elections) would mean the eventual loss of power of many individuals within these institutions.

In the chicken-and-egg debate about whether institutional change or individual change must occur first for peace to take hold, it seems that both need to occur more or less simultaneously. Individual change can only be undertaken in a sustained and active manner when the institutions that they belong to begin creating credible new incentives; the former will strengthen the latter, and vice versa. Individuals establish a new organizational structure and then learn how to function differently within that structure.[26] In this way, they strengthen each other, push each other further, and iteratively create solid foundations for lasting change. The new institutions and organizations become more solid because they are created and transformed by people who believe in them. Changes in people's attitudes and beliefs are more durable since they are congruent with and reinforced by institutions and organizations.

The BLTP facilitated increased cooperation and understanding between individuals with incentives to do so. It did not cause the cooperation, but took an environment conducive to cooperation and helped it to happen by showing that a win-win approach was possible with the right tools and attitude. This gave old and new players in the Burundian political game new confidence. This is not to say that the BLTP was not of major importance. At best, it acted as a catalyst for change, allowing people to overcome individual and social barriers that could have undermined fragile institutional change. In doing so, it strengthened and substantiated these nascent institutional changes, making them less fragile, allowing them to move on.

Ripeness for Cooperation and Compromise

Institutional ripeness—at the level of the conflict and peace process and at the level of specific organizations—mattered for the BLTP's success. Our concept of "institutional ripeness" builds on I. William Zartman's concept of conflict ripeness—the moment when key decision-makers that are party to a conflict become ready to negotiate.[27] It refers to an institution's readiness for a particular type of peacebuilding intervention. One can assess the degree of ripeness by assessing the *fit* between the characteristics of peacebuilding intervention and the characteristics of the target institution.

Generally, Burundi was entering a phase where a military stalemate, and the economic pain inflicted on almost all people, rich or poor, meant that the overwhelming majority of people were ready for change. The Arusha and Pretoria agreements, and the constant international pressure to implement them, created a climate that was strongly in favor of compromise and collaboration—if only people had the tools to work together more effectively. This was very different from Rwanda a decade earlier, where both major sides to the conflict, the Rwandan Patriotic Front and the National Revolutionary Movement for Development, believed that war would serve them best and that total victory was possible. In Burundi, war had been tried for ten long and miserable years, and it was clear to all that the military option had been a costly failure. In this ripe climate, people were interested in participating in the process that the BLTP offered.

Still, even in this favorable context, a major gap remained between individual change—no matter how profound—and the creation of macropolitical change. For this reason, the impact of the Ngozi (I–III) workshops is hard to demonstrate. That said, it seems that more was possible here, both in pushing for macropolitical change and in documenting it. For this reason, some of the targeted workshops were most successful because they were microclimates of ripeness, allowing the macropolitical change to take place immediately. As a result, apart from the quality of the workshops, three factors explain the success of the targeted workshops. First, institutional and organizational incentives favored compromise. Second, important and highly specific problems needed to be addressed within the targeted organizations. Third, most of the important people who needed to address these problems could be trained. Once these factors were addressed, major progress was made—institutional transformation was promoted—which created enthusiasm and confidence for more of the same. Thus, country-, institution-, and organization-specific ripeness was instrumental in the success of the targeted workshops.

Replicability

Can the success of the BLTP be replicated in other countries and contexts? It will depend on how the new context and program design aligns with the major factors that led to the program's successes: the staff; the contextual, organizational, and institutional ripeness; and the political receptivity of the country to the BLTP team and its supporters.

It should be reiterated that the political clout and credibility of Howard Wolpe and Eugene Nindorera were crucial in getting the BLTP off to a good start. Indeed, a key factor in the program's success was the presence of two well-known, widely respected, experienced, and committed political leaders who were able to negotiate political buy-in, seek institutional opportunities that were ripe for the BLTP process, and maintain credibility in the eyes of all of the leaders.

Contextual, organizational, and institutional ripeness also matter. Several BLTP participants said that the program would have been useful prior to and during the Arusha peace negotiations because of the poor negotiation and communication skills of the people around the table. Indeed, the BLTP could have been an effective tool in prenegotiation processes, particularly if it had trained everyone who would be present at the negotiation table. Nonetheless, the dynamic of the workshops' impact likely would have been different during this prenegotiation phase when the incentives were not in favor of cooperation and compromise. It is unlikely that the participants would have been so open to the BLTP approach or that it would have resonated so clearly with them. The dialogue sessions that took place during the war, such as International Alert's CAP (Compagnie des Apôtres de la Paix), were surrounded by much more secrecy than the BLTP and took much longer to achieve the interpersonal results that the BLTP facilitated in a relatively short time.

Finally, the home country of the program staff and the identities of the major donors matter. One aspect of the BLTP that contributed to its success was its perceived neutrality. It was able to bring a politically and ethnically diverse group of people together without too much suspicion about ulterior motives (although there is always some talk). The credibility of the BLTP staff greatly enabled this difficult task, but the relationship between Burundi and the staff members' home countries also improved its outcome. A group of Americans running a BLTP-like program in Iraq or Afghanistan would have a very different experience; the project would likely have a much narrower degree of success. This international political context should be taken into consideration when deciding whether a BLTP-type program could be applied to other countries and contexts.

Future leadership training initiatives can learn an enormous amount from the BLTP. The abovementioned evidence shows that individual transformation can lead to institutional transformation under the right conditions. Open communication between former enemies can have a profound effect not only in the moment but also in the future. An empowerment alternative can provide critical support and encouragement to embattled transitional leaders charged with seemingly impossible political tasks. Yet so much of the BLTP's contribution depended on *how* it navigated the complex political context in Burundi. The specific training and dialogue tools and techniques were of secondary importance to the program team's understanding of the needs and concerns of the leaders of Burundi's transition, and their ability to reach out to these leaders. The BLTP's contribution derives from how it situated itself within Burundi's dynamic political context, built on earlier lessons learned, and brought Burundi's leadership together with courage and determination.

With a successful project, the risk is that the real lessons that should be learned will be lost in the effort to replicate its successes in other locales. Others could be tempted to duplicate the BLTP's program directly. The lessons to be drawn from the BLTP are the importance of a deep understanding of the political situation in the country; the need to learn from feedback about the project and changes in this situation; and contextual, institutional, and organizational ripeness. There is also the risk of falling into the traps of either overattribution or cynicism. The BLTP did not build peace in Burundi. It did not transform all of Burundi's leaders into peace-loving, cooperative individuals. At the same time, it was not a waste of time and money. It helped several leaders build relationships and gain tools that, in conducive institutional and organizational contexts, helped to achieve significant breakthroughs and increase understanding and confidence. If this nuanced understanding of the factors that contributed to the BLTP's success, and what that success entailed, can be conveyed to others seeking to roll out similar initiatives, then these initiatives may have a chance to make an important contribution to another country's difficult emergence from war.

Followup and Conclusion

Since the evaluation that this chapter is based on was completed, the BLTP's influence has diminished. After Pierre Nkurunzia was elected president in 2005, the Burundian government, attempting to establish its hegemony, was no longer receptive to being "trained" by the BLTP team or receiving advice from other international actors.[28] Over the subsequent ten years, a tug-of-war ensued between authoritarian practices and democratic dialogue, with the former gradually winning out.[29] During this period, the BLTP offered crucial support to dialogue efforts organized by the UN and international NGOs but did not lead its own high-level consultations or workshops.[30] Now a national NGO, the BLTP has become a conflict resolution training organization, stepping away from the specific role it played as "the" convener of Burundi's political class in 2003 and 2004. The BLTP team no longer has the influence it once had, and the Burundian government is no longer as open to international dialogue efforts as it once was. As the BLTP never developed a space where Burundi's leaders could address the real issues undergirding the country's political conflict, it has not had the capacity to mitigate the growing polarization among this political class. The effectiveness of organizations like the BLTP, which aim to transform the nature of political dialogue in war-torn countries, depends in large part on how their team and approach fit with fleeting opportunities in a rapidly changing political landscape.

Notes

1. Howard Wolpe and Steve McDonald, *Proposal for Renewing and Expanding the World Bank/WWICS Partnership in Post-Conflict Burundi*, (Washington, DC: Woodrow Wilson International Center for Scholars, July 2004), 1

2. In May 2004, the World Bank Post-Conflict Fund contracted Peter Uvin and Susanna Campbell to conduct an independent external evaluation of the Burundi Leadership Training Program (BLTP). The evaluation—*The Burundi Leadership Training Program: A Prospective Assessment*—was finalized on July 23, 2004. This chapter is based on the evaluation and uses some of the text of the final evaluation report. The report was based on interviews with forty-seven people: the project team, twenty-five participants chosen in proportion to their participation and at random from among their constituent groups (e.g., rebel, government, civil society), and sixteen observers primarily from international organizations. The authors also assisted at the Ngozi III workshop and at two followup workshops. Finally, both of the authors have worked in Burundi for years, and were quite familiar with the challenges the program was seeking to address.

3. The Tutsi-Hima were the lower-class Tutsi. René Lemarchand cites their perception of exclusion and disadvantage as a primary motivating factor for their capture of the postcolonial Burundian state. René Lemarchand, *Burundi: Ethnic Conflict and Genocide* (Washington, DC: Woodrow Wilson Center Press; Cambridge: Cambridge University Press, 1994), 4–5.

4. See Michael S. Lund, Barnett R. Rubin, and Fabienne Hara, "Learning from Burundi's Failed Democratic Transition, 1993–1996: Did International Initiatives Match the Problem?," in *Cases and Strategies for Preventive Action*, ed. Barnett R. Rubin, (New York: Century Foundation Press, 1998), 66. See also Jack Snyder and Robert Jervis, "Civil War and the Security Dilemma," in *Civil Wars, Insecurity, and Intervention*, ed. Barbara F. Walter and Jack Snyder (New York: Columbia University Press, 1999), 29–30.

5. Lund, Rubin, and Hara, "Learning from Burundi's Failed Democratic Transition," 48. See also Ahmedou Ould-Abdallah, *Burundi on the Brink, 1993–95: A UN Special Envoy Reflects on Preventive Diplomacy* (Washington, DC: United States Institute of Peace Press, 2000). A "jawboning delegation" refers to a delegation that aims to use its position and authority to persuade another individual or group to take action.

6. Lund, Rubin, and Hara, "Learning from Burundi's Failed Democratic Transition," 48.

7. Ibid., 73–75. Some of the most notable dialogue and facilitation efforts in Burundi were run by The Carter Center, the Community of Sant'Egidio, International Alert, Accord, International Center for Conflict Resolution, Search for Common Ground, International Crisis Group, Parliamentarians for Global Action, Swedish Agency for International Development Cooperation, United Methodist Church, Synergies Africa, and World Vision. These projects variously aimed to train politicians in the skills and values required by democratic institutions, promote human rights and humanitarian law, train Hutus and Tutsis in conflict resolution, teach a "culture of peace," promote reconciliation by helping people to work together to address common problems, disseminate conflict resolution and interethnic coexistence through radio programs, fund various indigenous NGOs (e.g., women's, peace movement, dialogue groups), encourage dialogue, take selected leaders on trips to study conflict resolution and interethnic or interracial projects in South Africa and the United States, produce educational materials on democracy, coordinate efforts and strategic thinking among the various organizations involved, work with elders to reintegrate displaced and dispersed people into their *collines* ("hills": the units of rural settlement in Burundi and Rwanda), and more.

8. At the time of Ambassador Dinka's appointment as the head of the Implementation Monitoring Committee, he was the Secretary-General's Special Representative and Regional Humanitarian Advisor for the Great Lakes Region. United Nations Information Service, "Biographical Note: Secretary-General Appoints Berhanu Dinka as His Special Representative for Burundi," United Nations, New York, July 24, 2002, http://www.unis.unvienna.org/unis/pressrels/2002/sga811.html.

9. Report by the working group of the Commission de Suivi de l'application de l'Accord d'Arusha/Implementation Monitoring Commission (CSAA/IMC) Executive Committee, together with other transition institutions, pursuant to its charter, 8th Session, April 22–26, 2002, quoted in International Crisis Group, *Burundi after Six Months of Transition: Continuing the War or Winning Peace?*, Africa Report No. 46 (Brussels: International Crisis Group, May 24, 2002), 7, http://www.crisisgroup.org/en/regions/africa/central-africa/burundi/046-burundi-after-six-months-of-transition-continuing-the-war-or-winning-peace.aspx.

10. See International Crisis Group, *A Framework for Responsible Aid to Burundi*, Africa Report No. 57 (Brussels: International Crisis Group, February 21, 2003).

11. Howard Wolpe and Steve McDonald, "Burundi's Transition: Training Leaders for Peace," *Journal of Democracy* 17, no. 1 (January 2006): 126–27.

12. "Training is a skill-building exercise to prepare participants to be more effective as they work out their dispute." Eileen F. Babbitt, "Contributions of Training to International Conflict Resolution," in *Peacemaking in International Conflict: Methods and Techniques*, ed. I. William Zartman and J. Lewis Rasmussen (Washington, DC: United States Institute of Peace Press, 1997), 368.

13. Like Kelman's problem-solving workshops, the BLTP sought to impact political negotiations. Unlike Kelman's problem-solving workshops, the BLTP took place in a

postaccord environment, and did not specifically address political issues or grievances or directly target any ongoing negotiations or specific conflicts. Herbert C. Kelman, "Informal Mediation by the Scholar/Practitioner," in *Mediation in International Relations*, ed. Jacob Bercovitch and Jeffrey Z. Rubin (New York: St. Martin's Press, 1992), 75.

14. Wolpe and McDonald, *Proposal for Renewing and Expanding the World Bank/WWICS Partnership*, 2.

15. Wolpe and McDonald, "Burundi's Transition," 126–27, 131.

16. Cheyanne Church and Julie Shouldice, *The Evaluation of Conflict Resolution Interventions: Part II: Emerging Practice & Theory* (Londonderry, UK: INCORE, 2003).

17. Further discussion of theory-based evaluation and evaluating the success of peacebuilding programming is found in Johanna D. Birckmayer and Carol Hirschon Weiss, "Theory-Based Evaluation in Practice: What Do We Learn?," *Evaluation Review* 24, no. 4 (August 2000): 407–31; and Thania Paffenholz and Luc Reychler, "Towards Better Policy and Programme Work in Conflict Zones: Introducing the 'Aid for Peace' Approach," *Journal of Peacebuilding & Development* 2, no. 2 (2005): 6–23.

18. The challenges of and opportunities for evaluating the impact of unofficial dialogue processes are discussed in Nadim N. Rouhana, "Interactive Conflict Resolution: Issues in Theory, Methodology, and Evaluation" in *International Conflict Resolution after the Cold War*, ed. Paul C. Stern and Daniel Druckman (Washington, DC: National Academies Press, 2000), 294–337.

19. Howard Wolpe with Steve McDonald et al., "Rebuilding Peace and State Capacity in War-torn Burundi," *The Round Table* 93, no. 375 (July 2004): 466.

20. As we wrote: "At some point, then (either at the end of the initial workshop or during the follow-up workshops), the BLTP needs to start dealing more explicitly with the concrete level, the compromises and sacrifices and intermediary steps and guarantees required." Peter Uvin and Susanna P. Campbell, *The Burundi Leadership Training Program: A Prospective Assessment* (Washington, DC: World Bank, July 23, 2004), para. 74.

21. Herbert C. Kelman, "Contributions of an Unofficial Conflict Resolution Effort to the Israeli-Palestinian Breakthrough," *Negotiation Journal* 11, no. 1 (January 1995): 19–27.

22. John Paul Lederach, *Building Peace: Sustainable Reconciliation in Divided Societies* (Washington, DC: United States Institute of Peace Press, 1997), 144–46.

23. I. William Zartman, *Ripe for Resolution: Conflict Resolution in Africa*, 2nd ed. (New York: Oxford University Press, 1989); I. William Zartman, "Ripeness: The Hurting Stalemate and Beyond," in Stern and Druckman, *International Conflict Resolution*, 225–50.

24. Lederach, *Building Peace*, 144–46.

25. International Alert, Saferworld, and FEWER, *Conflict-Sensitive Approaches to Development, Humanitarian Assistance and Peacebuilding: A Resource Pack* (London: Conflict Sensitivity Consortium, 2004).

26. Organizations are recognizable structures that may represent one or more institutions. According to W. Richard Scott, "institutions are multifaceted, durable social structures, made up of symbolic elements, social activities, and material resources." W. Richard Scott, *Institutions and Organizations*, 2nd ed. (Thousand Oaks, CA: Sage Publications, 2001), 49. Organizations "are collectives oriented to the pursuit of relatively specific goals and exhibiting relatively highly formalized social structures."

W. Richard Scott and Gerald F. Davis, *Organizations and Organizing: Rational, Natural, and Open System Perspectives* (Upper Saddle River, NJ: Pearson Prentice Hall, 2007), 29.

27. Zartman, *Ripe for Resolution*; Zartman, "Ripeness," in Stern and Druckman, *International Conflict Resolution*, 225–50; Dean G. Pruitt, *Whither Ripeness Theory?*, Working Paper No. 25 (Fairfax, VA: Institute for Conflict Analysis and Resolution, George Mason University, 2005).

28. See Susanna P. Campbell, *Organizational Barriers to Peace: Agency and Structure in International Peacebuilding* (Medford, MA: Tufts University, 2012).

29. Human Rights Watch, Pursuit of Power: Political Violence and Repression in Burundi (New York: Human Rights Watch, 2009).

30. Interview with BLTP staff member (B9).

Part III

Findings and Implications

Chapter 9

Learning from the Case Studies:
Impacts and Explanations

Michael Lund

Introduction

The first chapter of this volume presented the widely held view that international efforts often fall short of achieving sustainable peace because they fail to encourage sufficient local ownership of their peace processes and motivate a country's political leaders to embrace peace. The method of non-official intervention known as conflict transformation purports to narrow this gap by bringing together leaders across the lines of conflict in nonbinding, facilitated meetings that instill conflict resolution values and skills. The second chapter traced the expected logic through which this approach can help to motivate convened leaders to resolve their conflicts and build a sustainable peace. It identified certain intermediate conditions that would indicate concrete progress toward that end goal. It then laid out the questions, based on clues from existing research, investigated by each author of the subsequent case study chapters on six conflict transformation initiatives.

This chapter gathers together the rich and diverse findings of the case study chapters in order to develop a coherent picture of the lessons within. By combing through the evidence, it will uncover the main impacts of these

315

interactive interventions, their limits, and explanations for these results. First, the chapter collects the evidence on the impacts that the initiatives had on their participating political and social leaders and conflict environments, It then assesses these findings in light of the question raised in chapter 1: To what extent have the initiatives helped to achieve the ingredients of sustainable peace? The findings also provide a basis for ranking the six initiatives in terms of their comparative effectiveness. It concludes by identifying the chief reasons why some initiatives made more progress than others toward establishing a lasting peace.

Taking Stock of the Initiatives' Achievements: Case Study Evidence

Initial observations on the initiatives focus on the overall capabilities of this intervention method of sustained encounter, looking at whether it can make progress toward a peaceful, enduring resolution of the conflicts involved. The case study chapters addressed the same set of questions, but varied in how they organized their findings about the projects' impacts. To consolidate these findings, four distinguishable categories of possible impacts are given below. Two of the four categories relate to changes that affect workshop participants:

1. *Altering attitudes and imparting collaborative skills:* Reducing negative perceptions and beliefs that participants held toward the other side; fostering appreciation of the costs of the conflict and the perspective and anxieties of one's opponents, and increasing mutual trust; discovering common interests that boost confidence that solutions are possible; forging cross-group relationships that make cooperative actions possible; enhancing participants' empathic communication and problem-solving skills.

2. *Applying understandings and skills gained in the workshops to jointly address intergroup issues:* Applying improved attitudes and procedural tools to identify particular sources of the conflict; reach common stated principles; or craft substantive products such as agendas, options, and proposed steps to resolve the conflict or related problems.

The other two categories involve changes outside the workshops:

1. *Improving capabilities for conflict resolution in the wider society:* Organizing nonofficial workshops or other projects that address the

manifestations or sources of conflict, independently of official negotiations, such as by facilitating specific disputes, promoting peaceful
behavior, or undertaking economic development or other projects.

2. *Influencing official peace agreements or contested national policies:*
   Increasing the impetus to undertake authoritative negotiations for
   resolving the conflict; providing substantive ideas or proposals to the
   official negotiating parties or political decision-makers; having political leaders adopt such ideas in official peace negotiations or in public
   policies such as in legislation or governing practices; promoting public
   support for peace proposals being considered by officials.[1]

Based on these four categories, what did the initiatives achieve that likely
would not have occurred without their intervention?[2]

Altering Attitudes and Imparting Collaborative Skills

In all six initiatives, the participants' attitudes toward the other side appear
to have improved and new skills were introduced. But the projects displayed
some differences in the extent to which attitudes were transformed and
how the workshops drew upon these changes to impart concrete skills. The
Inter-Tajik Dialogue (ITD) in Tajikistan, the Burundi Leadership Training
Program (BLTP) in Burundi, and the Estonian dialogues facilitated by the
University of Virginia's Center for the Study of Mind and Human Interaction (CSMHI) and The Carter Center (TCC) brought about marked attitudinal change.

In the ITD, after tense initial sessions in which the sides aired grievances and expressed deep mistrust and suspicion, the experience of hearing
and being heard persuaded the participants of the value of listening to their
opponents, which elicited a more tolerant and civil discourse. Both parties
came to respect the other more and believe that they could actually fulfill
commitments. For the poorly organized Democrat and Islamist opposition
in particular, the initial meetings motivated representatives to come forward
and participate despite threats to their personal security. The potential of
the discussions led them to realize that they needed to get organized and
formulate a common position.

Similarly, the Hutu and Tutsi participants in the initial BLTP workshops
in Burundi were distrustful, hurt, and insecure. But because the workshops
provided an opportunity for the two estranged groups to talk informally, they
began to see each other as individual human beings rather than stereotypes.

The interpersonal communication led them to question long-held preconceived notions about the other group that had developed because of lack of contact. This change was especially evident in those who had fixed views, or had been in the bush or abroad and thus had been isolated from intergroup contact for many years. The interactions also inspired new thinking and hopefulness that a lasting peace was possible, which the followup workshops in Ngozi reinforced.

The Estonia CSMHI-TCC workshops also brought about discernible changes in perceptions between the Estonian- and Russian-speaking participants. For the first time, many participants came to understand the fears and hopes of the other side as well as recognize their own. The contending groups discovered that they actually shared some anxieties, such as a fear of Russia. The new mode of mutually respectful democratic dialogue helped the participants learn how to listen and speak more empathetically.

In Tajikistan, Estonia, and to a lesser extent Burundi, the act of convening an elite from across the political spectrum was a novel approach. These first-time encounters evoked major changes in the participants' perceptions. In Cyprus and Guyana, the changes were less dramatic because many participants had already met people from the other side in prior intergroup venues. Many participants in the Harvard Study Group (HSG) workshops in Cyprus, for instance, had been involved in bicommunal activities between the Turkish and Greek Cypriot sides. Mutual perceptions had already improved to some extent, so the impact of the project was less pronounced. Yet HSG participants reportedly gained an even deeper understanding of the priorities and preferences of the other side, and their hard-liners became more open and engaged. In Guyana, owing to the experiences of a few previous dialogues and the fact that the country's small population was concentrated along the coast, many participants in the Social Cohesion Program (SCP) workshops and related activities were already acquainted and had spoken with one another, at least professionally. Participants came to the workshops with considerable familiarity with people and views from the other side. Nevertheless, the norms of communication and the win-win concepts that the workshops introduced converted many participants to a new way of talking to each other and discovering common interests. For example, the youth leaders of Guyana's two main parties found that they shared certain concerns because they occupied the same roles in the country's political system, and the workshop experience increased their desire to learn how to work more collaboratively.

In the case of Sri Lanka's One-Text Initiative (OTI), the evidence of attitudinal change is less clear. The OTI hugely expanded the number of interpersonal contacts, communications, and working relationships among participants across the main Sinhalese-Tamil divide and between the national and local levels. It also created access to the peace process for the country's hitherto-unrepresented Muslim minority. OTI's centerpiece, the national stakeholder dialogues, established one of the few remaining places where such interaction could go on as renewed war further divided the country. The dialogues' scrupulous effort to work out basic principles and set up inclusive mechanisms and fair procedures for reaching agreements may have strengthened mutual trust and confidence, at least among those participants who valiantly continued to meet. As to the many other people involved in the OTI's activities, it is not known how much their attitudes were changed.

In addition to fostering more favorable perceptions and communications, all the workshops imparted some new skills. This effect was more obvious in the three initiatives that more deliberately "taught" specific procedures, such as those for group problem-solving. The organizers of the ITD in Tajikistan essentially tutored the participants by guiding them through analytical, consensus-building, and other interactive exercises. The ITD organizers assigned numerous "homework" assignments, such as writing memos to summarize the consensus in the discussions. To strengthen the weaker opposition side, the organizers provided special coaching in negotiating skills, which stimulated internal debate and greater cohesion. Several individuals who were to become government policy advisers and officials reportedly benefited in particular from the procedural techniques imparted by the workshop exercises. For both sides, the ITD's extensive exercises provided political education for an emerging elite—a virtual training ground for a new Tajikistan leadership base.

The SCP in Guyana also went beyond changing attitudes to show participants how to undertake collective tasks such as strategic planning and organizational development. In several workshops that convened members of the contending ethnic groups from single or multiple organizations—such as the Ethnic Relations Commission, trade unions, and business associations—team-building exercises enabled their members to bring deep-seated organizational problems to the surface, identify the various interests at stake, and devise ways to move beyond the problems. Intraorganizational or sector-wide interests were better able to address common challenges such as globalization, which often were overlooked in Guyana's ethnically divided politics. The HSG working groups in Cyprus also facilitated joint understanding and problem-solving on a number of concrete critical issues.

The Burundi, Estonia, and Sri Lanka cases differed, however. Although the workshops in these countries also modeled a more accommodative discourse and discussed substantive issues, they were less deliberate in imparting specific concrete conflict resolution and other procedural skills to the participants.

Applying Understandings and Skills from the
Workshops to Jointly Address Intergroup Issues

A new outlook on the conflict may help to elicit sufficient mutual trust among a workshop's participants, and new skills may bolster their confidence so that they feel motivated to address substantive issues. Gains in attitudes and collaborative skills mean little unless participants use them to improve their conflict environment by taking actions inside or outside the workshops. But even if the emotional and conceptual impacts of workshops create a bond within the group, that bond alone may not be enough to propel the group to collaborate on specific tasks.

The initiatives were even less consistent on this criterion of actually applying newly gained trust and skills to reach common views within the workshops. All six initiatives appear to have built closer relationships among the participants during the workshops. All of the initiatives were welcomed by the participants, and once the initiatives began, participants felt it useful to continue meeting. However, not all the initiatives reached internal substantive agreement. Among those that came to such agreement, moreover, the agreements varied as to whether the consensus was able only to define the outstanding problems and broad principles, or went further to propose specific remedies.

Four initiatives produced group agreements on the outstanding issues or specific proposals to resolve the conflict. In the ITD workshops in Tajikistan, the trust created in a neutral political space and exposure to new skills emboldened the participants to proceed to work intensively on resolving a number of issues and come up with proposals. This effect was especially pronounced for the opposition side, which grew more united in determining who would speak for them, formulated common goals between the secularist Democrats and the Islamists, and defined bargaining positions for the official negotiations. A new platform that formed the basis of an opposition alliance was produced within two months of the dialogue's fourth meeting.

When the official-level negotiations started in 1994, the ITD participants were asked if they saw value in continuing the nonofficial workshops, and the overwhelming response was affirmative. The ITD participants were able to explore issues in greater depth in the workshops than during the official negotiations, and they raised sensitive issues, such as questions about refugees, that were not being discussed at the talks. The workshops generated many issue papers, group memos, and public statements on various options, and many of these from the first five years were published. During the post-agreement period, the participants' joint work went on to help outline a postwar national vision and set an agenda for Tajikistan, such as regarding political parties and the role of civil society. The workshops thus acted as a forum for a range of independent voices from an emerging but still weak civil society. The ITD constituted both a "holding net" to preserve the still-fragile focus on peace and a policy forum for new issues that were coming up.

The HSG participants in Cyprus also moved beyond defensive arguments to hammer out several new options that might satisfy both the Turkish and Greek Cypriots, thereby creating a zone of possible agreement endorsed by the participants on both sides. As the study group workshops shifted the participants' perspective from an adversarial stance to a mutual gains-based framing of issues, they strengthened the participants' desire to reach agreements.

The SCP workshops in Guyana also applied the learned skills to substantive topics, but these workshops varied in how much they went beyond agreeing on the outstanding issues to proposing specific remedies. The high-level workshop and workshops with political party leaders and their youth wings resulted in partial convergence on the problems of the country and general directions in which it should go, as well as a stated determination to work together to advance them. However, differences arose when it came to considering the details of how to take this shared motivation a step further. More substantive progress was made at the middle- and local-level workshops involving professional organizations in specific sectors, such as the Ethnic Relations Commission, businessmen, the police, and regional development councils. As a result of the strategic planning done in several cases, concrete decisions were made to change the practices of these organizations, ways to implement the practices were devised, and some of these implementation plans were carried out. Examples of such changes include the Private Sector Commission's more unified and assertive lobbying strategy and Region 10's more participatory process for formulating a development plan.

In Burundi, the participants in the initial and followup BLTP workshops increasingly moved from the initial interactive exercises to discuss some of the country's problems. Over time, these discussions focused less on interethnic perceptions and more on policy issues facing the country such as justice and disarmament. But while the initial and followup workshops broached these problems, the workshop discussions remained general and noncommittal, and reached few explicit understandings on how to approach the problems. However, in the targeted workshops with the army and police, the discussion not only delved into problems but also developed specific options for the security agencies. As in Guyana, the workshops for particular "ripe" institutions provided the opportunity for their members to develop concrete solutions to sectoral problems and how to implement them.

By virtue of the large number of working committees and venues that the OTI organized in Sri Lanka, this initiative was the most elaborately structured of the six. As illustrated by the 132 consensus decisions that were agreed upon up to 2005, the OTI was also likely the most prolific in the sheer number of substantive documents and proposals that were discussed and agreed upon. Its many working units raised and explored multiple key issues that stood in the way of peace and hammered out numerous written statements proposing possible solutions. Several issues were raised for the first time, including the interests of Muslims, the 2005 elections, and reconstruction. The mission statement and shared values document were regarded as a possible foundation for postwar intergroup reconciliation by affirming principles such as popular sovereignty and equal participation. However, many of these products and recommendations ended up staying at a rather general level, perhaps in part because of the need to reach wide consensus on so many topics.

In Estonia, the CSMHI-TCC workshops did not develop written products on either substantive issues or specific proposals, nor did they seek to formulate such products. They avoided pressing for group consensus on substantive issues; instead, the workshops apparently continued to plumb into the underlying anxieties and fears that were regarded as driving the sides' diverging views on the substantive issues.

Improving Capabilities for Conflict Resolution in the Wider Society

One "transfer" effect of such workshops might be that the participants will seek to spread conflict resolution ideas and skills outside the workshops.

Indeed, all these initiatives intended to reach out to the wider society and general population, independent of the political process, so as to enlarge the neutral public space for citizen-level intergroup reconciliation. These activities to "transplant" conflict resolution in society can be distinguished from efforts to promote public support for proposed official agreements or policies. Such outreach actions could be taken jointly or by individuals.

All six initiatives inspired at least some of their participants, in small groups or as individuals, to spread the influence of conflict resolution norms and ideas into other arenas so as to affect more people. Participants generally felt energized to disseminate attitudes, values, behaviors, skills, and ideas from the workshops to their respective personal and professional arenas or wider publics. Yet the initiatives appear to have differed in the amount of contact that the participants initiated outside the workshops and the extensiveness and scale of the outside activities.

In two of the initiatives, activities to build wider capacities outside the workshops were extensive. In Guyana, groups like the Ethnic Relations Commission and Private Sector Commission applied their newly found internal collaboration from the SCP to take steps to relate to other groups, the public, and the government. On the largest scale, the Ethnic Relations Commission organized a nationwide dialogue process. This Multistakeholder Forum organized and facilitated a from-the-ground-up series of consultations starting at the local and regional levels and culminating in the National Conversation, a two-day conference near Georgetown. The intent was to stimulate Guyana's civil society to identify and address widely recognized problems at all these levels. But few sustained working relationships were by-products of the SCP-organized activities. Some SCP-convened workshops did spawn cooperation among groups, such as the Bikers for Peace and the Peace Builders Network, but the extent of such groups is not known, and they do not appear to have constituted a major network or "peace coalition" that continued to press for reconciliation.[3] The OTI in Sri Lanka also undertook to spread conflict resolution processes into a "track-three," grassroots effort. Tapping into the networks of four Sri Lankan NGOs, these activities launched numerous public and "people's" forums in local communities that involved thousands of people in tolerance training, economic development, and local decision-making. The OTI created a channel to represent the Muslim minority, banded together to help certain individuals being held by the government, and, after a major outbreak of local violence in Trincomalee, prompted two members from opposed parties to jointly call for peace.

On a smaller scale, the Estonian CSMHI-TCC participants also sought to pass on to the wider society their new understandings of how to listen to and speak with one another with more empathy. The common interests and fears that the workshops elicited gave way to brainstorming about concrete remedies. These sessions reportedly fostered some personal and professional relationships beyond the workshops that kept open communication and an exchange of views across the two communities. Thus, a few individuals took ideas away from the workshops and used them to set up "extracurricular," local interethnic projects: a community cultural house for holding multiethnic events, a pilot Estonian-language program for Russian-speaking children in kindergarten, and an NGO that organized interethnic tourist attractions and church renovations. Workshop participants took pains to publicize these projects as promising examples of Estonian-Russian cooperation.

Likewise, in Tajikistan the ITD facilitators hoped that their participants would interact in between the meetings, but such interaction was difficult during the war. Several individuals reportedly took its tools and ideas into their places of work: government, opposition circles, a negotiating forum, citizen discussions to invite civil society views, and the media. The workshops also sensitized the group to the need for local economic development programs. Some participants helped to develop political parties and set up NGOs for civic education and research, stimulate dialogues through other donors, and organize local dialogues. However, the extent to which these spinoff dialogues reflected the skills learned was noted as unclear.

Although the initial BLTP workshops in Burundi introduced only basic principles, some participants reported applying them in their family lives and workplaces such as for teaching and management. Some individuals worked together to do a local development project, conflict resolution and dialogue work in two provinces, and new training for Muslims. Not mentioned in the chapter was training organized to prepare the political parties for the 2005 elections. These efforts resulted in a code of conduct for the elections and interparty commitments to give joint addresses to reassure the electorate of the parties' desire for an election without violence or intimidation.

Capacity-building efforts in Cyprus mainly consisted of several HSG participants visiting a border town inhabited by Turkish Cypriots that would be given to Greek Cypriots if a reunification agreement was agreed upon. Despite the possibility that the residents would be dislocated following unification, the town subsequently supported the Annan peace plan.

Another capacity-building effect involved immediate efforts to avert the outbreak, escalation, or continuation of organized armed conflict or intergroup violence. Only one initiative had a dramatic impact of this sort. Violence had occurred in all of Guyana's past elections, but an array of SCP-sponsored activities was substantially responsible for avoiding violence around the 2006 elections. As the elections neared, media efforts supported by SCP-backed groups saturated the public with the message that the elections should be conducted peacefully, and this message made a clear difference in preventing election-related violence. The OTI presents a less clear example of violence prevention efforts. Many local forums in Sri Lanka may have helped to prevent instances of intergroup violence and in one particular case an intercession in Trincomalee in 2005 may have helped curtail an outbreak of violence. However, the OTI was unable to keep the military forces of the government and the Tamil Tigers from reverting to war, thus limiting the OTI to issues that were caused by war such as displaced persons and humanitarian aid. Similarly, an ITD participant in Tajikistan interceded with local commanders to encourage them to enforce an agreed cease-fire, and this intervention may have reduced the potential that other cease-fire violations would occur and aggravate the wider war. In Burundi, most of the same BLTP participants continued to attend the followup workshops, sending a reassuring signal during a critical period that may have reduced the potential for renewed fighting among the groups participating. The BLTP had no influence, however, in the continued fighting with an armed group that had not signed the Arusha Peace and Reconciliation Accord of 2000.

Compared with the examples of Guyana, Sri Lanka, and Burundi, neither Estonia nor Cyprus was in similarly great danger of armed conflicts or violence. Violence was feared in Estonia only if the grievances of the Russian-speaking communities were totally ignored. However, the CSMHI dialogue teams that went into Russian-speaking local communities may have had a dampening effect on the potential for violence by making their conflict resolution efforts visible. The Cyprus conflict had been "frozen" for several decades and a UN peacekeeping force was in place, so there was little immediate prospect of a return to violence and the HSG's actions were not needed to prevent local flareups.

Influencing Official Peace Agreements or Contested National Policies

Another transfer effect has to do with actions taken by the workshop participants to influence the making of official decisions by either key leaders engaged in peace negotiations or governmental policymaking authorities. Initiatives could realize such impacts by (1) increasing the *impetus* or momentum to initiate or continue official deliberations, (2) shaping the *content* that is considered, and (3) promoting the formal *adoption* or ratification of agreements. These impacts could occur through direct channels, or indirectly, by boosting popular support.

On this score, the six initiatives were the least consistent. Two initiatives had significant effects on official deliberations. The ITD in Tajikistan had the most significant effects, as it increased the momentum for negotiations, shaped the content of specific provisions in the official agreement being discussed, and enhanced the chances for the agreement's acceptance by the parties. The ITD workshops, which started before any official talks were organized, emboldened the sides to see promise in undertaking negotiations. The quality of the intergroup dialogue persuaded the government side to accept the opposition groups as legitimate negotiating parties with real interests and views and thus to negotiate with them—despite protest from its own hard-liners—rather than write off the opposition as a collection of irresponsible rebels. For the northern elite, the ITD also provided a seat at the table that allowed it to preserve some standing during a time when it was under challenge and on the defensive. "After six meetings, it was no longer possible to argue credibly that negotiation between the government and the opposition was impossible."[4]

The ITD workshops then helped to define the official negotiation agenda by supplying answers to basic questions, such as the purpose of the negotiations. This included exploration of delicate issues that the two sides preferred not to discuss, particularly the government's reluctance regarding the refugee problem and power-sharing with the opposition. The workshops explored such issues in depth and developed options and scenarios that the official talks could not go into for reasons of time, thereby making it easier to avoid surprises and reach decisions. As a result, the essence of several ITD ideas became cornerstones in the June 1997 peace agreement: the Commission on National Reconciliation, four working subcommittees, and the concepts of power-sharing and of a postsettlement transition period. Presidential speeches reportedly also reflected some of the workshops' ideas, since a few ITD participants served Tajik president Emomali Rahmon as advisers. This influence was achieved largely through direct channels. The ITD was not only an important source of solutions for ending the war; it also raised and discussed postagreement issues. This additional topic helped to integrate elements on each side into a national policy dialogue, eventually touching on emerging topics such as relations between the public and private spheres.

Similar to the ITD, the HSG's early meetings both helped to stimulate official negotiations in Cyprus and contributed much basic content to the reunification agreement being negotiated under the UN. By instilling confidence that solutions were possible, the study group's early meetings added to the political impetus behind reviving talks at the official level, even though the Turkish parties had banned cross-line contact and the Turkish Cypriot leader did not want to talk about anything other than confederation or two sovereign states. Specific ideas from the study group also informed the prosettlement Turkish Cypriot party's positions such as on constitutional issues and the right of return, and it adopted these ideas after its leader was replaced. In this way, the study group's several products shaped the agenda by giving the mediators a sense of the parties' priorities, possible balances or tradeoffs among issues, prospects for a zone of compromise and agreement, and likely sticking points. As a result, several proposals from the study group discussions—including the notion of a federal republic with constituent states, ideas for allocating federal and state authority, and the reconciliation commission—found their way into the Annan Plan that was agreed on in the peace negotiations. In addition, the workshops stimulated a public campaign to promote support for the Annan Plan, mainly on the Turkish Cypriot side. The interchanges in the workshop supplied the prosettlement participants with answers to likely questions and criticisms from their respective constituencies about the proposed solutions and how the other side might react to specific options. Despite these efforts, the HSG initiative was not able to get the UN's reunification plan ratified by the Greek Cypriot public in the referendum.

In comparison, the Burundi, Guyana, and Estonia initiatives had less influence on official-level peace agreements or national policymaking, although they did influence some participants' government agencies and other organizations., In Burundi, the Arusha Accord of 2000 had left crucial issues like disarmament, the presidency, transitional justice, and election law unresolved or unimplemented. Although the high-level BLTP workshop did not work on specific solutions to these issues, several workshop alumni moved into high political, governmental, and other positions. It is impossible to trace their subsequent behavior back to the workshops, but notions from the workshops such as the importance of effective communications and inclusivity may have influenced their thinking and actions. More evidently, the targeted workshops influenced specific policy changes at the sectoral level. These changes dealt with significant issues concerning integration of the armed forces, such as how to define a "combatant" and to harmonize the ranks. The workshops then established mixed teams of observers to oversee the integration process. No major public advocacy efforts by BLTP participants were reported.

Similar to the BLTP, in Guyana the SCP project was launched in part to advance constitutional issues that previous official-level mediations had left unresolved. Political party leaders were deliberately engaged in both the initial high-level political leader meetings and the subsequent party-level workshops, and many SCP activities were well known among the political class. However, its activities did not lead to further agreement on the outstanding constitutional reforms that the opposition wanted and the government opposed. Instead, the country-wide National Conversation generated a long list of issues and recommendations. As the National Conversation's organizers did not check to see which recommendations were already adopted or being considered by the government, the final document resembled a wish list of unfocused demands. This process seems not to have moderated the polarizing discourse of national politics; political debate in the media continued to resurrect the contentious constitutional issues between the two main ethnically divided political parties. Yet as in Burundi, some changes in government practices in Guyana were achieved where a specific government agency, namely the police, had leaders who were motivated to seek advice.

Although individual Estonia workshop participants gained important insights from the conversations and brought them to policymakers, including parliamentarians and the President's Roundtable on Minority Issues, the CSMHI's evident impact on the substance of official policy was indirect and modest. To influence public opinion and discourse, individuals wrote op-eds and articles, spoke with other influentials, and participated in forums on interethnic relations and related topics. A few participants organized local interethnic projects, in part to provide possible examples of how to achieve reconciliation and to address the language education problem. These successful models were publicized as a way to persuade national decision-makers. The joint Russian-Estonian kindergarten program that one participant undertook was subsequently funded by the government and illustrated ways to implement legislation of the kind that the Estonian Parliament subsequently passed to ease the transition of the language of instruction from Russian to Estonian in Estonian secondary schools.

Compared with the other five initiatives, the OTI in Sri Lanka did not succeed in having any of its many working group agreements adopted in official channels (such as the peace negotiations, political parties, or the legislature) or as sectoral-level policy changes. The numerous products of the stakeholder dialogues were widely publicized, but the OTI's advocacy of reconciliation met with strong resistance from the nationalistic Sinhalese parties and militant Tamil elements. Any hopes for exerting influence were soon preempted as the government stepped up its prosecution of the war and eventually defeated the Tamil Tigers on the battlefield. As the war ensued, the OTI still hoped that the agreements might become the basis for a peace settlement, but these hopes proved unrealistic.

Summary of Impacts

Table 9.1 summarizes the case-study findings above by rating the impacts of the initiatives in each of the four areas as high, medium, low, or none. Although the information in the table is drawn from only six cases, it provides a picture of the general capabilities and possible limitations of this type of intervention.

Looking horizontally along the bottom row labeled "Totals of the Initiatives," we see that, with one exception, all six initiatives affected all four dimensions of change to some degree. Evidently, this type of interactive intervention can ameliorate several aspects of conflict. However, as shown in the Totals of Impacts column, the four areas of impact were affected to varying degrees. The initiatives affected attitudes and skills the most, followed by joint efforts within the workshops to identify issues and propose remedies. The remaining two categories—impacts on societal capacities for conflict resolution-building and on officialdom—were less consistently achieved.

Progress toward Sustainable Peace?

The assembled evidence about the initiatives' impacts allows us to return to the question raised in chapter 2: How well do these initiatives perform in achieving their espoused goal of a sustainable peace? Recall that social science research shows that certain core conditions are essential for achieving that ultimate end-state: effective, impartial security; elite agreement on power-sharing; channels for representation; functioning public services and judicial procedures; and some improvement in the general standard of living. Examining the impacts of the six initiatives through this lens reveals very uneven and generally modest accomplishments.[5]

Table 9.1.   *Extent of Impacts Achieved (high, medium, low, none)*

	Burundi BLTP	Cyprus HSG	Estonia CSMHI-TCC	Guyana SCP	Sri Lanka OTI	Tajikistan ITD	Totals of Impacts
Were attitudes improved and new skills imparted?	Medium	Medium	Medium	High	Medium*	High	2 Highs, 4 Mediums
Were understandings and skills applied in the workshops to address concrete issues and propose specific remedies?	Low	High	Low	Medium	Medium	High	2 Highs, 2 Mediums, 2 Lows
Were the wider society's capacities for conflict resolution strengthened?	Low	Medium	Medium	High	Low	Low	1 High, 2 Medium, 3 Lows
Were official peace agreements or public policies influenced?	Medium	High	Low	Low	None	High	2 High, 1 Medium, 2 Lows, 1 None
Totals of the Initiatives	2 Mediums, 2 Lows	2 Highs, 2 Mediums	2 Mediums, 2 Lows	2 Highs, 1 Medium, 1 Low	2 Mediums, 1 Low, 1 None	3 Highs, 1 Low	

*Such effects are implied by the chapter with regard to participants in the stakeholder dialogues.

SECURITY

In Tajikistan, the ITD participants helped to reach a peace agreement that stopped a continuing armed conflict. Major armed violence has not returned, although local episodes have occurred.[6] The BLTP helped implement Burundi's Arusha Accords by facilitating a solution to the key problem of integrating rebel and government forces into a national army and training to increase their cooperation. The country's overall security improved, but violent deaths still occurred due to sporadic clashes between the army and a rebel force and to rising criminal activity. For many Burundians, abuses by the security forces have been a source of insecurity. In Cyprus, the presence of the UN peacekeeping force continued to ensure security; yet it is unclear whether armed conflict or violence would return if the force were removed. As reflected by the persisting international negotiation efforts to resolve the conflict—emboldened perhaps by the near miss of the Annan Plan—the UN, European Union, United States, and other third parties are highly invested in the island's circumstances and, increasingly, its economic opportunities. Although they would likely act to forestall any escalation to armed conflict, their efforts might simply maintain the status quo. In Guyana, the SCP headed off electoral violence in 2006, thus setting a precedent and standard for the peaceful 2011 and 2015 elections. Ethnic-based political violence has declined. Yet gains from the SCP's police training in mediation and human rights have been overwhelmed by violent crime due to drugs and arms trafficking, and police brutality still occurs. In Sri Lanka, the OTI failed to halt the trajectory of all-out war. In Estonia, the prospect of political violence was little affected by the CSMHI initiative.

POWER-SHARING

The ITD coalesced the opposition around a proposal to grant them a portion of offices in government, and the dialogues injected the need for power-sharing into the official negotiations. But once the peace accord was signed and power-sharing deals were made, the ITD had little influence on its implementation, such as fulfilling the opposition quota, releasing political prisoners, and subsequent matters of governance. The HSG in Cyprus incubated the idea in the Annan Plan of distributing formal powers to constituent states under a united republic, but failed to persuade one of the sides to adopt it. The BLTP, during the uncertain postaccord period of transitional government, helped foster cooperation among the competing leaders who shared power at that time. However, it was hard for an interactive intervention facilitated by outsiders to have an impact on the concrete material interests of powerful individuals that were at stake. Following the 2005 elections, the initial cooperation did not translate into respect by the contending political parties for rule-governed and peaceful electoral competition, and political violence reemerged. On its part, the SCP did not effect any change in the existing allocation of constitutional authority that the opposition party felt excluded them from meaningful decision-making. The CSMHI in Estonia and the OTI in Sri Lanka brought no change in their countries' basic structures of power.

POLITICAL PARTICIPATION

The effects of the initiatives on strengthening representative government were minimal, indirect, or transitory. By helping to authorize and support political parties and multiparty elections, the ITD and BLTP introduced the principle of wider access to government decision-making. Yet subsequent elections produced ruling parties and increasingly autocratic leaders that dominate the organs of government, so the channels of access narrowed to favored factions. The OTI also articulated a democratic vision for a united Sri Lanka, but the proposed structure was eclipsed by a populist-based, militant Sinhalese nationalism. Although the president who pursued the war was voted out of office in 2015, it is unclear whether the OTI had any role in that change. Similarly, in Guyana, it is unclear whether the SCP inspired individual participants to help organize or vote for the emerging and increasingly successful cross-ethnic opposition parties. Local elections, emblematic of grassroots democracy, have yet to be held. The HSG not only articulated a democratic vision for a united Cyprus, but directly helped to mobilize Turkish Cypriot opinion behind the UN plan. This may have strengthened the role of mass influence on politics, at least on that side. In Estonia, the CSMHI modeled democratic processes on the small scale of its own consultations.

By the related standard of promoting an active but politically autonomous civil society, the results may be more encouraging. One expectation of this method is that the bonding and learning that occur in the workshops can carry over into an ongoing network of individuals that undertakes collective action outside the workshops, such as a peace movement that pressures political parties and officials. The SCP and OTI, for instance, were able to energize particular civil society groups, although these groups did not coalesce into sustained, organized movements to promote resolution of the issues between governments and oppositions. The HSG did somewhat better by fostering concerted public pressure in support of a solution, although only on the Turkish side. The ITD's follow-on civil society projects had little apparent impact on Tajikistan's postconflict politics.

PUBLIC SERVICES AND JUDICIAL PROCESSES

Only the SCP made specific efforts to improve public and judicial services. Its stimulation of local youth projects and community consultative processes for development in distressed areas may have increased the confidence and legitimacy of those local authorities. Its human rights training for magistrates may have increased judicial fairness to some degree.

STANDARDS OF LIVING

Following the initiatives, all six countries saw their economies improve, poverty reduced to some degree, and income distribution not worsen. But these trends appear to be due largely to other factors. The initiatives themselves accomplished little along these lines: two initiatives spawned local economic development projects, which in one case continued in the form of local youth projects, but in another foundered.

In sum, some of the initiatives helped to reduce major armed conflict and to stop election-related violence, but not all political violence or major violent crime, so citizen security was not assured. Although several initiatives helped to foster interim power-sharing among top leaders and espoused democratic principles, the initiatives rarely got beyond conflict issues to help ensure a self-sustaining peace through institutionalizing violence-free electoral competition and rule-governed pluralistic policymaking. In two of the cases, subsequent elections reinforced the dominance of ruling parties. In the other cases, broad representative channels already functioned and no one party has stayed in power, so it has been shared by various parties or coalitions, and the initiatives may have given a boost to popular participation. However, there was scant evidence that the interactive initiatives improved the efficacy or accountability of public and judicial services, or effected change in national-level government policies. The two possible exceptions occurred where secure officials in relatively powerful ministries, such as for security, could exercise autonomy in their decision-making.

In short, these initiatives can make significant inroads but they meet serious limits beyond which they seem unable to go. They can fill important gaps for a time but cannot build new democratic institutions or do much to consolidate existing ones. In terms of instilling "local ownership" for building peace, the initiatives clearly succeeded in having the participating leaders drive their joint discussions in the workshops, but this feat did not empower those participating leaders sufficiently either to establish competitive but self-regulating peaceful political processes or to implant a responsibility for peacebuilding in the wider society.

Ranking the Initiatives

Although this instrument had only scattered effects in creating essential ingredients of a sustainable peace, it is still useful to compare the extent to which the initiatives affected the four kinds of impact and thereby rank them in terms of their overall effectiveness. This ranking can provide a basis for deriving lessons about why some initiatives were relatively more effective than others.

Looking down the columns under each of the six initiatives in table 9.1 reveals that these initiatives differed greatly in how much they affected each of the four areas and which areas they affected. No initiative achieved high impacts in all four areas. The ITD had high impacts in three areas but was weak in the fourth; the SCP had two high impacts. The HSG had high or medium impacts in all the areas. The remaining three had various medium, low, or no impacts.

One lesson that might be drawn from this picture is that each initiative has strong and weak points. Some readers might conclude that almost any version of this type of intervention should be judged on its own terms and is worth doing, as long as it has some positive benefit and does not create new problems. From this perspective, there is no objective basis for rating the overall effectiveness of the six initiatives. An initiative's effectiveness would depend solely on which areas of impact the observer values—for instance, a group's solidarity, societal capacity-building, or official actions. Thus, one approach is as good as another. The moral of the story would be "each to his own." Unfortunately, this conclusion is not very illuminating for improving practice. It offers no guidance for deciding how to apply limited resources to maximum effect in varying contexts. The abovementioned logic would regard the four kinds of impact as equally significant. However, it would be more useful to be able to compare the initiatives through some way of tallying their total effectiveness. In fact, there are theoretical and empirical grounds for such a measurement, beyond simply adding up the high, mediums, or lows in table 9.1 and comparing the total scores.

One way to compare the initiatives is to consider that each of the six country situations presented the initiatives with different paramount challenges, or primary deficits, and that these priorities had to be tackled before a country could move any closer to a sustainable peace. For example, some countries faced all-out war or the prospect of imminent violence, while in others that scenario was less threatening. Cyprus, Estonia, Guyana, and Sri Lanka had functioning democratic processes and institutions such as regular elections and organized political parties, whereas Burundi and Tajikistan lacked democratic legacies and had weaker political institutions. These varying circumstances of countries are implied by the terminologies in the peacebuilding field that refer to differing stages on the way to a sustainable peace such as conflict prevention, crisis prevention, crisis management, peacemaking, peace enforcement, conflict resolution, and peace consolidation. The premise here is that at a given time in their development, although these societies have manifold problems, these problems are not all equally imperative, of strategic importance, or even amenable to change.

Using these notions, one can then ask how well the initiative in a particular country addressed that country's paramount challenges and made progress toward their amelioration. Although we have seen that the initiatives' accomplishments fell considerably short of achieving the elements of a sustainable peace, it is worth knowing which initiatives made the most progress toward mitigating their countries' respective challenges. As each country's situation called for somewhat differing needs, the question is how much each initiative helped to fill these deficits and thus moved the needle the furthest in the most important directions. Using these criteria, the following is a tenable ranking of the comparative effectiveness of the six initiatives.

1. Inter-Tajik Dialogue, Tajikistan
2. Harvard Study Group, Cyprus
3. Social Cohesion Program, Guyana
4. Burundi Leadership Training Program, Burundi
5. Center for the Study of Mind and Human Interaction–The Carter Center, Estonia
6. One-Text Initiative, Sri Lanka

On balance, the ITD appears to have achieved the greatest overall range and depth of impact, notwithstanding its fading influence on Tajikistan's post-settlement politics. The pressing priority in Tajikistan was to terminate an active civil war that was tearing the country apart. This required a cease-fire and some political rapprochement between the warring parties. The dialogue brought the warring sides together for the first time, forged the opposition groups into a bargaining partner, led the parties to see that a peace accord was possible, and hammered out key substantive ideas that appeared in the official peace agreement.[7] In short, the ITD made it possible to reach agreements that halted fighting that, unless ended, would make progress of any other kind impossible. The ITD also may have helped create a new political class and fledgling civil society in Tajikistan, and enunciated principles for democratic governance.

In Cyprus, the HSG initiative also scores relatively well. The main challenge was to find a mutually attractive governing formula that could thaw the "frozen" conflict between the two estranged communities on the island. Their long-standing separation posed some risk of renewed violence if the international peacekeepers were withdrawn, and it was holding back the island's economic and social development. The HSG helped to reactivate official-level negotiations and infused specific solutions into those talks. HSG participants themselves also rallied popular movements on both sides to support the Annan Plan, and the Turkish Cypriots endorsed the plan. Unfortunately, the HSG miscalculated the amount of support for the plan among the Greek Cypriots, and the plan's ultimate failure prevented the island's communities from breaking the stalemate and unifying the two communities in a new constitutional structure.

In the middle ranks are the Guyana and Burundi initiatives, though their relative positions are less easily decided. Guyana faced increasing political polarization between its two dominant ethnic-based parties, a loss of control over national politics to the street and politically influenced violent crime, and continued economic decline. The SCP awakened elements of a latent civil society around the theme of national cohesion and, notably, prevented election violence for the first time in Guyana's history. But the SCP could not bring the two clashing political parties together on the contentious constitutional issues. Though the economy improved and a new multiethnic opposition has come to power, it is plausible but unknown whether the SCP influenced these developments. In Burundi, the main fear was that the 2003 peace accords would not be fulfilled and would give way to renewed civil war. The BLTP created a nucleus of cooperating individuals with varying influence and helped integrate the largest rebel group into the army. Yet other rebel groups continued fighting in the bush, and the cohesion achieved among the workshop participants did not prevent the rise of political violence in the years following the 2005 elections.

In Estonia, as it was reasserting the national independence it once enjoyed, the chief challenge was enacting legislation that did not discriminate against its Russian-speaking minority, thus avoiding possible escalation to violence and Russian government interference. The Estonia initiative altered the outlook of the participants, but the lobbying and community projects undertaken by individual workshop members influenced the substance of government policies only indirectly and marginally.

The OTI initiative in Sri Lanka is at the bottom of the list. As the cease-fire agreement was failing and all-out war was returning, the OTI's dialogues reached consensus among many stakeholders on numerous proposed solutions, at least on paper. Yet it failed to moderate the actions of militant nationalists driving the two belligerent sides. Consequently, the OTI's extensive efforts were sidelined as the government decided to pursue a military victory. It is unclear whether the many seeds of local interethnic reconciliation that the OTI planted had any independent effect on the later electoral defeat of the president or on the prospects for postwar reconciliation.

Chances and Choices: Explaining Effectiveness

If certain factors are especially significant in determining the outcome of conflict resolution initiatives such as those described in this volume, they offer lessons on how to make future initiatives of this kind more effective. This section looks through the cases to see if certain factors vary in ways consistent with the differing impacts. A few factors emerge as pivotal.[8]

Favorable Contexts

The initiatives' ability to ameliorate their respective conflicts is significantly explained by domestic and international settings that were either favorable or unfavorable for reaching a settlement or accommodation on the issues. These "givens" were at work regardless of any actions taken in the initiatives, but those that favored an official resolution provided an opening in which the initiatives could make a difference if they took advantage of the opportunity.

The most fundamental contextual factor was the extent to which the most influential leaders on the conflicting sides saw compromise on the core issues as being in their political interests. In some cases more than others, the advantages of accommodating their opponents' demands came to be seen as greater than the advantages of pursuing their own agendas through armed conflict, unilateral acts, or maintenance of an objectionable status quo. The calculations of these leaders were shaped in turn by two factors: (1) whether the *domestic political gains* of compromising outweighed the costs of concessions; and (2) whether global and regional actors were *unified* in offering incentives to the parties through particular channels, rather than pushing in separate directions, dispersing their influence, or taking little interest in the conflict. These domestic and international influences on the leaders' motivation configured differently in each case, but they stand out more than other frequently cited contextual factors, such as the level of physical hostilities in the conflicts and extent of democracy in the countries.

LEADERS' DOMESTIC INTERESTS

First, the parties' receptivity to a settlement was influenced by whether making concessions was seen as the only way to achieve domestic political advantages, or whether there were other military or political ways to achieve those interests. In at least three of the six initiatives, the parties were relatively open to the possibility of making concessions and thus were willing to consider what options an unofficial process might present to them. The main issues in contention also contributed to these calculations. Disagreements over basic constitutional changes, such as those regarding control over a nation's territory or the reallocation of governmental authority, were more difficult to agree on than were issues about a group's treatment by particular government policies.

These domestic interests took different forms in the six initiatives. In the three armed conflict cases—Tajikistan, Burundi, and Sri Lanka—the potential balance of military power on the battlefield greatly influenced the parties' perceptions of where their interests lay. If the parties believed that they could not make further gains by continuing to fight, this deadlock or the prospect of a lengthy, costly struggle made the conflict "ripe for resolution."[9] If either or both sides believed that victory could still be achieved, they were less open to negotiating.

Tajikistan was still at war when the initiative started in 1993, but a kind of "mutually hurting stalemate" had emerged between the two sides. Though the worst fighting was soon over, the opposition still constituted a threat and could drag the war on for some time. The military standoff between the UTO forces in the mountains and the government forces in the plains left the options of either a protracted guerrilla war or a negotiated settlement. Both sides had sizable public constituencies, but Tajik society as a whole was suffering from the effects of conflict dislocation and desired peace and the restoration of normal services. Spillover of the factional conflicts in Afghanistan was feared, but the Tajik state was seen as capable of restoring normalcy in most areas rather than leaving a vacuum of law and order. Consequently, save for some extremists in the United Tajik Opposition, the parties began looking for a way to resolve their conflict and restore peace.

The issues at stake also influenced their openness to negotiations. Except for their radical elements, the leadership on both sides wanted a united Tajikistan under secular rule that accommodated Islamic principles and interests. This outcome could be achieved through power-sharing with opposition figures, who could benefit from a settlement by gaining personal wealth through access to government positions. Consequently, President Rahmon was willing to negotiate and reached out to the United Tajik Opposition and its regional supporters. As a result, even though emotions were high and the parties on their own were unwilling to talk to each other, the ITD could capitalize on their latent desire to reestablish contact and explore the possible resolution of the outstanding issues.

By the same token, the ITD's influence waned when these incentives to settle weakened. Once the peace accord was signed in June 1997 and power-sharing deals were agreed on, the ITD had less influence on the implementation of the settlement and other policies of the resulting government. Though the chances for ITD influence were enhanced when several participants took up political or government positions, they did not stay in office much after the dialogue concluded, and the opposition members were coopted by their government positions and thus soon lost their outside leverage. The ITD could not press the government to fulfill the agreed-upon opposition quota or to release political prisoners. It was also unable to strengthen aspects of democracy such as political parties, which were not well organized and had no active constituencies.

In Burundi at the time the BLTP started, the existence of an armed stalemate was less clear, despite the signing of the Arusha Accords. However, a broad consensus existed on the overall goal of peace, as most Burundians were sick of war and wanted to get on with life after conflict. In addition, signals were coming from the military leaders in the integrated chiefs of staff that a resolution of the reintegration sticking points was desirable. Thus, Burundi's leaders felt pressure to show that they were complying with the Arusha agreement. The immediate issues were about carrying out transition government tasks, and the elites who participated in the workshops also had more to gain by being part of a transition government than by returning to the bush. Thus, the BLTP's success stemmed in large part from its ability to convene a particular group of people at a critical time in Burundi's history.

Of all six initiatives, the OTI in Sri Lanka had the most extensive activities, encompassed the most domestic actors, and showed the most courage in view of the dangers the participants faced. Yet its size and scope did not overcome the impetus for war, as the government leaders who held power had few incentives to settle and the LTTE Tamil Tigers forces resisted any compromise on the main issues. The armed conflict on the ground was not at a stalemate but was instead reverting to all-out war. Military commanders were persuading the top government leaders from the Sinhalese ethnic majority that the LTTE could be defeated by continuing the armed campaign. Although the state had lost all influence in many Tamil-dominated areas in the north and east, Sri Lanka's overall economy was thriving. On its side, the LTTE was driven by its armed militants. Also, the central issue presented a major hurdle—whether the Tamil minority could carve out a homeland on the island—so there was little possibility of integrating the opposition into the government. In short, the Sri Lankan government's leaders saw nothing to lose from fighting on and nothing to gain from a settlement. Given their perceived advantage, the government leaders balked at using any unofficial peacebuilding process, and in fact tried to sabotage it.

In the three nonarmed conflicts (Estonia, Guyana, and Cyprus), military considerations were not relevant, but the will to settle was shaped primarily by the perceived costs of conceding on the substantive issues in contention. The leaders' views were shaped by the extent to which they saw compromise as the best way to achieve or preserve their domestic political interests, or whether they had alternative ways to advance their position. Of further importance to these calculations was the weight of public sentiment for accommodation or resisting policy change, which could be influenced by the perceived effects of conflict on the domestic economy at large.

In Estonia, the leaders on the conflicting sides were willing to talk, their positions on the issues had not hardened, they showed restraint and urged peaceful solutions, and they were interested in finding a remedy for their impasse. The Estonian government was open to considering policy concessions to address grievances, and found the general idea of compromise acceptable—it was confident that it would remain in a dominant political position with regard to the Russian-speaking minority, which also was not well organized—so it felt no serious threat to its status by making policy changes. The disputes concerned the relatively more manageable question of whether a minority group would be treated more equitably by government policies. On their part, the Russian speakers' grievances were partly absorbed by Estonia's electoral system, which encouraged candidates to appeal across ethnic lines. The growth of the Estonian economy also depended on cooperation between the sides. In short, the government had relatively little to lose from engaging on the issues, and reinforced by the positive incentives offered by international actors (described below), it had a lot to gain.

In the two other cases, however, the net advantages of reaching a political settlement were not as compelling. In Guyana, although the government party had a larger political constituency than the opposition party, it was not as large as the political majority in Estonia. Thus its periodic elections constituted a major "battlefield," as the parliamentary form of government and party lists system intensified the winner-take-all nature of the competition and the polarization of Guyana's electorate around its two ethnic-based political parties. Although the governing People's Progressive Party had won every election since 1992, its continued control of government power was not assured. At the same time, however, the People's Progressive Party made the principled argument that Guyana's long-standing provision in its democratic constitution for periodic elections was the only legitimate way to decide who was to govern, and it had won three successive elections fair and square. Shielded by its electoral mandate, the government was not under great political pressure to negotiate and compromise on the core issues in contention. Moreover, those issues were difficult to compromise on: they involved not only perceived discrimination of minorities under government policies, but also a reallocation of governing authority to the opposition, which would give the opposition a more direct role in decision-making. Previous official efforts at mediating these constitutional issues had made little progress. Guyana's conflict was based not simply on mistrust, but given the availability of normal electoral competition it was stuck in a kind of "democracy trap" arising from established democratic procedures. In addition, Guyana's basic security was not immediately at risk. Although the threat of continued social unrest prompted the government to allow and to participate in the SCP initiative, the state was functioning in most areas, and the security forces could be counted on to avoid any escalation to major violence. Furthermore, the emigration of many educated people created a kind of safety valve that reduced the pressure to reach a settlement. Granted, there was a desire to avoid repeating in the next elections (to be called within five years) the violence that had occurred in the 2001 elections, but the political deadlock had reached a kind of satisfying equilibrium that, though suboptimal, was not "hurting."[10]

The result, in Guyana, was that the SCP workshops led to concrete policy changes only when the participants had discretion to make decisions on sectoral or intraorganizational issues that were largely technocratic and politically nonthreatening. As in Burundi, remedies were reached where there were pockets of "organizational readiness" within the government. The Ethnic Relations Commission was the only one of the four proposed bipartisan commissions that was adopted. The commission showed that the government was willing to address certain issues of discrimination, but the issues in the other constitutional reforms could not be conceded because the ruling party resisted sharing political power.

In Cyprus, both sides could have gained from a settlement, but the long-standing status quo was also not hurting. The Cyprus conflict was between two long-separated communities, and UN peacekeeping troops had kept the sides apart, largely reducing any threat of impending violence. A mutual settlement was almost achieved but ultimately was vetoed by one of the two communities because, as in Guyana, one side's political leaders and their followers did not regard the settlement as a net gain. The consensus that the HSG successfully incorporated into the UN's Annan Plan was not equally shared by both sides. The proposal also presented a major obstacle regarding territory: whether to give up partition and move to a new kind of confederation. Thus, a referendum allowed the Greek Cypriot leaders to counsel their constituency against a carefully cultivated, yet wrenching, Annan Plan.

On the whole, the respective workshops were more likely to be able to provide possible solutions where domestic political reasons made the parties more receptive to concessions and settlement. The receptivity of standing officials had a lot to do with whether the options at play would support their incumbency, or alternately could reduce their control over governing authority or even unseat them.

COHERENT EXTERNAL INCENTIVES

Another strong influence on the conflicting leaders' readiness to settle, and thus the ability of the workshop initiatives to exert leverage, was the extent to which external actors were unified in their actions toward the conflict and provided robust, consistently prosettlement incentives targeted at the leaders in power. External actors such as other countries in the region, major powers, and multilateral organizations can be aligned behind the search for a settlement, neutral or ambivalent toward the conflict, or pushing in opposite directions. In the six cases, one approach used by external actors in favor of a settlement was to channel their pressures in such a way that the leaders in conflict were required to talk to each other through a single negotiating channel. A specific high-level process would be a target and receptacle for the workshops' ideas.

Tajikistan's peace settlement in 1994 benefited from cooperation between the United States and Russia, which was reflected in the ITD's US-Russia team. In particular, Moscow put considerable pressure on Dushanbe to induce the Tajik government to stop fighting and to engage with the opposition to seek a peaceful resolution of the conflict. Iran pressured the opposition side.[11] The security provided by the presence of a Commonwealth of Independent States peacekeeping force on Tajikistan's south border also helped prevented the conflict in Afghanistan from potentially abetting the cause of the Islamist side, and a subsequent UN observer mission reinforced the peace agreement.

In Estonia, the CSMHI started when international observers persuaded the Estonian government that the language and citizenship issues affecting the Russian-speaking minority had a potential for ethnic violence. Because of its geopolitical salience, Estonia became the focus of multiple official-level preventive mediation and technical assistance by the United States, the Conference on Security and Co-operation in Europe, the other Baltic states, the UN, and the Council of Europe, all of which were essentially united in their purpose. Estonia was also willing to address the issue because it feared that continued infringement of the Russian-speaking minority's rights could also put at risk the attractive prospects of its EU and NATO membership. Furthermore, financial aid was provided to enable the withdrawal of Russian troops, thus removing the possible threat of internal pressure from the Russian military. At the same time, however, these multiple channels of discussion scattered the impact of the CSMHI initiative on national policies.

The Cyprus case was unique among the six to the extent that two countries in the immediate region, Greece and Turkey, were vying for political influence in the conflicted country, which tended to pull their respective Cypriot parties apart. However, the crafting of the UN's reunification and federation plan showed resolve at the global level to finally move beyond this frozen conflict. The EU offer of accession was also intended as a powerful incentive that would galvanize all Cypriots behind supporting the

UN's Annan Plan in referendums. In this case, however, these two international influences led to an inconsistency. The UN plan ultimately failed because, contrary to expectations, the prospect of a united Cyprus did not appeal equally to the leaders of both communities. Because the EU had never recognized the earlier Turkish military takeover of the northern part of the island, the accession offer was brought to the Greek Cypriot government, even though it only governed the north de jure. So although the Turkish Cypriot population endorsed the plan, the Greek Cypriots, aware that their EU membership did not hinge on approval and worried that the less-developed Turkish side of the island would drag down their economy, were swayed by their leaders to reject it.

In Burundi, the regionally mediated Arusha accords reduced the ability of extremists on all sides to act as spoilers of the peace. Knowledgeable observers believe that the unified leverage exerted at the beginning of the Arusha process could have brought the antagonists into a less tenuous implementation of the settlement. However, the coherence of the multilateral monitoring committee waned in the succeeding years. In Guyana, pressures from the Caribbean region to resolve the conflict between the ethnically oriented political parties had also attenuated. Initially, official-level international mediations by the Commonwealth nations, the Caribbean Community, and The Carter Center had reflected international interest, but these interventions had made little progress and no further high-level international diplomatic assistance or incentives were provided. Lacking pressure from a formal peace process, Guyana's politicians were left largely to their own devices. The Guyanese government was open to the initiative being suggested by the UN factfinding team, but unlike in Estonia and Cyprus, potential economic aid was not offered as an inducement to settling the issues. International donors such as the US Agency for International Development and the British Department for International Development tried to use their individual democracy and development programs to promote peace, but no aid was conditioned on progress at the policy level. The main burden of addressing the conflict was left to the SCP initiative.

In Sri Lanka, foundering official mediation also left the field largely to a nonofficial initiative. Although several major regional and international actors took an interest in stopping the conflict, they did not speak with one voice, and the lack of external unanimity failed to outweigh the Sri Lankan government leaders' one-sided domestic incentives to seek military supremacy. Moreover, no international peacekeeping force was present to restrain the politically popular government from using force.

Strategies and Tactics

The above contexts provided major opportunities or constraints that greatly affected the initiatives' ability to influence the parties in conflict. But these contexts alone are not sufficient to explain the initiatives' varied performances. Within those parameters, the initiatives' effectiveness was also determined by their implementers' own decisions about certain design and implementation aspects. Some of the initiatives took fuller advantage than others of the opportunities their contexts presented.

The case study chapters show that the six initiatives had many common basic characteristics. All six initiatives were designed and implemented by nongovernmental organizations dedicated to conflict resolution, and they all convened influential leaders and other professionals in the country's politics and society who came from opposing sides in its main conflict. All aimed to increase the participants' motivation and ability to resolve and move beyond their domestic conflict. The workshops also endeavored to directly or indirectly contribute to some formal resolution of the conflict on the part of official representatives of the contending parties. These face-to-face workshops were conducted periodically for at least two years and engaged in a non-imposed process aimed at creating new space for contact, communication, and interaction. All initiatives were premised on the limitations of power bargaining, and deliberately used nonbinding "conflict transformation" techniques that were applied by skilled facilitators. The chapter authors generally complimented the respective organizers and facilitators as dedicated, skillful, and respected.[12] To encourage communication and camaraderie, all of the initiatives deliberately arranged for special meeting places that lay outside the normal procedures and interactions of politics, organizations, and social life. In one way or another, the workshops were designed as retreats so the parties could talk with each other without distractions.[13]

Several chapters attribute the effectiveness of their initiatives to their shared characteristics, such as prior due diligence to ensure local buy-in, careful preparation, sustained workshops, and study tours.[14] These commonalities offer valuable guidelines, but because they characterized almost all of the initiatives they do not help to explain their comparative effectiveness. However, a close comparison of the case studies reveals that the initiatives actually varied in how they handled certain tasks, and these variations were crucial determinants of their differing performances.

The differing impacts stemmed in part from each initiative's particular strategy for effecting change. It is obvious that an initiative's strategy would have consequences, but particular variations led to differing results. The six initiatives' strategies diverged in four crucial operational respects: their missions and methods, their congruence with high-level decision-making processes, the extent to which they incorporated two-way communications with officialdom, and the composition of workshop participants.

MISSIONS AND METHODS

A key factor was the basic goals the initiatives set as most important for the workshops themselves to achieve—that is, the tasks that the implementers mandated the workshops to undertake, rather than leave them to other processes outside of or subsequent to the workshops. A close comparison shows that the six initiatives differed markedly in how they prioritized the respective goals of exploring the workshop groups' attitudes and enhancing communication skills, stimulating efforts outside the workshops to leverage change, and nudging the group toward politically realistic solutions. Some of the initiatives' strategies saw their main priority to be changing the attitudes, mutual perceptions, and communication skills of the participants and building relationships within the workshops, and therefore these initiatives chose to leave any subsequent actions by their participants up to other moments, channels, and venues, whose prospects were thus uncertain. Other initiatives sought to a greater extent to stimulate wider public actions as the route to change. A third group saw its main job to be deliberate and continued efforts to reach as much closure as possible around specific policy solutions that were politically palatable at the official level, and to communicate those results to the decision-makers. The proportional emphasis that the workshops put on these three functions of group therapy, wider capacity-building, and closure around viable policy options made a definite difference in their relative effectiveness. Less-refined ways to capture these variations are psychology versus substance, training versus dialogue, and societal versus policy change.

These differing balances in the initiatives' goals were reflected in the respective mixes of techniques their facilitators used and their range of expertise. In five case studies (Burundi, Cyprus, Estonia, Guyana, and Tajikistan), the chapter authors noted that one feature leading to their programs' success was the highly elicitive, nonpressuring approach to setting the agenda and governing the pace of the discussions. This approach effectively disarmed the participants' initial resistance to talking and gained their ownership of the process. Several chapters also credited facilitators with astuteness and flexibility in sensing when the participants were ready to move toward some common understanding, and then coaxing them to pursue such avenues while staying mindful of the parties' state of readiness to commit. But actually, the initiatives varied noticeably in how much their facilitation methods included procedures to work out options that were feasible for official decision-makers to adopt.

The Tajikistan and Cyprus initiatives, for instance, aimed directly at encouraging and influencing their respective peace negotiations while ensuring that the initiatives would complement, not compete with, the official talks. Ostensibly, the ITD's main intent was to build relationships among the Tajik government and opposition, but in practice, as openings arose and confidence was built, it deliberately introduced selected substantive issues. It meticulously followed a five-step methodology that first sought to build relationships as the way to frame specific issues. The method also entailed looking for openings to elicit a realistic consensus on particular points. The team broached easier issues, such as the return of refugees, before tackling more difficult subjects, such as power-sharing. Varied techniques were used to encourage the group gradually to take the reins, including nondirective questions, homework, small breakout group work, and random grouping. The mix of psychological focuses with substantive issues, as well as assignments to develop responses, produced documents such as summary memoranda and draft memos for further consideration. The US moderator would even challenge particular participants to do individual assignments: "What can you personally do to overcome these obstacles?" Ideas for resolving the issues were sometimes offered. In short, although the ITD facilitators described their task as being "to generate analysis from within the conflict itself, and not to impose their own analytical framework on the conflict,"[15] in fact they were moderately assertive. This mixed approach worked well because it generated a sense that the participants were making headway despite the ups and downs of the conflict. As the participants agreed to certain solutions during the meetings, these accomplishments in turn reinforced the growing trust and increased confidence that peaceful solutions were possible. Thus, while the ITD provided a school or training ground for leaders in communications and negotiations skills, it also infused several concrete ideas into the peace settlement.

The HSG initiative in Cyprus also involved problem-solving exercises to encourage the group to set the agenda and frame the issues. It set its sights on developing workable substantive ideas to finally decide the relationship of the two communities on the divided island, and these ideas were reached with relatively less initial emphasis on catalyzing attitude change or building relationships and trust. Early on, the focus turned to substance and involved methods for joint analysis and framing of detailed options on difficult issues such as power-sharing, security, refugees, and boundaries. Like the ITD, the HSG used a wide range of techniques, including tools of conflict resolution, training exercises, briefings from outside technical experts, working groups, and homework. These exercises were still nonbinding; formal commitments were not expected. At one point, when the study group made a cautious but interventionist move, participants rejected the ideas from the organizer.[16] Nevertheless, the Cyprus project's emphasis on discussing concrete details of possible solutions elicited several viable ideas for a proposed settlement. In view of the lack of a hurting stalemate and the major constitutional change that the Annan Plan could have represented, the HSG achieved an impressive degree of substantive progress.

The initiatives in Estonia, Burundi, and Guyana all concentrated more heavily on the social, psychological, and value dimensions, putting less emphasis on deepening participant discussion and forging agreement on substantive issues. The psychopolitical dialogues in Estonia inserted some diplomatic and academic content, but its core activity was the breakout groups that probed into the mutual fears of the Estonian- and Russian-speaking populations. In contrast to the more legalistic approach taken by the official international efforts to the human rights grievances in Estonia, these underlying anxieties were viewed as obstacles that needed to be removed before participants would be free to make progress in rational discussion of difficult policy issues. However, even though efforts to bring out the submerged feelings among influential individuals were intended to affect the political climate, the initiative stopped short of getting deeply into substance and judged that trying to actively influence the official deliberations was best left to the participants' individual discretion.

The methods of the Burundi workshops also stressed conflict resolution training more than third-party-facilitated dialogue. The BLTP sought to strengthen its participants' ability to take on the difficult tasks of peace consolidation and institutional transformation by providing them with the attitudes, perspectives, and relationships that it hoped would make participants more capable of conducting the complex negotiations going on in the transitional government. The workshops were based on the view that a "zero-sum, winner-take-all" wartime mindset, mistrust between key group leaders, and the lack of consensus on the rules of power-sharing and public decision-making all called for the lines of communication and understanding to be reestablished between Burundian elites. The participants in the initial retreat workshops were led through a process that started with interactive exercises to build trust and imparted communications and negotiations skills, and then invited them to identify the country's problems and list ways to address them. Over time, through the series of followup workshops, the issues discussed were less about interethnic perceptions and more about policy issues such as justice and disarmament.

Nevertheless, unlike in Tajikistan and Cyprus, where the initial workshops broached the country's problems, the BLTP did not specifically address political issues or grievances or directly target ongoing negotiations or any specific conflicts.[17] No pressure was applied to produce consensus around specific agreements; the brunt of the work focused on improving the participants' mutual perceptions and relationships. As substantive issues and solutions were less emphasized, the workshop discussions often did not get beyond "general, noncommittal discussions."[18] The facilitators' choice not to press BLTP workshop participants to achieve greater substantive agreement, even though the conditions for further progress seemed evident, was one of the relatively few missed opportunities that were noted in the six case studies. Participants might have made further progress but the initiatives did not take up the opportunity or turned to other matters. Only later, during the targeted workshops for sector-specific groups such as the army and for political parties in the run-up to the August 2005 elections, did the BLTP produce formulations about how to address specific problems. The security sector workshops were organized to help unblock negotiations regarding the integration of rebel and national armies and advanced decision-making within the security ministries. Revealingly, these substantive discussions were not planned by the facilitators but were undertaken at the urging of the military professionals themselves.

The Guyana chapter noted a similar missed opportunity. The nonjudgmental, nonbinding character of the SCP's workshops fostered a willingness to produce tangible results. The SCP undertook an ambitious effort to seed its values and skills in several government arenas and more broadly in organizations and groups of civil society, but its methods did not push participants vigorously to come to specific agreements, although a few did. The SCP did not seek to directly influence specific official issues, nor did it promote, as a complement to its methods, the idea of restarting formal talks at the official level. The National Conversation produced a long list of social and economic problems but did not seek agreement on how they should be pursued (nor would such efforts have been feasible for its large number of participants). The one exception to this dearth of substantive followup was the outstanding effort to avert election violence; this campaign did not evolve out of the original workshops, but emerged as an offshoot activity.

Overall, the HSG was faulted for possibly pushing too hard in one instance, whereas the BLTP and SCP were faulted for not pushing hard enough. In view of the excellent connections and favorable context of the CSMHI workshops in Estonia, it might also be questioned why that initiative did not discuss specific aspects of relevant policy issues that may have been left unaddressed by other third parties or the government. Apparently, this opportunity was forgone because the facilitators did not regard that as their mandate.

The Sri Lanka initiative, like the other five initiatives, did not pressure its participants. Unlike the other initiatives, the One-Text methodology essentially leapfrogged any initial step intended to build trust and relationships before turning to other tasks. Instead, it saw its main purpose as providing a protected venue in which many participating "stakeholders" could come to agreement on the substance of the conflict's many issues.[19] As it happened, frequent objections or resistance kept the group from achieving full consensus on many issues, and so laborious internal consultations and special efforts were required to break deadlocks. Consequently, the resulting endorsements often lacked a sense of compelling commitment. The easing of the consensus rule was not done until later.

In sum, an important explanation of the initiatives' differing effectiveness involved the fundamental purposes of their workshops and the respective balances they struck among the facilitation techniques that the initiatives employed. This does not mean that any initiative could induce participants to agree upon courses of action on which their respective political leaders differed, as seen in the few instances when the facilitators unsuccessfully tried to press the participants for such agreement. Even when the ITD and HSG participants agreed among themselves, they anticipated the likely responses of their respective higher officials and subjected their own conclusions to self-censorship: memos were tempered so as to be acceptable to officials. In Tajikistan, for instance, hot topics such as electoral violations were raised at the meetings but were not included in meeting agendas.

An associated difference lay with the mixes of expertise that the initiatives' facilitators brought to the workshops. The teams of facilitators in Tajikistan and Cyrus combined knowledge of the local players, substantive issues, official negotiation, and diplomacy, as well as psychological dynamics and conflict resolution. The ITD was directed and facilitated by former diplomats who were not only schooled in conflict resolution techniques but also well prepared to discuss the regional issues and frame the substantive issues. The HSG included an international relations scholar as well as conflict resolution professionals, and the latter had also followed the island's local politics. These "deep benches" allowed for a wider, multidimensional range in focuses and techniques. Though the Burundi and Guyana initiatives were headed by diplomats who were informed by regional knowledge, their participants' interactions were facilitated almost solely by conflict resolution professionals, as was the Estonia initiative.[20]

CONGRUENCE WITH HIGH-LEVEL OFFICIAL DECISION-MAKING PROCESSES

Another consideration for conflict transformation project organizers is when to start such a project in relation to the timetable of official peace negotiations or other high-level political processes. All six initiatives acted upon an assumption that a promising window of opportunity had arrived for conflict resolution efforts. But a close look at the cases suggests that the initiatives' relative influence depended on whether they proceeded simultaneously with an ongoing high-level process or when strong prospects for some high-level official processes existed. Initiatives that preceded official-level talks and continued during them (Tajikistan, Cyprus) had somewhat greater impact on the resolution of the main issues than did initiatives that followed formal agreements (Burundi), or that sought in effect to substitute for the breakdown of formal negotiations and did not press to restart such processes (Guyana, Sri Lanka). Where prospects existed for official talks, the initiatives added momentum. When official talks were simultaneous, they created a target and receptacle for initiative products.

The Tajikistan and Cyprus initiatives were classic cases of prenegotiation to assist official processes to bring a conflict to resolution. In the first case, the conflict was being pursued militarily, and in the second, the armed conflict had ended decades before but had concluded without a mutually acceptable settlement. The ITD sought to develop the agenda of the official negotiations while stopping short of undertaking actual negotiations.[21] Likewise, the HSG also had an official process to focus on, as a series of failed official negotiations had led to deadlocks but at the international level there was a desire to restart them. Earlier local-level bicommunal activities and conflict resolution training had also failed to reshape the diplomacy and balance of opinion that were preserving the island's ethnic division. The HSG therefore sought to facilitate the start of official negotiations and inform it by feeding in policy suggestions. In fact, the UN's Special Adviser to the Secretary-General himself stimulated the Cyprus initiative by asking its eventual organizer to hold an initial conference to pinpoint the issues that divided the island and the reasons for stalemate, and to come up with new ideas. This one-day conference grew into the longer study group project.

In Burundi, a peace agreement had been signed two years earlier, but virtually all parties had expressed reservations about it, a cease-fire was not in place, and few people expected the agreement to hold. The BLTP was intended as a way to advance the transitional government's implementation of difficult provisions in the accord, such as demobilization and reintegration of the opposed forces, transitional justice, electoral law, and the constitution. But the international mechanisms that were supposed to oversee the implementation of the provisions, and through which the parties episodically negotiated implementation issues, lacked continuity and strong leadership, which provided a less coherent focus. Even if those channels had been more vigorous, however, the BLTP did not set out to address specific political issues or grievances in the ongoing negotiations.

In Estonia, the CSMHI operated simultaneously with a number of diplomatic initiatives that were engaging Estonians and Russians at the track-one (official governmental) level on issues such as language and citizenship laws. But nevertheless, as discussed above, the initiative did not choose to target a particular process or substantive issue. Those issues were unresolved, but the initiative saw itself as uniquely concentrating on an emotional aspect of the conflict that was not being addressed in the official, more legalistic deliberations being conducted through diplomatic channels, but rather than as a deliberate conduit for arriving at substantive agreements.

The Guyanese and Sri Lankan initiatives lacked designated official counterpart processes. Although the projects' organizers could not command such processes to start or to continue, they also did not try to press for an official channel to be created or seek out an existing one. In Guyana, several international mediations had failed to resolve the main issues. But even though no high-level negotiation processes were continuing or being restarted, the SCP initiative was inaugurated in the hopes of advancing a resolution for the issues at stake. Because the initiative did little to connect its several achievements to provide a cumulative momentum and focus, its various efforts remained piecemeal and dispersed. In Sri Lanka, the Norwegian-led mediation had broken down and only a fragile and deteriorating cease-fire was in place. The OTI organizers sought to fill the vacuum by creating an alternative channel through which the parties could continue to explore the prospects for common ground, but apart from any particular official process. However, the OTI found it impossible to get the most influential politicians to participate, and it was not able to create channels to inform the still-existing multinational mediating team or press for a more robust process to complement and support. Proceeding on its own but lacking sufficient standing and influence, the OTI was vulnerable to being eclipsed by the outcome of the 2005 elections, in which a leader appealing to Sinhalese nationalism came to power.

TWO-WAY COMMUNICATIONS WITH OFFICIALDOM

Another crucial feature of the initiatives was whether they had ongoing, intensive, and iterative communications with official high-level decision-makers. Direct contact could be secured as initiative participants moved into official positions or the initiatives' organizers made deliberate efforts to maintain regular communications with certain decision-makers. To be sure, the existence of an official negotiations process makes it easier to create a connection to and coordinate with an authoritative, decision-making focal point, but such congruency does not automatically produce a direct connection and special efforts need to be made. Initiatives that do not have such processes as a target could still endeavor to communicate with specific incumbent officials such as chief executives, their staffs, and key cabinet members.

Here again, a pattern seems to be evident. The high-ranking Tajikistan and Cyprus initiatives both had close ties to official levels and maintained regular two-way communications with key official figures. The middle-ranking Guyana, Burundi, and Estonia initiatives did not undertake systematic interactions. In low-ranking Sri Lanka, the highest-level officials were not looped into the OTI and effectively shunned it.

In Tajikistan and Cyprus, the tight linkages were afforded both by the good access that the organizers initially had to major powers and UN mediators and by continuing efforts to keep the official negotiations informed. The US chair of the ITD approached the UN Assistant Secretary-General to explain the interactive process and highlight the compatibility of the dialogue process with the official talks. Analytical memoranda sent to the UN Assistant Secretary-General provided the UN with regular information about the substance of the dialogue sessions. The UN, in turn, recognized the value of the informal dialogue process.[22] In addition, several ITD participants were included in the official delegations, while others provided advice to the decision-makers. To test the political feasibility of proposals on which there was joint agreement in the workshops, such as about a State Council, the participants floated trial balloons with specific officials. Various options were summarized and communicated to officials in private, not in public.

In Cyprus, the HSG also achieved its influence through direct and ongoing communications with the international negotiators and with the Turkish Cypriot and Greek Cypriot governing authorities. Detailed summaries of the HSG deliberations were regularly shared with the UN Special Representative mediator and the US embassy. The Turkish Cypriot participants communicated ideas directly to the leader of that community, to political parties, and to officials in Ankara. The Greek Cypriot participants also used their direct access to their government. Two participants who went into the Greek Cypriot government remained with the initiative. The negotiations also apparently picked up study group ideas via other decision-makers on both sides with whom the HSG communicated and the UN consulted. Significantly, the workshop participants adjusted their work in order to respond to the evolving negotiations and political situation. In Estonia, the CSMHI participants also made some direct contacts such as through the President's Roundtable on Minority Issues, but this type of outreach was less regularized. In the targeted security sector workshops in Burundi and certain sectoral workshops in Guyana, good linkages existed because of the often direct involvement of representatives in the workshops of the target organizations. As a result, the participating organizations were already well acquainted with the issues to be discussed and motivated to use the workshop products. However, in the Burundi case, no systematic effort was undertaken to communicate results with the post-Arusha implementation forum. Although many Ngozi participants were high level decision-makers and the workshop may have influenced the tone of the implementation negotiations, these discussions did not get deeply into the substance of issues and thus did not generate usable ideas. In Guyana, high-level officials such as cabinet members were not regularly apprised about the positive atmosphere and products of the sectoral workshops. The SCP influence was expected to occur largely through public channels. The vice president and other incumbent officials attended the culminating National Conversation conference at the end of the Multistakeholder Forum process, but they were passive recipients of a vast collection of recommendations.

At the other extreme, the Sri Lanka OTI was focused heavily on middle-level consensus and advocacy with regard to policymakers, but it had little if any contact with the official mediating partners or highest government officials.

INCLUSION OF POLITICALLY INFLUENTIAL PARTICIPANTS

Another crucial decision facing the initiatives involved the kinds of people to invite to participate in the workshops. It is often argued that to have lasting results, peace negotiations need to be inclusive. However, it is usually not made clear how much and what kind of inclusiveness is necessary. Unlimited participation is obviously infeasible. In these six cases, effectiveness was not a function of the number and breadth of the groups engaged. More was not necessarily better, and in some cases it was worse.

The Burundi, Cyprus, Estonia, and Tajikistan chapters mentioned as important the deliberate selection of participants from the ranks of influential and capable members of the elite that cut across the political spectrum. The choice of influentials gave the initiatives greater status, thus attracting other participants; it helped to ensure that official negotiators and government policymakers would take the initiatives more seriously; and it created channels to other influential people who were active in the ongoing official conflict resolution processes. For example, in Burundi, the BLTP's methodical selection of participants for the initial workshops was made by interviewing more than seventy institutional heads about the most influential people from across the political spectrum, and it resulted in ninety-five chosen "leaders" who were deemed to be influential. This approach conferred prestige on the processes and attracted other participants. Workshop participants were thought to be potential key players in Burundi's transition, and representative of main parties to the conflict.

However, the six initiatives differed notably in whether they were composed principally of higher-level political figures or a large number of mid-level and grassroots participants. The cases can be distinguished in terms of their main "tracks." As mentioned, the Tajikistan and Cyprus initiatives were explicitly intended as "track-one-and-a-half" diplomacy. Burundi initially targeted track-one officials in their individual capacities, and later worked on a track-two level. Estonia was a track-two initiative. The Guyana and Sri Lanka initiatives combined track-two and track-three activities, embracing professionals and ordinary citizens at the community level. In other terminology, Tajikistan, Cyprus, Burundi and Estonia looked mainly to "key" people, whereas Guyana and Sri Lanka went to great lengths to involve "many" people in addition to some "key" people.[23]

Comparing the differing compositions of the workshops, there appears to be a strong relationship between their overall performance and the extent that the initiatives' core group contained high-level political influentials. In Tajikistan, the ITD was among those credited for carefully picking people of the right caliber. The ITD participants were intellectuals and experts with personal political credentials, and some had direct access to power-holders even if they were not decision-makers themselves. They included individuals from both sides of the conflict, some of whom were also members of the delegations in the UN-chaired official negotiations or served as advisers. Ethnic Uzbeks were left out, but that may have actually increased the chances that the concurrent negotiations would accept the workshops' ideas. Similarly, the Estonia initiative chose high- and mid-level participants who had access to official decision-makers and to the Russian-speaking community.

In Cyprus, the HSG incorporated a spectrum of the political elite from both sides, including parliamentarians, party leaders, and former officials who had specific connections to their political superiors, as well as business interests and hard-liners who had not been previously represented in workshops. Three people were or would become second-level decision-makers in both parties; several were key figures in the prosettlement coalition in 2000. At the same time, the HSG mixed in compatible outsiders who were reflective and creative, and it sought gender balance. However, the study group did not rely on these members to carry the ball. HSG participants also carried out advocacy work to influence public opinion, such as public speaking, writing op-eds, appearing on call-in shows, and joining mass rallies, the last of which allowed them to connect with grassroots constituencies and leaders. But unlike in Guyana and Sri Lanka, this mobilization activity was not seen as an alternative to communicating with the high-level leaders, but rather as an auxiliary measure. Regrettably, this outreach focused mostly on the Turkish side, in order to buttress the emerging prosettlement parties in selling the UN plan to the Turkish public. The HSG was faulted for not doing more to cultivate the Greek Cypriot community's leaders or to lobby its constituents to support the Annan Plan.

In Burundi, many BLTP workshop participants were very high-level. Indeed, the initial workshops included the entire new Burundian government, with the president, two vice presidents, twenty cabinet ministers, the appointed secretary-general of the government, military and civilian chiefs of staff, and several senior advisors to ministries, as well as some civil society leaders. As the study authors stated, "No leadership training project has ever reached so high a political level."[24] Training workshops were also organized specifically for the Burundian security sector.

Guyana and Sri Lanka clearly differed from the other initiatives in that both explicitly set out to be especially inclusive and thus to involve a broad swath of actors, not just a politically influential elite or specific agency decision-makers. The assumption was that bringing a large number and variety of actors into the workshop experience to address multiple problems would help to increase the influence of the initiative and build civil society capacity. In Guyana, high-level government and opposition political party heads and deputy heads were engaged at the outset, but many other groups were subsequently involved in activities down to the grassroots level. Yet that inclusiveness did not change the contested government policies. Although the Sri Lanka OTI procedure for choosing participants was more systematic and required the approval of the four participating main political parties, its multiple venues and types of meetings were even more broadly inclusive of national- and local-level participants. The OTI failed only to entice participation by two right-wing Sinhalese parties and small Tamil parties. But trying to encompass so many participants with differing positions and setting up a complex set of rules and procedures to ensure explicit consent to the agreed-on texts made the overall OTI process extremely cumbersome and greatly slowed it down. Also, many OTI participants wielded unequal degrees of influence within their various roles in officialdom, so the consensus statements that the initiative labored to produce often were said to lack credibility and authority and failed to influence the official positions of the parliamentary parties. So even though the OTI pursued consensus through its formalized structures and procedures, it lacked the de facto participation of key influentials who could translate its resolutions into actual policies. Top political leaders resisted participation and indirectly threatened participants.[25] Even the three peace secretariats it created did not work in unison. In sum, both the Sri Lanka and Guyana initiatives sought inclusiveness at the cost of efficacy.

This is not to say that the more effective initiatives were always perfect in their choices of key influentials. Among the missed opportunities noted, two had to do with parties that were excluded. In both the Tajikistan and Cyprus initiatives, individuals representing certain interests such as important political parties were left out of the workshop process because of the preferences of the initial participants. These early decisions contributed to subsequent problems. On its part, the ITD included only one Uzbek, as both of the principal sides feared Uzbek influence in Tajikistan's politics. This choice precluded the ITD from making any provision to ensure Uzbek access to positions of power or to enact policies favorable to Uzbeks or other ethnic minorities. A more inclusive regional-level dialogue was considered, but was rejected for several reasons. But the omission left a "structural factor with future conflict potential," and subsequently, majority-minority tensions resurfaced and remain a source of potential conflict.[26] The chapter also faults the ITD for failing to include hard-liners and the powerful Tajikistan military, for that put at risk the possibility that the latter could act on their resentments if the political situation changed. More consequentially, in the Cyprus case, invited participants who were unable to attend the initial HSG meetings were subsequently left out; the group voted to maintain its existing composition so as to avoid losing momentum. But this decision meant that the HSG initiative excluded two important political parties on the Greek side that represented 40 to 50 percent of the Greek Cypriot population. As a result, the HSG was more vulnerable to these parties' nationalist sentiments and its participants overlooked the possibility that the prosettlement sentiment on the Greek side was not strong enough to support the UN's reunification plan. The participants assumed wrongly that the most intransigent parties were on the Turkish side, and failed to lobby the wider Greek Cypriot community equally. Greater insistence on including significant participants from those parties might have bridged the gap between the "yes" and "no" camps on the Greek Cypriot side and moderated the rising Greek opposition that was expressed in the Annan Plan referendum. This omission also may have contributed to the failure to anticipate how the prospect of EU accession could reduce the Greek Cypriots' incentive to settle the conflict. Their inclusion might have introduced more political realism into the discussion.

In these two cases, tradeoffs were made between short-term gains and possible future problems. The chapters do not definitively judge whether the initial exclusions could have been avoided without damaging the amount of substantive progress that was made, or whether early inclusion of the particular parties would have limited that progress. However, neither chapter argued that inclusion going beyond what has been called an "inclusive enough coalition" would have been more effective.[27] In all, a great difference was made by the proportional emphases put on seeking collaboration among leaders of groups who were especially well connected politically, compared with efforts to include a broad swath of groups. The key to initiatives' effectiveness did not lie in the numbers or breadth of the participants, but in the amount of de facto political weight that the individuals possessed at the time.

Inadequate Theories

Interestingly, the evidence from these cases indicates that certain leading alternative explanations of the six initiatives' effectiveness are informative but ultimately inadequate. One important characteristic that one body of theory might invoke is the amount of hostility expressed by the parties in conflict. The spectrum of interactions can range from peaceful disputation to all-out war. Compared to contentious but nonviolent demonstrations or even to violent protests, for example, war between organized armed forces brings bloodshed and fatalities and poses the possibility of total extermination at the hands of one's enemy. As the destruction and casualties from a conflict mount, mutual animosity and suspicion will increase. The level of hostility might affect the success of a nonofficial initiative because the hatred and fear felt by the participating sides makes it harder for them to even speak to each other, much less come to agreement. These antagonists may resist engaging altogether, give only lip service to the effort, or even obstruct or undermine efforts to resolve the conflict by intimidating anyone on their side who wishes to seek compromise.[28]

To capture such gradations, Ronald Fisher usefully distinguishes between four stages in conflict relationships: discussion, polarization, segregation, and destruction.[29] These gradations reflect the extent to which the parties in conflict are entrenched in their opposed positions, are politically organized into separate groups, have developed a moral justification for their cause, have armed themselves, engage in or threaten physical violence, and are single-mindedly dedicated to destroying the other side. As shown in the box below, the main conflicts in the six countries varied a great deal in their levels of hostility at the time the respective initiatives began.

EXTENT OF THE HOSTILITY OF THE CONFLICTS

Discussion

1. **Estonia's** conflict had surfaced following the restoration of its independence in 1991, and had caused no deaths but was raising concern over possible escalation into violence.
2. Since its independence in 1966, **Guyana** had experienced episodes of violent unrest and repeated election violence, causing a small number of deaths, but the country was peaceful most of the time.

Polarization

3. Following several major interethnic massacres since its independence in 1962, **Burundi's** first multiparty elections triggered an
officers' coup and rural massacres that escalated into civil war,
causing an estimated 300,000 deaths. Except for skirmishes with
one holdout insurgent group, a cease-fire had ended the war but the
peace agreement was uncertain.

Segregation

4. Following a long history of intercommunal violence and opposed
armed groups before and following independence in 1960, a Turkish military invasion of **Cyprus** in 1974 ended with a cease-fire and
physical separation of the two Cypriot populations on the island,
maintained by a UN peacekeeping force.

Destruction

5. **Tajikistan's** postindependence factional civil war was unprecedented but was actively being waged.
6. **Sri Lanka's** decades-long armed conflict between a majority-led
government and a militant rebel force faced a deteriorating cease-
fire and an increase in armed skirmishes.

As shown above, the Estonian conflict was at one extreme; although contentious, it had always been entirely peaceful. At the other extreme was Sri
Lanka, a conflict that fits what the literature refers to as "intractable."[30] The
remaining cases varied considerably in terms of past or recent bloodshed. If
these differences were significant, then it would be expected that the most
escalated conflicts, in Tajikistan and Sri Lanka, saw the least impact from
their initiatives, and the nonviolent conflict in Estonia would show the highest impact. The Guyana, Burundi, and Cyprus initiatives would perform
better than that in Sri Lanka but less well than that in Estonia.

However, there is no consistent relationship between the differing levels
of hostility and the initiatives' ultimate achievements. The Sri Lanka initiative's impact was negligible during its escalating war, but Tajikistan's was
high during its active war. Cyprus's initiative, despite a long-standing unresolved conflict that had separated the two communities, helped formulate a

peace proposal that came very close to being adopted. Yet in another post-conflict situation, Burundi's initiative had less impact. The two least hostile conflicts were influenced only modestly by their initiatives: Guyana's amid sporadic incidents of violence, and Estonia's during a period of complete peace. From this evidence, the extent of hostility does not determine the influence of the initiatives.

A second major candidate explanation, derived from "democratic peace" theory, would presume that initiatives in democratic countries would be better received than those in nondemocratic countries. Popular sovereignty and political representation such as through elections provide peaceful channels for expressing and reconciling differences, and so opportunities to seek compromises would be more welcome than those offered to more authoritarian regimes. Interestingly, in the case studies the channels for popular representation played a minor or sometimes a negative role in increasing official receptivity to a settlement.

The leaders in Estonia, Cyprus, Guyana, and Sri Lanka were more or less accountable to popular pressures through constitutions, political parties, elections, and referendums. Some of these electoral institutions had operated since before their country's independence. However, these structures also gave constituencies such as ethnic nationalists and other partisan majorities substantial influence over the conflict-related policies of incumbent officials, and these popular forces tended to exacerbate as much as or more than mitigate the conflicts. In the semidemocratic systems of Cyprus, Guyana, and Sri Lanka, the populations were politically mobilized around major identity groups that leaders often could manipulate through party and patronage channels. Thus, the influence of mass opinion was usually to thwart peace agreements rather than push for them. By reflecting if not amplifying ethnic divisions, majoritarian democracy outweighed the efforts of cross-cutting civil society actors to bridge the differences between the sides. Because democratic procedures actually erected barriers to changing the status quo, the ability of the nonofficial initiatives to alter the leaders' calculations was vitiated. Even in the more institutionalized democracy of Estonia, executive officials were more accommodating of the Russian minority's rights than the Parliament was.

To be sure, the initiatives in Cyprus and Guyana worked to mobilize mass publics in support of resolving the conflicts, as illustrated by the prosettlement campaign of the Turkish Cypriots and the effort to promote peaceful elections in Guyana. These activities apparently helped to reduce hostile rhetoric and behavior, but they focused on immediate, transitory issues and were short-lived. In Cyprus, moreover, a popular referendum on one side led to the defeat of the proposed resolution plan. These campaigns had limited impact on the greater resolution of the conflicts.

In the noninstitutionalized democracies of Burundi and Tajikistan, a "public" hardly existed, as mass sentiments were unorganized, diffuse, and weak. Their leaders were more inclined to seek deals, but not because they were being pressed to do so by popular sentiments through representative processes. Because their countries were in conflicts or barely beyond them, the leaders still lacked full governing authority in the country and were vying to obtain it. In Burundi in particular, the participants often were not representative of broad interests, and instead were operating under conditions of what the chapter authors describe as "near-Hobbesian institutional anarchy" and using any tool to ensure that they would have a seat at the table and a portion of the power that was available to them if they went along with the peace settlement. Both these initiatives created a venue through which the participants could allocate governing power among themselves.[31]

Conclusion

Keeping in mind the small sample of initiatives presented in this volume, this close review of the case study chapters suggests several generalizations about the contributions that nonofficial interactive interventions can make toward a sustainable peace and the main factors that maximize their efficacy. Several of these conclusions provide added support and expand upon findings in existing research, and some depart from previous findings. This study also leaves unanswered one question for further inquiry.

All told, this method of bringing adversaries together in nonbinding, facilitated communication is capable of softening the perceptions and stances of the workshop participants toward each other and in making them more open to accommodate each other's interests. More significantly, in some circumstances the methods can encourage the conflicting parties represented in the workshops to enter into higher-level, potentially more binding peace negotiations, and initiatives have succeeded in inserting into those negotiations mutually accepted substantive solutions to major sticking points. The workshop experience also inspired participants in some instances to lobby their respective leaders to accept specific solutions, or to organize public campaigns to rally wider support for proposed settlements or for other peaceful actions. However, even though these methods contributed to the conclusion of crucial power-sharing pacts among core leaders, they were not able to ensure that the resulting agreements were complied with, and they had only occasional effects in institutionalizing other crucial elements needed for sustaining a peace. Generally, the provisional agreements did not lead to less politicized and more effective security forces, enforceable procedures for ensuring citizen representation, more competent judiciaries and public services, or economic benefits.

Certain favorable domestic and international contexts increased the chances that the initiatives could persuade conflict actors to talk rather than fight, come to an agreement, and thus begin to take steps to build enduring peace. The first condition was whether the political leaders of the contending groups saw compelling domestic political advantages in adopting a peace settlement or accommodative policies, rather than persisting in confrontation or conflict by pursuing unilateral gains or maintaining a contested status quo.[32] Interestingly, certain heads of ministries were especially receptive to initiative ideas because these incumbents apparently felt secure in their positions (rather than concerned about losing them through elections or other means), and thus they could invest themselves in solving their organization's problems. Other domestic factors do not adequately explain the relative amenability of the conflicts to the initiatives' influence: the depth of the conflicting groups' societal differences, the conflict's level of hostility,[33] and the extent of democratic representation and accountability in the country.[34] Whatever these contexts, the calculations of key leaders determined the amount of influence on conflict resolution.

The thrust of external influences also was pivotal. For the leading decision-makers on both sides of the conflict to come to agreement, global and regional state-based actors had to be willing to proffer powerful positive incentives. A vigorous and united international front in support of peaceful conflict resolution was critical, and the international actors needed to back it up with attractive rewards through a coherent diplomatic channel, rather than evince contradictory goals or half-hearted interest.[35] Instilling "local ownership" of peacebuilding required robust external commitment. Where present, these unequivocal inducements offered through designated channels shaped the leaders' decision-making preferences even when an asymmetric balance of power favored government leaders over opposition leaders. Conversely, international incentives that were weak (as in Guyana), uneven (as in Burundi), or contradictory (as ultimately in Cyprus) reduced the chances of achieving the fullest conflict resolution. These favorable contextual factors reinforced each other.

Within those parameters, the interventions' choices of priority goals and of workshop "curriculum" made a significant difference. The more effective cases did not refrain from coaxing the participants to take on substantive issues. They took advantage of available openings to astutely engage the participants in formulating solutions that were politically feasible for official decision-makers to adopt.[36] The workshops started with trust- and relationship-building methods, but used a series of diverse but linked activities to cautiously engage participants in formulating concrete, politically realistic resolutions of outstanding issues.

The organization and conduct of these nonofficial initiatives also stood the best chances of fostering a resolution if—

- They recruited participants from government and civil society who had political sway with their leaders and in their base constituencies in the respective societies.[37]
- The initiatives maintained ongoing iterative communications with the official international mediators and the domestic leaders with effective decision-making authority. Nonofficial consultations needed to be aligned with existing or potential official negotiations or authoritative policymaking processes and to respond sensitively to the evolving topics and pace of those deliberations.[38]
- The proposed actions are actually adopted by the recognized decision-makers at the highest levels of political power. Few situations will achieve an overall peaceful resolution if they fail to achieve agreement by authoritative officials.[39]
- The initiatives promoted but did not rely primarily on midlevel or grassroots intergroup cooperation as a surrogate for failed or weak official processes, or as a source of pressure on political leaders to reach such agreements.[40] Cross-cutting activities scattered in the general population and intended to have a bottom-up effect were only faintly heard.[41]

Other features such as an initiative's international stature were important for gaining local access, attracting participants, and starting a conversation, but these features had no consistent effect on comparative effectiveness.[42] This study review ends with a paradox: the ability to affect domestic political power and wield international influence—aspects of *realpolitik* that the unofficial methods theory often tend to view as obstacles to sustainable peace and therefore to disregard—turns out to be paramount determinants of whether the methods can expect to achieve the cherished goal of sustainable peace.

Notes

1. In the language of program evaluation, this is a "summative" evaluation. The categories define what the initiatives' workshop activities ("outputs") may have yielded in initial "outcomes" directly affecting the participants and further "impacts" resulting from those outcomes. The classification draws in part on Tamra D'Estree Pearson, "Changing the Debate About 'Success' in Conflict Resolution Efforts," *Negotiation Journal* 17, no. 2 (April 2001): 101–13

2. The following analysis is based almost entirely on the evidence reported in the case-study chapters and seeks to reflect them as faithfully as possible. The interpretations and conclusions are this author's responsibility.

3. Such networks and coalitions are described in Tharia Paffenholz, ed., *Civil Society and Peacebuilding: A Critical Assessment* (Boulder, CO: Lynne Rienner, 2010), 53–54; Ronald J. Fisher, ed., *Paving the Way: Contributions of Interactive Conflict Resolution to Peacemaking* (Lanham, MD: Lexington Books, 2005) 216. Possibly, the ideas that the SCP injected into the public discourse helped to inspire individuals to engage in the cross-party politicking that helped form the multiethnic PNC Coalition and Alliance for Change, and their better showing in the 2011 and 2015 elections. But such influences would be very diffuse and difficult to verfiy, requiring confirmation through large-scale, intensive surveys.

4. Randa Slim and Harold Saunders, "The Inter-Tajik Dialogue: From Civil War towards Civil Society," in *Politics of Compromise: The Tajikistan Peace Process*, ed. Kamoludin Abdullaev and Catherine Barnes (London: Conciliation Resources, 2001), 46.

5. The factors essential for achieving a sustainable peace were most closely associated with gains in the third and fourth impact categories in table 9.1.

6. See, e.g., Kirgizbek Kanunov, "Tajikistan After Reconciliation: 17 Years Without War or Peace," *CACI Analyst* (Washington, DC: Central Asia–Caucasus Institute and Silk Road Studies Joint Center, August 5, 2014).

7. As Anna Matveeva states in her chapter in this volume, "If the dialogue had not taken place, it is unclear how long it would have taken before the sides decided to negotiate, how slow and painful the formal talks would have been, how much time would have been wasted, and how the peace agreement would have been designed" (163).

8. This analysis cannot determine the exact degree to which the identified key factors contributed to the differing impacts, as it is not possible to hold other factors constant. But it can yield grounded hypotheses about the most important factors associated with greater effectiveness. An alternative way to search for significant factors is to compile what the case study authors judge to be most important in their own case. However, these factors may be idiosyncratic to individual cases. If several authors point to the same or similar features of the initiatives, these may be worthy of being replicated, but such factors do not necessarily explain the differences in impacts or reveal possible patterns of variation.

9. I. William Zartman, *Ripe for Resolution: Conflict Resolution in Africa*, 2nd ed. (New York: Oxford University Press, 1989); I. William Zartman, "Ripeness: The

Hurting Stalemate and Beyond," in *International Conflict Resolution after the Cold War*, ed. Paul C. Stern and Daniel Druckman (Washington, DC: National Academies Press, 2000), 225–50.

10. Zartman, *Ripe for Resolution*; Zartman, "Ripeness."

11. As Vladimir Goryaev of the UN Department of Political Affairs observed: "Despite the apparent complexity of international interventions in the Tajik conflict, clear mandates and effective coordination prevented duplication and 'competition of initiatives.'" Vladimir Goryaev, "Architecture of International Involvement in the Tajik Peace Process," in Abdullaev and Barnes, *Politics of Compromise*, 32.

12. These common attributes suggest that all six initiatives were "powerful" by Fisher's criteria; see *Paving the Way*, 226.

13. Most of these places were physically separated from the participants' usual places of work. Most were in-country, but some convened a few meetings abroad: the ITD met occasionally in Russia as well as Tajikistan, and the HSG met in Israel, Jordan, Northern Ireland, and the United States. Although two groups in the Guyana SCP went on trips abroad, most of the SCP venues were in Guyana and several were in the participants' workplaces.

14. For example, in Cyprus, Estonia, and Tajikistan, effectiveness was attributed to the continuity afforded by the regular workshops sustained over several years; in Burundi and Guyana to the extensive due diligence before launching the initiative; in Tajikistan to the ITD facilitators' thorough preparation prior to each session; and in Cyprus and Guyana to providing a comparative international perspective through study tours. Other features mentioned were the organizers' painstaking interactions to invite local interest in the prospective workshops.

15. Harold Saunders, "Evaluating Sustained Dialogue," in *A Public Peace Process: Sustained Dialogue to Transform Racial and Ethnic Conflicts* (New York: Palgrave Macmillan, 2001), 226.

16. Toward the end of the HSG workshop series, the project director handed out a draft of possible joint recommendations for the study group's consideration. The harm was not in making that suggestion; the text was leaked to the press months after it had been withdrawn, and the ideas in it were largely acceptable to the participants. However, this step fell victim to grumbling outside the workshops on the Greek Cypriot side about the secrecy of UN negotiations and to accusations from opponents on both sides that the US government was using the study group to manipulate the negotiations, and thus to interfere in Cyprus's internal affairs. The episode undermined the work of the study group and its three Greek representatives, and the US government and UN Office for Project Services felt compelled to dissociate themselves from it.

17. See footnote 13 in Susanna Campbell and Peter Uvin's chapter in this volume.

18. See Susanna Campbell and Peter Uvin's chapter in this volume, 296.

19. As Hannes Siebert and Chanya Charles state in their chapter in this volume, the OTI "created a mechanism and working space . . . to collectively explore and discover common ground and ways to constructively propose and deal with critical issues without having to take formal positions on issues" (204–5).

20. It might be thought that the longer that initiatives are in operation and thus can be assessed, the greater opportunity the participants have to hold meetings, pursue tasks, apply a wider range of techniques, experience trial and error, and thus be able to demonstrate more achievements. The case study period of the ITD was more than ten years; the other cases ranged from two to four years. However, each initiative

expressed certain distinct assumptions and ways to organize at their outset, and these plans largely predicted the activities that they carried out in the years examined. Also, the initiatives' operating period does not necessarily circumscribe the number of workshops they could hold.

21. As Anna Matveeva states in her chapter in this volume, the ITD did not take the place of formal talks but rather made the formal process "more productive, more efficient, and less frustrating" (157).

22. "In addition to facilitating the official Inter-Tajik negotiations, UN mediators also maintained liaison with the 'second track' dialogue initiated by Ambassador Saunders of the Kettering Foundation." Goryaev, "Architecture of International Involvement in the Tajik Peace Process," 32.

23. Mary B. Anderson and Lara Olson, *Confronting War: Critical Lessons for Peace Practitioners* (Cambridge, MA: The Collaborative for Development Action, 2003), 56.

24. See Susanna Campbell and Peter Uvin's chapter in this volume.

25. It is unclear whether the OTI failed to capitalize sufficiently on the opportunity to reach into higher levels of government leaders, whether this effort was fruitless, or whether it might not have made a difference either way.

26. As Anna Matveeva states in her chapter in this volume, the Uzbek issue was not a prominent part of the ITD, but "remains a driver of potential conflict" (185).

27. The World Bank coined this phrase to refer to coalitions that are less than all-inclusive and thus feasible to form, but that encompass sufficient relevant interests to gain support for policy reform. See World Bank, "Restoring Confidence: Moving Away from the Brink," ch. 4 in *World Development Report 2011: Conflict, Security and Development* (Washington, DC: World Bank, 2011), 119–21.

28. This explanation is analytically distinguishable from one that points to underlying, long-term socioeconomic and cultural (often called "root" or "structural") causes of conflict. In all these conflicts, the wider constituencies of the leaders in the workshops were estranged because of diverging lineage, historical, socioeconomic, or cultural differences. Although these cleavages have been attenuated by integrating forces such as urbanization and intermarriage, in this view, they would continue to fuel the groups' antagonism. If such fault lines were determinative, then the conflicts in the most divided societies should be the least amenable to influence. To the extent that societal cleavages were deep, one would expect more obduracy against a settlement and greater difficulty in reaching a mutual understanding. Some of the conflicting identities were compounded by territorial separation, such as geographically divided Sri Lanka and Cyprus and to a lesser extent Estonia and Tajikistan, compared to Guyana (where intermingling has increased) and Burundi (which largely has been ethnically mixed geographically). A qualitative ranking of the six case study countries in terms of their group differences suggests the following gradation from *least* to *most* divided societies:

1. Tajikistan: Southern Islamist and Democrats versus northern secularists (religion, region)
2. Burundi: Hutu versus Tutsi (ancestry, class)
3. Estonia: Estonian-speaking versus Russian-speaking (language, economy, region)
4. Guyana: Afro-Guyanese versus Indo-Guyanese (ancestry, class, religion)
5. Cyprus: Cypriot Greeks versus Turkish Cypriots (language, religion, region)
6. Sri Lanka: Tamils versus Sinhalese (language, religion, region).

Examining the importance of these factors, the positions of Tajikistan and Sri Lanka mirror the earlier ranking of the initiatives' effectiveness. But other than those extremes, the relative depth of these cleavages and the respective initiatives' performances do not correspond.

29. Fisher, *Paving the Way*, 206, 208.

30. "Intractable" conflicts such as the Israeli-Palestinian conflict are not impossible to resolve, but are extremely difficult cases because they are fed by multiple historical and dynamic factors. These include long-standing grievances that have not been accommodated, a strong sense of respective communal identities, a legacy of years of violent conflict and multiple failed peace negotiations, external actors supporting different sides, uncompromising behavior, high stakes for a perceived "victory," the perception that there is no way out, and a feeling of hopeless and despair. See for example, Heidi Burgess and Guy M. Burgess, "What Are Intractable Conflicts?" in *Beyond Intractibility* (Beyond Intractability Project, University of Colorado, November 2003), http://www.beyondintractability.org/essay/meaning-intractability.

31. Susanna Campbell and Peter Uvin's chapter on the BLTP describes the differing stakes involved in transitioning polities compared to institutionalized democracies: "Once it was clear that the peace process was progressing, many high-level members of the military saw the integration of the army as a way to secure a seat in power by ensuring that they had a position in Burundi's strongest governmental institution. . . . In other transitional institutions, such as the Burundian Parliament and the political parties, the incentives for change were much weaker because progress (such as elections) would mean the eventual loss of power of many individuals within these institutions" (304–5).

32. This is consistent with the notion that mutual hurting stalemates are conducive to third-party influence. See Fisher, *Paving the Way*, 230.

33. Some previous studies conclude that the level of violent conflict generally reduces the success of initiatives by civil society (Paffenholz, *Civil Society and Peacebuilding*, 430). However, other studies find that the success of unofficial conflict resolution initiatives in particular are not determined by the level of violence or a conflict's intractability (Fisher, *Paving the Way*, 221–22).

34. That the extent of democracy in the country does not increase the initiatives' effectiveness casts doubt on a claim that even if civil society groups have only indirect access to official peace negotiations (such as by participating in a nonofficial track-two process), their involvement will still increase the chances of sustained peace in a country with a democratic political system. In that view, the elites who are bargaining at the official level are themselves responsive to the country's democratic institutions. See Anthony Wanis-St. John and Darren Kew, "Civil Society and Peace Negotiations: Confronting Exclusion," *International Negotiation* 13, no. 1 (2008) 30–31.

35. Third party mediations are more effective in achieving peace when they invest more resources in their efforts. See Tobias Böhmelt, "The Effectiveness of Tracks of Diplomacy Strategies in Third-Party Interventions," *Journal of Peace Research* 47, no. 2 (2010): 167, 175.

36. Group dialogues need to address concrete issues if they are to have sociopolitical impact; Anderson and Olson, *Confronting War*, 70.

37. Similarly, "eminent" leaders in politics, religion, and other spheres are crucial for national facilitation between the main conflict parties. Paffenholz, *Civil Society and Peacebuilding*, 428–29.

38. This finding expands on the notion that these initiatives work best when they are complementary to official processes (Fisher, *Paving the Way*, 227). The combination of

unofficial and official third-party processes is more effective than action on independent tracks (Böhmelt, "The Effectiveness of Tracks of Diplomacy," 175).

39. Achieving agreement among top leaders makes it more possible to ensure grass-roots support (Böhmelt, "The Effectiveness of Tracks of Diplomacy," 175). Agreement on some sort of elite power-sharing in particular, although no guarantee of a sustained peace, appears to be a prerequisite. Real reforms may flow from elite leaders who are relatively secure, have the capacity to act, and find policy changes politically appealing. See, e.g., Diane de Gramont, *Beyond Magic Bullets in Governance Reform* (Washington, DC: Carnegie Endowment for International Peace, November 2014), 12–17.

40. For example, free-floating training exercises for ad hoc assembled groups of individual leaders tend to have little impact unless they are connected to specific, organized activities for exercising the newly gained commitments. See e.g., Anderson and Olson, *Confronting War*, 78; and Paffenholz, *Civil Society and Peacebuilding*, 426–27. This conclusion suggests caution for the view that promoting various civil society activities in order to effect political and policy changes is an effective or feasible route to achieving a sustainable peace. The expectation that civil society will bring about social and political change faces enormous collective action problems, especially in poorer, noninstitutionalized democracies in developing countries. These problems include aggregating preferences across diverse interests; stimulating concerted action by many ordinary poor people who must attend to basic daily tasks; meeting the objection that nonelected people and organizations are unrepresentative and therefore lack legitimacy; and obtaining ongoing funding for broad-based civil society organizations. Efforts to build a common *civil* society also confront many diverging interests, traditions, and groups, some of which take parochial, militant, and violent forms (Wanis-St. John and Kew, "Civil Society and Peace Negotiations," 13). As the case studies show, relatively poor autocratic or semidemocratic countries are often fragmented along the lines of estranged (if not antagonistic) identity groups. Political leaders often "instrumentalize" the divisions in society by controlling the state apparatus, doling out patronage, and wielding other means of hegemonic control. Peacebuilding literature distinguishes between "key" or "eminent" people versus "many" people because it recognizes that power is held unequally in poor and conflict-prone societies with weak states and non-institutionalized democratic processes.

Realistically, actors in high positions generally affect the course of events more than do small groups or poorly organized collections of ordinary people. Politically influential individuals or groups that are persuaded to adopt an initiative's ideas generally will have more net effect on the wider society than actions by an ad hoc collection of ordinary individuals of whatever size. Although masses of people may assert themselves through popular uprisings or social movements that can exert a tempering influence on current conflicts, these episodes tend to be temporary and may reflect highly partisan interests. It is better to view civil society as a way to fulfill and deepen an established enforceable peace over the long run, not as an immediate remedy. The issue is not whether to ignore fostering particular civil society organizations, but what factors actually bring about civil societies and give them political weight. The influence of civil society actors depends on whether their activities are allowed to operate under stable conditions, such as the rule of law, broad-based political parties, democratic institutions, the media, professional militaries, and competent administration (see, e.g., Paffenholz, *Civil Society and Peacebuilding*, 428). Because the emergence of a vibrant and unified civil society depends upon economic growth, a middle class, a democratic culture, and an encompassing state to maintain some order among competing societal interests, civil society is mainly an effect rather than a cause of these other forces in these societies' development. As such, it should not be presumed to have a comparative advantage over these other entry points for international influence. It is more promising to prioritize political agreement among elites and to directly build accountable institutions following such agreements, rather than look to civil society actors to bring about these institutions simply by exerting pressure on elites.

41. This study leaves one unanswered question for further research: Did the seeds that some initiatives sowed in their wider societies sprout in multiple ways that eventually brought about significant social and political changes? In Guyana and Sri Lanka, for example, did the highly dispersed graduates and activities of the unusually inclusive multileveled initiatives play significant roles—independent of other factors—in bringing about the broad multiethnic support that later led to the electoral defeats of the very leaders and parties that had largely resisted conflict resolution when the initiatives were operating? Were the dispersed activities of these initiatives crucial for avoiding the "unlearning" that apparently occurred among the high-level graduates of the Burundi initiative? That said, it would be extremely difficult to pursue this question without doing extensive surveys.

42. It might be conjectured that initiatives headed by respected diplomats, with their international stature, can have more impact on their in-country audiences than those led by academics or professionals such as conflict resolution practitioners. The Burundi, Guyana, and Tajikistan chapters noted that the initiatives' direction by experienced and effective former diplomats gave the initiatives prestige and credibility from the start, thus attracting participants. However, the Tajikistan initiative had a higher impact than either the Burundi or Guyana initiatives. Moreover, both the high-impact Cyprus and low-impact Estonia and Sri Lanka initiatives were led by nondiplomats. It might also be hypothesized that initiatives associated with a major power, especially the United States, can wield more influence than those with multilateral sponsors. (The reverse notion is also plausible, depending on the host country's view of US involvement, as in the Cyprus case.) However, both US-sponsored and multinational initiatives had greater and lesser impacts. One of the two diplomats who co-led the Tajikistan initiative was American, but it was the reputation of its bilateral predecessor organization, the Dartmouth Conference, that brought it attention in Tajikistan. The Cyprus initiative was directed by an American academic, and even though it suffered some credibility when it was accused (wrongly) of being an instrument of US policy, it still had high impact. The middle-ranking Burundi initiative was led by an American diplomat who was highly respected in the region, while the middle-ranking SCP in Guyana was headed by a respected non-American who served as the UN country representative, which allayed suspicion that particular nations' interests lay behind it. It seems that the combination of multilateral and diplomat sponsorship may make some difference. The highest impact Tajikistan initiative was multinational and directed by former diplomats. At the other extreme, the OTI in Sri Lanka was neither diplomat-led nor seen as clearly multilateral. In short, initiatives benefit greatly when they are perceived locally as having legitimacy, but that access can be achieved by several kinds of sponsors.

Chapter 10

Contemporary Implications:
From Trust-Building to Institution-Building

Michael Lund

Introduction

Chapter 9 identified potential progress toward sustainable peace, achieved by applying the methods of interactive conflict resolution under certain conditions and in certain ways. It also noted the limits to this approach. For international policymakers and funders, the comparative analysis of the case studies yielded considerations about whether and where to support these initiatives; for the practitioners who carry them out, it suggested ways to design and implement them. This book could conclude by simply urging the organizers and funders of such projects to consider that advice, and thus look for propitious opportunities to apply the lessons while implementing the existing model. But one more question can be profitably addressed: Are this distinctive methodology and its theory of change still relevant to the changing global trends in conflict and challenges to sustaining peace? Do those who contemplate using this method need to modify it to achieve its potential? Proponents of this method have urged that it be applied more deliberately and systematically in international responses to conflict situations,[1] but less has been said about how to come to terms with contemporary realities and what ways can overcome the limitations of this approach.

This chapter takes up that challenge by detailing how initiative organizers, international policymakers, funders, and host countries can capitalize on the strengths of this type of engagement, and attend to its weaknesses, in order to address the challenges of violence and state-building in contemporary conflict-prone societies. Despite the limiting conditions in which this tool for intervention can show concrete results, it deserves to be utilized more widely than it is, if applied in more modest and realistic ways. In a nutshell, the idealistic values and unique strengths of methods of interactive conflict resolution can best be put to work when used pragmatically as a catalyst for endogenous processes to build effective and legitimate institutions, backed by incentives, expertise, and support from international actors.

The Changing Face of Intrastate Conflict

The conflict transformation methods studied in this volume originated in labor-management issues and other domestic applications in the United States and other Western advanced democracies and derive their intellectual inspiration mainly from the field of social psychology. Since the end of the Cold War, they have been used as an unofficial way to try to get around deadlocks in intractable national conflicts, to end conflicts between proxies of the competing superpowers, and to settle emerging conflicts between governments and aggrieved groups. Although these methods benefited from the post–Cold War quest for peace and democracy after the collapse of communism, that global consensus has eroded in an increasingly multipolar world, The changing nature and arenas of conflicts in the twenty-first century call for a consideration of whether these methods still have special value and what adaptations might be required to realize their promise.

The main forms of international conflict have been changing. Since the mid-1990s, major civil wars have declined, although some earlier wars persist or reerupt and new intrastate national-level conflicts emerge. There are many fragile states that have had no recent conflicts yet are especially susceptible to conflict. A large category is the formerly authoritarian regimes that have evolved into mixed "semiauthoritarian" or "semidemocratic" systems. Worldwide, authoritarian regimes have declined in number and democracies have increased, but these mixed "anocratic" regimes have remained at about the same number.[2] Although these hybrid polities are widely presumed to be "transitioning" to democracy, they are at especially high risk of debilitating violence and political instability. Many of these postcolonial, authoritarian, or postauthoritarian quasi-democracies—exemplified not only by Afghanistan and Iraq but also by countries such as Thailand, Ukraine, and Zimbabwe—are vulnerable to political instability and regression on the long road to *stable* democracy. Researchers noted this pattern years before the so-called Arab Spring arose in the Middle East in 2011, and it has been repeated in Egypt, Libya, Syria, and Yemen. Popular uprisings against tyrants express aspirations for democracy but also greatly increase the chances of civil war, mass atrocities, state breakdown, political extremism, terrorism, or the return of repressive autocracies. Such diverse countries as Azerbaijan, Bangladesh, Cambodia, Cameroon, Eritrea, Ethiopia, Madagascar, Myanmar, Pakistan, the Philippines, Russia, South Sudan, Sudan, Uganda, Uzbekistan, and Venezuela hold elections. But because rule-governed yet pluralistic institutions have not fully taken root in these countries, competing political factions within or outside the state can threaten intimidation and violence in pursuit of political supremacy, often triggering factional violence or repression. These countries may not be at the top of the current global agenda, or even of fragile state indexes, but they continue to be vulnerable to various degrees and forms of serious instability.

In addition, subnational forms of violence persist or are increasing in many postconflict and other fragile states. The World Bank's 2011 *World Development Report* turned the spotlight onto less salient forms of conflict and violence such as intercommunal and sectarian clashes; kidnapping, murder, and assassinations arising from organized crime and radical groups; land disputes over expropriation of valuable natural resources for export; youth gang violence; and gender violence.[3] Intranational and transnational terrorism has also increased, although its rise has fluctuated in recent years. Arising from manifold global, national, and local sources, these several faces of conflict tend to be localized, episodic, and of elusive origin. Yet they not only cause many deaths, humanitarian crises, and social displacement, they also perpetuate political distrust and widespread societal insecurity, discourage investment in productive income-producing opportunities, and block social betterment—all of which are conditions that must be overcome to ensure a stable state.

These forms of contemporary violence—whether seen in armed challenges to states, regime repression of opposition, or community strife—have led to the emergence of an analytical perspective that focuses on the weaknesses of the institutional environments in which violence occurs, a perspective encapsulated by the term "state fragility." In fragile states, governmental legitimacy and effectiveness are seriously deficient or absent, thus inviting political uncertainty and social instability. In failed or near-failed states, large areas may lie beyond the effective reach of a functioning government and basic public services, including control over physical security. Where central authorities exert little or nominal influence at local levels, warlords or similar figures command local allegiances by distributing economic favors and maintaining private militias. Even if poorly institutionalized states are newly democratic, legitimacy as well as security may be low because governmental functions are politicized and feeble. Law enforcement is often corrupt or nonexistent, and competing systems of justice may operate. Although more authoritarian states may exercise greater control over their territories, state services are likely to serve the most well-connected groups through their elites, and divide-and-rule policies maintain only a tenuous rapprochement among estranged ethnic groups or regions. In all these settings, a surface stability hinges on the uncertain, often deadly competition between ethnic, sectarian, and clan networks over the revenues and other "rents" that access to government assets provides. Eventually, conflicts and violence are likely to be triggered by economic or political crises and polarizing political factionalism, the single most powerful predictor of ensuing civil war, genocide, and state failure.[4]

In these cases, governments do not operate through a system of agreed-upon enforceable rules and are not sufficiently accountable to a broad-based citizenry. Recent empirical research on economic and political development and state formation has concluded that effective and legitimate *institutions*, both governmental and social, hold the key to economic growth as well as to the political stability that makes growth possible by managing change peacefully.[5]

From Trust-Building to Institution-Building

Can interactive conflict resolution methods be used to fill these institutional deficits that permit security threats and generate violence in postconflict societies and other fragile or failed states, including the hybrid "democratizing" countries? For these problems, nonofficial third-party conflict resolution initiatives such as those examined in this volume might seem to have limited utility, as they usually address specific disputes or conflicts between two distinct organized parties with defined interests. In fragile and failed states, however, the threats to stability and development are often more diffuse and slow-moving; they do not always appear as time-specific conflicts or crises typified by discrete groups in overt confrontation. Even though nonofficial actions are still useful for responding to ongoing major crises, the contemporary context seems to call for less focus on the grievances and antagonisms of particular opposed parties and more focus on the low-intensity dysfunctional political, policy, and institutional deficits that enable conflicts and other violence. The challenge is not simply how to resolve specific conflicts, but how to fill gaps in effective self-governance. Crucial priorities include ensuring fuller physical security of citizens, strengthening absent or grossly corrupt law enforcement and public service delivery, depoliticizing courts and rationalizing judicial administration, and expanding income-producing opportunities for large numbers of ordinary people across the divisions in a population. Unfortunately, the initiatives in the case studies, notwithstanding their several effects, generally were found to be limited with regard to altering their respective countries' governmental policies and institutions and depended on considerable international reinforcement. Even the Tajikistan project, judged on balance as the most successful of the six cases, was unable to prevent postconflict Tajik politics from coopting the opposition into what has become an increasingly authoritarian regime.

Much of the reason for the seeming irrelevance of the conflict resolution methodology may be that it arose in response to intergroup disputes within already wealthy, developed, liberal democracies. These nations took several centuries to establish democratic state institutions and a complex framework of laws within which relatively stable and pluralistic political competition and legal protection of basic rights operate. But in countries that have not developed such institutions or have only weak ones, a method that relies on achieving social-psychological change and closer relationships within small groups cannot be expected to create deep-rooted institutions and routine procedures for managing societal tensions.

Actually, a fundamental condition in fragile state and transitional settings is not simply a lack of interpersonal trust, cohesion, and relationships among key individuals who are engaged in active conflicts. Interpersonal relationships and allegiances exist in many forms. Informal patron-client relationships and elite cooperation based on ethnic, regional, party, clan, family, or other loyalties often largely determine who wields real authority

and how socioeconomic advantages are allocated. Through patronage practices and clientelist networks that pervade a country's politics and markets,
these relationships determine what public business does or does not get done
and how it is transacted. In fact, these informal arrangements elicit a degree
of cooperation and a modicum of development essential for survival. They
often keep social tensions from escalating into open violence and may be
locally accepted as generally adequate and legitimate. Although they are
often inequitable and uneven in their benefits, these less-than-ideal, home-
grown processes and practices of "good enough governance," some argue,
may be the most realistic foundations on which to begin to build better societies, economies, and governments.[6]

However, these arrangements are good only in the short run, while more
durable and formal laws and efficient administration are established. These
allegiances and marriages of convenience are shifting and ultimately unstable. When economic shocks or other crises arise, they often cannot avoid
degenerating into destructive violence and societal breakdown. The deeper
problem is that the prevailing political systems in fragile states lack the kinds
of enforceable rules that, in more secure and productive societies, promote
"public goods": activities that produce wider benefits to society. Examples
of such rules and policies are not merely orderly and genuine elections, but
also reliable laws and administrative regulations that sufficiently enforce
contracts and property rights and thus can encourage investment in major,
economically productive enterprises. In contrast, endemic corruption, for
example, is a result of the lack of alternative opportunities for income; competition over existing sources; the ability to exploit one's office; and the
inability of individuals to resist the prevailing short-term, self-regarding
mores and instead create alternative norms. Even when participants are converted to other values through workshops, once they leave that venue and
reenter their daily lives, the predominant practices exert pressures on them
to comply if they are to maintain their positions and sources of support in
their existing society.

To stabilize these environments of fragile states, collective action is
required in order to establish and enforce superordinate rules and public
policies. In sum, the underlying challenge is to shift from relationships of
personalistic rule and other informal ways through which elites and their
clients relate to more rule-governed and thus predictable procedures that
characterize public institutions that are more widely accepted and largely
accountable to a general citizenry.

Prologue to Progress: Steps to Making a Difference

In fact, there are ways to apply these same interactive methods by setting modest expectations to address the need for institution-building.[7] In fragile states, informal relationships and processes often are stabilizing in the short run but counterproductive over time, which suggests a focus for achieving sustained peace and development. International actors must examine how they can work with or through endogenous processes. It is essential to have contextualized strategies that "go with the grain" of the existing relationships and resiliencies but gradually adapt them to meet ultimate threats to stability by taking on greater development and state-building tasks.[8]

What would such a process look like? Essentially, the envisioned processes target actual or potential conflicts and other fragility problems in relatively amenable countries that are subject to debilitating conflicts and violence. They use the usual trust- and relationship-building techniques in workshops to engage leaders, but these workshops are merely the opening wedge in sustained country-led but internationally supported processes that catalyze collective actions to remedy specific institutional weaknesses. This hands-on approach requires an extended series of workshops over several months or possibly years, headed by persons with international stature and contacts. The following outline describes major steps for translating changed participant attitudes into incremental efforts to build more effective and legitimate states.

1. SCAN: Identify countries where conditions of fragility and conflict threaten stability and development, but where proactive efforts to strengthen country resiliencies could make headway.

To remedy institutional deficits in fragile states, engagement must come early and be sustained. For international actors, this form of engagement means going beyond the reflexive practices of concentrating mainly on major "postconflict" countries or responding with special diplomatic efforts only when "crises" arise. The proactive examples in Estonia and Guyana in this volume are still exceptions; the prevailing tendency is to respond belatedly at the highpoints of conflicts. This habit commits outside actors to a continuing series of Herculean, cost-ineffective struggles that are exhausting the scarce resources of the willing international actors, so they can never get ahead of the game. The current international approach is like playing the carnival game of "whack-a-mole": constantly trying to respond to the latest threat that pops up, but failing to act quickly enough to be able to score.

To identify fragile states that may yet offer prospects for conflict resolution and institution building, a useful starting point is the several available conflict early warning and fragile state indexes that identify countries that are especially vulnerable to institutional breakdowns and related conflicts. These cross-national databases periodically rank countries based on indicators of conflict risk and state fragility, and some offer judgments on the weakest areas within given countries, such as security, legitimacy, and organizational capacity.[9] However, initiatives should not be launched in these places indiscriminately. The celebrated accomplishments of conflict resolution and peacebuilding initiatives in contexts such as the transition from apartheid in South Africa do not automatically ensure that other initiatives will have positive results in contexts that lack enabling peaceful conflict-resolution and institution-building ingredients. Before supporting an initiative, organizers and funders should look for and capitalize on opportune places and moments when authoritative or influential leaders of estranged communities or interest groups face obstacles to improving their circumstances or are at a standstill, may be looking for ways to reach an acceptable settlement or other policies, and could be receptive to serious political bargaining if offered plausible ideas and meaningful incentives and support (see further below).

2. IDENTIFY: Once certain vulnerable countries are selected, use a diagnostic process to identify problem areas that appear to be blocking peaceful change owing to the weakness or absence of conflict-regulating institutions.

This country-specific analysis should identify significant sources of conflict that if reduced would constitute concrete improvements, but are not so entrenched as to resist any domestic and international influence. Major areas of importance include strengthening security, improving basic government functions, and reducing disincentives in the political economy that stand in the way of development. They also should include an assessment of a country's relevant social and institutional resiliencies and internal capacities that can be built upon to remedy the identified problems. Almost always, some existing pockets of political will and built-in capacities for action can be found that may help halt deterioration, prevent the escalation of violence, or point to avenues for improvement. This preliminary diagnostic procedure thus brings to light the main social and institutional gaps—as well as resiliencies—that could be addressed to reduce the causes of conflict and state fragility.

The specific issues to be tackled may vary greatly and could arise at national or subnational levels. Diverse examples might be land conflicts, disputes over the use of natural resources, the challenges of economic liberalization and opportunities afforded by economic globalization, and the allocation of authority between central and provincial governments. Likewise, election commissions might need help to become independent or establish candidate codes of conduct, and a massive civic education campaign might help to make upcoming elections meaningful expressions of voter preferences. This process of identifying target issues should combine extensive consultation with well-informed elites and grassroots individuals, in addition to analysis of relevant studies, to find a workable balance between significant problems and political feasibility.

3. ENGAGE: After identifying the candidate issues, invite an appropriate mix of relevant, influential individuals from government and civil society to participate in one or more joint processes of relationship- and skill-building, followed by problem diagnosis and strategy development.

For this step, it is crucial to involve well-connected, generally respected leaders not only in the wider society but also in political parties and the government who represent powerful identity groups or other interests. The World Bank argues that it is crucial to obtain buy-in from an "inclusive enough" coalition of the political elite that is sufficient to support any new rules of the political game.[10] This task thus means more than simply satisfying some general principle of inclusiveness; it requires a substantive, in-depth political assessment of the interests that are driving the main actors who are competing or cooperating to affect a particular situation, and those actors' receptivity to possible engagement.[11] Dialogue and trust-building exercises are vulnerable to cooptation or only nominal commitment if they do not speak to the interests of those who influence or wield power and hold authority, as well as those who do not but crave it.

This step must also engage the participants initially in training in interactive conflict resolution and awareness-raising concepts and tools. Here, the techniques of facilitating interpersonal trust-building and relationships have a comparative advantage over more intrusive international policy instruments. By offering a dedicated political space for convening special groups of key influentials who may interact officially or professionally but seldom develop trusting, ongoing working relationships, these methods provide a missing link in the standard preconceived international programs for peace processes and economic and political development. A major impediment to capitalizing on any latent motivations to change a problem situation is the simple absence of organized but nonconfrontational venues to undertake sustained communication and action. Unless specific opportunities and concrete incentives are created to encourage intensive action, individuals and small groups are not likely to assemble on their own to undertake the kind of collective efforts that can make a measurable difference.

The nonthreatening methods used to sensitize participants to crucial notions such as the tendencies and pitfalls of misperception and miscommunication, the importance of empathetic listening, and the costs to all of dysfunctional problems such as unequal resource distributions can start up conversations about potential collaborative efforts. These sensitization methods introduce the alluring idea that mutual understanding of shared interests, effective negotiation skills, and active cooperation may yield practical, concrete gains for the benefit of both individual participants and their country by beginning to tackle national policy problems and political disagreements. By offering a special venue for contact and a set of skills and tools, such workshops create an opportunity for leaders to discover their own reasons to more fully dedicate themselves to dealing with certain challenges—allowing them to come to terms with the advantages of doing things differently and emboldened by the awareness that they are not alone in the effort.

Such opportunities to convene also make it possible for country leaders and international actors to address issues, disagreements, and tensions earlier and more quickly, smoothly, and productively. Without such a jump start, the relationships within the usual governing processes are susceptible to the turbulent, dissonant, unilateral, and often coercive politics of postconflict and other weak states, where default assumptions about incompatible zero-sum interests, mutual suspicions, and abiding resentments frequently lead to passive aggression and disruptive disputes that block or slow down progress. The methodology can create a nucleus of participants who are developing a collaborative mindset and experiencing mutual confidence and motivation, and thereby becoming open to addressing problems together. Such efforts to convene special groups can achieve what more formulaic programs do not, which is to transform indigenous but poorly functioning processes so that a country can begin to modify its political and governing practices.

An initiative that starts by leveraging attitudes and relationships can go on to address and bring about larger changes. Preliminary meetings can gradually turn to wider, longer-term activities. However, a few initial workshops for relationship-building do not provide enough time for the participants to examine and work through concrete, feasible solutions to specific issues. Further structured opportunities are needed if the participants are to continue to see value in meeting together. Although the workshop methods introduce the idea that cooperation can bring mutual gain, the methods cannot themselves formulate options that begin to transform the prevailing informal, largely systemic rules of the game. Their new outlooks need specific procedures through which to be applied to concrete problems. Beyond their initial convening and energizing efforts through mainly social-psychological methods, the initiatives need to introduce further procedures and tools. Otherwise, the amicable demeanor exhibited in such dialogues can be mere window dressing that evades or postpones meaningful accommodations on real issues and does not change the political relations of the contending parties, much less policies that affect the lives of ordinary people.

Conventionally, a frequent next step after initial trust-building workshops is to do more training of a generic nature with more individuals and groups in a country, such as "training of trainers" through the same conflict resolution techniques. However, once a project establishes trust and instills skills and values in a particular group or several groups, a better alternative is to work with the original groups to focus on understanding and making progress in addressing substantive political or policy issues—that is, to give the training more depth and less breadth—rather than simply extending the method to ever-wider circles of initiates. The training and association of the influential people who are now "converted" will likely have more impact if their solidarity is put to work through efforts to probe into specific, urgent issue areas. Thus, one should not expect that changed attitudes and newly created relationships will on their own spill over to produce significant changes in peace negotiations or government policymaking. This assumption puts too great a burden on the social and psychological changes in the group and on the gumption of individual members to persevere by working toward political agreements. It is true that moving to resolve substantive issues and expecting to reach agreements too quickly, without building relationships, can backfire and discredit the effort. However, even though a new conflict transformation perspective and fostered relationships may make agreement on substantive issues more possible, the former alone does not ensure the latter. A more assertive stance is needed to exploit openings in which to press participants to settle more substantive and difficult peace and policy issues.

The engagement step can capitalize on the experiential learning that participants have gained by turning to examine specific substantive policy or organizational problems and conflicts in their country. This process could start with a macro-level envisioning exercise to stimulate national goal-setting, followed by some type of conflict and fragile state analysis that shows how disputes, political interests, stalemate, and other constraints stand in the way of achieving greater benefits, but where preemptive actions could avoid potential dangers and take advantage of opportunities.

For these purposes, one of several readily available analytical tools can be used as a common framework of questions for assessing common sources of state fragility and conflicts.[12] An analytical framework that is empirically based on cross-national research is an essential starting point to avoid being diverted into myriad amorphous, peripheral complaints. Although initially it will be essential to tap into pent-up grievances and local perceptions, the unstructured discussion of such issues will not necessarily focus on the most important priorities. Instead, the discussions should turn to defining certain major problems threatening the country's overall stability. Of course, the particular answers to the framework's questions will be country-specific and inevitably will be politically tinged. But such tools provide a systematic and neutral touchstone for participants to develop a sense of the especially critical political, security, and economic problems in their countries, and to identify the specific structural, proximate, and triggering sources of these problems, as well as countervailing factors. This step then concentrates the collective energies of the workshop groups on an intensive search for possible solutions to selected problems. It is inadequate to ask the participants on the last week or so of a workshop to draw on the analytical tools, problem-solving frameworks, transformed relations, and communications skills they have been using simply to make a list of their country's institutional and political challenges and possible ways to address them. Such workshops may conclude with individuals' express commitments to move forward, but the lack of specific follow-up can allow their energy to dissipate and looks to indefinite and random actions for results, thus forfeiting the opportunity to maximize the group's collective prominence for resolving major issues. Instead, facilitators should exploit their opportunity to train and engage participants in cooperative problem-solving. To this end, facilitators must do more than allow the participants to set the pace, without providing explicit encouragement and specific guidance. It also calls for staffing a "deep bench" of facilitators with technical expertise in international relations, official diplomacy, particular public policies, and domestic politics, in addition to various facilitation techniques. The initiatives, which sponsor this process, need to expand their range of techniques to take on a larger task of designing and possibly organizing wider initiatives through which the "converted" workshop participants can apply their skills.

One way to connect this assessment of crucial issue areas to more concrete action is by setting up state-society working groups on selected problems and offering to support the most workable proposals and policy changes that the groups develop. Working groups could tackle particular political and policy issues identified by the diagnostic analysis and formulate concrete proposals to remedy these problems. These groups would be composed mainly of interested and appropriate participants in the original workshops, but could draw upon other technical and political expertise as needed. These groups would be invited to also create feasible implementation plans with built-in accountability measures.

Proposed actions could include authoritative policy analyses or more action-oriented initiatives, such as organizing substantive debates on public policy options or interventions to resolve particular policy disputes. Other actions might seek to remove organizational bottlenecks to economic development or other policies in key functional or geographic areas. Projects might profit by working with especially willing and strategically placed government ministries, as was done in Burundi with the armed forces.[13] This work would draw upon the facilitation, mediation, or negotiation skills that were stressed in the initial workshops. One example of a methodology for tackling such policy or organizational problems is organizational development, which could be used to change a ministry's standard operating procedures and practices at the "business end" of its work. In some cases, proposals might call on international backup such as mediation, quiet diplomacy, good offices, observer missions, development assistance, and security.

4. INCENTIVIZE. Organize concerted international support behind the processes.

Using workshops as an indigenous problem-solving process requires resources and incentives early on to generate sufficient domestic political will. Both the participants in the nonofficial workshops and the targeted government officials must show willingness by being open to consider and work through the options that the workshops formulate. Institution-building must reconcile deeply conflicting political and material interests within newly emerging but as yet unformed and uncertain political and institutional arrangements. Given the continuing dominance of politics in the economy, "reforms" that are pushed from the outside raise the prospect of gain for some and threaten political and economic loss for others. Basic economic, political, or even physical survival is often at stake. To the extent that the efforts described here aspire to make a difference, they will encounter potential resistance, subversion, or cooptation. This is where the influence of outside governments and international actors other than the initial workshop organizers and their methods has an essential role and must come into play. If the workshop process is to generate the kind of policy and institutional change that reshapes existing practices, international actors need to support it in three ways: monetarily, diplomatically, and strategically.

First, the locally developed strategies need influential international actors to provide concrete positive incentives or pressures in order to stimulate and reinforce progress on the targeted problems such as security and economic development. International support through development and other funds not only needs to be ready to conduct the basic "curriculum" in the initial workshop meetings, but also should be offered as an inducement for the more substantively focused diagnostic step and formulation of followup proposals. One possible incentive to proposal development would be to ensure that the most meritorious proposals will receive operational funding for getting the recommended actions actually adopted and implemented. Thus, donor support would provide both the initial political space and positive incentives to produce concrete visible solutions to host country problems.

Second, the ambassadors in the embassies in the host country should be brought into the process at the outset and regularly apprised of the workshops' and working groups' goals and achievements. These diplomats need to use their official channels to urge the host government to support this work by engaging in the workshop activities. Ideally, the process could also benefit from political support from multilateral bodies such as the United Nations or regional organizations and any associated country "group of friends."

Third, this overall process of supporting influential leaders from within these countries to assess the "state of their state" and tackle major gaps presents an attractive opportunity for the international actors as well. Failed states and conflicts occur in many countries and areas for multiple reasons, so individual projects of international actors that are shaped along preformed lines and are scattered around the world have limited effect in any one place. The process outlined here provides a vehicle for actually operationalizing not only the widely espoused international goals of supporting local ownership and creating country capacities, but also for generating integrated and tailored "whole-of-government" strategies that incorporate complementary efforts in development, defense, diplomacy, and democratic institution-building. Donors and diplomats should not view the working groups laid out in this chapter simply as discrete projects that are operating alongside the usual international programs in various sectoral areas. Multilateral and bilateral donors, peacebuilding organizations, and other international actors in the country could build on the local momentum created by the workshops to fulfill their oft-stated aspirations to better align their sectoral priorities and programs with locally owned development plans and achieve more international complementarity. The endogenous processes create a platform for international actors and the host country leaders to consult each other in order to review how their respective actions could lead to a more coherent, integrated, and cost-effective national strategy. Thus, the role that a proposed initiative can serve within a larger, robust diplomatic international or regional strategy needs to be considered.

The process also affords an opportunity for local and international actors to assess whether existing international and domestic programs and policies are helping or hurting to advance institution building and reduce major sources of conflict and violence. In doing so, it may help to integrate conflict sensitivity into international policies. Many handbooks, toolkits, and other guidelines provide instruction on how to adapt the programs for specific sectors such as agriculture, economic growth, health, and infrastructure in order to both target conflict generators and avoid doing harm. In effect, by developing locally decided and strategic priorities, the workshops constitute a participatory process for formulating the substantive elements in an unofficial but potentially official country-led institution-building strategy.

An added advantage is that the international commitments in fragile state contexts may not necessarily need more resources, but rather can benefit from more cost-effective ways to spend what is already being disbursed. Support for the proposed process need not involve large new expenditures—various bilateral and multilateral programs and resources are already available—but existing programs may need to be modified in order to support the locally developed strategy.

Fortunately, the United Nations and other governmental and nongovernmental organizations already have a long history of offering face-to-face and online training programs in conflict analysis and conflict-sensitive program formulation for their staffs, often on an interagency basis. These training programs have "graduated" thousands of international professionals who are conversant with key concepts and tools for addressing conflict and fragility. What is not clear is how much such skill-building at the personnel level has modified these organizations' standard operating procedures and existing regulations. Such procedural changes are needed to enable these well-prepared staff to actually utilize their training in conflict-sensitive analysis, planning, program design, and evaluation. The workshop processes proposed here provide a needed procedural mechanism to enable these trained staff members to actually get together in a country and work across their ordinarily separate structures. One possible approach, akin to the country-specific "donor conferences" that decide on joint aid packages, would involve multinational teams and coalitions formed among international financial institutions and nongovernmental organizations on a country-by-country basis. These actors could then jointly fine-tune and galvanize their existing programs and agree on a division of labor in order to support and implement the locally developed strategies.[14]

5. PUBLICIZE: Increase support and reduce resistance by demonstrating tangible results.

It is crucial for peacebuilding programs to disseminate their interim and eventual results through informal channels and the formal media. The visible benefits from successful activities can have multiplier effects. The process could publicize the achievements of successful efforts, such as the passage of promising legislation or a resolved policy dispute, as something for others to emulate. Such successes can inspire others and provide prototypes for them to replicate. The World Bank argues that if new reform initiatives clearly "signal" that widely needed actions are actually being taken, and that such activities follow through in the short term by making "concrete commitments," these initiatives can restore confidence, start to reverse vicious cycles of conflict and instability, and encourage virtuous cycles.[15] An effort that is shown to have results can also expand its support base and attract further funding. Moreover, where the working groups include both government and nongovernmental participants, well-publicized models of successful nongovernmental projects can attract high-level government and political attention; important officials who hear about the results of popular initiatives may be encouraged to become identified with the activity and want to emulate it and give it government support.

6. MOBILIZE: Build constituencies behind adopting, implementing, and sustaining the activities, while holding them accountable.

Efforts to extend the original model to try to influence changes, even if incremental, will run up against prevailing political interests and policy prerogatives at all stages. To avoid the dangers of backlash or capture, and to avoid being pulled back into the debilitating environment of earlier practices, the new ways of handing public business that have been developed need to be sustained and protected so they can be "locked in" to the institutional fabric of the society. Research on institution-building in fragile states suggests that for the desired institutions to be created, effective leadership is needed that combines a vision of what is needed with political skill in mobilizing support for specific plans.[16] Previously mentioned sources of support include financial incentives and political backing of the resident diplomatic community, as well as a domestic constituency that is served by the activities and is invested in defending them.

This step does not mean simply reaching out to a diffuse array of civil society groups to gain consensus on outstanding issues or forming a broad peace lobby to mount pressure against incumbent politicians. These approaches tend not to be aggregated or focused enough to outweigh the influence of partisan domestic politics and the dominant power of political elites. As mentioned, simply pushing for democratic elections—as if that puts countries on automatic pilot toward harmony—often exacerbates divisions. Although media campaigns and political action may be needed to promote particular alternatives, these actions should not be limited to increasing civil society pressure on what are often poorly functioning governments. Specific objectives can be achieved and reinforced by mobilizing particular latent constituencies.

Public accountability procedures must be built into the support for new activities. This accountability means more than strict procedures for management oversight and financial integrity and monitoring and evaluation. Part and parcel of the task of changing prevailing governance practices is establishing and enforcing transparent rules of accountability, such as performance standards for officials and civil servants. One source for holding the activities accountable is the constituencies that the initiatives are designed to serve. To counterbalance the potential capture of program resources by closed elites, guidance from the Organisation for Economic Co-operation and Development's Development Assistance Committee advises donors that are supporting government capacities for local service delivery to ensure that locally serviced constituencies are able to hold the administrative agencies directly accountable. Transparent arrangements are needed to establish a "double compact" that ensures accountability both to the country's citizens and to international funders.[17]

Here again, tools are available for identifying particularly interested parties and mobilizing them as a constituency. For example, the "managing policy reform" framework distinguishes the management of policy change from project and program management.[18] It regards the context of programs as inevitably political, in need of resources, and without a specific actor fully in charge. It is applicable to many sectors and to policy, legal, and regulatory reform. The suggested steps provide guidance to leaders and donors for converting general policies into actions through policy management steps that address political threats to programs. These steps have been used in a number of countries to help organizations or agencies identify the political and organizational assets and obstacles that affect policy implementation, analyze stakeholder interests, engage citizens, increase transparency, and resolve disputes over policy changes.

Conclusion

Within generally favorable parameters, the procedures outlined for organizing workshop processes can make a considerable difference. Well-conceived steps can provide opportunities for participants in interactive conflict resolution workshops to apply their skills in concrete, focused ways that demonstrably address the larger challenges of institution-building while being appropriately contextualized. Workshops that start by building trust and relationships and are sustained can go on to affect specific structural problems. Even in apathetic, ambivalent, or resistant environments, rule-governed behavior and other alternatives to debilitating existing practices can become institutionalized through combinations of local legitimacy, international incentives, tangible benefits, and constituent pressure. More states and societies will be able to draw upon the inner capabilities and resources of their own governmental and social actors to adjust to and address new threats and opportunities. Indeed, this whole process could start experimentally in a pilot effort in one country. Even a partially collaborative effort could set an example that jump-starts, operationalizes, and legitimates the notion of complementarity, providing cover for other actors to join in or motivating new actors to sponsor similar integrated engagements in additional places. In sum, these steps put the leaders of host countries in the driver's seat by giving them incentives for change and holding them accountable, thus also achieving the international norms of local ownership and responsible sovereignty.

Notes

1. Ronald Fisher and Herbert Kelman, "Conflict Analysis and Resolution," in *Oxford Handbook of Political Psychology*, ed. David O. Sears et al. (Oxford: Oxford University Press, 2003), 346.

2. Monty G. Marshall and Benjamin R. Cole, *Global Report 2014: Conflict, Governance and State Fragility* (Vienna, VA: Center for Systemic Peace, 2014), 22–24.

3. World Bank, *World Development Report 2011: Conflict, Security and Development* (Washington, DC: World Bank, 2011), http://www.worldbank.org.

4. Jack A. Goldstone et al., "A Global Model for Forecasting Political Instability," *American Journal of Political Science* 54, no. 1 (2010): 190–208.

5. See, e.g., William Easterly, "Can Institutions Resolve Ethnic Conflict?" *Economic Development and Cultural Change* 49, no. 4 (June 2001) 687–706; and Ashraf Ghani and Clare Lockhart, *Fixing Failed States: A Framework for Rebuilding a Fractured World* (New York: Oxford University Press, 2009).

6. Merilee S. Grindle, "Good Enough Governance Revisited," *Development Policy Review* 25, no. 5 (2007): 533–74.

7. This section draws also on an assessment of another leadership capacity-building initiative in the Democratic Republic of Congo: Michael Lund and Howard Wolpe, *Engaging Leaders for Statebuilding: The Case of the Democratic Republic of Congo* (Washington, DC: Woodrow Wilson International Center for Scholars, 2010).

8. Similarly, the World Bank urges support for participatory endogenous processes that mobilize key governmental and nongovernmental actors, nationally and locally, to tackle urgent community problems and threats to local livelihoods and security (World Bank, *World Development Report 2011*).

9. See, e.g., "State Fragility Index and Matrix," in Marshall and Cole, *Global Report 2014*, 45–51.

10. World Bank, *World Development Report 2011*, 119–21.

11. International actors are urged to analyze "the nature and interests of elite groups, possible incentives to influence elite bargaining positions, the potential for alliances between some elites and excluded groups, and opportunities to build links with reform-minded elites." Clare Castillejo, *Promoting Inclusion in Political Settlements: A Priority for International Actors?* (Oslo: Norwegian Peacebuilding Resource Centre, 2015), 8.

12. Existing analytical tools, such as the US government's Interagency Conflict Assessment Framework, assess typical conflict drivers and sources of state fragility. Other analytical tools measure democracy, good governance, and socioeconomic development. A current challenge is synthesizing these tools to take account of emerging knowledge about the internal dynamics in fragile, failed, and transitioning states and

integrating their differing criteria in order to provide a coherent picture of the kinds and degrees of actual and potential conflict and fragility in particular countries, thereby establishing a sound basis for contextualized program designs.

13. Projects might also concentrate on troubled geographic areas. Assuming there is sufficient security, an example would be to organize local government-citizen forums that address local needs in a number of chosen communities in order to stimulate and enforce more responsible local governments. Participatory community development processes involving government officials and ordinary citizens could provide models for promising local citizen-government joint vehicles for local problem-solving.

14. The fact that a few major multiactor activities, such as multidonor evaluations, actually have been undertaken in certain countries in recent years shows that such donor collaboration is not utopian.

15. World Bank, *World Development Report 2011.*

16. See Ghani and Lockhart, *Fixing Failed States*, 230; and Grindle, "Good Enough Governance Revisited," 570f. See also Thomas Carothers and Diane de Gramont, *Development Aid Confronts Politics: The Almost Revolution* (Washington, DC: Carnegie Endowment for International Peace, 2013).

17. Ghani and Lockhart, *Fixing Failed States.*

18. Derick W. Brinkerhoff and Benjamin L. Crosby, *Managing Policy Reform: Concepts and Tools for Decision-Makers in Developing and Transitioning Countries* (Bloomfield, CT: Kumarian Press, 2002).

Contributors

Susan H. Allen is associate professor of conflict analysis and resolution at George Mason University, where she serves as director of the Center for Peacemaking Practice. She previously taught at American University, and engaged in conflict resolution practice and evaluation of conflict resolution initiatives at The Carter Center and the Alliance for Conflict Transformation. She holds a master's degree and doctorate in conflict analysis and resolution from George Mason University. She currently convenes Georgian–South Ossetian confidence-building workshops.

Susanna Campbell is a postdoctoral researcher at the Centre on Conflict, Development and Peacebuilding at the Graduate Institute of International and Development Studies in Geneva, and was previously a visiting postdoctoral scholar at the Saltzman Institute for War and Peace Studies at Columbia University. She is also currently a principal investigator for two large research projects funded by the Swiss Network for International Studies and the Swiss National Science Foundation, both of which expand on her dissertation research. She received her PhD in 2012 from the Fletcher School at Tufts University, with her dissertation "Organizational Barriers to Peace: Agency and Structure in International Peacebuilding." She has been studying international intervention in violent conflict since 1996. During this time, she has worked for, carried out studies for, and evaluated numerous intergovernmental organizations, donors, and nongovernmental organizations (NGOs). She has published widely on peacebuilding, statebuilding, and conflict prevention, including with the Council on Foreign Relations Press, *The Journal of International Peacekeeping*, *The Journal of Peacebuilding and Development*, Routledge, and through reports, policy articles, and conference papers. In 2011, she co-edited with David Chandler and Meera Sabaratnam, *A Liberal Peace?: The Problems and Practices of Peacebuilding* (Zed Books). For more information, see www.susannacampbell.com.

Diana Chigas is co-director of the Reflecting on Peace Practice Program at CDA Collaborative Learning Projects in Cambridge, Massachusetts, and a professor of the practice of international negotiation and conflict resolution at the Fletcher School of Law and Diplomacy at Tufts University. From 1994 to 2002, as program director at Conflict Management Group, she facilitated bicommunal conflict management training and dialogue in Cyprus.

Michael Lund, senior associate, conflict and peacebuilding with Management Systems International, is author of *Preventing Violent Conflicts: A Strategy for Preventing Diplomacy* (United States Institute of Peace Press, 1996); coeditor and contributor to four other books, including *Engaging Fragile States: An International Policy Primer* (Woodrow Wilson International Center for Scholars, 2010) and *Security and Development: Searching for Critical Connections* (Lynne Rienner, 2009); and author of chapters in other volumes on conflict and peacebuilding in fragile states. For numerous governmental, intergovernmental, and nongovernmental organizations, he has assessed sources of intrastate conflicts and conflict management capacities; evaluated diplomacy, development, and security policies and early warning systems in preventing or mitigating conflicts; and researched other topics in conflicts and peacebuilding in sub-Saharan Africa, the Balkans, the Caucasus, and Central and East Asia. He has taught at Cornell University; UCLA, University of Maryland, Baltimore County; George Mason University; and Johns Hopkins University; and was founding director of the Jennings Randolph Program and senior scholar for preventive diplomacy at the United States Institute of Peace. Lund has a M.Th. from Yale

University Divinity School and a Ph.D. in political science from the University of Chicago.

Anna Matveeva is a visiting senior research fellow at the Department of War Studies, King's College London, and an Honorary University Fellow at the Department of Politics, University of Exeter. From 2003 to 2004, she served as the United Nations Development Programme regional peace and development adviser in Central Asia and in 2010 headed the Research Secretariat of the international Kyrgyzstan Inquiry Commission. She has published extensively on Central Asia and the Caucasus, including "Exporting Civil Society: The Post-Communist Experience," in *Problems of Post-Communism* (2008); "Legitimising Central Asian Authoritarianism: Political Manipulation and Symbolic Power" in *Europe–Asia Studies* (2009); and "Russia's Changing Security Role in Central Asia" in *European Security* (2013).

Steve McDonald is currently a Global Fellow at the Woodrow Wilson International Center for Scholars, a freelance writer, and an international consultant. Until recently, he was the director of the Africa Program and the Project on Leadership and Building State Capacity at the Wilson Center in Washington, DC, where he worked from 2002 to 2014. McDonald helped to design, initiate, and manage the Center's leadership capacity building and postconflict resolution programs in Burundi, the Democratic Republic of Congo, and Liberia.

Hannes Siebert is an international consultant, trainer, facilitator and mediator who has worked in Africa, the Middle East, the Balkans, South Asia, and the United States. In addition to cofounding and helping to facilitate the "One-Text" process in Sri Lanka, he has facilitated dialogue initiatives and advised the peace processes in Nepal and Kosovo. He is chairman and director of the Peace Appeal Foundation and director and cofounder of the Media Peace Centre, which produces media projects supporting peacebuilding and conflict initiatives. Between 1991 and 1994, he headed the media and youth divisions of South Africa's National Peace Secretariat, a multiparty body to reduce violence and promote dialogue during the run-up to the country's first democratic elections. In the late 1990s, he was a member of the World Economic Forum's "Transitions to Peace" initiative on South Africa, the Balkans, Northern Ireland, and the Middle East. A former newspaper editor and television producer, Siebert has been a fellow at the Center for War, Peace and the News Media at New York University, initiating and coordinating the West–Dar al Islam Dialogues between media institutions in the United States and Middle East. He continues to produce children's animation projects and helped start a project to support orphanages for victims of war and human trafficking in war-torn areas of South Asia.

Peter Uvin is vice president for academic affairs and dean of the faculty at Claremont McKenna College. Prior to joining Claremont, he was provost and professor of political science at Amherst College, academic dean and Henry J. Leir Professor of International Humanitarian Studies at the Fletcher School of Law and Diplomacy at Tufts University, and the founding director of Tufts' Institute for Human Security. He is the author of four books and numerous articles dealing with development aid and its relation to human rights and conflict, war in the African Great Lakes region, NGO scaling-up, and hunger and food aid. His most well-known book is *Aiding Violence: The Development Enterprise in Rwanda* (Kumarian Press, 1998) which received the 1998 African Studies Association's Melville J. Herskovits Award for the most outstanding book on Africa. His subsequent book, *Human Rights and Development* (Kumarian Press, 2004), took this argument further in a normative direction. In 2006, he was awarded a prestigious Guggenheim Fellowship to analyze young people's lives in post-transition Burundi, which led to his latest book, *Life after Violence: A People's Story of Burundi* (Zed Books, 2009).

Index